£40—
#4247

THE FRANCO-PRUSSIAN WAR
AND ITS HIDDEN CAUSES

ÉMILE OLLIVIER
1825–

THE FRANCO-PRUSSIAN WAR

AND

ITS HIDDEN CAUSES

BY

ÉMILE OLLIVIER

Translated from the French
With an Introduction and Notes by
GEORGE BURNHAM IVES

WITH ILLUSTRATIONS

 BOOKS FOR LIBRARIES PRESS
FREEPORT, NEW YORK

First Published 1912
Reprinted 1970

INTERNATIONAL STANDARD BOOK NUMBER:
0-8369-5612-5

LIBRARY OF CONGRESS CATALOG CARD NUMBER:
71-140369

PRINTED IN THE UNITED STATES OF AMERICA

PREFACE

SOME two or three years ago I happened to read in the *Revue des Deux Mondes* the chapter of his History in which Émile Ollivier told of the publication of the news, in July, 1870, that Prince Leopold of Hohenzollern had been offered and had accepted the throne of Spain. Previously, I had had a vague idea that M. Ollivier was commonly held up to obloquy as being mainly responsible for the War of 1870; but I was not aware that he had been engaged for many years in writing a history of the Second Empire which was to be at the same time a defence of his own brief administration.

My interest being once aroused, I began to read back, and to read collaterally, and so convinced myself that in the common attribution of responsibility to M. Ollivier much injustice had been done; and that, in this country at least, save among historical students, there is little acquaintance with the actual causes of the conflict. Believing that M. Ollivier should have an opportunity to plead his own cause in English to those who might be alarmed by the many volumes of his work, I entered into correspondence with him as to the possibility of making extracts therefrom suitable for translation, which should set forth clearly the story of this Hohenzollern candidacy and its sequel. Eventually M. Ollivier himself made up the volume which is here presented in translation.

It seemed to me, while preparing the translation, that, in addition to supplying, as well as I could, the annotations necessary to explain allusions to past events, it was advisable to accompany what is, inevitably and indeed confessedly, an *ex parte* narrative, with parallel views of the same events derived from other sources. Curiously enough, the frantic partisans of the war, and the extreme Republicans who, after doing their utmost to make war inevitable, claimed to have been mortally opposed to it united in making scapegoats of the Ministers who were forced into declaring it; and especially of their titular head. Many of the so-called histories of the period can be fairly characterized in the terms applied by M. Ollivier to Taxile Delord's *Histoire du Second Empire* — as political broadsides against the Empire and the Liberal Ministry. Jules Favre's *Gouvernement de la Défense Nationale* is, in addition, a labored plea in favor of his own disinterested devotion to the cause of his country; while the embittered tone of M. Welschinger's very recent work — *La Guerre de 1870* (1910) — I can attribute only to the publication of the fourteenth volume of M. Ollivier's *L'Empire Libéral*. The exhaustive work of M. Pierre de La Gorce, — *Histoire du Second Empire*, — however, is admirably moderate and impartial, while it certainly does not err on the side of lenity, and I have found it difficult to restrain the temptation to quote from it at great length.

I have not presumed to attempt to write history; but simply to present M. Ollivier's defence, in his own words, together with the views of other writers on the same events, for purposes of comparison. It has often seemed to me that he has omitted in his abridgment some passages of his main work which could less well be spared than some of those included, and I have added a good many of these in the notes.

M. Palat ("Pierre Lehautcourt") has printed a bibliography of the Franco-Prussian War, including everything that has been written on the subject, so far as he could discover. It is a volume of some three or four hundred pages, so that I need hardly say that it has been impossible to make an exhaustive examination of the authorities; but thanks to the generous treatment accorded by the authorities of the Harvard Library to even the humblest of investigators, I had their collections at my disposal, and I have tried to make a fair selection therefrom.

The following works are cited frequently in the notes by their authors' names only: —

P. de La Gorce, *Histoire du Second Empire;* Albert Sorel, *Histoire Diplomatique de la Guerre Franco-Allemande;* Duc de Gramont, *La France et la Prusse avant la Guerre;* Comte Benedetti, *Ma Mission en Prusse;* "P. Lehautcourt" (Palat), *Histoire de la Guerre de 1870–71;* Henri Welschinger, *La Guerre de 1870.* By the "Memoirs of the King of Roumania," frequently cited, is designated the most important of all the authorities as to certain phases of the Hohenzollern question; namely, *Aus dem Leben Königs Karl von Roumanien* (1895).

All notes in brackets have been supplied by the translator; those without brackets are always in the language of M. Ollivier himself: those in quotation marks being additional passages from the text of *L'Empire Libéral,* those without such marks being footnotes from the same work; all footnotes having been omitted from the volume here translated. In many cases the authorities cited in M. Ollivier's notes have not been consulted or the citations verified, the works in question not being readily available. As they are not always consistent with each other, their accuracy is not vouched for, but it seemed the better way to insert them as I found them. The references to Bismarck's Autobiography (*Reflections and Reminiscences*) I have generally been able to verify.

SALEM, MASS., October, 1912.

CONTENTS

		PAGE
PREFACE		v
TRANSLATOR'S INTRODUCTION		xiii
INTRODUCTION		1

CHAPTER
I.	BISMARCK CONTEMPLATES WAR WITH FRANCE	13
II.	BISMARCK TAKES UP THE HOHENZOLLERN CANDIDACY ANEW AFTER THE PLEBISCITE IN FRANCE	27
III.	THE HOHENZOLLERN SCHEME EXPLODES AT MADRID	42
IV.	THE HOHENZOLLERN SCHEME EXPLODES AT PARIS	48
V.	THE HOHENZOLLERN CANDIDACY AROUSES INDIGNATION IN FRANCE AND REPROBATION IN EUROPE	63
VI.	OUR INABILITY TO NEGOTIATE. OUR PERPLEXITY	72
VII.	DECLARATION OF JULY 6, 1870	81
VIII.	THE FOUR PACIFIC NEGOTIATIONS	101
IX.	GRAMONT'S NEGOTIATIONS WITH THE POWERS	117
X.	THE NEGOTIATIONS WITH THE KING OF PRUSSIA AT EMS	132
XI.	THE NEGOTIATION WITH PRINCE ANTONY. THE WITHDRAWAL	169
XII.	EFFECT AT PARIS OF THE ABANDONMENT OF THE CANDIDACY	188
XIII.	THE DEMAND OF GUARANTIES	215
XIV.	THE EMPEROR'S LETTER TO GRAMONT ON THE DEMAND OF GUARANTIES	230
XV.	THE MORNING OF JULY 13 AT EMS. THE KING OF PRUSSIA BRUSHES ASIDE THE DEMAND OF GUARANTIES	241
XVI.	THE MORNING OF JULY 13 AT PARIS	248
XVII.	THE EVENING OF JULY 13 AT EMS	266
XVIII.	THE EVENING OF JULY 13 AT BERLIN. BISMARCK'S SLAP IN THE FACE	276

CONTENTS

CHAPTER		PAGE
XIX.	THE EVENING OF JULY 13 AT PARIS. PACIFIC MEASURES PREVAIL	295
XX.	EXASPERATION AT PARIS CAUSED BY THE EMS DESPATCH	308
XXI.	OUR REPLY TO BISMARCK'S SLAP IN THE FACE. THE DECLARATION OF JULY 15	334
XXII.	UPON WHOM SHOULD THE RESPONSIBILITY FOR THE WAR FALL—FRANCE OR GERMANY?	366
XXIII.	SUMMARY AND JUDGMENTS	384
XXIV.	CONCLUSION	400

APPENDICES

A. LETTER FROM ÉMILE OLLIVIER TO PROFESSOR HANS DELBRÜCK, OF BERLIN 407
B. THE SPANISH REVOLUTION OF 1868 419
C. THE HOHENZOLLERN CANDIDACY FOR THE SPANISH THRONE . 422
D. PRINCE LEOPOLD OF HOHENZOLLERN 435
E. THE DUC DE GRAMONT 438
F. PRINCIPLES OF INTERNATIONAL LAW APPLICABLE TO THE HOHENZOLLERN AFFAIR 445
G. THE DECLARATION OF JULY 6 451
H. BISMARCK'S CIRCULAR NOTE OF JULY 18 TO THE POWERS . 461
I. THE NEGOTIATION AT EMS 468
J. I. THE DUC DE GRAMONT'S CIRCULAR NOTE OF JULY 24 TO THE POWERS 476
II. BARON WERTHER'S REPORT OF HIS CONVERSATION WITH GRAMONT ON JULY 12 480
K. THE EMS DESPATCH 484
L. INTERVIEW BETWEEN COUNT BISMARCK AND LORD A. LOFTUS, BRITISH AMBASSADOR 491
M. THE COMMISSION OF JULY 15 AND THE EMS CORRESPONDENCE 495

INDEX 505

LIST OF PORTRAITS

ÉMILE OLLIVIER	*Frontispiece*
	PAGE
MARSHAL PRIM	14
LEOPOLD OF HOHENZOLLERN	54
DUC DE GRAMONT	88
COMTE VINCENT BENEDETTI	132
NAPOLEON III	216
WILHELM I	244
PRINCE VON BISMARCK	282

TRANSLATOR'S INTRODUCTION

THE book of which this is a translation consists of extracts from the thirteenth and fourteenth volumes of the author's elaborate work, not yet completed, *L'Empire Libéral*, preceded by an introductory chapter taken from the exordium in the first volume of that work. It was published in Paris in 1911, under the title *Philosophie d'une Guerre*, for which a more descriptive and more accurate title has been substituted.

Between fifteen and twenty years ago, being already seventy years old, M. Ollivier, who had lived practically in retirement since the overthrow of his Ministry on August 9, 1870, after the news of the first serious reverses of the French arms, began the publication in the *Revue des Deux Mondes* of the series of articles which, expanded and elaborated, with notes and appendices, have been reprinted, year by year, in the successive volumes of *L'Empire Libéral*. Fifteen of these volumes have already appeared, the last of which (1911) discusses exhaustively the question whether France was prepared for war, and describes vividly the deplorable conditions that obtained in the French armies at the outset, and the hesitation about taking the offensive until the opportunity was gone forever. In the spring of the present year (1912), M. Ollivier being now eighty-seven years of age, the *Revue* printed the usual number of articles dealing with the first great battles of the war, Woerth (or Reichshoffen) and Spicheren, and narrating with abundance of moving detail the story of the downfall of the Ministry of January 2. These articles will soon appear as volume sixteen.

L'Empire Libéral is, in fact, a history of the Second Empire, and the first eight or nine volumes are occupied exclusively with the acts of the imperial government when it was still the "Empire Autoritaire," and before it had acquired any right to the title of Liberal. But the later volumes, from 1865, perhaps, may fairly be considered, generally speaking, M. Ollivier's *Apologia pro vita sua;* and, from whatever standpoint one considers them, one can hardly withhold one's admiration of the spirit and energy and eloquence with which this venerable statesman of a past generation maintains the sincerity of his Liberal opinions and the rectitude of his conduct from the beginning of his public career to its premature close, under the shadow of what he at least believes to be unmerited obloquy, when he was still in the prime of life.

Émile Ollivier was born at Marseilles, July 2, 1825. His father, Demosthène Ollivier (1799–1884), was a merchant in that city, and sometime municipal councillor. In April, 1848, the father was elected to the Constituent Assembly from the Bouches-du-Rhone. He sat with the Extreme Left, and bitterly opposed the policy of Louis Napoleon as President of the Republic. For protesting vigorously against the *coup d'état* of December 2, 1851, he was in great danger of transportation to Cayenne, but was saved therefrom by the exertions of his son, through his relations with Prince Napoleon, and was simply expelled from France, whither he returned in 1860.

Émile Ollivier was bred to the bar and began to

practise in Paris. In February, 1848, by the influence of his father's friend and fellow republican, the celebrated Ledru-Rollin, he was made Commissioner of the new Republic in the department of the Bouches-du-Rhone, resident at Marseilles. That he displayed great activity in that post is beyond question; but his administration is praised or condemned, apparently, according to the personal prejudices of the critic. He was recalled by General Cavaignac in July, and appointed prefect of the department of Haute-Marne. On the election of Louis Napoleon as President (December, 1848) over Cavaignac and Ollivier's patron, Ledru-Rollin, he lost his prefecture and resumed his practice at the bar of Paris.

He became favorably known as an advocate, no less by his talent than by his eloquence, and covered himself with glory in several important political trials, besides conducting a large private practice. In 1857 he was chosen deputy for one of the "circumscriptions" (the 3d) of the Seine, and for several years thereafter, until 1863, he was one of the famous *Five*,[1] who alone constituted the opposition during those years. He was, in fact, the leader of the little band that "struggled so vigorously for the recovery of the public liberties." Endowed with liberal instincts, overflowing with liberal enthusiasm, as the great majority even of his critics admit him to have been, it is difficult to see why he should not have been drawn toward the Empire when he saw, or thought that he saw, indications of a purpose on the part of the sovereign to restore the public liberties.

[1] The other four were Louis Alfred Darimon, J. L. Hénon, Ernest Picard, and Jules Favre.

The best brief summary that I have found of the successive steps in the liberalizing of French institutions in the sixties is that given by Sir Spencer Walpole in his *History of Twenty-Five Years*, volume ii, page 473 and following pages. He says: —

"The little group of deputies — the five of 1857 — had gradually become a power in the land; and the principles which they had hardly dared to enunciate in the beginning were becoming the commonplaces of Imperial policy. In 1859 the ranks of the Opposition were recruited by the return to France, under an amnesty, of the exiles of 1851; in 1860 discussion was made effective by the concession to the Chamber of the right to address the Crown; by the appointment of Ministers specially selected to defend the Imperial policy in the Legislature, and by the publication, in the *Moniteur*, of the debates. In 1861, the Chamber obtained a closer control over the finances of the State by the division of the supplies into sections, each of which was separately voted. At the general election of 1863, the five developed into a compact opposition of thirty-five, and the Emperor found himself in the unusual position of looking to the more moderate members of the Opposition for a defence of his policy. In 1867, he actually made M. Ollivier, the most prominent person among the original five, an offer of office.[1] In 1868 the Emperor went a step farther and gave the Chamber the right of questioning his Ministers, who were authorized to attend the Chamber, and defend their own action; and, what was still more striking, he removed the restrictions which, since 1851, had paralyzed the newspaper press,

[1] As Minister of Public Instruction. Naturally, the offer was declined.

TRANSLATOR'S INTRODUCTION xvii

and accorded, on certain conditions, the right of holding meetings to discuss questions of public policy."

It was on November 24, 1860, that the Emperor issued a decree permitting the publication of the debates in full in the then official organ, the *Moniteur*. "The Liberal Empire had been inaugurated," says M. de La Gorce,[1] "by a memorable decree, that of November 24, 1860, and by a personage eminent among all, M. de Morny.[2] Morny had prematurely disappeared. In that great void, the man who had been the associate of his plans, the confidant of his latest views, M. Émile Ollivier, did not despair. A few days after the funeral, March 27, 1865, he invoked the memory of the departed, and proclaimed that true wisdom lay not in resisting the wishes of public opinion but in yielding to them in time; then, when the *Address* was under discussion, he announced that, breaking with the opposition, he would move a favorable vote; it would not, he said, be a vote of entire agreement, but a vote of hope."

The last four of the concessions enumerated by Walpole in the passage quoted were announced by the Emperor in a letter of January 19, 1867, to the Minister of State (Rouher).

"It is said that on the morrow of the Emperor's letter, Prince Napoleon exclaimed: 'If the Emperor

[1] *Histoire du Second Empire*, vol. v, p. 346.

[2] The Duc de Morny, an illegitimate son of Queen Hortense and uterine brother of Napoleon III, is often said to have been the instrument of M. Ollivier's adhesion to the Empire. The post of councillor to the Viceroy of Egypt in the matter of the Suez Canal, which M. Ollivier held in 1864, and which occasioned the abandonment of his legal practice, is sometimes charged to have been a bribe offered by M. de Morny. He died in March, 1865. He was the original of the Duc de Mora in Daudet's romance *Le Nabab*.

wishes to be consistent with himself, there is nothing for him to do but form a new cabinet with Émile Ollivier.' Extraordinary, premature, as this solution may have appeared at that moment, strict logic would have explained it." [1]

The partisans of the "Empire Autoritaire," headed by M. Rouher, founded a club on rue de l'Arcade (whence the name "Arcadians"), where they discussed methods of maintaining the old imperial phalanx and barring the road to the Liberals. Their motto was: "Let us indulge the Emperor in his Liberal whims, since he absolutely insists upon them, but let us do it as cheaply as possible; let us yield to him, but paralyze him at the same time, and above all let us protect him against those who would destroy him." [2]

"Of all the liberals," says La Gorce, "M. Émile Ollivier was the most bitterly attacked. As they could not deny his oratorical powers, they denounced his ambition. He had striven, they said, to raise himself high enough to grasp a portfolio; but high office would elude the 'parliamentary Tantalus' many another time, and for a long while, if not forever, he would remain a fixture on his 'bench of patience.' Others, the better to assure the aim of their shafts, concealed them under an appearance of praise. 'Émile Ollivier,' they said, 'has talent, great talent; really, it's a great pity that he is unpopular, like all turncoats; that he lacks authority, that he lacks it to the extent of endangering every cause that he claims to serve.'"

In 1868 the law restoring the liberty of the press occasioned great agitation. Introduced in fulfilment

---

[1] La Gorce, *ubi sup.*
[2] *Ibid*, vol. v, p. 349.

TRANSLATOR'S INTRODUCTION xix

of the Emperor's promise in the letter of January 19, 1867, it was bitterly attacked in the Chamber, notably by M. Granier de Cassagnac, and was so lukewarmly defended by ministers that it would have been defeated, but for Napoleon's determination to support it despite the opposition of the Empress, and of M. Rouher himself.[1]

Despite the vigorous resistance of the inveterate partisans of the personal power of the sovereign, the years 1868 and 1869 witnessed the irresistible progress of Liberal ideas. Such incidents, among many others, as the founding of the *Lanterne* by Henri Rochefort (suppressed after the third issue) and the subscription in honor of Baudin, the deputy killed in the barricades in December, 1851 (in connection with which Gambetta delivered the great speech in defence of Delescluze, which made him famous in a moment), sufficiently indicated the trend of affairs. The International Association of Working Men made its appearance as a political factor. In anticipation of the elections of 1869, all the elements of opposition coöperated, save only the intransigent Royalists and the radical Republicans.

In the 3d circumscription of the Seine, M. Ollivier, a typical representative of liberal reform, was opposed by M. Bancel, a no less typical representative of the revolutionary tradition. "Both were in the full maturity of age and talent. By a singular coincidence they had a similar past, both having suffered from the *coup d'état* and having lived amid tales of exile. But

---

[1] The debates on this law, as well as those on the law concerning the right of assembly, which was passed under somewhat similar conditions, are interestingly summarized by M. de La Gorce, in vol. v, pp. 351-369.

Bancel, settled upon foreign soil, had remained in the legend of 1792, and had confined himself to disguising its commonplaces beneath eloquent phrases. Ollivier had speedily set himself free from the legend, and in his reconstituted mind had kept but one cult, that of liberty."[1]

M. Ollivier was defeated by 10,000 votes, but was returned for the department of the Var. The election resulted in the return of a sufficient number of "official" candidates to assure a majority, "on the sole condition that that majority should retain its confidence in itself, and find leaders to guide it."

"The drift towards parliamentary government was steadily gaining force," says Walpole, although the Emperor, while "ready to remove every restriction which hampered the expression of opinion, either in Parliament, or in the press," was "unwilling to part with the executive power which he still retained. He was ready to trust a Chamber elected by the people, but he could not bring himself to trust a Minister selected by himself. He was ready to invest a legislature with almost sovereign powers of control; and he hesitated to take the final plunge by making his advisers responsible to Parliament. . . .

"After the general election of 1869, the moderate men of all parties joined hands in desiring a parliamentary Ministry, and no fewer than one hundred and sixteen deputies signed an interpellation demanding the appointment of a Ministry responsible to the Legislature.[2] Napoleon III, even in the hour of his

[1] La Gorce, vol. v, p. 481.
[2] The interpellation was decided upon by a meeting of 42 deputies, and was drawn by a committee consisting of MM. Buffet, Chevandier, Plichon,

TRANSLATOR'S INTRODUCTION xxi

strength, might have found it difficult to resist this movement. In 1869 he endeavored to meet it halfway. On the 12th of July, when the session began, he instructed M. Rouher to make fresh concessions giving the Legislative Chamber greater control over legislation, over finance, and over its own business. In order to mark more clearly the importance of these reforms, he followed them up by removing M. Rouher from the office which made him the spokesman of his master's policy, and by choosing a new, and — in a political sense — somewhat colorless ministry. Ever halting, however, between two opinions, he accompanied these concessions with a stroke which irritated the very men in whose favor they were made. On the 12th he had endowed the Chamber with new powers; on the 13th he prorogued it to an indefinite date."

The Senate was summoned, however, to confirm the reforms announced in the Emperor's message of July 12, and after weeks of discussion they were sanctioned by the *Senatus Consultum* of September 8.

"What the decree of November 24, 1860, had begun, what the letter of January 19, 1867, had continued, the message of July 12, 1869, completed. These three acts, inseparable from each other, marked the three stages of the liberal evolution. . . . By the act of July 12, Napoleon most nobly surrendered what was left of his absolute power." [1]

The Emperor's concessions, however, still fell short of full ministerial responsibility; he "could not yet

Segris, Louvet, and Ollivier, all of whom were to be members of the hapless Ministry of January 2.

[1] La Gorce, vol. v, p. 494.

make up his mind to yield the titles to his pilots, and stand on the quarter-deck of the ship of State, in the uniform of an admiral, but without the admiral's power. When the Chamber was at last suffered to meet, on the 29th of November, he unfolded his own views in one of those phrases which he knew so well how to coin. 'France,' he said, 'desires liberty, but liberty and order. For order, I am responsible. Help me, gentlemen, to endow her with liberty.' Every day, however, showed him that the views of the Chamber were gravitating more and more directly to the institution of a Ministry which, if it represented the cause of liberty, should relieve the Emperor of his responsibility for order. Within a month of the meeting of the Legislature, Napoleon found it necessary to part with the provisional cabinet of the summer, and to entrust M. Émile Ollivier with the task of forming a new Ministry, prepared to act in the spirit as well as on the letter of the *Senatus Consultum* of September."[1]

The negotiations between the Emperor and M. Ollivier began early in the autumn, and were carried on at first through Duvernois and others; and after October 31 partly by personal intercourse. They are detailed at great length by M. Ollivier in chapters 5, 6, and 7 of his twelfth volume. It is only fair to say that from the beginning he firmly refused to lend his assistance to prop the reactionary *ad interim* ministry by accepting office therein, and that his steadfast insistence upon a thoroughgoing change of system, to be evidenced by a similar change in the Cabinet, triumphed at last. It is interesting, too, to

[1] Walpole, vol. ii, pp. 477-481.

follow the turns and windings of the affair, which led finally to the compulsory inclusion of MM. Buffet and Daru from the Left Centre, the majority of the new ministers being taken from the Right Centre, to which M. Ollivier belonged — the son of an exiled republican and himself the one-time leader of the Five. Not until the last hours of January 1, 1870, were the arrangements finally made, to be announced in the *Journal Officiel*, on the following day, which gave its name to the new Ministry.

"The new Ministers," says La Gorce, "so far as they were known at all, were known for honorable men, of perfect integrity and enlightened mind, and there was no reason to doubt that they would be loyal servants of the Prince and the country. Moreover, they represented a new element in the Emperor's government, and every novelty awakens the idea of hope. Thus the Imperial act was greeted with remarkable favor. And thus opened, under the reposeful auspices of peace and liberty, that year 1870, which was to be the last of the Empire, and of all the years of our history as a nation the most tragic." [1]

The same judicious historian, after a brief sketch of each of the new Ministers, continues: "Among all these men, M. Émile Ollivier stood prominently forth. He was not President of the Council, and, indeed, the deputies of the Left Centre had exerted themselves to prevent or to neutralize any suggestion of superiority. These precautions denoted neither antipathy nor jealousy, but simply a slight distrust. They feared his inexperience, his enthusiasms, his changeableness, his superb flights which were of an artist rather than

[1] Vol. v, pp. 527, 528.

a statesman: hence the idea of holding him in check, of hedging him about with his equals in authority, of maintaining a sort of equilibrium between the various temperaments and groups which would mutually counterbalance one another.[1] But despite this effort, public opinion attributed a preponderant position to the former deputy of the Left. It was he to whom the Emperor had entrusted the commission to form the new administration. It was he who, as Keeper of the Seals, had countersigned the appointments. Among the advisers of the Crown he was the only one whose name was known to the masses, some being accustomed to extol his liberalism, others to revile his backsliding. That which more than all the rest would place him in a rank apart would be his admirable eloquence, always ready to attack or to retort, which no incident, even the most unexpected, could disconcert. And so, without the official title, he appeared, in the eyes of the nation, the real head of the Cabinet; and from the first day the ministry of January 2 was known as the Ollivier Ministry."[2]

Lack of space forbids more than the briefest reference to the rude shock that the ministry received before they were warm in their seats, by the killing of the journalist Victor Noir by Prince Pierre Bonaparte, the Emperor's cousin. The revolutionary party seized upon the incident as a pretext for a determined effort

---

[1] "In the facility with which I deigned to submit to these precautions," says M. Ollivier himself (vol. xii, p. 227), "there was more scorn than humility. I felt that I was the stronger. . . . They might, therefore, claim as much as they pleased that I was admitted as a favor to the Daru-Buffet Ministry. I was sure that the Ministry of January 2 would be the Ministry of Émile Ollivier." [2] Vol. vi, pp. 2, 4.

TRANSLATOR'S INTRODUCTION xxv

to overthrow the Empire and proclaim the republic.[1] It was thwarted, however, by the vigorous preparations of the ministry, assisted by the timely prudence of Rochefort and others of the leaders.

The Ministry of January 2 found still in force but one important remnant of the *autocratic* régime — the exclusive power of the Senate to amend the Constitution. The Emperor, acting upon the advice of his ministers, signified to the Senate, in February, his wish that the Constitution should be revised in this respect; and by the *Senatus Consultum* adopted on April 20 the power of changing the Constitution was transferred to the Legislature as a whole. By the advice of M. Rouher the Emperor decided to give greater significance to this decision by asking the people to pronounce on the reforms that had been adopted. After much discussion, in which the various parties and groups exhibited curious differences of opinion,[2] the vote was taken throughout the country on May 8, upon this proposition: "The people approve the liberal reforms introduced in the Constitution since 1860, by the Emperor, with the concurrence of the great governing bodies of the State, and ratified by the *Senatus Consultum* of April 20, 1870." There were 7,358,786 affirmative and 1,571,939 negative ballots — a vote nearly as large as that by which the introduction of autocratic Imperialism had been sanctioned eighteen years before.

That the idea of the plebiscite was at first unpalatable

[1] In the *Souvenirs d'un Homme de Lettres*, of Alphonse Daudet, there is a chapter on Émile Ollivier, in the author's best vein, which contains a vivid paragraph or two concerning the commotion caused by the death of Noir, and an account of an interview with M. Ollivier on that subject. The whole chapter is well worth reading.

[2] The different views are described by M. de La Gorce, in vol. vi, book 18.

to M. Ollivier, and made doubly so by its suspicious source, is undoubtedly true; but he made the best of it, and the energies of the Ministry were devoted to securing the largest possible majority. Unfortunately M. Buffet's opposition to the plebiscite was too great to be overcome, and while the discussion was pending, he resigned, to be followed almost at once by Comte Daru and the Marquis de Talhouët, the former of whom was succeeded by the Duc de Gramont. However, the result of the ballot seemed to be generally accepted as proof that the Empire was as solidly established as ever.

In the spring of 1870, M. Ollivier was chosen a member of the Académie Française in place of Alphonse de Lamartine. He is said to have been the only person ever admitted by a unanimous vote. The war and its consequences caused the postponement of his "address of reception" until 1873; and public sentiment was even then in such an excited state that the characteristically vigorous defence of the Emperor which he introduced into his eulogy of M. de Lamartine aroused bitter recrimination. For many years now, M. Ollivier has been the dean of the Academy.

M. de La Gorce draws a sympathetic and attractive picture of the new Minister of Justice, as he appeared at the ministerial receptions at the Chancellery, "going from group to group, good-humored, expansive, radiant, smiling on everybody, smiling also at his good fortune, and overflowing with a confidence which then seemed justified. In those fleeting hours everything prospered as he would have it, and his young wife, at his side, completed the image of his happiness."[1]

[1] Vol. vi, p. 21. M. Ollivier's first wife was a daughter of Liszt, the illustrious composer and pianist. He had married for the second time, in 1869, the daughter of a merchant of Marseilles.

TRANSLATOR'S INTRODUCTION xxvii

The following sketch is drawn by M. Welschinger as a companion piece to that of the Duc de Gramont, quoted at the end of Appendix E.: —

"Less self-satisfied [than M. de Gramont] and yet as sure of his own infallibility, but more fidgety and feverish, appeared M. Émile Ollivier. Tall and thin, always dressed in black as if he were on his way to somebody's funeral, with gold-bowed spectacles over eyes always in motion, a sallow, pale face encircled by thin black whiskers, a strong, firmly set mouth and high forehead; quick and emphatic in gesture, incisive and hurried in speech, always ready to retort, upheld by his great reputation as a lawyer and political orator, defying any opponent whomsoever on any field, and accepting at every moment contests of the most diverse nature, without a sensation of fatigue. . . . Blessed with a self-assurance due to his impassioned eloquence and alert intellectual resources, he had accepted the heavy burden proffered him, with the hope, nay, the certainty of triumphing over all obstacles."[1]

Lack of competence, even more than lack of space,

[1] *La Guerre de 1870*, vol. i, p. 94. This called forth the following reply from M. Ollivier, printed in the *Éclaircissements* to vol. xv, p. 599: — "*My gold-bowed spectacles.* — I have been represented as always dressed in black, wearing gold-bowed spectacles — a sort of cross between a countryman and an undertaker's 'mute.' Dear readers, who have followed me kindly for so many years, let me tell you that none of the chosen friends among whom I have lived have ever seen me so. To be sure, being near-sighted, I have worn spectacles since my youth, but not with gold bows — modest spectacles, with bows of burnished steel. It has sometimes happened with me, as with other men, that on days of mourning I have worn a black coat; but ordinarily I have never worn anything but dark blue or dark gray clothes and if I have endured cruel suffering during my life, I have always made it a point not to display it in the lugubrious aspect of my outer man."

deters the translator from attempting to give even a bare sketch of the external relations of France from 1865 to 1870. He can hope to do no more than explain some of the allusions in the text — especially, perhaps, the repeated reference to a battle between Prussia and Austria as an event for which France was entitled to seek revenge. The summary that follows is taken mainly from Professor Macvane's translation of Seignobos's *Political History of Europe since 1814*, chapter xxvii, pages 798 ff.

"The question of the duchies of Schleswig-Holstein . . . was reopened by the extinction of the Danish dynasty in 1863. The German states supported the Duke of Augustenburg; the European powers defended the integrity of the Danish monarchy; Austria and Prussia took an intermediate position. . . .

"The Danish government was counting on European intervention." But England and France could not agree, and Prussia and Austria began war against Denmark in January, 1864. The peace of Vienna (October 30) ceded the duchies to Prussia and Austria.

"Austria and Prussia had been in conflict since 1860, when reform of the Confederation had been attempted. But the Austrian government, having fallen out with the German states . . . had made overtures to Prussia.

"The conflict began again with the question of determining the disposition of the duchies they had conquered together. A special council of the Prussian ministers, July 21, 1865, declared Austria's concessions insufficient and advised immediate war. But King William was unwilling to attack, and Austria, having no money, wished to avoid a war. The Gastein convention in August settled the question provisionally by dividing the duchies. France protested against this act as a violation of the principle of nationalities and the popular will, and as a revival of a procedure that had become obsolete in Europe. . . .

"Napoleon had made advances to Italy, bringing up the Roman question by the September Convention, 1864. The peace party, which had held the ministry since 1862, hoped to reconcile Italy with Austria by inducing the latter to give up Venetia. But the Italian government wished to keep its army ready, and Austria still refused to recognize the Kingdom of Italy.

"Bismarck tried to conclude an alliance with Italy against Austria. Italy could do nothing that France did not approve; Napoleon's authorization must therefore be obtained. Bismarck came to ask it of him. The Biarritz interview of October, 1865, was the decisive act of this negotiation. Napoleon resumed his personal policy: to bring about the national unity of Italy, to fortify Prussia against Austria,. and to profit by the conflict to gain territory and destroy the treaties of 1815. Bismarck's game was to encourage these hopes without making any formal engagement. He prevailed on Napoleon to promise the neutrality of France."[1]

After much difficulty Bismarck succeeded in obtaining an alliance with Italy for three months (April 8, 1866). "Italy promised armed support to Prussia's plans for the reform of the Confederation, and Prussia

---

[1] The details of the Biarritz interview have never been disclosed. Whoever is curious to read the story of Bismarck's handling of the many-sided negotiations of 1865–66, will find it told in illuminating but not tedious detail, especially with reference to the Chancellor's beguiling of Napoleon, by Sir S. Walpole in vol. ii, chapter 10 of his *History of Twenty-five Years*.

promised to secure the cession of Venetia. . . . Napoleon promised neutrality.

"Austria's policy was to delay a rupture in Germany in order to force Prussia, by taking the aggressive rôle, to alienate the German states (which plan succeeded), and in Europe to isolate Prussia by satisfying Italy. She proposed to Prussia, on April 25, that both sides should disarm, but not in Italy. She left France the hope that she would cede Venetia if Italy remained neutral. As compensation for Venetia she spoke of taking back Silesia from Prussia."

Napoleon in his perplexity proposed a European congress, "to revise the map of Europe. England and Russia agreed; Prussia and Italy, from regard for Napoleon, had agreed beforehand. Austria defeated the scheme by demanding that no increase of territory should be discussed and that the Pope should be invited."

The rupture was provoked on the very eve of the expiration of the three months' alliance with Italy. The Six Weeks' War of 1866 was decided in a single day, by the overwhelming defeat of the Austrians at Sadowa, or Königgrätz, on July 3.

"The Austrian government . . . ceded Venetia to Napoleon, begging him to negotiate peace with Italy. Napoleon seemed to be the arbiter of Europe. The Minister of Foreign Affairs (Drouyn de Lhuys), who favored Austria, urged him to mobilize and stop Prussia by threatening to take possession of the left bank of the Rhine, which was unprotected. But the Minister of War confessed that the army was disorganized by the Mexican expedition, and that he could not get together more than 40,000 men. Napoleon, who was

TRANSLATOR'S INTRODUCTION xxxi

in ill health, hesitated between two policies; whether to impose peace on Prussia or negotiate with her to secure advantage for himself. He thus let slip the moment for intimidating Prussia by a demonstration on the Rhine. The policy of the Prussian government was to put Napoleon off with vague promises, keeping him passive while the Prussian army was marching on Vienna.[1]

"Napoleon first tried to check Italy by threatening to join Austria against her: Italy replied that she could agree to nothing without Prussia and refused an armistice. Napoleon then sent to the Prussian camp to ask the King to authorize a truce for Italy. He then (July 14) proposed the bases of a peace: integrity of Austria, dissolution of the Confederation, confederation of Northern Germany, and cession by Austria of her right to the Duchies. On these conditions all were agreed. The difficulty was in arranging additions of territory; Prussia wished to annex several German states, but Austria dared not abandon her allies to that fate. Napoleon wanted to secure some territory to compensate France for the increase of Prussia. But Bismarck knew that Prussia's army made her mistress of the situation, and he stood out for his own terms.

[1] See Walpole, vol. ii, pp 256 ff. "With some misgivings, but with some hope he [Napoleon] decided to trust to Count von Bismarck's spoken promises, and with this object to instruct M. Benedetti, the French Ambassador in Berlin, to repair to the headquarters of the Prussian army, and to preach the wisdom of moderation: with some misgivings, for the Emperor could not conceal from himself that M. Benedetti did not speak with the authority of a nation prepared to enforce its counsel in arms; with some hope, for the Emperor recollected the specious prospect which the Prussian Minister had held out to him at Biarritz and was disposed to credit other men with the weak benevolence of his own character." P. 259.

xxxii THE FRANCO-PRUSSIAN WAR

"By the preliminary peace of Nikolsburg, July 26, Austria withdrew from German affairs, ceding her right in the Duchies and leaving Prussia free to establish a new confederation, and to annex the North German states except Saxony. Bismarck made concessions of form: 1. The German states south of the Main, left out of the new confederation, should have the right to form a union of their own. 2. The northern districts of Schleswig should be restored to Denmark if their population so wished. The final peace of Prague, of August 23, preserved these two clauses, but they remained illusory.[1]

"Napoleon asked Prussia for a territorial enlargement, and the Prussian envoy let him hope for one (July 19).[2] When the Tsar proposed a congress to settle the changes in Germany, it was Napoleon that refused, hoping to gain more from Prussia. He offered a secret understanding for mutual enlargement: France to have the possessions of Bavaria and Hesse on the left bank of the Rhine. Bismarck insisted upon a written draft of the scheme (to use against Napoléon), then refused it, and later published it in a conversation with a correspondent of the *Siècle*. In face of the commotion in Germany, Napoleon withdrew his

[1] It was the second of these two clauses to which the charges of violation of the Treaty of Prague, reiterated in the debates during the crisis of July, 1870, referred.

[2] The Prussian envoy referred to was the Prussian Ambassador to France, Count von Goltz, "a man almost as remarkable as Count von Bismarck himself." This statement of Walpole (vol. ii, p. 261) is amply borne out by his account of this conversation of July 19, in which Von Goltz "succeeded so well that he persuaded the Emperor to agree to the transfer of Hanover, Electoral Hesse, and Frankfort, or of some 4,500,000 people, to Prussia; and to postpone for the moment any negotiation on the compensation which should be awarded to France." P. 263.

TRANSLATOR'S INTRODUCTION xxxiii

project, denied the rumors of negotiation (August 12), and turned to Belgium. He proposed (August 20) that Prussia should aid France to acquire Belgium and Luxemburg. Bismarck had the plan written out at Napoleon's dictation; he published it in 1870 to embroil England and Belgium with France.[1]

"The South German States were isolated and quickly crushed by Prussia. They at once asked for the mediation of France; but Bismarck showed them Napoleon's plans for annexation at their expense, and in August induced them to conclude with Prussia secret treaties of offensive and defensive alliance.

"Napoleon therefore obtained no positive result, and Prussia, by a single war, acquired first place in Germany."

Bismarck continued to play upon the hopes of the Emperor during the summer of 1866, while he was negotiating the secret treaties of alliance with the South German States, which assured him of a united Germany in case of a foreign war. It became evident, at last, that "the objects at which the Emperor had originally aimed were unattainable. Prussia had no intention of surrendering an inch of territory on the Rhine to satisfy French ambition, or to heal the wounds

---

[1] The publication of this draft treaty, which Bismarck caused to be photographed and distributed in facsimile soon after the outbreak of war (it appeared in the *Times* of July 25), had a decisive effect on public opinion in England. It was in Benedetti's handwriting throughout, and was declared by him to have been written at Bismarck's dictation and by his suggestion. "When M. Benedetti had laid down the pen, M. de Bismarck folded the document and put it away as one does with a thing that may be of use. A second time, he had, in accordance with the recommendation of the great Frederick, *procured something in writing*." La Gorce, vol. v, p. 69. See also Walpole, vol. ii, pp. 447-449.

xxxiv THE FRANCO-PRUSSIAN WAR

of French discontent; and Prussia had equally no intention of moving a man or a gun to facilitate a French attack on Belgium." Thereupon Luxemburg presented itself as offering perhaps the very compensation that the Emperor desired. It was still garrisoned by Prussia (under a doubtful claim of right, the old Germanic Confederation having been dissolved). It belonged to the King of Holland, not to Holland, and he was anxious to sell it. "Napoleon grasped at the opportunity to secure additional territory. He believed that the Prussian government was only awaiting a pretext to withdraw its garrison in such a way as not to offend public opinion; Bismarck left him under this delusion. The King of Holland agreed to sell, provided Prussia would consent. Bismarck did not refuse distinctly. . . . He told the King of Holland that he would leave to him the responsibility for his acts. The King, believing that Bismarck wished only to have his hand forced, notified Napoleon that the sale would be made (March 30, 1867).

"The treaty of cession had been drawn up and announced to Europe, when an interpellation was made in the Reichstag on the rumor of a sale of German territory by a prince of German blood. Bismarck replied that nothing had yet been arranged and sent word to the King of Holland that in the present agitated condition of opinion in Germany the cession of Luxemburg would mean war. The King withdrew his consent in spite of French insistence." [2]

[1] Walpole, vol. ii, p. 453.
[2] Seignobos, p. 804. A clear and concise account of these various transactions is contained in the first chapter of Albert Sorel's *Histoire Diplomatique*, etc. For the most judicious and lively detailed account, see books 30 and 32 of vol. v, of La Gorce.

In the end, Luxemburg was neutralized, in accordance with the conclusions of a congress, held at the instance of England; but another item had been added to the Emperor's list of grievances against Prussia.

The years from the conclusion of the Luxemburg affair to the accession to power of the Ollivier Ministry were marked principally by the attempts of France to form an alliance with Austria and Italy; the sole result being a promise by each of the three sovereigns to conclude no other alliance without notifying the other two.

On accepting office M. Ollivier declared himself in favor of depriving Bismarck of every pretext for seeking a quarrel: of refraining from espousing the cause of the Danes and from interfering with the progress of the unification of Germany. "German unity so far as we are concerned is complete. . . . What interest have we in preventing the democrats of Würtemberg and Bavaria from boring Bismarck to extinction in his parliaments, since, on the day of battle, all Germany would be against us?"[1]

Early in February, at the instance of the French Foreign Office, Lord Clarendon, then Foreign Secretary, undertook to transmit to Berlin a proposition looking to eventual disarmament. Bismarck gave a most discouraging reply to the overtures of Lord A. Loftus; but a fortnight later the French ministry appealed again to Lord Clarendon, announcing at the same time that the "contingent" force of the army for 1870 would be reduced by 10,000 men. This attempt had no better

[1] *L'Empire Libéral*, vol. xii, pp. 134, 135. See La Gorce, vol. vi, pp. 175–177, on the pacific disposition of the ministry and the consequent disturbance of Bismarck's designs.

success than the earlier one, but the proposed reduction was carried out none the less. It was during the debate in the Chamber on this reduction, on *June 30*, that M. Ollivier, in reply to a question from Jules Favre, made his often-quoted statement: "In whatever direction we turn our eyes, we see no irritating question in dispute, and never at any time has the maintenance of peace in Europe been better assured."

Less than three weeks later, France and Prussia were at each other's throats; in another three weeks the Ministry of January 2 was overthrown after the first victories of the Prussian arms; and before another month had passed the Emperor was a prisoner and the Empire dead.

"It was between the 12th and 14th of July that war was morally declared," says one of the few defenders of the action of the Emperor and his ministers, "not by the will of the Ministry, but by the imperious, impatient will of the country, expressing itself at the same moment through all its organs: the Chamber, the press and public manifestations."[1]

It is absolutely certain that, if M. Ollivier and his pacifically inclined colleagues had resigned their posts when they found, on July 13, that they were being driven into a position that must inevitably lead to war, their places would have been filled by ministers chosen from the rabidly bellicose Right, the "Arcadians" or extreme Bonapartists, who believed in the

[1] Fernand Giraudeau, *La Vérité sur la Campagne de 1870* (1871), p. 58. This little volume is particularly valuable because it gives copious extracts from the newspapers, in Paris and the provinces, amply confirming M. Ollivier's statements in the text as to the general attitude of the press.

necessity of a foreign war to solidify the dynasty no less than Bismarck believed in a similar necessity to forward the unity of Germany. It may be well for Americans to recall the events of 1898, when an equally reluctant administration allowed itself to be forced into war, by a similar clamorous demonstration of the public will "through all its organs." Then, perhaps, we shall be better prepared to judge the conduct of men the sincerity of whose patriotism, as well as of their desire for peace, no historian save the bitterest partisan has failed to acknowledge.

Of all the persons who played a leading part in the critical days of July, 1870, only M. Ollivier and the Empress Eugénie are still living in this year, 1912.

THE FRANCO-PRUSSIAN WAR AND ITS HIDDEN CAUSES

INTRODUCTION

"As there is, in all human affairs, something that paves the way for them, something that determines one to undertake them, and something that causes them to succeed, the true science of history consists in taking note of those secret combinations which have paved the way for great changes, and of the momentous conjunctures which have caused them to come to pass. In truth, it is not enough simply to look at what is going on before one's eyes; that is to say, to consider only those great events which suddenly decide the fate of empires. He who would thoroughly understand human affairs must begin further back."

Whosoever would understand the War of 1870 should bear in mind this precept of Bossuet. If one would discover the real causes of a war which overturned the territorial arrangement of Europe, which restored the ancient international law of the barbarians, which arrested the regular forward movement of civilization, which forced the nations to undergo the discomfort of armaments that they abhor, and imposed upon Germany the penalty of a victory beyond her moral strength, it is all the more important not to look simply before one's eyes, but to begin further back, to observe the secret combinations from which the successive events resulted; because sooner or later this drama of 1870 will prove to be, whether at home or abroad, but the prelude of crises no less grave, whereby the form and fortunes of empires will once again be changed.

There has been much declamation concerning the expedition to Mexico — that the real cause of our catastrophe dates back to that. It is said that we were beaten in 1870 because the Empire "had squandered all our blood, all our gold, all our strength, on the plains of Mexico." [1] Now what was the average figure of our effective force in 1866? Four hundred

[1] Jules Simon, *Gouvernement de la Défense Nationale*, p. 377. Moltke, too, who is ordinarily inaccurate as to anything in which we are concerned, because he repeats the assertions of the enemies of the Empire, says, in his *Memoirs of the War of 1870*, that the Mexican War "cost enormous sums and disorganized our military strength."

In the *Memoirs* of Marshal Randon, vol. ii, p. 75, we read: "On December 13, 1862, the Mexican expedition comprised 28,000 men, 5845 horses, 549 mules, 8 12-pound siege guns, 6 12-pounders in reserve; 24 campaign 4-pounders, and 12 mountain guns. This force was not afterwards increased by more than a few thousand men, and the *matériel* was not increased at all." See also pp. 169 and 228.—In another official report that I have before me the number of mountain guns is given as 16 instead of 12, and there are 2 Mexican mortars in addition, making a total of 56 pieces.

[The best account in English of the ill-fated enterprise of Maximilian in Mexico may be found in Sir Spencer Walpole's *History of Twenty-five Years*, vol. ii, pp. 69-100. "The prince, who was shot in America, was the victim," says this distinguished historian; "the Emperor, who survived at Paris, was the instigator of the crime. And the shuttle of destiny was already weaving the warp of fate into the woof of Napoleon's winding sheet. The dream which the dreamer had dreamed was dissolved, not only in Mexico, but in Europe. The Mexican enterprise had eaten up the resources of the Empire, and had deprived Napoleon of the power to exert his will nearer home. The crowd, indeed, who only recollected the past, still regarded him as the master of many legions, the man on whose will the future of Europe depended; men more intimately acquainted with politics were already perceiving that his power was waning, and that his own faith in his destiny was yielding to circumstances" (p. 99).]

INTRODUCTION 3

thousand men. How many cannon were there in our arsenals? There were 10,944 brass guns, besides nearly three thousand of iron. How many men were employed in Mexico? From 35,000 to 40,000. How many guns? Fifty!! As for the expense, it was adjusted, during Thiers's presidency, at three hundred millions, from which it is proper to deduct what those 35,000 to 40,000 men would have cost for their keep in France — that is to say, nearly one half. That is how Mexico devoured all our blood, all our gold, and all our strength! Moreover, the losses of that campaign, in men and *matériel*, were abundantly repaired by the results of the Niel military reform of 1867.[1] That expedition impaired the personal prestige and the infallibility of Napoleon III, but even if it reflects little honor on the history of the Second Empire, its influence was no more unfortunate, no more decisive, than that of the Chinese, Cochinchinese, and Syrian expeditions was fortunate.

According to others it is to the Italian War of 1859 that we must attribute the beginning of our downfall, because it led us, by the way of Italian unity, to German unity.[2] In reality there was at that time no necessary connection between the Italian movement and the Germanic movement; and even if we had not gone down into Italy to prevent Austria from

---

[1] [An excellent brief account of the plans of Marshal Niel, and of the resistance which those plans encountered and which led to their practically complete failure, will be found in volume six of P. de la Gorce's *Histoire du Second Empire*, pp. 133–147. Niel died in August, 1869.]

[2] [A most lucid and informing narrative of the circumstances which led Napoleon III to join Italy against Austria in 1859, and of the result of that war upon his subsequent policy and fortunes, is given by Mr. W. R. Thayer in his recent work: *The Life and Times of Cavour*. Boston, 1911.]

becoming definitively mistress there, German unity, the intense desire for which Chateaubriand had noticed at the time of his embassy to Berlin, would not have interrupted its progress, daily more determined, which no opposition from without or within could have prevented from triumphing sooner or later.

No, the War of 1859 was not the prelude to our decline: it added some noble pages to our military annals, it restored two splendid provinces to the mother-country, and showed us to the world as being what we have always been, under the old monarchy as under the Republic, save for a few rare moments of aberration, the defenders of the weak, the protectors of the independence of nations, and "the morning bugle-call of the world."

Others again have assumed to refer the succession of our misfortunes to the supineness of our government in the affair of the Danish Duchies.[1] This is to ascribe undue importance to a trivial event, the solution of which, whatever it may have been, was not

---

[1] The controversy concerning the status of the duchies of Schleswig and Holstein, which had passed through many phases during the mid-nineteenth century, reached its most acute crisis in 1863, when the death of Frederick VII of Denmark brought a change of dynasty and the accession of Christian of Glücksburg. The war of 1864 between Denmark and Prussia resulted in the handing over of the duchies to Prussia and Austria, and in the eventual absorption of both by Prussia. The whole Schleswig-Holstein question, which at one time seemed likely to lead to a general European war, is said by Sir Spencer Walpole to have been "one of the most complicated matters recorded in history. The facts are so involved, the merits of the dispute are so confused, that it is difficult to make them intelligible or to pronounce a confident opinion upon them." (*Life of Lord John Russell*, vol. ii, p. 396). France, although her interests, like those of England, were associated with the cause of Denmark, failed, as did England, to go to her aid — hence the charge of "supineness." For a bird's-eye view of the whole complicated subject, see Walpole, *op. cit.*, vol. ii, pp. 371–397.]

of a nature to prolong its influence on the development of affairs. Napoleon III would have been mad enough for a strait-waistcoat, if alone, abandoned by England, he had, on that occasion, endangered the fortunes of France in a war with all of Germany; for at that time the Germanic Confederation, that is to say, the States of the South and Austria, would have gone with Prussia.

The first cause of the War of 1870 is to be found in the year 1866. It was in that year, to be marked forever with black, it was in that year of blindness when one error was redeemed only by a more grievous error, and when the infirmities of the government were made mortal by the bitterness of the opposition; it was in that accursed year that was born the supreme peril of France and of the Empire. If the year 1870 is the terrible year, 1866 is the fatal year.[1] The Romans, according to Cicero, considered the battle of the Allia more disastrous than the taking of Rome because that last misfortune was the result of the first.

Everybody, in all Europe as well as in France, is in accord touching the importance of the fateful year, and this historic truth is not contested. But everywhere the error committed by Napoleon III is mistakenly characterized. It was his chimerical loyalty to the principle of nationalities, people say, which led him to allow Prussia to constitute a great power that was a menace to ourselves. Say just the contrary, and you will be in the right. It was his disloyalty to the principle of nationalities that was the source of all of Napoleon III's misfortunes and our own.

[1] [See the translator's Introduction, *supra*.]

People would not deny it if they had a better comprehension of this theory of nationalities, which everybody talks about without understanding it, or understanding it all awry. The theory of nationalities may be reduced to a few maxims of luminous simplicity: —

Every freely constituted nation forms a sovereign, intangible organism, however weak, which cannot be placed under foreign domination without its consent, or be kept there against its will. It does not recognize conquest as a legitimate means of acquisition. Only the will of the people has the power lawfully to create, to transform, to diminish, or to increase kingdoms.

Whence it follows: first, that no nation has the right to meddle in the affairs of another, to object to its international arrangements, to prevent it from separating from a state to which it was united by force, or from annexing itself to another to which it is drawn by its sympathies or its interests. Furthermore, Europe, assembled in congress or conference, is not possessed of a collective right of its own, which is denied to each nation separately, on the pretext of preventing any nation from disturbing, at its pleasure, the general system to which it belongs.

The underlying principle of the theory of nationalities is easily distinguishable from others with which it is too often confused — that of great agglomerations, of natural boundaries, and of race. The will of the people concerned may, if it seems fitting, constitute great agglomerations, but it may constitute small ones as well. It does not recognize natural frontiers. The real frontiers are those established by the will of the people; the others are the walls of a prison, which one has always the right to tear down. Woe to the country that drags a province in its train like a millstone about its neck; woe to that one whose people do not bask in its sunshine with free and joyful hearts. To create moral unity is more essential than to satisfy the strategic demands of a mountain-chain or a stream.

Nor does the theory of nationalities recognize a pretended right of race, manifested by a common language or by historic tradition, by virtue of which all the nations born of a common stock and speaking the same language must needs, whether they will or no, and without being consulted, be united in a single state. The idea of race is a barbarous, exclusive, retrograde idea, and has nothing in common with the broad, sacred, civilizing idea of fatherland. Race has limits which cannot be overstepped; fatherland has none: it may expand and develop unceasingly; it might become all mankind, as under the Roman Empire. On our European continent races long since became blended in fatherlands, and it would be impossible to undo the mysterious process from which have flowed the beautiful products of that blending.

There is an ineffable sweetness in the word fatherland, just because it expresses, not a preordained aggregation, but a free, loving creation, wherein millions of human beings have placed their hearts for centuries past.

The will of the peoples, then, is the one dominant, sovereign, absolute principle, whence the modern law of nations in its entirety should flow by a series of logical deductions, as from an inexhaustible spring.

It is the principle of liberty substituted in international relations for geographical and historical inevitableness.

Of course the principle of nationality does not do away with all wars. There remain the wars waged for honor, for religion, for the diversion of despots; but it eliminates the most common and most dangerous sort, — those of conquest; and it tends toward the progressive abolition of other wars, by virtue of the civilizing principle which is its inspiration. It should be cultivated everywhere with respect, and propagated by men of progress and liberty. In France it should be a national dogma, since it is our incontestable right to reconquer our dear Alsace, brutally wrested from us by conquest, and annexed to the foreigner without her consent.

Were the events that occurred in Germany in 1866 the logical outcome of the principle of nationalities? Was it by virtue of that principle as we have defined it, that Prussia annexed the Danish Duchies, the free towns, Frankfort, Hesse-Darmstadt, and Hanover, although it was the declared desire of the peoples thereof to retain their autonomy? No, it was by virtue of a denial of that principle that those annexations were carried out. Bismarck, who was not fond of hypocritical euphemisms of speech, said in so many words, "It was by right of conquest." The year 1866, therefore, was not the triumph of the principle of nationality, but its defeat, and the victorious resurrection of the principle of conquest. The real error of Napoleon III consisted, not in forwarding that civilizing principle, which had already raised him so high, but in becoming the compliant tool, in the hope of a reward, of those who were rending it with their swords.

He was at liberty not to oppose by force the conquests of Prussia, if he did not consider that the interest of France demanded it; but he should have seconded the efforts which others (Russia, for example) were making to arrest them, and, in any event, should not have approved, much less have encouraged them, and, less still, have demanded a reward for that encouragement. But that is what he did: he gave Prussia his formal assent, refused to second Russia in suggesting the assembling of a congress, and solicited, as a reward, first the left bank of the Rhine, then Belgium, and finally Luxembourg.

Prussia welcomed his adhesion with sarcastic cordiality, and refused with insolent ingratitude the wage, even when it was reduced to the minimum. She did more: she snapped her fingers at the man to whose kindly neutrality she was indebted for not being crushed on the battle-field, and she instantly disregarded the promise she had made at Prague to arrest her predominance at the Main: she passed that boundary, in a military sense, by means of treaties of alliance, and thus constituted the military unity of Germany — the only form of unity which was dangerous to us.

The Emperor, disconcerted by the failure of his plans, regretting that he had favored fruitlessly the principle of conquest, and had imprudently abandoned the principle of nationality, wavered from 1867 to 1870 in a state of incoherence and indecision, daring neither to accept nor to repudiate the results of his fatal complaisance.

It was my ambition, when he honored me with his confidence, to restore to the Empire the ground that it had lost since 1866, by returning definitively to the principle of nationality, which, since the irrevocable events of 1866, bade us not to oppose the internal transformation of Germany, even though it must end in rounding out, by political unity, the military unity already constituted. In a letter addressed to Walewski[1] on January 1, 1867, and intended to be shown to the Emperor, I said: —

"I criticised and regretted the events of last year, and the ill-advised circular note which passed them over; but I now consider German Unity as an irrevocable, predestined fact, which France can accept without danger or humiliation. So long as I shall not desire to ruin my country by fallacious counsel, I shall not urge her to contemplate joining exhausted Austria in a new Seven Years' War, in which we should find Russia by the side of Prussia, without being certain of Italy's following our lead. Whatever we may attempt agianst Prussia will facilitate her work instead of hampering it: even a Jena would not impair it. Peace without any mental reservation — such is the only external policy to which I can adapt myself."

My language in my conversations with the Emperor, when I was forming my ministry, was no less explicit.

"Our policy," I said on November 1, 1869, "should consist in depriving Herr von Bismarck of any pre-

---

[1] [Comte Alexandre Walewski, reputed to be an illegitimate son of Napoleon I, was Minister of Foreign Affairs for several years previous to 1860, and afterwards president of the Corps Législatif.]

INTRODUCTION 11

text for picking a quarrel with us, and for making his King eager for war, which he is not now. There are two firebrands of war already lighted, and we must stamp them out: in the North the question of Schleswig; in the South that of the line of the Main. Although sympathizing deeply with the Danes, we have no right to involve our country in a conflict in order to ensure a quiet life to a few thousands of them who are unjustly oppressed. As for the line of the Main, it was crossed a long while ago, at least so far as we are concerned. Have not the treaties of alliance [1] brought about the military unification of Germany, and the renewal of the Zollverein its economic unity? German Unity, as against us, is complete; that which remains to be completed, political union, concerns Prussia alone, to whom it will bring more embarrassment than strength. What interest have we in preventing the democrats of Würtemberg and the Ultramontanes of Bavaria from annoying Bismarck in his parliaments, when, in the day of battle, all of Germany would be united against us?"

The sovereign, who recognized his own ideas in mine, approved my policy, notwithstanding some reservations, and the ministry of January 2 was formed, not to make ready for war with Germany, but to make such a war impossible.[2]

[1] [This term refers to the secret treaties between Prussia and the various South German states, after Sadowa, whereby Prussia acquired complete control of the military forces of all Germany in case she should be attacked or her territory even threatened. See Albert Sorel, *Histoire Diplomatique de la Guerre Franco-Allemande*, vol. i, pp. 43–44.]

[2] [The members of the ministry as originally constituted were: Émile Ollivier, *Keeper of the Seals* and *Minister of Justice*, Comte Daru, *Foreign*

12 THE FRANCO-PRUSSIAN WAR

And yet it was that ministry which was compelled to declare it. One is reminded of the musicians in *Romeo and Juliet*, who, being invited to the marriage feast, arrived just in time to sing the burial music. There are few tales so tragic as this. I propose to tell it.

Affairs, Buffet, *Finances*, General Le Bœuf, *War*, Admiral Rigault de Genouilly, *Marine*, Chevandier de Valdrôme, *Interior*, Segris, *Public Instruction*, Louvet, *Commerce*, Marquis de Talhouët, *Public Works*, Maurice Richard, *Fine Arts*, Parieu, *President of the Council of State*. Comte Daru and Buffet resigned in April, and were soon followed by the Marquis de Talhouët. The vacancy in the Foreign Office was filled for a short time by Ollivier, but he handed the portfolio to the Duc de Gramont in June ; Segris was transferred to the Department of Finance and Plichon took his place as Minister of Public Instruction. The ministry suffered no further change during its brief life. For characterizations of the different ministers see La Gorce, vol. vi, pp. 3, 4, 117, 216, 217.]

CHAPTER I

BISMARCK CONTEMPLATES WAR WITH FRANCE

IN 1866, on the field of Sadowa, Austria not only lost her former preponderance in the Germanic Confederation, but was excluded therefrom. The intervention of France prevented the victory of Prussia from being complete: she was allowed to annex certain territory, but the States of the South were set outside of her Confederation, and the Main became the artificial boundary between the two sections of Germany. Thenceforth Bismarck's policy had but one object: to destroy that boundary and to throw bridges across the Main whereby the two sections of Germany might be united. With keen and intelligent foresight, he saw that there could be no drawing together of the States of the North and those of the South so long as the gory memories of 1866 stood between them. A campaign made by them in common against France seemed to him the only means of wiping out all trace of these internal dissensions.

For some time he hoped that France would seek such a rencounter, and would try to recover the preponderance of which the victory of Sadowa had deprived her; but France perorated, sulked, and did not stir.

The accession to power, on January 2, 1870, of the liberal ministry definitively blasted that hope of Bismarck's of an aggressive policy on our part. He determined thereupon to assume himself the responsibility for aggression which we declined, and to force us to the field of battle. As soon as it appeared that it was our policy not to oppose the internal transformation of Germany, he was unable to conjure up any cause for war in that direction. He set his wits at work, therefore, to find one in Spain.

Queen Isabella had just been dethroned, and as the republicans were not in a majority, Spain was in search of a king.[1] Pending his discovery, the Cortes had made Serrano Regent of the kingdom; but the actual dictator of Spanish policy was the Minister of War and President of the Council, General Prim.[2] Bismarck, by means of hard cash,[3] came to an understanding

---

[1] [See, *infra*, Appendix B, "The Spanish Revolution of 1868."]

[2] [For a brief history of the Hohenzollern candidacy, from its first conception, see, *infra*, Appendix C.

General Prim, in his youth, fought in the army of Maria Christina (widow of Ferdinand VII, and Regent during the minority of her daughter Isabella II) in the Carlist troubles of 1833-40. He was prominent in the overthrow of the Regent Espartero in 1843. Having attained high rank in the army, he won the victory of Los Castillejos in the Moroccan War of 1860, and was made a marquis in honor thereof. He commanded the Spanish forces sent to Mexico in 1862 to act in conjunction with the English and French; but he did not approve of Napoleon's plans, and took his troops back to Spain, where his action was sanctioned by the Cortes. As leader of the Progressists, he was one of the triumvirate which assumed control on the overthrow of Isabella — the others being Admiral Topete and Francisco Serrano y Dominguez, who became Regent. As commander in chief of the armies of Spain, in addition to his high civil posts, Prim was the most powerful and influential man in the kingdom until his death, by assassination, in December, 1870. "He was the active man, and, as was said in Europe, 'the king-maker.'" La Gorce, vol. vi, p. 199.]

[3] One of the best informed of English publicists, Sir Rowland Blennerhassett, contributed to the *National Review* for October, 1902, a remarkable study on the "Origin of the Franco-Prussian War." He says: —

"It has often been asked whether, at this time or some other (when Lothar Bucher and Versen were sent to Spain in April, 1870), money was supplied

Marshal Prim, Marquis de Los Castillejos
1814 – 1870

with him to put forward the candidacy for the Spanish throne of a prince of the Catholic branch of the house of Hohenzollern-Sigmaringen: a mediatized house, closely allied to the royal family of Prussia by the bonds of filial obedience, and with sons serving in the Prussian army. The head of this branch was Prince Antony, a very shrewd person, ambitious and wealthy, and it was his oldest son, Leopold, whom Bismarck and Prim jointly chose as a candidate for the crown of Spain.[1]

Both were well aware that France would not endure that a Prussian prince should be set up, a Prussian sentinel, across her southern frontier, so that she would be caught between two fires in the event of a war on the Rhine. "France will never put up with such a candidacy," was Prince Antony's reply to the first overtures made to him for his son. Bismarck knew it as well as he, and that is precisely why he contrived the scheme.

by the Prussian agents to forward the Hohenzollern candidacy. I have reasons for thinking that a very considerable sum was expended for that purpose. Indications of this might be found in the papers of the late Lord Acton, and proofs could be furnished by a certain banking house which I could name."

In the more extensive work from which the present volume is taken, M. Ollivier says: —

"The arguments of Bismarck's agents were not of the sort to convince a gentleman of his (Prim's) stamp — a gambler and libertine, corrupt in every way. He required chinking arguments. None of those who have gone to the bottom of this affair doubts that Bismarck made use of them. It is not probable that history will ever acquire proof of the fact: one does not ordinarily go before a notary and set down such arrangements in a contract under seal. In Bernhardi's memoirs everything relating to this negotiation is omitted, and in the writings of Lothar Bucher, the decisive agent in the last stage of the affair, all that has reference to this, the most important episode in his career, is not printed." *L'Empire Libéral*, vol. xiii, p. 38.

[1] [See, *infra*, Appendix D, "Prince Leopold of Hohenzollern, his Family and Relationships."]

The negotiations which were thereupon entered into, with profound secrecy, were unknown to Napoleon III.[1] Prim commissioned a Spanish Deputy, Salazar y Mazaredo, who was subsidized, like himself, to take to Berlin the words which he did not choose to put upon paper. Salazar arrived in January, 1870, supplied with letters of introduction to Bismarck and the King.

He was received without delay by Bismarck, for he was his agent. But he found the King's door closed. William, having read Prim's letter, refused to receive his envoy, and wrote to Bismarck. "The *enclosed*

---

[1] "If," says M. Ollivier, "Prim's designs were disinterested and avowable, why should he have concealed them from Olozaga, his former comrade in political battles? and from me, whom he knew to be so well disposed to oblige him? Why should he not have revealed them to the Emperor, from whom, despite his desertion of him in Mexico, he had received so many proofs of good-will, and whose loyalty in keeping a state secret he had fully tested? . . . And why that threat to the one man from whom he was not in a position to conceal anything — Salazar: 'If you open your mouth, I'll blow the lid off your brain'?" *L'Empire Libéral*, vol. xiii, pp. 39, 40.

[The truth seems to be that Prim, in common with every one else concerned, was perfectly well aware what would be the effect upon French opinion of the announcement of the candidacy, and it is supposed that, expecting to meet the Emperor at Vichy in July, he desired to be the first to mention the subject to him, hoping that he might, by making the most of Prince Leopold's kinship with the Bonapartes (see Appendix D), bring about a peaceful solution of the affair. See the article by H. Leonardon, "Prim et la candidature Hohenzollern," in the *Revue Historique*, vol. lxxiv (1900), pp. 287–310; and see also, *infra*, Chap. iii, p. 42, note. — "Improbable as it may appear, he flattered himself that he could win over Napoleon III to his plans. Emboldened by his parliamentary triumphs, full of confidence in his dexterity, he said to himself: 'I will persuade the Emperor as I persuade my majority. After he has heard me, he will accept my candidate, who is his kinsman; if not I will make him buy me off by a formal promise to quiet the apprehensions of the Court of Florence and to give me the assistance which he has hitherto refused me in my negotiations to secure an Italian prince.'" C. Victor Cherbulliez, in *L'Espagne Politique*, cited by Sorel, vol. i, p. 57.]

BISMARCK CONTEMPLATES WAR

letter shocks me like a thunder-clap in a clear sky. Here is another Hohenzollern candidacy! and for the crown of Spain! I had no suspicion of such a thing. I was joking not long ago, with the prince's heir, about the previous mention of his name, and we agreed in rejecting the idea as a jest. As you have heard details from the prince, we will confer about it, *although on principle I am opposed to the thing.*" (February 26, 1870.)[1]

The King was, in truth, opposed to this enterprise, which, in the first place, he considered hazardous, and in which it was repugnant to him to compromise the dignity of his house. He was well aware that it would offend the Emperor Napoleon, whose predilection for Alfonzo, as heir to the Spanish throne, was notorious; and lastly, considering the disposition of French opinion, he feared serious complications, and he wanted nothing of the kind.

If he had held to his first impulse, the business would not have been begun. According to existing statutes and treaties, the princes of the Catholic branch of the Hohenzollerns were strictly bound to enter upon no important act of their lives, public or private, without the formal approval of the head of the family first obtained. On no occasion did those princes deny this disciplinary obligation; on the contrary, they deemed it to their honor and glory to submit to it. If therefore the King had uttered a formal *no*, he would have put a stop to the whole affair, especially

[1] Sybel, whose whole narrative is a constant distortion of the truth, says that the King knew nothing of the negotiation, which was carried on behind his back, until after it was at an end; that, consequently, he could not have informed Count Bismarck of divers incidents thereof, because he had no knowledge of them himself. [Von Sybel, English trans., vol. vii, p. 319.]

18   THE FRANCO-PRUSSIAN WAR

as that was the inclination of the princes themselves.[1] But Bismarck's whole policy hung upon the success of his Spanish plot, and his influence over his master was then more predominant than at any other moment of his career. He argued against the veto. At first his arguments did not avail to overcome the King's repugnance. The concession that he obtained was that the King would not utter a definitive *no;* that he would place himself again in the position he had taken in 1866, at the time Prince Charles assumed the throne of Roumania, saying neither yes nor no, leaving the princes at liberty to accept or decline, and declaring himself ready to approve their decision.

Consequently he summoned them to Berlin, and on March 15 there was held a council at the Royal Palace, where the Hohenzollerns had, as their custom was, taken up their abode. Prince Antony described the meeting to his son Charles of Roumania in terms which deserve to be given literally : —

"I have been for a fortnight immersed in family affairs of the greatest importance: they concern nothing less than the acceptance or refusal by Leopold of the Spanish crown, which has been officially offered to him by the Spanish government under the seal of a European state secret. Bismarck favors acceptance for dynastic and *political* reasons, but the King does not

---

[1] "Sybel is the only serious historian who has maintained the dishonest position that the King's consent was not necessary. 'That the King, as head of the family,' says Ottokar Lorenz (*Wilhelm I*, p. 212), 'could forbid the Prince's acceptance of the crown, cannot be questioned by anybody.' — 'It is certain,' says Hans Delbrück, 'that no Hohenzollern prince would have come to such a decision without having inquired anxiously of the King's wishes, and without being guided entirely thereby.' ('The Secret of the Napoleonic Policy in 1870': in *Preussische Jahrbücher*, Oct. 1895, p. 28.)" — *L'Empire Libéral*, vol. xiii, p. 42. See also, vol. xiv, pp. 67, 68, and notes.

BISMARCK CONTEMPLATES WAR 19

wish it unless Leopold so decides of his own free will. On the 15th a very interesting and important council was held under the presidency of the King, in which the following took part: the Prince Royal, we two, Bismarck, Moltke, Roon, Schleinitz, Thile, and Delbrück. The council resolved unanimously in favor of acceptance, *which means the performance of a patriotic Prussian duty.* After a great struggle Leopold refused. *As they want, above all things, in Spain, a Catholic Hohenzollern,* I proposed Fritz."[1]

The deliberation was followed by a dinner at Prince Antony's. "If Napoleon takes this in ill part, are we ready?" asked Jules Delbrück. To which Moltke

[1] [*Aus dem Leben Königs Karl von Rumanien* (Stuttgart, 1894), vol. ii, p. 72; French translation (Bucharest, 1899), vol. i, p. 570. An abridged English translation, by Sidney Whitman, was published in 1895. Count Bismarck, in his address to the Federal Council on July 16, 1870, after war had been practically declared, said that the negotiations concerning the candidacy of Prince Leopold "had been brought unofficially to the knowledge of the King of Prussia, on the express condition that he would keep them secret. As they concerned neither Prussia nor the Confederation of the North, the King agreed to that condition, and therefore he did not speak of the affair to his government, as it was to him simply a family matter." And in his Circular Note of July 18 to the Powers, he said: "The statement is also untrue that His Majesty the King communicated the candidacy of Prince Leopold to me, the undersigned Chancellor of the Confederation. *I was casually informed in confidence of the Spanish offer by a private person concerned in the negotiations.*" See the full text of the Note in Appendix H. When the Memoirs of the King of Roumania appeared, they presented a categorical denial, notably in the letter quoted in the text, of the Bismarckian theory of the relation of the Prussian King and government to the candidacy. In the Appendix to vol. xiii of *L'Empire Libéral* (pp. 639–641), M. Ollivier quotes from Bismarck's *Reflections and Reminiscences*, vol. ii, p. 90, as follows:] "The Memoirs of His Majesty the King of Roumania are not exactly in accord with the details of the part played by the ministry in the matter. This council of ministers held at the palace, of which they speak, never took place. Prince Antony was quartered in the palace as the King's guest, and he had invited the sovereign and some of his ministers to dine with him. I am inclined to think that the Spanish question was hardly

replied in the affirmative, with cheering confidence.[1] That the Emperor would take it in ill part, no serious-minded man doubted, especially in Spain; and the Prussian minister, Kaunitz, announced from Madrid that "many perils would spring from that candidacy."

Leopold, who had been treated by Napoleon III with the utmost kindliness, confidence, and affection, could not make up his mind to the felonious act, unworthy of a gentleman, into which Bismarck's craft would have hurried him. In truth nothing could be less honorable than the motives appealed to by Bismarck, as Prince Antony describes them. "It was," he says, "the performance of a patriotic Prussian duty." What patriotic Prussian duty could there be to be performed in Spain at that precise moment,

mentioned at the table." "If," comments M. Ollivier, "there were an absolute contradiction between Prince Antony and Bismarck, it would be impossible to hesitate a moment between the testimony of Prince Antony, a truthful person, writing to his son at the time of the occurrence, and Bismarck the liar, writing many years later, from vague memories, whose inaccuracy is described by Lothar Bucher" (see *infra*, p. 23, note). "But, in reality, there is no contradiction between the two. Bismarck says that there was no council of ministers, and he is right; but Prince Antony does not say that there was: he speaks only of a council of high officers of State, whom he names, and among whom there is hardly a minister. Bismarck talks about a dinner, during which he thinks that hardly an allusion was made to the Spanish question. Again he is right: it is certain that they did not discuss the question whether Prince Leopold should or should not accept the Spanish crown, before servants standing behind their chairs or serving courses. But Prince Antony speaks of a council and not of a dinner-party, and the dinner-party referred to by Bismarck did not take place until after the council. Bismarck dares not deny the fact of that council; he omits to mention it, and thereby confirms it. . . . In reality he impliedly confirms, although he pretends to contradict them, the explicit memoirs of Prince Antony. And so Lothar Bucher, Ottokar Lorenz, and, one may say, all Germans, regard Prince Antony's narrative as one of those historical facts which are beyond all question."

[1] Hans Delbrück, in *Preussische Jahrbücher*, Oct., 1895.

BISMARCK CONTEMPLATES WAR 21

if not to stir up that war against France without which German Unity would have to come to anchor?

The revelations of Prince Antony concerning the council of March 15, under the presidency of the King of Prussia, strike at the root of the structure of glittering falsehoods intended to prove that "Leopold's candidacy was a *palliative* family affair, entirely Spanish, of which the Prussian government knew absolutely nothing."

"The French have always been convinced," says Hans Delbrück, "that the Hohenzollern candidacy was Bismarck's work; in Germany people did not choose to believe it, and I myself, as well as Sybel, protested earnestly against that reproach. But facts have demonstrated that, in this instance, the reproach of the French was well founded. The King of Roumania, for reasons by no means easy to comprehend, they say, thought it his duty to relieve his family from all responsibility for the affair, but the secret which the Ministry of Foreign Affairs at Berlin had kept with a solicitude that was never relaxed, is now disclosed, and there is no longer the slightest doubt upon this point: namely, that, although the first suggestion came from Spain, the candidacy was, nevertheless, the work of Bismarck." [1]

It was natural that the King should consult Bismarck about a private matter, as he consulted him about everything. But what concern in a question of this nature had that areopagus of diplomatists, warriors, and administrative officers, whom the King,

[1] Hans Delbrück, *ubi sup.* It is a mistake to say that the first suggestion of the candidacy came from Spain. It came from Lisbon, having reached there from Germany and Brussels. [But see, *infra*, Appendix C.]

who was very jealous of his authority as head of the family, would certainly not have convoked and consulted, if it had been a matter of some simple intimate affair of no international importance?

It is unquestionable, therefore, that the King, as soon as he was informed of the candidacy of Prince Leopold, considered it an affair of state, and that he consulted upon it the most influential men of his government, under the seal of secrecy. It is unquestionable, too, that Bismarck had not chosen Leopold because of his presumptive capacity to govern Spain wisely, or because of his alliance with the royal family of Portugal; but solely because he belonged to the royal family of Prussia and bore the name of Hohenzollern. He had thought at first of Prince Charles, then of Prince Leopold, and if need were, would content himself with Prince Fritz. Whether he was capable or not mattered little; the essential point was that his name was Hohenzollern; that is to say, that his name would cause alarm in France and would wound her sensibilities. In very truth there would be neither justice nor loyalty nor common sense in this world if, in presence of such facts, one could still ask one's self from whom came the provocation to that terrible war.

While they were waiting to learn whether Prince Fritz would be more compliant than his brother Leopold, Salazar was requested to leave Berlin and return to Madrid, without awaiting a *final* answer, "lest some one might find out that a Spaniard was having numerous interviews with Prince Bismarck."[1]

[1] Memoirs of King Charles of Roumania [French trans., vol. i, p. 571. And see Leonardon, "Prim et la candidature Hohenzollern," in the *Revue*

BISMARCK CONTEMPLATES WAR 23

The Chancellor was not of those who are discouraged by obstacles. He did not choose to allow others to be more discouraged than himself, or that Prim should be disturbed by Leopold's negative response, of which Salazar was the bearer. He wished also to dispel the objection of the King and the princes based upon the perils of the undertaking; and in the early days of April he despatched as agents of the Prussian government, although their quality was concealed under *incognitos*, two men in his confidence, Lothar Bucher and Major Versen.[1] The former, a keen, close-mouthed

Historique, vol. lxxiv: "Salazar had already set out for Spain, fearing to arouse suspicion by a longer sojourn in Berlin, and by his numerous visits to Bismarck."]

[1] [Dr. Moritz Busch (1821-95) who became attached to the service of Bismarck early in 1870, as a sort of what would be called to-day "publicity agent," diligently kept a diary, which was eventually published, first in an English version in 1898, under the title: *Bismarck: Some Secret Pages of his History;* then in French, and finally in German, in 1899. He was closely connected in his service with Adolf Lothar Bucher (1817-1892), through whom the Chancellor's memoranda for newspaper articles to be written by Busch were generally delivered to the latter; and on pages 433 ff. of volume one of the two-volume English version will be found a lifelike sketch of that able and trusted fellow-worker of the Chancellor. He had had a stormy youth of a sort that seemed unlikely to lead him to that relationship: a revolutionist in 1848; imprisoned, then practically an exile in London, where he lived until the amnesty of 1860 enabled him to return to Berlin. In the *Éclaircissements* to his 13th volume (pp. 634-636), M. Ollivier tells the story, from Poschinger's *Life and Works of Lothar Bucher, a Forty-Eighter*, of Bucher's entering the government service:] "At a meeting of the ministry, Count Lippe, then (Aug. 1864) Minister of Justice, said: 'Something extraordinary happened to-day. Lothar Bucher has asked to be employed in the bureau of law. Naturally I can't accept that fellow.' — 'What's that?' cried Bismarck, 'Bucher wants to enter the service of the State; very good! if you don't take him, I will.' General amazement. Thereupon Bismarck wrote to Bucher. The latter, who, as every one knows, was one of the founders of the National Association, then wrote to Bismarck: 'Your Excellency knows my national point of view, which I shall never abandon.' — Bismarck replied at once: 'I am perfectly well aware of your national point of view; but I

man, of wide experience, acquainted with all the windings of Bismarckian politics, who had retained from his demagogic origin an intense aversion to Napoleon III; the second, a soldier of great decision of character, who was wonderfully conversant with the Spanish tongue. They were to place themselves in communication with Salazar and Bernhardi, encourage Prim, travel through the country, and report on the chances of success of the candidacy. This step, no less than

need just that to carry out my policy, and I shall employ you only in doing things which lie within the sphere of your national opinions.' Bucher hastened to inform Bismarck that, in that case, he gladly accepted the position offered him." [For more than twenty years he filled many important posts and performed many arduous and delicate tasks, under the Chancellor, to whom he was perfectly loyal after his fall, in 1890, and whom he assisted in the preparation of his memoirs.

M. Ollivier notes the interesting fact that the English edition of Dr. Busch's book is much the most complete, many passages being suppressed in the French and German editions, especially in the former. He gives many examples of such suppressions, mainly statements made to Busch by Bucher concerning Bismarck's failure of memory. One instance must suffice. "It is not only that his memory is unreliable," said Bucher to Busch, "but he also purposely gives a false turn to the simplest proved facts. He will not admit that he ever had a share in anything that turned out ill; and he thinks that nobody is of any consequence compared to himself except possibly the old Emperor, to whom, *in order to annoy the young Emperor*, he assigns a higher place than he deserves. . . . Even where his policy succeeded brilliantly, he is unwilling to admit the truth, as, for example, in the matter of the trap set for Napoleon in the Spanish business. He denied his letter to Prim until I reminded him that I myself handed it to the general at Madrid. The whole Hohenzollern candidacy was represented as a private affair of the court, and he was obliged to confess that it was discussed at a session of the Council of Ministers."

Major von Versen "accepted with joy, being of those who love adventures full of glory," according to his biographer, Freiherr von Werthern: *General von Versen, aus hinterlassenen Briefen und Aufzeichnungen zusammengestellt*. For Versen's investigations and favorable conclusions, see La Gorce, vol. vi, p. 205, and Leonardon, "Prim et la candidature Hohenzollern," heretofore cited. As to the unpopularity of Prim's selection, as evidenced by caricatures and puns, Welschinger, *La Guerre de 1870*, vol. i, p. 42.]

BISMARCK CONTEMPLATES WAR 25

the council of March 15, "proves that it had been decided at Berlin to follow up the Spanish affair in all seriousness, and that the government was more deeply involved in it, than it had publicly and officially admitted." [1]

While Versen and Bucher are pursuing their inquiries in Spain, Fritz von Hohenzollern, having been found, arrives at Berlin from Paris. But Fritz is more recalcitrant than his brother, for the very reason that he is just from the Tuileries, where he has been overwhelmed with courteous attention. He will accept only if the King so commands — otherwise he will decline. The King does not choose to command. Fritz declines. Prince Antony telegraphs his decision to Lothar at Madrid, and writes mournfully to his son Charles of Roumania: "A great historical moment for the house of Hohenzollern has past — such a moment as never presented itself before and will never occur again." [2]

Lothar Bucher and Versen had been received with exceptional warmth and cordiality; they were taken about, cajoled, and taught their lesson. They saw things as Prim showed them, and they returned to

[1] Ottokar Lorenz, p. 246.

[2] [Prince Antony's letter was dated at Berlin, April 26. "The Spanish question has brought me here again," he says, "it is now approaching its decisive stage. After Leopold refused the offer for weighty reasons, Fritz's candidacy was seriously taken in hand. An immediate settlement was necessary, as pressure was brought to bear from Madrid; your brother, however, most decidedly declared that he could not undertake the task! The matter must therefore be allowed to drop, and a great historical moment, etc. . . . If the king had commanded, Fritz would have obeyed; but as he was left free to decide, he thought best to refuse. Now it is all over, and this episode will fall into oblivion until some historian of our family shall revive it in the distant future." *Aus dem Leben Königs Karl von Rumanien;* cited by La Gorce, vol. vi, p. 206; French trans., vol. i, p. 578.]

Berlin on May 6, convinced that the candidacy offered the best chances of success: there was no reason for not accepting it.[1]

They did not find Bismarck at Berlin. Exhausted by his labors, by his Gargantuan appetite, he had been obliged to lay aside public affairs temporarily, and to go to Varzin to restore his digestion. In default of Bismarck, it was to the King that Versen made his report. The King, left to himself, recurred to his original repugnance, and attached but the slightest importance to Versen's favorable conclusions; he attributed their "rosy hue" to the courtesies with which his envoys had been overwhelmed. Meanwhile he questioned Prince Fritz anew, who repeated his reply: "If the King had commanded, I would have obeyed; he did not, so I decline."

[1] [The visit of Bucher and Versen, early in April, followed very close upon an event which really put an end to Montpensier's candidacy, although it was momentarily resurrected in June (*L'Empire Libéral*, vol. xiii, 565 ff.). He killed his brother-in-law, Don Enrique de Bourbon, in a duel, was tried by a council of war, and sentenced to pay a fine and to a month's exile from Madrid; a cabinet crisis followed, resulting in the retirement of his partisans. See *L'Empire Libéral*, vol. xiii, pp. 51, 52.]

CHAPTER II

BISMARCK TAKES UP THE HOHENZOLLERN CANDIDACY ANEW AFTER THE PLEBISCITE IN FRANCE

ALTHOUGH the plebiscite [1] did not settle directly the question of peace or war, since neither the government nor the opposition had submitted that question to the people, it was indirectly a pacificatory event by reason of its soothing effect upon the internal situation of the country. It had intensified, if such a thing were possible, our inclination for peace. We were moved by the confidence and loyalty of the country people, and as peace is their principal concern and their most unvarying desire, we felt more than ever bound to safeguard it with great care.

To claim that the plebiscite was one of the causes of the war is devoid of common sense, so far as France is concerned. On the other hand, it is quite true, if we consider it from Bismarck's standpoint. The victory of Napoleon III was an unpleasant surprise to him; he had supposed that the liberal administration would lead the Empire to its ruin; he found, on the contrary, that that administration had strengthened the Empire.[2] The guaranties which the Emperor's success

---

[1] [A very brief account of the plebiscite may be found in the translator's Introduction, *supra*, p. xxv.]

[2] [The subject is elaborated by M. Ollivier in his 13th volume, pp. 546 ff. See also La Gorce, vol. vi, pp. 176, 177, where Bismarck's discomfiture is attributed rather to the whole initial policy of the ministry of January 2, than to the plebiscite alone. The Chancellor was disturbed at the time by

afforded of the continuance of peace, escaped nobody in Germany. At Berlin people asked one another if they would not be forced to abandon the idea of the conquest of Germany, and content themselves with being just Prussia and no more. "The internal situation," Ottokar Lorenz admitted, "could not be relieved except by an attack from France." Now it was becoming certain that France would not be the first to make the attack which, since 1867, Bismarck had vainly awaited. It had not come; it would not come; it was necessary, therefore, to provoke it. He resolved to wait no longer, but to bring matters to a head.[1]

As soon as he had recovered, he left his retirement at Varzin and attended the last sessions of the Reichstag of the Confederation of the North (May 22).

Versen, who had taken a fancy to the Spanish enterprise, and had found no consolation for the contempt with which the King had received his report and

the growing spirit of autonomy in the States of the South, notably Bavaria and Würtemberg. "In his domestic embarrassments, France had hitherto been his main resource." (La Gorce.) See also Sorel, vol. i, pp. 48, 49.]

[1] "In 1867 Bismarck avoided war because he thought that Prussia was not strong enough. In 1870 that difficulty was out of the way, Germany was sufficiently armed. The Arcadians desired war, the Ultramontanes, with the Empress at their head, were striving ardently to the same end. France was visibly strengthening her army and seeking alliances. If hitherto we had been able to rest our hope on delay, such delay was now becoming a danger, and thence resulted for the true statesman the duty of substituting for a policy that postponed decisive action a policy that hastened the coming of what was absolutely inevitable. In the interest of Germany, and no less in the interest of all Europe, it was essential to find some means of surprising the French, who were not entirely prepared for the contest, in such wise as to force them to lay aside their reserve." [Moritz Busch, cited by Ollivier, vol. xiii, pp. 548, 549. The ultra-Bonapartists were called "Arcadians," because their club was on rue de l'Arcade.]

BISMARCK AND THE CANDIDACY 29

broken off the negotiations, had attempted to take up the affair secretly with the Crown Prince, under whom he had served. He had striven to such good purpose, that he had won the Prince over to his cause.[1] He had no doubt that Bismarck, fortified by this new concurrence, would go on with his scheme. As soon as he learned that the Chancellor had returned to Berlin, he hastened to the Palace of the Reichstag and told him of his report and of the King's refusal to take any notice of it.

Bismarck, greatly displeased by this check, said that the affair must be set in motion again forthwith. "For Germany it was an object the attainment of which was unconditionally desirable and worthy of being striven for."[2] First of all Prim's confidence must be restored and he must be given the countersign. To this end Lothar Bucher was sent to him once more, bearing an autograph letter from Bismarck. "Prim will be ill-advised to consider the Hohenzollern candidacy abandoned; it depends upon him alone to revive it. The essential point is never to involve the Minister of Foreign Affairs, or the Chancellor of the Empire, or Bismarck himself. If he has any communications to

---

[1] [Versen obtained from the Crown Prince a letter to Prince Antony, then at Düsseldorf, and left Berlin May 20. He finally found the Prince at Nauheim, and argued with him so strenuously that he succeeded in convincing him that all was not lost; then he induced him to write to the Crown Prince a letter, wherein, instead of reiterating his former refusal, he manifested uncertainty and hesitation — hesitation which asked nothing better than to be overcome. . . . On May 26, writing to Charles of Roumania, Prince Antony confides to him his budding hope: "The affair is not yet altogether buried; it hangs by a few threads, but they are only spiders' webs." La Gorce, vol. vi, p. 207, citing Werthern's *General von Versen,* and the Memoirs of Charles of Roumania (French trans., vol. i, pp. 584, 587).]

[2] Ottokar Lorenz, p. 247.

make, he has only to forward them through Salazar or the Doctor (Bernhardi)." [1]

For the plot to attain its full fruition, only the consent of the princes was now lacking. Bismarck bent his energies in that direction. Prince Antony being already favorably disposed, the Crown Prince set about indoctrinating his friend Leopold, who, under his urgent arguments, began to discover some scruples touching his refusal, *in the first place because of his duty to the house of Hohenzollern*, and secondly because of his country and its prestige. Finally he reached the point of semi-assent (May 28).[2]

Meanwhile the Spaniards were losing patience. Every day Salazar pressed Lothar Bucher to obtain a definite answer. "Never mind that," said Lothar; "let us go together in search of the assent that they don't send us." They did both set out, travelling separately so long as they were in France, for fear that some one might recognize them, and not meeting until they were on German soil.

They went first to Reichenhall. They added their entreaties to the half-victorious ones by which Leopold was beset, and had the satisfaction of extorting his full acceptance. Leopold determined "*to set aside all per-*

[1] [As to the letter from Bismarck, see *supra*, chap. i, p, 24 n.] This letter was not Bismarck's first reply to the overture brought to Berlin by Salazar in February. Prim had already received one or more letters; but after Bismarck went to Varzin, the King and the Hohenzollern princes, despite Versen's favorable report, had broken off the negotiation. There had been a long silence, and Prim might well have feared that the scheme was abandoned. It was against this apprehension that Bismarck reassured him· [Major Bernhardi was councillor to the Prussian embassy at Madrid. See *L'Empire Libéral*, vol. xiii, pp. 575, 576, for his previous employments and his "anti-French sentiments."]

[2] [See La Gorce, vol. vi, pp. 207, 208.]

sonal considerations, and allow himself to be guided only by necessities of greater moment, because he hopes to render his country a great service."[1]

What was the great service to be rendered to his country, what were the exigencies of greater moment, which impelled him thus to lay aside personal considerations; that is to say, to play the part of a man without honor with reference to the Emperor Napoleon? Let the German historians and their French

[1] [Many years later (1883), Bucher described to Busch his second journey to Madrid and back. "It was a rush hither and thither, in zigzag, accident playing a large part in delaying and hindering as well as in promoting my purpose. Salazar came to me on the Saturday and wanted to have the Prince's final decision by Monday. I replied that it would not be possible in such a short time, particularly as I did not know where the Prince was staying at the moment, and of course he would have to be consulted first. . . . He said that he knew the Prince was at Reichenhall, and added: 'Selon ce que vous me dites, je renonce.' I replied: 'I assume that you will write a statement of what has passed between us, which will find its way into the Spanish archives, and as they will one day be open to historians, I should not wish to take this responsibility upon myself. I will travel with you first to Madrid [improbable, but so I understood], and then to the Prince of Hohenzollern.' He said he would take with him one of his liegemen, a man who would fling himself out of window without hesitation, if he bade him. . . . Well, we started for Reichenhall, travelling first in separate compartments, so as to avoid notice in Paris, and afterwards together, as he did not understand German and his companion spoke only Spanish." They failed to find the Prince at Reichenhall, but finally ran both him and his father to earth at Sigmaringen. "They both agreed. They could, however, decide nothing without the consent of the King, who was at Ems. We went thither, and were received by the old gentleman, who was very gracious to me and agreed to what I submitted to him. I then went to Varzin to report to the Chief." *Bismarck: Some Secret Pages of his History*, vol. ii, pp. 367 ff. As will be seen, this account varies in some of the details from that given in the text. And see La Gorce, vol. vi, pp. 209, 210. This author names Salazar alone as the one who removed Leopold's last scruples.

These random notes upon different phases of the mysterious scheme are but supplementary to M. Leonardon's full narrative of the whole matter of the Hohenzollern candidacy, in the *Revue Historique*, summarized in Appendix C.]

copiers answer this question; let them tell us, in unequivocal terms, what great service a Hohenzollern could render to his country at that moment, unless it were to compel France to make that attack which was demanded by the internal condition of Germany. That is the *leit-motif* of this narrative: I shall recur to it unweariyingly.

The Prince's consent being obtained, the two envoys separated. Lothar Bucher went to Berlin with Prim's reply, and Salazar returned to Madrid bearing the assent of the princes. But everything was not settled by this twofold assent at Madrid and Sigmaringen.

While the underground plot was being laid, the King of Prussia unexpectedly left his capital on June 1, and, attended by Bismarck, went to Ems to meet the Czar,[1] who was on his way to Würtemberg.

On June 4, Bismarck was back in Berlin, whence he set out again for Varzin, where Lothar Bucher and Keudell joined him. Ordinarily he went there to rest, and turned away those advisers who might bring his thoughts back to the anxieties of the day. On this occasion he works harder than ever there. He plans, writes, sends messengers, receives telegrams in cipher. Keudell and Bucher spend more than half the day deciphering, and when they are no longer equal to the work, Bismarck himself lends a hand,

[1] [Alexander II was the son of Princess Alexandra of Prussia, King William's sister. "The Emperor Alexander professed a chivalrous admiration for his uncle William; King William had always manifested a warm affection for his nephew. The union of the two courts had been a tradition since 1813." Sorel, vol. i, p. 45. — Whether or not the probability of war between Prussia and France was discussed at this interview at Ems, it seems certain that the two sovereigns reached a complete understanding subject to certain conditions, notably with reference to the States of the South. Sorel, pp. 47, 48; *L'Empire Libéral*, vol. xiii, pp. 555 ff.]

BISMARCK AND THE CANDIDACY 33

as does his daughter, the Countess Marie. The scheme soon to be put in execution is definitely decided on.[1]

The action is to be begun by Prim. He will send Salazar to make a formal offer of the crown to the Prince; he will hold the Cortes in session until Salazar's return, will announce to that body Leopold's acceptance, and will carry by storm the vote that will proclaim him King. Leopold will come at once to take possession of his throne. Meanwhile the utmost secrecy will have been preserved: France will have no suspicion of the candidacy until it is proclaimed by the Cortes; thus Napoleon III will be unable to throw himself in the path of the undertaking and thwart it. France, being rudely awakened, will be angry; her government will request the King to forbid his kinsman and subject to go to Spain; but the French Ambassador will find at Berlin neither the King, who is at Ems, nor Bismarck, who is under cover at Varzin; he will be forced to appeal to Thile, the mute of the seraglio. Thile will affect amazement: he knows nothing about it; the Prussian government has nothing whatever to do with Leopold's candidacy; the choice of a king is the business of the Spaniards alone; Prussia is too careful of her independence to inflict a blow on that of other nations.

He had no doubt that we would refuse to allow ourselves to be hoodwinked thus, and that we would insist upon our demand; thereupon he would come out of his mole-hill, would shriek about provocation, would stir up Germany, and would summon Spain to the rescue, whose interest would be made identical with that of Prussia by our prohibition. If we should

---
[1] Poschinger, *Life and Works of a Forty-Eighter.*

commit the stupid blunder — of which he liked to believe us capable — of taking Spain to task, then Prim would enter upon the scene, would cast to the winds the mouth-filling phrases of his hidalgoesque rhetoric, would reply to our protests by hastening on the result against which we were protesting, and Bismarck would hurry to the assistance of the German Prince, who had become, by a free election, the head of a friendly nation. Thus, whatever course we might take, he would force us into inextricable embarrassments; and he was confident that, having lost our heads, not knowing with whom to deal, finding ourselves subjected on all sides to unprecedented humiliations, we should discover no other issue from this no-thoroughfare than the war which was necessary to him, and which we should be obliged to wage on the Pyrenees and on the Rhine at one and the same time.

This diplomatic plan of campaign was as admirably conceived as Moltke's military plan. Every contingency was provided for. There was no external interference to be feared. Gladstone was not anxious to exert a European influence, and would have done so only to the profit of Prussia; if Clarendon should give way to his French sympathies, Gladstone would hold them in check.[1] Beust, active only with the pen,

[1] [Gladstone's first ministry had been in power since 1868, Lord Clarendon being Foreign Minister. Clarendon died on June 27, 1870, just before the Hohenzollern "bomb" exploded, and was succeeded by Earl Granville, who received the seals only on July 6, just in time to hear from Lord Lyons in Paris that the Spanish crown had been offered to Prince Leopold. "The death of Lord Clarendon occurred at a singularly unfortunate moment, both for this country and for France. . . . So far as France was concerned, no man in England — perhaps no man in Europe — was held in higher esteem at the Tuileries. Lord Clarendon, in fact, spoke to the Emperor and the

BISMARCK AND THE CANDIDACY 35

had about his ankles two balls and chains, Hungary and Russia, which would keep him from stirring.[1] The Roman Question, mooted in Italy by a ministry devoted to Prussia, would overcome the grateful good-

Empress with an authority to which no other statesman could pretend. Excellent as was the advice that the Emperor received from Lord Granville, it would have carried more weight if it had been given by Lord Clarendon. There is no use speculating on the course which events might have taken in other circumstances. But it is possible that, if Lord Clarendon had survived till the autumn of 1870, and Lord Cowley had remained at the English Embassy at Paris, the united influence of these two men might have saved the Emperor from the rash policy which led to the disastrous war of 1870." Walpole, *History of Twenty-Five Years*, vol. ii, p. 481, n. 3.]

"An important event, which caused no immediate sensation, brought a new element of luck to Bismarck's game. This was the death of Clarendon. Bismarck considered him a formidable adversary. Whether Clarendon would have had the strength to resist the combined wills of Gladstone and the Queen may be doubted; at all events, his successor, Granville, did not even attempt it. Granville's pacific sentiments were no less earnest than Clarendon's, who was called the 'travelling salesman of peace'; he was as amiable and as generally liked, but he had less skill in handling men, attracting them, and convincing them; he had not the same spirit of initiative or the same consistency, and he readily allowed himself to be led from one party to another; he knew Europe less well, and did not exert the same authority there. . . . He knew our country, our language, our statesmen, and the Emperor; he had no ill-will against us, but was not disposed to be sympathetic any further than he was permitted to be by Gladstone, and above all by the Queen, . . . whom he had served against his chief, Palmerston." *L'Empire Libéral*, vol. xiii, pp. 611, 612.

[1] [Count Friedrich Ferdinand von Beust (1809–1886), by birth a Saxon, was especially distinguished by one trait, hatred of Bismarck. He was responsible for Saxony's joining Austria in the War of 1866. He entered the Austrian service and was Francis Joseph's first minister from 1867 to 1871. The Duc de Gramont, who was Ambassador of France to Austria, 1861–1870, being equally hostile to Bismarck and Prussia, worked zealously to effect an alliance between France and Austria during the critical years after Sadowa. See La Gorce, vol. vi, pp. 149 ff. "When two years had passed in these mutual coquetries, it became necessary to cut loose from prolegomena. There are some books which are all preface. The Franco-Austrian alliance was one of those books" (p. 151). See also Sorel, vol. i, pp. 37–40; Welschinger, vol. i, pp. 198 ff.]

will to France of Victor Emanuel.¹ Failure could not ensue unless the King, the Hohenzollerns, or Prim himself, should allow themselves to hesitate and should fail to carry out energetically his or their part in the common task. And there seemed no reason to fear that on the part of any one of them.

There was some hesitation as to the best moment for putting the plan in execution. Should it be in June or in October? June was preferred, first, because it was the time of year when the general dispersal of sovereigns and diplomatists would make explanations difficult, notably at Berlin, where the exodus would be most complete; secondly, because secrecy, an essential condition of success, would become less and less assured, as the number of persons admitted to the secret was increased.²

---

¹ [In December, 1866, the French garrison, which had been maintained at Rome ever since the stamping out of the Roman Republic of 1848 by French troops under General Oudinot, was withdrawn in accordance with the Convention of September, 1864. (See Walpole, *History of Twenty-Five Years*, vol. ii, pp. 217 ff.) But in October, 1867, a second expedition was despatched to defend the Pope against the threatened invasion of Garibaldi's revolutionary bands. The revolution was defeated at Mentana in November, and the French troops remained in Rome. It was hardly conceivable that Victor Emanuel would form an effective alliance with France except on the condition that the Roman garrison be withdrawn, which alone prevented the realization of Cavour's dream and his own, of Rome as the capital of a united Italy. While he owed Napoleon much for his coöperation in the War of 1859, he was indebted to Prussia for the recovery of Venice in 1866. After Sedan the French troops in Rome were hastily summoned to the defence of their own country, and the Italians entered the city that has ever since been their capital.]

² [See La Gorce, vol. vi, p. 210. "A single question remained, but one of extraordinary importance, namely, at what moment and in what shape the intrigue, thus far kept secret, should be disclosed. The shrewdest plan seemed to be to spring the dénouement suddenly, and to take advantage of the Cortes being in session to carry the election in that body by surprise.

BISMARCK AND THE CANDIDACY 37

Bismarck communicated this plan to Prim, and numerous despatches and letters were exchanged, if not directly, at all events through intermediaries. At this juncture arrived Salazar from Sigmaringen, bringing the assent so ardently desired. Prim accepted Bismarck's plan, as well as the time fixed, and agreed with him as to the smallest details. Prim sent Salazar again to Sigmaringen, where he arrived on June 19. As he did not speak German, Versen went along to act as interpreter. Leopold would have preferred to postpone his election to the autumn, but Salazar explained to him the necessity for hastening the consummation: the Cortes were in session and awaiting his reply; there was not an instant to be lost. The princes at once agreed to take the last step indispensable according to the statutes of the family, with which they had always complied, and Leopold asked the King, then at Ems, for his sanction: he insisted upon the sacrifice he was making to the glory of his family and the welfare of his country. Prince Antony himself wrote and begged the King to approve his son's decision. These letters were taken to Ems by Salazar and Versen.

Versen relates that, at the supreme moment of cutting the cable and setting the affair adrift amid the tempest, "the King fought a great inward battle." His uneasy conscience, abandoned to itself at a distance from Bismarck, detected the disasters which, with a

In this way, all parties would be bound simultaneously — Spain and Prussia and the Prince himself. As for Napoleon, he would find himself caught off his guard, facing an accomplished fact; and his embarrassment would be twofold, as he would be confronted not only by Prussia, but by the Spanish government whose freedom of choice he would be reduced to the necessity of contesting."]

simple word, he could hold in check or unloose. He had not the courage of his honesty of intention, and he granted the fatal approval on June 20.[1]

Salazar had announced to Prim the Prince's acceptance subject to the King's assent. This assent being obtained, he telegraphed to the President of the Cortes that he would reach Madrid on June 26, "that the *election would take place forthwith*, and that a delegation of fifteen members of the Cortes would journey to Sigmaringen to offer the crown in solemn form to the Prince."

[1] [There is much uncertainty as to the dates of these various transactions, and the actual order of the steps in the negotiation is more or less a matter of conjecture. M. Ollivier says in a note to his larger work that all this part of the Hohenzollern plot has been laid bare by Werthern's *General von Versen*, previously mentioned.] "But the editor of those memoirs has combined with the documents, whose authenticity is unquestionable, some errors as to the dates to which they should be assigned, which I have corrected by the aid of what I have gathered from other sources, especially the memoirs of Salazar, Bucher, and Bernhardi." [But Bismarck covered his tracks very carefully, and they remained covered until the publication of the memoirs of King Charles of Roumania disclosed a large part of the secret, and led to the cynical admissions of the Chancellor's own Memoirs and to the revelations of Dr. Busch's diary. The subject was eminently one for a special study, and M. Leonardon's monograph (see Appendix C) probably comes as near to the full truth of the matter as we are likely to arrive. It will be noticed that in the paragraphs preceding this note there is no mention of Bucher as Salazar's companion in the last, successful mission to Sigmaringen, and thence to the King at Ems. See Bucher's statement to Busch, *supra*, p. 31 n. In Bucher's account of his gracious reception by "the old gentleman," who "agreed to what I submitted to him," there is no trace of the "great inward battle." But see La Gorce, vol. vi, pp. 209, 210. The date, June 20, given by M. Ollivier as that of the King's notification of his approval, is probably too early, although the date given by Sorel and others, June 28, is certainly too late, as Salazar's telegram announcing his arrival in Madrid for the 26th was not despatched until the King's assent had been obtained. According to Sybel (*Die Begründung*, etc., English trans., vol. vii, p. 312), the King confined himself to saying: "If he has a bent that way, I have no right to oppose it."]

BISMARCK AND THE CANDIDACY 39

And now, all is ready, each of the accomplices is at his post. Salazar is crossing France with the brand which is to set the whole country on fire. As soon as he shall have reached Madrid, the explosion will take place. Moreover, no one has a suspicion of the drama which is on the eve of performance.[1]

And yet, amid the general tranquillity, one fact, to which the public paid no heed, attracted the attention of close observers. The Prussian Ambassador at Madrid, who had been granted a leave of absence, received on June 30 orders to remain at his post, and allowed his wife to set out alone for The Hague. Mercier [2]

---

[1] [At this point M. Ollivier has omitted some thirty pages of his larger work (vol. iii, pp. 582-617), in which he touches upon several matters of great interest, among others, the debate in the Corps Législatif early in June on the participation of Germany in the construction of the St.-Gothard railway. But the most significant passage bearing on the special subject of this work, and especially on the genuineness of the Emperor's inclination for peace and his hearty coöperation with his ministers, is that relating to the mission of General Lebrun to Vienna in June, 1870, following the visit of Archduke Albert to Paris in May. The details of this last vain effort to gain Austria as an ally are given in General Lebrun's report to the Emperor of June 30, and by innumerable writers upon the war; but the extraordinary fact is that the secret of the mission was confided only to Le Bœuf, Minister of War, and a general or two, and that it never came to the knowledge of M. Ollivier, then titular head of the government, until five years later!] "It was not until 1875," he says, "that I first learned of this. Having heard that Lebrun was preparing his memoirs, I asked him to read them to me. When, in his reading, he reached his mission to Vienna, I uttered an exclamation of surprise. 'Why, didn't you know that story?' he said. 'If I had known that, I wouldn't have read it to you.'" [But M. Ollivier attributes the Emperor's silence to his being "so far from believing in the imminence of the danger, in prevision of which" he had taken the step, "that he did not deem it necessary to inform his ministers, not even Gramont, of General Lebrun's mission, its origin, its nature, and its results."]

[2] [M. Mercier de Lostende was French Ambassador to Spain. His suspicions apparently had not been aroused by the presence in Spain of Bucher and Versen, if, indeed, he had be en aware of it. (See *L'Empire Libéral*, vol.

advised Gramont of the fact, but his confidence in Prim's word was still so great that he was not alarmed. "I have not heard a word of the Hohenzollern candidacy," he added (July 1). And yet that was the little cloud that announces the storm.

xiii, pp. 53, 54.) On June 11, Prim made a speech to the Cortes in which, after detailing his various disappointments in his search for a king, he alluded to another candidate whom he could not name, but whose qualifications he described in such terms as to leave little doubt of his identity. He represented, however, that he had as yet had no better success in this direction. "The ministry has not been fortunate; it has no candidate to present for the crown; at least, it has none for the moment, but will it have to-morrow? That I cannot say." M. Ollivier, who gives a great part of the speech (*L'Empire Libéral*, vol. xiii, pp. 568 ff.), says that this was false because, when he was speaking he knew from Salazar that Leopold would accept, and was discussing with Bismarck the details of the election. But this does not accord with the dates given above of Salazar's various journeys, and it is a fair question whether Prim, even at this time, had not begun to realize that he had got himself into a scrape. (See Appendix C.) At all events, the Emperor, having read Prim's speech in the *Journal des Débats*, with Prince Leopold's name supplied, bade Gramont write to Mercier to find out whether it was true that there was a well-matured plot to seat a Prussian prince on the Spanish throne. M. Ollivier quotes at considerable length from the correspondence between Gramont and Mercier, but he seems hardly to do full justice in his conclusions to the latter's discernment. Mercier wrote that he suspected that there was an intrigue in progress at Madrid tending to some such result; that, although it had never been taken seriously by prominent men, and it seemed strange that Prussia should care to take such a risk, still we [France] ought to be the more suspicious of her, because Prim in despair may decide to recur to the Hohenzollern. "He talked to Prim himself, who seemed annoyed, as if he were afraid that he was detected; he denied the intrigue, declared that he no longer had a thought of the Hohenzollern, and, to put the Emperor's vigilance altogether to sleep, gave Mercier his full confidence: he expected to go to Vichy in July and hoped to see Napoleon there . . . who alone could get him out of his scrape. . . . Mercier was convinced that, even if the candidacy was not definitively abandoned, there would be nothing new until after the interview with the Emperor. Being reassured himself, he set Gramont's mind at rest," says M. Ollivier. But in the next sentence he quotes a confidential letter of Mercier of June 24: "I have very strong reasons for beliving that this [Hohenzollern] project has existed, and for fearing that it may spring up again after being aban-

A few days later the heavens were ablaze. "The season of perfidy draws nigh; the way lies open; they will reign by craft, the wretches, and the noble heart will be caught in their snares."[1]

doned, but it seems to me, for the moment, to be laid aside. However, there's something in the wind, that is clear, and we cannot be too much upon our guard." *L'Empire Libéral*, vol. xiii, pp. 571–579.

Whatever Prim's real inclination may have been at this period, he was so far involved with the Hohenzollerns and Bismarck that he could not well draw back, and he evidently set about hoodwinking Mercier; but after reading the correspondence as given by M. Ollivier one can but wonder that the "explosion of the bomb" should have caused so much amazement in certain quarters in Paris.

M. Welschinger cites an article in the *Temps* of January 11, 1910, in which M. G. de Coutouly, "one of our most distinguished publicists," who was in Madrid in the spring of 1870, gives his recollections of the state of public opinion there concerning the candidacy of Prince Leopold, and of Mercier's views thereon; vol. i, p. 42.

Sorel says (vol. i, p. 57), àpropos of the great parade in Madrid of cordial sentiments toward France, that there was some talk at this time of bestowing the Golden Fleece on M. Ollivier.]

[1] Goethe, *Goetz von Berlichingen.*

CHAPTER III

THE HOHENZOLLERN SCHEME EXPLODES AT MADRID

SALAZAR arrived at Madrid, bubbling over with delight, on the day announced by him by telegraph — June 26. He called upon Prim, failed to find him, and hastened to the Department of the Interior. "The President is hunting," said Rivero; "I am acting in his place." "If that is so, let me tell you that I have brought Leopold of Hohenzollern's acceptance of the throne." And he displayed to the thunderstruck Rivero a letter from Prince Leopold himself, saying that he was highly flattered by the overtures that had been made to him and would be most happy to accept the crown of Spain if it were offered him by the majority of the Cortes; thenceforward he would be a Spaniard and nothing else. "We must see to it that the Cortes vote forthwith," added Salazar. "But the Cortes have adjourned!"[1] "Then they

[1] [There is more or less mystery attending the adjournment of the Cortes. Salazar had sent, through Major Versen, two despatches, as stated in the text, one to Prim, and one to Señor Zorrilla. M. Leonardon concludes that they must have been sent on the 19th or 20th of June. "On the 21st Prim and Zorrilla allowed a motion by their friend Martos to be presented and adopted, authorizing the President to put an end to the session whenever he should see fit. On the 23d Zorrilla declared the session closed, in view of the absence of important business, and expressed a decided hope that in November the constitutional edifice would be crowned.

"To explain this procedure the Spanish government pretends that Salazar's despatch announcing his return for the 26th reached Madrid with a change in the wording which caused *July 9* to be substituted for June 26

THE SECRET DIVULGED AT MADRID   43

must be recalled at once!" exclaimed Salazar, much discountenanced.

Rivero wrote to Zorrilla, the President of the Cortes, and told him the news. He was no less surprised than his colleague. But the Cortes could not be summoned

in deciphering it. For fear that the affair would become known, they dared not hold the Cortes in session so long, the members being anxious to adjourn.

"Considering the end that Bismarck had in view, that error, if it really occurred, was deplorable. For the complete and unequivocal success of the Prussian scheme, it was necessary that the Hohenzollern candidacy should be presented while the Cortes was in session. When that assembly was officially informed, no backing out was possible on the part either of Prim or of Prince Leopold, and the protests of France, by offending the Spanish deputies' sense of their sovereign independence, might well result directly in the immediate election of the Prince. If thereupon Napoleon III should call the Prussian government to account for its share in the intrigue and should go so far as to declare war, Spain and her new monarch could not evade the obligation to take up arms, and a diversion in the Pyrenees would help to ensure Prussia's success.

"We venture to doubt the error in deciphering Salazar's telegram to Zorrilla. Prim was perfectly well aware that the Hohenzollern candidacy could not be agreeable to France. Witness the absolute ignorance of Salazar's negotiations in which he kept the Spanish Ambassador at Paris, Olozaga, whom he well knew to be most friendly to France. But he expected to see the Emperor in July; he knew of the friendship that Napoleon professed for Prince Charles of Roumania, Leopold's brother, and he probably hoped that by making the most of the relationship between the Hohenzollerns and the Bonapartes [see Appendix D], he might win his consent. This was an illusion which Bismarck himself had helped to keep alive: at the beginning, the Augsbourg *Gazette* (in April, 1869), and afterward Salazar, in his deliverance of October of the same year, had called attention to those bonds of kinship.

"To arrive at this friendly solution, Prim needed time to talk to the Emperor; it was essential that he should be the first person to mention the candidacy to him, and that he should not assume the attitude of proposing to force his hand. When he realized that Bismarck wished to force him to take the decisive step more quickly than he had planned to do, he tried to dodge, and it was in order to secure the necessary time and freedom of action that, in concert with Zorrilla, he brought the session of the Cortes hurriedly to a close, on a trumped-up pretext. . . . He himself, being supposed not to expect Salazar until July 9, left Madrid June 25 for his country estate in the mountains of Toledo." The above-quoted conclusion of M. Leonardon (in

without Prim's sanction; so that the urgent thing was to send for him. The messenger chosen was Herreros de Tejada, the only person who was in the secret. It would have been wise not to spread the news before the marshal's arrival, but Zorrilla did not feel called upon to keep a secret which he had not been asked to keep, and he informed his friend Ignacio Escobar, editor of the *Epoca*. A confidential communication to a newspaper man is at once spread broadcast. In a moment it burst out at the very centre of gossip, the Puerta del Sol, and everybody exclaimed: "Ya tenemos Rey!" (We have a king.)

Prim, being advised of what had happened, hastened back to the capital during the night of June 30. Victor Balaguer, the deputy, and two friends, were awaiting him at the station. They expressed their joy. Prim frowned, twisted a glove that he held in his hand, and exclaimed in a lugubrious tone: "Trouble thrown away! the candidacy has fallen through! God grant that that is the worst of it!"[1]

the *Revue Historique*) is adopted by La Gorce (vol. vi, p. 211), but many authorities simply state the error in deciphering the despatch as a fact which led to the adjournment of the Cortes, and thereby interfered with Bismarck's plans. See, for instance, the memoirs of Charles of Roumania (French translation), vol. i, p. 589. M. Leonardon's views as to Prim's disposition toward Bismarck at this time may be found in Appendix C.]

[1] Muniz, vol. ii, p. 117. [All the other authorities that I have seen give the night of July 1-2 as the date of Prim's return to Madrid. Leonardon says that it was Balaguer who described the scene at the station. The unexpected disclosure of the plan compensated in a measure, from Bismarck's standpoint, for the ill-effect of the inopportune adjournment of the Cortes, in that Prim was equally forced to show his hand. According to La Gorce (vol. vi, p. 212), Mercier *had* heard the rumors afloat in the city. "On July 2, rumors came to his ears, vague at first, then more distinct. They had a candidate! That candidate was a Hohenzollern. A little later in the day a deputy wrote him that the Cortes would undoubtedly be summoned forthwith, and would pro-

THE SECRET DIVULGED AT MADRID

In truth, at the first step the scheme had met with a setback, which might ruin the whole business. It had been agreed with the King and Bismarck that the secret should be kept until the communication to the Cortes and their immediate vote, so that the panic-struck Emperor could not defeat the conspiracy. Doubtless Salazar, who had been so discreet up to that time, would not have been so indiscreet had he known that the Cortes was not in session.

If something goes wrong in the execution of a maturely devised plan, men of little decision of character take fright, halt where they are, and improvise a new and insufficiently thought-out scheme, which increases the confusion; men of daring are not disconcerted, but persist, and, by the vigor of their action, checkmate the malicious whim of Fortune. Thus did Prim, who was that day a worthy associate of Bismarck. He recovered himself, picked up the scattered fragments of his glove, and hurried on the execution of his plan.

It was impossible longer to postpone the communication to the French Ambassador; he no longer sought to avoid it. That first step was the least agreeable.

ceed to the election of a king. Late in the afternoon, it was known that a council of ministers was in session. Instinctively alarmed, M. Mercier did not wish to wait until morning to obtain a confirmation or contradiction of the news. Although the day was far advanced he went to Prim's house." M. de Gramont speaks of Prim having published the scheme himself on July 3, because of his impatience, and says that his premature action so displeased and embarrassed the Prussian government that there was some thought of abandoning the whole undertaking. *La France et la Prusse avant la Guerre* (1872), pp. 24, 25. But Gramont wrote very soon after the war, when very little material for the accurate ascertainment of facts was available; moreover, his work is often marred by carelessness, or something worse, even in matters of greater importance than this.]

The trustful Mercier had not heard the rumors afloat in the city. On Saturday, July 2, in the evening, he went to pay his respects to Prim. He found him in his salon, his manner unwontedly constrained. After a few moments of halting conversation, the marshal said: —

"Come with me; I must have a talk with you." And he led him to his study. "I have to speak to you," he continued, "of a matter *which will not be agreeable to the Emperor, I fear, and you must help me to prevent his taking it in too ill part.* You know how we are situated. We cannot prolong the interregnum indefinitely, nor indeed can we appear before the Cortes without some solution to propose to them. We must have a king, and here, at the moment of our greatest embarrassment, one is proposed to us who fulfils all the conditions, — Leopold of Hohenzollern, a Catholic, of royal lineage, thirty-five years of age, married to a Portuguese princess, and with two sons, which will inevitably prepossess men's minds greatly in his favor; furthermore, comely of person and a soldier. You understand that I cannot let this last chance of averting revolution escape, especially under such conditions. How do you think the Emperor will take it?"

"There are no two ways of taking it," Mercier replied. "But first of all let me remind you that I cannot consent to talk on this subject as ambassador; for, having no other instructions than simple abstention, I have no right to speak for the Emperor. But, if you allow me to give you my personal opinion, I shall not hesitate to say that you could not take *a more momentous step, or one likely to bring in its train*

THE SECRET DIVULGED AT MADRID

more disastrous consequences. In France the election of a Prussian prince to the throne of Spain, in view of the present state of the public mind with regard to Prussia, cannot fail to produce *an extraordinary effect. National sentiment will see therein a downright insult;* and be assured that a Napoleon cannot leave the national sentiment in distress."

Thereupon ensued between Prim and Mercier a conversation in which Mercier, speaking like a true ambassador of our glorious France, made an admirable display of dignity, plain-speaking, and decision. Prim thought to embarrass him by referring to the Montpensier candidacy.

"Very good! rather Montpensier!" cried Mercier.

"What! you believe that the Emperor would prefer Montpensier to a Hohenzollern?"

"He never told me so, but I have no doubt of it. The Emperor is a Frenchman first of all."[1]

[1] [Practically the whole of the interview as reported by Mercier to the Foreign Minister on July 3 (see Gramont, *La France et la Prusse avant la Guerre*, pp. 360–365), is given by M. Ollivier in his vol. xiv, pp. 11–15, and by La Gorce, vol. vi, pp. 212–215. In reply to Mercier's representations as to the sensitiveness of French opinion, Prim remarked: "Bah! as for the consequences so far as France is concerned, I would accept them, but it's the Emperor whom it would be extremely painful for me to offend." — "Do you imagine, pray, that, in such a matter it is possible to separate France from the Emperor?" — "In that case, what are we to do? Take the *Almanach de Gotha* and try to find a prince there with whom we can make shift!" — Prim's method of referring to the Montpensier candidacy was to say slyly: "If we let this opportunity escape, we are thrown back perforce on Montpensier or the Republic."]

CHAPTER IV

THE HOHENZOLLERN SCHEME EXPLODES AT PARIS

ON the evening of July 2 the *Gazette de France* published the following paragraph: "The Spanish government has sent a deputation to Germany to offer the crown to the Prince of Hohenzollern." On the 3d, in the afternoon, the Havas Agency in its turn presented the information: "A deputation sent to Prussia by General Prim has offered the crown to the Prince of Hohenzollern, and he has accepted it. This candidacy will be proclaimed independently of the Cortes."

Still the government knew nothing officially. The first advice that came to hand was a telegraphic despatch from Mercier, Ambassador at Madrid, on the morning of July 3. It said: "The Hohenzollern business seems to be well advanced if not actually concluded. Marshal Prim himself told me of it. I am sending Bartholdi to Paris with the details and to receive your instructions."

On receipt of this despatch Gramont[1] hastened to Saint-Cloud. Francheschini Pietri, who was present, described to me the Emperor's extreme astonishment at that unexpected blow; up to that time he had received no suggestion of the project either from Prince Leopold or Prince Charles or Prince Antony.[2]

[1] [As to Gramont, see Appendix E, *infra*.]
[2] The assertion of Keudell to the contrary, already impliedly contradicted by the absolute silence of the memoirs of Charles of Roumania concerning the alleged communication, is formally contradicted by Hans

THE SECRET DIVULGED AT PARIS 49

When others had spoken of it, he had asked questions, but had stopped at the first word of denial, in the conviction that if ever the Hohenzollern princes, to whom he had always shown so much affection, should conceive such an idea, he would be informed of it by themselves. So it was that the Empress wrote to me: "The candidacy exploded like a bomb, *without warning.*"

The Emperor was even more distressed than offended by this disloyal act which he did not anticipate. He authorized Gramont to send despatches of exploration to Madrid and Berlin.

On leaving Saint-Cloud, Gramont called on Olozaga,[1]

Delbrück, in the *Preussische Jahrbücher* for October, 1895: "His Royal Highness Prince Leopold informed me explicitly that the statement to the effect that the late Prince Charles Antony informed the Emperor of the proffer of the throne of Spain, is altogether erroneous." [Note of M. Ollivier in vol. xiv, p. 16.]

[1] [The fact that Don Salustio Olozaga, the Spanish Ambassador to France, had been kept in complete ignorance of the Hohenzollern affair has been previously mentioned in these notes. On July 4, Lesourd, the French *chargé d'affaires* at Berlin, telegraphed to Gramont: "I learn that M. Olozaga telegraphed yesterday from Paris to the Spanish minister at Berlin [Rascon], that in his opinion the report of the offer of the Spanish crown to the Prince of Hohenzollern is untrue. M. de Rascon declares here that he shares that opinion, and that that step would be of a nature justly to excite our susceptibility." Gramont, pp. 19, 20.

On July 3, Prim made a virtue of neccessity and wrote Olozaga a letter in which he freely admitted his belief that the news would create an unfavorable effect in France, and urged Olozaga to do his utmost to bring the Emperor around to a favorable view of it. The letter is given in full by M. Ollivier (vol. xiv, pp. 18–20), who adds:] "In this letter as in his conversation Prim recurs again and again to the displeasure which the Emperor is sure to feel, and thus once more the fable accredited by the memoirs of Marshal Randon, that the Emperor, in September, 1869, advised that candidacy, is flatly contradicted."

[On July 19, after war was declared, Bismarck, in pursuance of his unceasing efforts to make out a case against France, dictated to Busch the following among other items "to be worked up for the German newspapers

but did not find him. He then went to the chancellery, but was no more successful in finding me. July 3 was Sunday, and I had gone to Egli, a small village in Seine-et-Oise, to the house of my chief clerk and friend, Adelon, to be present at the christening of a church bell of which my wife was the godmother. On my return to Paris in the evening of that single day of rest that I had enjoyed for several months, I found the following letter from Gramont: —

July 3, 10 P.M.

MY DEAR OLLIVIER, — I am writing at your desk to say that I came to inform you that Prim has offered the crown to the Prince of Hohenzollern, *who has accepted it!* It's a very serious business! A Prussian Prince at Madrid! I have seen the Emperor — he is greatly disturbed. While maintaining *officially* and *ostensibly* our rôle of abstention, we must defeat this intrigue. I like to believe, and I am tempted to

outside Berlin, such as the *Kölnische Zeitung*, and for the English and Belgian papers: . . . 'It now appears to be beyond all doubt that the French Government was aware of the candidacy of the Prince of Hohenzollern for months past, *that they carefully promoted it*, and foolishly imagined that it would serve as a means of isolating Prussia and creating a division in Germany. No trustworthy information has been received as yet as to whether and how far Marshal Prim had prepared the way for this intrigue, in agreement with the Emperor Napoleon. But doubtless that point will ultimately be cleared up by history. The sudden disappearance of Spain from the political field as soon as the difference between France and Prussia broke out gives matter for reflection and suspicion. It cannot but be regarded as strange that after the zeal shown by the Spanish Government in respect to the Hohenzollern candidacy had been raised to boiling point, it should suddenly have fallen below zero, and that the relations of Marshal Prim to the French Cabinet should now appear to be of the most friendly character, while the Spaniards seem no longer to feel any irritation at the interference of France in their internal affairs.'" Busch, *Bismarck: Some Secret Pages of his History* (English trans., vol. i, pp. 38, 39).]

THE SECRET DIVULGED AT PARIS

believe, that Olozaga knows nothing of it; but at Madrid they have hoodwinked Mercier. To-morrow we shall begin a *prudent*, but effective campaign in the press. Further details to-morrow. I have been to Olozaga's, but could not find him.

Yours ever.

On reading this letter I was more moved than Gramont was while writing it. I had a violent paroxysm of anger and despair. For four years in the tribune, for seven months in the ministry, I had striven laboriously to avoid every subject of irritation, to smooth over the unpleasant incidents between Prussia and ourselves by patience and courteous conduct, and to turn aside definitively the barbarous war which so many declared to be inevitable. And behold, Prim and Bismarck had suddenly destroyed what I was, after such painful efforts, on the point of achieving, and, seizing me on the shore where I hoped at last to breathe freely, hurled me back into the waves! All my labor thrown away! The most distressing presentiments assailed me. "It was Bismarck," I said to myself, "who engineered this candidacy; henceforth, whatever we may do, he will not withdraw it; and, on the other hand, however pacifically inclined we may be, it is absolutely impossible for us to tolerate it. And then?" Afraid to utter the word, I yet felt in my heart the lamentable on-coming of a war, of that war which I held in horror! Labor thrown away! labor thrown away!

This paroxysm of emotion lasted but a moment: with me anger is like the spark made by striking a stone, and dies out instantly. Well aware that lackadaisical manners do not persuade, I have always put passion into my speeches and my acts; but, as Darimon [1] observed, who formerly had much intercourse with me and who has spoken disparagingly of me, I retain my lucidity of mind at moments of difficulty. In the course of that crisis I was destined to pass through many agonizing moments, to know much mental torture, to be obliged often to make up my mind quickly; but at no time did I lose control of myself; I acted as if I had a problem in geometry or algebra to solve: inaccessible to any influence, whether of the press, or of the Emperor or Empress, or of my friends or my enemies; paying no heed to what people would say or would not say, following my own initiative, and determining my course solely by considerations deriving from my duty to my country and to mankind.

It was fortunate that Gramont did not find me at my office, and was obliged to write to me, for his letter manifests moderation and bears witness to the elevation of his sentiments. It is not the outcry of an irascible man, on the watch for a long-awaited pretext for insulting a destested nation; it is the reflection of an honorable minister, wholly master of himself, who thinks only of turning aside from his own country and from Europe the calamities of war. He does not exclaim as Cavour did in 1859 and Bismarck in 1866: "At last we have our *casus belli!*" He says simply: "It's a serious business; we must defeat this intrigue." And the campaign that he advises is not a

[1] Darimon, *Notes pouvant servir à l'Histoire de la Guerre de 1870*, p. 173. [Darimon was one of the "Five," of whom Ollivier was the chief, who alone represented the opposition in the Chamber of 1857. See translator's Introduction, *supra*, pp. xv, xvi.]

THE SECRET DIVULGED AT PARIS 53

campaign on the Rhine but a campaign in the *Constitutionnel*.[1] To make him out an impulsive, irascible man, is surely a most ridiculous biographical perversion. Gramont was a placid creature, too well broken to public affairs to allow himself to be excited by them. Like us all, he was anxious and preoccupied; at no time did we see him irritated and giving way to violent, unconsidered impulses, resulting from old grudges held in check since 1866.

On returning to his department he sent the two despatches agreed upon with the Emperor to Mercier and Lesourd.[2] To Mercier he said : —

"This intrigue plotted by Prim and Prussia against France must be effectively fought, and to succeed in defeating it requires no less of tact, prudence and discretion than of adroitness and vigor. Act upon the press and through your friends, without compromising yourself. The Prince of Hohenzollern is the grandson of a Murat. Make the most of the second of May.[3] Do not show any temper, but manifest some distrust while protesting your respect for the declared will of the Spanish people."

[1] [The *Constitutionnel*, edited by Robert Mitchell, "customarily received inspiration from M. Émile Ollivier," says La Gorce (vol. vi, p. 230). It was the only Parisian newspaper which could possibly be called an organ of the government, and that only in a very limited sense. For Gramont's first note in that paper, see Ollivier, vol. xiv, pp. 27, 28. And see *infra*, p. 68. n. 2.]

[2] [Lesourd was in charge of the embassy at Berlin, Comte Benedetti, the Ambassador, being then absent at Wildbad. Bismarck was at his country estate at Varzin, and Herr von Thile, Under-Secretary for Foreign Affairs, was his locum tenens.]

[3] [Prince Leopold's paternal grandmother was a niece of Joachim Murat, King of Naples, who commanded the French troops in Spain in 1808, and on the 2d of May in that year put down the insurrection in Madrid against the French domination.]

THE FRANCO-PRUSSIAN WAR

To Lesourd he telegraphed: —

"We learn that a deputation sent by Marshal Prim has offered the Spanish crown to the Prince of Hohenzollern, who has accepted it. We do not consider the candidacy as put forward seriously, and believe that the Spanish nation will reject it. But we cannot see without some surprise a Prussian prince seeking to seat himself on the Spanish throne. We should prefer to believe that the Berlin cabinet is not privy to this intrigue; in the contrary event, its conduct would suggest to us reflections of too delicate a nature to be mentioned to you in a telegram. I do not hesitate, however, to say to you that a bad impression has been created, and I urge you to express yourself to this effect. I await such details as you may be able to give me of this regrettable incident." (July 3.)[1]

The next morning, the 4th, Gramont saw the Spanish Ambassador and told him the news that had come from Mercier the night before. Olozaga's stupefaction proved even more convincingly than his protesta-

[1] [The sending of this despatch to Berlin seems to have been the first of the several steps, each more disastrous than the last, which M. de Gramont took without consulting his colleagues in the ministry — or, at least, without consulting those most concerned. M. Ollivier says that the Foreign Minister had conferred with the Emperor, but it is clear that he himself knew nothing of it, and M. de Gramont does not mention even the Emperor, although he speaks of the despatch as "the attitude assumed at the outset by the government," *La France et la Prusse*, p. 28. "Thus did M. de Gramont express himself at the first moment, and, as it were, *ab irato*," says La Gorce. "Did he consult his colleagues? At all events, this despatch, which already smelt of war, was sent without the knowledge of the man who presided over the affairs of the army. Not until the next day, when he arrived at the Palais-Bourbon, did Marshal Le Bœuf learn, from the conversation of the deputies, that a new question, called 'the Hohenzollern question,' had arisen in Europe." Vol. vi, pp. 218, 219, citing Le Bœuf's deposition in the *Inquiry concerning the 4th of September*.]

LEOPOLD OF HOHENZOLLERN
1835–1905

THE SECRET DIVULGED AT PARIS 55

tions that he knew nothing of it. He complained bitterly that negotiations of so serious a nature should have been carried on without his even being informed of them, and he admitted to the Minister of Foreign Affairs that he was unable to give him any explanation of a matter which he knew of only through what the minister himself had just disclosed to him. Gramont repeated to Olozaga the protests made by Mercier to Prim, and bade him repeat them without delay to his government.

That same day he called upon Werther,[1] who was about to start for Ems. He begged him to inform the King that France would not tolerate the seating of the Prince of Hohenzollern or any other Prussian prince on the throne of Spain. He adjured him to exert his utmost efforts to induce his Majesty to compel his nephew to refuse the Spanish crown. I, in my turn, saw the Prussian ambassador, and besought him to help us extinguish this dangerous firebrand. We found him (and that fact ruined him in Bismarck's esteem) in a most conciliatory frame of mind. Without expressing his opinion touching the actual crux of the controversy, he manifested genuine good-will, to

[1] [Werther and Gramont were old acquaintances, having been colleagues at Vienna. According to Lord Lyons, the British Ambassador, Gramont informed him "that he had declared categorically to Baron de Werther that France would not tolerate the establishment of the Prince de Hohenzollern or any other Prussian-Prince on the Throne of Spain." Lyons to Earl Granville, in the British government publication, *Correspondence respecting the Negotiations preliminary to the War between France and Prussia*, 1870 (hereafter cited as *Blue Book*), p. 1. This agrees with the text, but M. de Gramont himself says: "I let him see, *without, however, making an explicit assertion to that effect*, that France could with difficulty resign herself to accepting a state of things on her frontier which might at any moment endanger her security." *La France et la Prusse*, p. 35.]

such a degree that Gramont felt justified in asking him to inform him by telegraph of the result of his mission.

No minister of foreign affairs, being placed unexpectedly in such a thorny position, could have acted with more decision and at the same time more self-possession and prudence. Unfortunately, at Madrid as at Berlin, our judicious conduct was confronted by a scheme as powerfully devised as it was resolutely executed.

Realizing the impossibility of replying to our objections to the anti-French candidacy, Prim hastened to remove it from the domain of confidential interviews, and to convert it at the earliest possible moment into a *fait accompli,* beyond discussion or defeat. On July 4 he issued an urgent summons to the ministers to meet at La Granja, under the presidency of the Regent. One and all, including the latter, were unadvised of the secret negotiation. Prim unfolded it to them in his own way, dissembled and belittled its dangers, and obtained their unanimous approval and the summoning of the Cortes for July 20. He reckoned the certain majority at two hundred votes. Although warned of our opposition, on the 5th he sent word to Prince Leopold, by Vice-Admiral Polo de Barnabè, of the decision of the council of ministers. On the 6th he notified it by telegraph to all the diplomatic representatives, insisting upon the advantages which Spain would reap by her alliance with a military power of the first rank.[1] These measures signified that our

[1] [See the letter of July 7 from Earl Granville to Mr. Layard, British minister at Madrid, in *Blue Book*, p. 5. "I have seen the Spanish minister to-day. He translated to me a telegram which he had received from his

THE SECRET DIVULGED AT PARIS

observations would not be listened to, that they would not consent to discuss the matter with us, and that we were face to face with an irrevocable determination.

At Berlin Gramont's overture had no better success. On July 4 Lesourd called upon Thile. At his first word on the Hohenzollern candidacy, Thile interrupted him with extraordinary warmth. If he (Lesourd) were instructed to demand officially explanations from him touching the matter that he mentioned, then he (Thile) must, before replying, take the King's commands.

Government announcing that the Crown of Spain had been offered by them to Prince Leopold of Hohenzollern, and that the offer had been accepted by his Highness, and expressing the conviction that the choice thus made by them of a Sovereign for Spain would be agreeable to all the Powers of Europe.

"I told Señor de Rances that I had been surprised by the news, which I had received two days ago; . . . it was impossible not to have foreseen that such a choice, secretly made and suddenly announced, would create great irritation in France."

After the British Foreign Minister had requested Rances to lay before his government the urgent wish of Her Majesty's government that they would not give effect to a step which "might, on the one hand, bring on great European calamities, and which, on the other, was almost certain to render the relations of Spain with a Power which was her immediate neighbour, of a painful, if not hostile character . . . Señor de Rances explained that the project was one which had not been intended as hostile to France; that it was the natural result of other combinations which had failed. . . . But he begged me to remark that it was only a resolution of the Ministers with a view to put some proposition before the country; that the Cortes would have to decide; that there was no reason to suppose they would take any rash or injudicious step."

On the 5th, Mr. Layard had telegraphed to Lord Granville the decision of the Spanish ministers, adding: "The Cortes is summoned for the 20th of this month, and it is expected that he [Leopold] will be accepted by the requisite majority." *Ibid.*, p. 1.

M. Leonardon is of opinion that at this time Prim was already trying to find some means of getting rid of the candidacy. His conclusions, with the grounds on which they are based, will be found in Appendix C, *infra*.]

Lesourd replied that he did not intend as yet to give such weighty significance to the step he was taking; but that, being informed of the excitement caused at Paris by the news that he had referred to, he had it in view simply to inform the Duc de Gramont of the rôle which the Prussian government proposed to assume in the negotiation which had just come to light.

Thereupon Thile, one of the members of the council of the 15th of March, at which the candidacy had been resolved upon, in an indifferent tone which resembled irony, affected the most absolute ignorance. He had, it is true, read now and then the name of the Prince of Hohenzollern among the candidates for the Spanish throne, but he had attributed so little importance to such rumors that he was still wondering to which of the two princes they referred — the Hereditary Prince, who was married to a Portuguese princess, or Prince Fritz, a major of cavalry in the Prussian army. The Prussian government was entirely in the dark touching the affair; so far as that government was concerned it did not exist; consequently he was not in a position to give the French government any explanation; the statesmen and people of Spain had a right to offer the crown to whomever they chose, and to that person alone, to whom the offer had been made, belonged the privilege of accepting or declining.[1]

Lesourd imagined that Thile was embarrassed because he had not as yet received his instructions from the King and Bismarck, and that he would have

[1] Lesourd to Gramont, July 4. [For Thile's version of the interview, as given to Lord A. Loftus, British Ambassador to Prussia, see Loftus to Granville, July 6, *Blue Book*, p. 13.]

THE SECRET DIVULGED AT PARIS 59

spoken differently if he had had them. As a matter of fact, Thile spoke solely by virtue of explicit instructions from the King and Bismarck. According to Schultze, his reply was a result of Bismarck's plan to manœuvre so that the wrath of France could find nobody in Prussia to respond to its demands until the affair had reached its conclusion at Madrid. Bismarck, for his part, avowed later his reason for referring us to Spain through the medium of Thile. "It was difficult," he says, "for France to find a pretext in international law for intervening in the election of a king of Spain. I reckoned that the sensitive Spanish honor would revolt against such intervention."[1]

Thile made no secret of his reply. He repeated it at once to Loftus, the English Ambassador, and one after another to the foreign ministers who came to discuss the matter with him. Like a soldier carrying out an order, he repeated imperturbably to all that "the Prussian government denied all responsibility with respect to the candidacy of Prince Leopold, and that that candidacy could not be the subject of official communications among the different governments."[2]

This reply was forthwith transmitted and emphasized at London by the Prussian Ambassador, Bernstorff. He went to Granville and said to him that "the government of the North German Confederation did not desire to meddle in the affair; that it would leave to France the business of taking such measures as seemed fitting, and that the Prussian

---

[1] Bismarck's *Reflections*, etc. [English trans.], vol. ii, pp. 89–93.

[2] [See p. 58, n. 1.] Also, Granville to Lyons, July 8, *Blue Book*, p. 9; Granville to Loftus, July 15, *ibid.*, p. 30; Loftus to Granville, July 16 (No. 81), *ibid.*, p. 51.

representative at Paris had received orders to abstain from taking any part. The government of North Germany had no wish to stir up a war of succession; but if France should choose to make war upon that government on account of Spain's choice of a king, such a proceeding on her part would demonstrate her inclination to make war without a lawful cause. However, it was premature to discuss the question so long as the Cortes had not decided to accept Prince Leopold as King of Spain."[1]

At the same time there began in Prussia a skilfully organized newspaper campaign. Bismarck issued instructions to the effect that the tone of the official and semi-official sheets should continue to be most reserved, but that all the other journals, not known to be under his influence, should hold the most insulting language toward France and its government. These articles, inspired by Bismarck and written by Lothar Bucher, were sent from Varzin to Busch for publication.[2]

[1] [Granville to Lyons, July 8, *Blue Book*, p. 9. I have in this one instance translated M. Ollivier's French version of Earl Granville's despatch; the sense is unchanged.]

[2] ["Immediately on the commencement of the difficulties with France respecting the election to the Spanish throne of the Hereditary Prince of Hohenzollern, letters and telegrams began to arrive, which were forwarded by Bucher under instructions from the Chief. These consisted in part of short paragraphs and drafts of articles, as well as some complete articles which only required to be retouched in the matter of style, or to have references inserted with regard to matters of fact. . . .

"*July 7, evening.* — A telegram to me from Varzin: 'The semi-official organs should indicate that this does not seem to be the proper time for a discussion of the succession to the Spanish throne, as the Cortes, who are alone entitled to decide the question, have not yet spoken. German governments have always respected Spanish independence in such matters, and will do so in future as they have no claim or authority to interfere and

THE SECRET DIVULGED AT PARIS 61

All these manœuvres, as Ottokar Lorenz admits,[1] placed Gramont in an extremely embarrassing position:

lay down regulations for the Spaniards. Then, in the non-official press, great surprise should be expressed at the presumption of the French, who have discussed the question very fully in the Chamber, speaking as if that assembly had a right to dispose of the Spanish throne, and apparently forgetting that such a course was as offensive to Spanish national pride as it was conducive to the encouragement of republican tendencies. . . . It would appear as if the Emperor, who has instigated this action, wanted to see the outbreak of a new war of succession.'

"A letter from Bucher, which was handed to me on the evening of the 8th, further developed the idea contained in the last sentence. . . . 'Previous to 1868 Eugénie was pleased to play the part of an obedient subject of Isabella, and since the September revolution that of a gracious protectress. She unquestionably arranged the farce of the abdication [of Isabella], and now, in her rage, she incites her consort and the ministers. As a member of a Spanish party, she would sacrifice the peace and welfare of Europe to the intrigues and aspirations of a corrupt dynasty.

"'Please see that this theme, a new war of succession in the nineteenth century, is thoroughly threshed out in the press. The subject is inviting, especially in the hands of a correspondent disposed to draw historical parallels, and more particularly parallels *ex averso*. Have not the French had experience enough of Spain with Louis XIV and Napoleon? . . . Have they not excited sufficient hatred by all those wars and by the Spanish marriage of 1846?

"'Bring personal influence to bear . . . on the editors who have been intimidated by the Stock Exchange, representing to them that if the German press takes up a timid and hesitating attitude in presence of the rhodomontades of the French, the latter will become more insolent and put forward intolerable demands in other questions affecting Germany still more closely.' . . .

"The following was a third subject received from Varzin on the same day: 'Is Spain to inquire submissively at the Tuileries whether the King whom she desires to take is considered satisfactory? Is the Spanish throne a French dependency? . . . In France, where on other occasions so much is said of national independence, the attempt of the Spanish people to decide for themselves has immediately revived the old diplomatic traditions which led to the Spanish war of succession 160 years ago.'"

Busch, *Bismarck: Some Secret Pages of his History*, vol. i, pp. 26–28.]

[1] Whenever it is possible, I shall allow the Germans themselves to pass judgment on the facts I shall narrate. [Note of M. Ollivier.]

whatever happened, the Empire was driven, by the attitude of Prussia, to the brink of the precipice. The observation is true: at our first step in the negotiation we were stopped short. At Madrid as at Berlin we were told that no heed would be paid to our observations. At Madrid, they went forward as if we had said nothing; at Berlin they shut the door in our face and mocked at us. How then could we avoid falling into the pit that Bismarck had dug before our feet?

CHAPTER V

THE HOHENZOLLERN CANDIDACY AROUSES INDIGNATION
IN FRANCE AND REPROBATION IN EUROPE

WHAT made our deliberations more difficult was the fact that the walls of our offices were assailed by a storm of indignation which demanded extreme measures on our part. Public opinion, much less in control of its feelings than we were of ours, manifested once more the prominent feature of our character, which has been noted by observers of all times. "The decisions of the Gauls are sudden and unforseen, and they resolve hastily upon war (*mobiliter et celeriter*)," wrote Julius Cæsar. "We are a volcanic nation," says Dumouriez.

On July 4, in the morning, there occurred one of these sudden, irresistible, volcanic explosions. The foreign ambassadors, unmoved and watchful observers, noted it. "When the news of the acceptance by Prince Hohenzollern of the nomination to the Spanish throne reached Paris," wrote Metternich, "it caused very sudden and very intense excitement. Men saw in it a scheme devised by Marshal Prim and Prussia." [1]

Lyons was more emphatic. "Without considering how far the real interests of France may be in question, the nation has taken the proposal to place the Prince of Hohenzollern on the throne of Spain as an insult and a challenge from Prussia. . . . [I observed that]

[1] Metternich to Beust, July 15.

we could not shut our eyes to the fact that the feelings of the French nation would now render it impossible for the government, even if they wished it, to acquiesce in the elevation of Prince Leopold to the Spanish throne."[1]

And Taxile Delord, in his "History of the Second Empire," rather a political pamphlet than a history, says: "This possibility was too menacing to the interests of France, for her government to neglect to use its utmost efforts to secure the renunciation of the candidacy of Prince Leopold of Hohenzollern."[2]

There was not a politician, not a military man, who did not express aloud his condemnation of the Prussian enterprise. Marshal Vaillant wrote in his notebook July 5: "We learn that Prim has offered the Spanish throne to the Prussian Prince of Hohenzollern. It seems to me that this means war, or something very like it." Doudan, laying aside his jeering tone, exclaimed: "In my opinion we could not in honor suffer the affront of a Prussian colonel reigning on the other side of the Pyrenees."[3] Jules Favre admitted, although the point was open to discussion, that the candidacy of the Hohenzollern prince to the throne of Spain might be a *casus belli*.[4] Jules Simon could not see how it was open to discussion. "France," he said, "could not without endangering her security and her dignity, tolerate Prince Leopold's

[1] Lyons to Granville, July 7. [*Blue Book* (Nos. 10 and 12), pp. 6 and 9. The last sentence is from a conversation between Lyons and Count von Solms-Sonnewalde, Prussian *chargé d'affaires* in Paris.]

[2] Vol. vi, p. 128.

[3] Doudan to Piscatory, July 10. [Doudan was "one of the keenest-sighted observers of the second Empire," according to La Gorce (vol. vi, p. 229).]   [4] *Gouvernement de la Défense Nationale*, vol. i, p. 25.

EFFECT OF THE CANDIDACY

candidacy."¹ Thiers said that "France must look upon that candidacy as an affront to her dignity and an enterprise adverse to her interests."² Gambetta was even more violent: he exclaimed that all Frenchmen must unite for a national war.³

The opinion of foreign statesmen, at that moment when selfish considerations did not restrain the sincere expression of their sentiments, declared itself on all sides as identical with that of French statesmen. "It was impossible," said Granville to the Spanish Ambassador to England, "not to have foreseen that such a choice, secretly made and suddenly announced would create great irritation in France."⁴ He was no less explicit with his agent at Berlin. "The strict secrecy with which these proceedings have been conducted as between the Spanish ministry and the prince who has been the object of their choice, seems inconsistent on the part of Spain with the spirit of friendship or the rules of comity between nations, and has given what her Majesty's government cannot but admit to be, so far as it goes, *just cause of offence*, which, it may perhaps be contended, it may be impossible to remove so long as the candidature of the prince continues."⁵

Beust, in an interview with the Spanish minister, earnestly expressed his surprise and disapproval. He telegraphed to his minister at Madrid: "The idea may be excellent in itself, but its effect would be deplorable and would endanger the peace of Europe."⁶

---
¹ *Origine et Chute du Second Empire*, p. 159.
² Speech of July 15.   ³ Police report.
⁴ Granville to Layard, July 7. [*Blue Book*, p. 5. See *supra*, p. 56, n. 1. Chapter 4.]   ⁵ Granville to Loftus, July 6. [*Blue Book*, p. 3.]
⁶ Beust to Dubsky, July 7.

The excellent Topete was exasperated with Prim. "What!" he said to Mercier; "why, to set about insulting France in our present condition is madness! We proposed to do something that might not be agreeable to the Emperor, but we were fully convinced that everything could be arranged without disturbing the relations between the two countries. If necessary, I will make my *mea culpa* before the Cortes. I will say that I repent of the part I took in the Revolution, and that I go back to Prince Alfonso."[1]

Maria of Hohenzollern, Countess of Flanders, the candidate's sister, wrote to Antony Radziwill: "*This would be a second Sadowa; France would not allow it.*"[2] The daughter repeated, on the explosion of the plot, what her father had said when it was still in the future: "France would not allow it." Thus was the French sentiment in some sort justified by those who had aroused it.

The Czar, who did not as yet fathom the full scope of his ally's purpose, avowed to General Fleury, in the first impulse of sincerity, that he realized how offensive the offer of the throne to the Prince of Hohenzollern was to France, and that, however insignificant the candidate, he would none the less become a battle-flag for Prussia at a given moment.[3]

The Minister of Foreign Affairs at The Hague, Roest van Limburg, when the Spanish Ambassador told him the news, "remarked that the choice appeared

---

[1] Mercier to Gramont, July 4. [Admiral Topete de Caballo was one of the triumvirate who divided the power in Spain after the fall of Isabella.]

[2] This fact is told by King William to Queen Augusta in a letter of July 5 printed by Oncken [*Unser helder Kaiser*].

[3] Fleury to Gramont, July 9.

EFFECT OF THE CANDIDACY 67

to be very unacceptable to the French government."[1]
And the Spanish minister at Berlin himself admitted that our dissatisfaction was justified.[2]

In Southern Germany Bismarck was unanimously regarded as the inventor of this unlooked-for candidacy; it was believed that Marshal Prim had been bought for hard cash by the Prussian minister, who drew, for all transactions of this sort, upon the funds derived from the sequestrated fortune of the King of Hanover. Even in the Confederation of the North, the Saxon minister considered our grievance well founded. He did not hesitate to say that the fact in itself, and the mystery with which it was surrounded, were of a nature to arouse, on our part, a just sense of injury, and that France was entitled to be displeased; the demand of France was, in fact, in conformity with the precedents of European international law. Although in his eyes the accession of a Hohenzollern to the throne of Spain seemed unlikely to cause any danger whatever to the interest of France, he none the less recognized the fact that it was for us to determine and measure the importance of that eventuality. He added that, "by invoking the sanction of a doctrine already accepted and confirmed several times by the great powers of Europe, the Emperor's government justified its resistance to the plan of the Spanish government, and gave proof of its desire for conciliation."[3]

The newspapers reflected these opinions of states-

[1] Vice-Admiral Harris to Granville, July 11. [*Blue Book*, p. 24.]
[2] Lesourd to Gramont, July 5. [See Gramont, *La France et la Prusse*, p. 30.]
[3] Châteaurenard to Gramont, July 9-10.

men with unrestrained vehemence. "The press," said Thiers, "is the voice of the nation."[1] If the press is in truth the voice of a nation, never did nation express its feelings more unmistakably. Nor could any one say that we were responsible for it, for, save the *Constitutionnel*, our official organ,[2] we had no influence over any of the journals. How much more impressive would be this stirring of the country's heart, of which the press was then the outward expression, if we could reproduce the words that were exchanged in the public squares, in salons, and in workshops! Public opinion had already gone beyond the last stages of submission.

I note this state of public opinion with the more freedom because I have no purpose of invoking it to evade my own responsibility. Public opinion

[1] In a speech in 1868. [In vol. xiv, pp. 41–48 and notes, M. Ollivier quotes many passages from the Parisian press in support of his thesis.]

[2] "Of all the newspapers whose opinions I have reproduced, there was not one which could have been called 'governmental.' The only one which could possibly be so described was the *Constitutionnel*, which its owner, Gibiat, had placed at our disposal, and whose editor-in-chief, my friend Mitchell, was devoted to a pacific policy from conviction. The *Patrie* ordinarily supported us, but with less zeal since it had pronounced against the plebiscite, and its editor Saint-Valry had not our confidence. In the other papers there were some men with whom I was on friendly terms, like Dalloz of the *Moniteur Universel*, Pessard of the *Gaulois*, and even Nefttzer of the *Temps* and Hervé of the *Journal de Paris*, who, despite their goodwill, were not by any means in love with my policy and followed individual opinions over which I possessed no influence. I was not in accord on the question of peace or war with [Émile de] Girardin — a true friend he, whose devotion I had tested. He had just given over the *Liberté* to his nephew by marriage, Léonce Detroyat, a former naval officer, a man of heart and intelligence, whom I hardly knew; he [Girardin] had reserved the right to express his own opinion in the paper when he chose, and that opinion, whenever foreign affairs were in question, would continue to be opposed to mine." *L'Empire Libéral*, vol. xiv, p. 48.

should be the rule and the law of a constitutional sovereign, as he is irremovable, and as his abdication would be a worse evil than an ill-advised political measure; moreover, as the last word must belong to the nation and not to him, he is constrained to yield to the national demand, even though it be not in conformity with his personal views. As ministers are removable, and as the stability of the state does not depend upon their remaining in power, they are not to be excused for yielding to the wishes of public opinion unless they deem those wishes just and reasonable. If they disapprove them, it is their duty to oppose them, especially as such opposition will perhaps set them right.

The justification of the Emperor Napoleon III is complete the moment it is established — and the evidence is overwhelming — that he opposed the Hohenzollern candidacy at all risks because an almost unanimous public opinion compelled him to do it. But the justification of his ministers is not even suggested by such demonstration. It remains for them to prove that public opinon was right in exercising that compulsion upon the Emperor. If it was in error, their duty constrained them to controvert it, to declare open war upon it, and, if they did not succeed in overcoming it, to retire and to leave to others the melancholy privilege of consummating an act of madness.

What importance should have been attached to the fact of a German prince taking his seat on the throne of Spain? Was it a fact devoid of menace so far as we were concerned, and without advantage to Prussia, and did we, by raising a great outcry over that possibility, make, as Scherr says, an elephant out of a flea ? That is the question that we considered, Gramont and I, in a few hours, which, because of the intensity of our mental toil, were equivalent to many long days.[1]

We reached this conclusion: that the press and the public opinion of France were not in error and were not simply yielding to a heedless impulse of Chauvinism by proclaiming their wrath against the Prussian candidacy, but that they were in error when, alleging an intimate connection between that candidacy and the events of 1866, they repelled it as the last drop, insignificant in itself, but formidable only because it falls into a vessel already full to the brim; it was a flood more than sufficient in itself to fill an empty vessel. Even if there had been no shadow between Prussia and ourselves, if our relations since Sadowa had been affectionate and trustful, that candidacy would none the less have retained its threatening character. We did not therefore "take a flea for an elephant," and we did not manufacture phantoms when we looked upon a Hohenzollern at Madrid as a serious menace to our safety.

We decided that we would not associate ourselves with those who saw in the Hohenzollern affair simply a pretext for making up for our inaction in 1866, for taking our revenge for Sadowa, and for blocking the ulterior developments of the Prussian victory; but

[1] [At this point, in his larger work M. Ollivier discusses the principles of international law applicable to the Hohenzollern candidacy, and, in connection therewith, the different cases of recent occurrence in which similar questions had arisen. He also considers at some length the question whether, irrespective of precedents, it would have been expedient, in this instance, for France to allow Prince Leopold to ascend the Spanish throne without objection. See Appendix F.]

that, on the other hand, we would second with all our might resistance to a candidacy which was at once a challenge and a danger.

Gramont, had he been free to follow his private inclinations as a diplomat of the old school, would not have been averse to generalizing the dispute, instead of confining it strictly to a particular question; but he would have done it at the cost of an immediate rupture with me, for I would never have agreed to become the foe of that principle of nationalities which I had championed for so many years. And in the event of a rupture, the advantage would not have been with him, for I had explained to him, before we took up the government, my policy of friendly abstention with respect to the Germanic movement, and he had acceded to it. As he was loyal, he did not try to go back on that agreement, and it was fully understood, that, whatever those about us might say, there should never be any question of Sadowa and its results, but solely of the candidacy and its impossibility. We agreed even more readily on the methods to be employed against it: they were to be only those which had been sanctioned by international law as then in force, and which Prussia herself, since 1815, had, in concert with the other powers, helped to establish. To be rid of the candidacy, we would not apply to Spain, but to Prussia.

Gramont and myself submitted to the Emperor the conclusions at which we had arrived. He approved of them absolutely, without any objection, and authorized us to put them in execution at once.

CHAPTER VI

OUR INABILITY TO NEGOTIATE — OUR PERPLEXITY

THE aggression being manifest, we had the right, without a word, to recall our reserves, to despatch them to the frontier, and, when they had concentrated there, to announce the beginning of hostilities by a flag of truce sent to the outposts. We gave a striking proof of our moderation by not making use of our undeniable privilege of immediate reprisals. We did more: instead of discussing the course to be pursued in case the Hohenzollern should actually become King of Spain, we tried to prevent him from becoming so. We determined to defeat the plot and to avoid war by diplomatic negotiations.

We encountered much incredulity in the experienced men to whom we confided our purpose. However, we persisted in our determination to negotiate, without knowing just how. Gramont and I had expounded the rules of international law; the Emperor had approved our theoretical conclusions; but that carried us a very short distance. It remained to discover the way to avoid falling over the precipice to whose brink Prim's haste and Thile's persiflage had driven us.

On the 5th, at ten in the morning, the Emperor summoned us — Gramont and myself — to Saint-Cloud, for consultation. If we had sought simply a pretext for war, the conversation would have been very short; we had that pretext at hand, and to make use of it would not have been difficult. But although we were

OUR INABILITY TO NEGOTIATE

resolved to forbid the Hohenzollern candidacy, even at the cost of war, we were passionately desirous that it should disappear without war.

Beust, whose prudence had been highly praised to us, proposed a most original plan: let the French government declare that, being offended by Prussia's action, it could do no less than forbid Prince Leopold to pass over its territory on his way to Madrid. Being unable to go through France, the prince-candidate would necessarily embark either on the Mediterranean or on the North Sea. Then let the French government, being on the alert and informed by its agents, cause the vessel bearing the Prince to be attacked at sea, and thus obtain possession of the *corpus delicti*. After that, they could negotiate and would speedily reach an understanding; for it went without saying that Prussia would find it a very simple affair, and the incident would be at an end.

I need not say that we did not discuss this comic-opera plot, in which the lover of practical jokes is easily recognized.[1]

Others advised us to announce simply that, in case the Hohenzollern should be elected, we should withdraw our ambassador, espouse the cause of the rejected pretenders, and allow Carlists and Alphonsists, horses, guns, and powder, to enter Spain across the open frontier.

Such tortuous tactics were not to our liking; we considered them degrading. Moreover, they had the disadvantage of making the affair a Spanish one, which we did not want, because Bismarck did want it. Nor, indeed, would Leopold's government have looked

[1] [See P. Lehautcourt, *Histoire de la Guerre de 1870–1871*, vol. i, p. 248, n. 3.]

dumbly on at our manœuvres; it would have complained, would have called upon us to put an end to them, and would have met hostilities with hostilities. In that conflict Prussia would have intervened, and we should have found ourselves at war with Spain and Germany united.

The only plan that we discussed seriously was that of a conference of the powers. If, before July 20, when the Cortes were to assemble, we had been able to convoke a conference, we should certainly have adopted that plan; for the first act of the powers would have been to demand from Spain a postponement of the date of the election, thus giving us time to turn round. But Spain and Prussia would have refused at the outset to agree to a conference. Spain would have invoked her right as an independent nation to govern herself as she saw fit, and Prussia would have supported her the more earnestly because she had always repelled the interference of Europe in the internal affairs of Germany. The other powers would, before entering into any engagements, have discussed the programme to be submitted to the plenipotentiaries, whence exchange of notes and despatches and duplicates and triplicates, and days and days absolutely wasted. And while all that scribbling was being done to no purpose, the 20th of July would have arrived, and, as Prim was pushing his affair with all his force, we should have learned at one and the same time that the Cortes had elected the Prussian aspirant, and that he, overflowing with gratitude and zeal, had taken possession without delay of his new realm. And by this process, as by the others, the affair would have become Spanish, and we should have been placed

OUR INABILITY TO NEGOTIATE 75

between an impossible submission and war against Spain and Prussia united. There was no one who did not realize this. Metternich said as much to Gramont: "If Prince Leopold arrives in Spain and is proclaimed there, then it will be Spain that you will have to make war on."

And so, in whatever direction we turned, we fell always into the abyss. We were, at this point, perplexed and anxious, when suddenly a gleam of light passed through my mind. I recalled that on May 3, 1866, on the eve of the war between Prussia and Austria, Thiers had said: "What course, then, should be followed with regard to the power that threatens the peace of Europe? I do not bid you to declare war on her. But is there no other way to make her confess the truth? I propose to consider all the methods, from the harshest to the mildest, and it seems to me that there is not one which should not be successful. I do not advise the harshest, but I know governments that would have resorted to it. In truth, *when one desires what is just and right, one can afford to be plainspoken;* and what could be fairer, for instance, than to say to Prussia: 'You are threatening the equilibrium of Europe, you are threatening the peace of the whole world; it is well known that you alone are responsible, and not Austria. Very good! we will not endure it!'" And recently, in the debate of June, 1870, he had recurred to the same idea: "We might have spared Europe that disaster [Sadowa], and a word would have been enough."

"Good!" I exclaimed to myself, "there is our course all marked out. Let us utter that word which Thiers blames the Emperor for not uttering to prevent the war of 1866. We cannot adopt the mild form, for that would necessitate a conversation, and that they refuse to allow. Let us not adopt the harsh form either, but let us hold to the firm, decided form. Our cause is just; let us say frankly what we will not allow. If we had no one to deal with but Bismarck, Prim, and Leopold of Hohenzollern, that word would be unavailing, and we should be forced into war none the less; for it is not supposable that either of the three conspirators will fail to keep his agreement with the others. But beside Bismarck there is the King, who, according to our information, has embarked reluctantly in this adventure; beside Prim there is Serrano, who is well-disposed toward us, and will not be sorry to play a trick on his mayor of the palace; beside Prince Leopold, there is Prince Antony, a very prudent man and easily alarmed. Outside of the powers immediately interested there is Russia, whose Tsar is emphatically desirous of peace, being convinced that war would unchain the revolution, his nightmare; there is England, whose ministers are opposed on principle to every warlike commotion. Tsar and ministers would perhaps rouse themselves from the supine attitude of indifferent observers if they should see the possibility of a conflict which they dread staring them in the face. And thereupon the negotiations, official or non-official, which are now denied us might be entered into. Since we are refused a diplomatic tête-à-tête, we have no other resource than to proclaim from the tribune to the two conspirator powers what one does not choose to understand and the other does not choose to hear, and to awaken a benumbed Europe."

OUR INABILITY TO NEGOTIATE

Gramont immediately entered into my idea, and found in his memory as a diplomatist examples of declarations which, in similar cases, had by their vigorous tone, ensured peace.[1] The Emperor instructed him to prepare a declaration to be submitted to the next day's Council, for our colleagues' approval.

On July 5, about two o'clock, Cochery, a deputy of the Left Centre, was proceeding quietly to the session of the Corps Législatif. Thiers, one of whose lieutenants he was, accosted him and called his attention to the gravity of the Spanish business and urged him to give notice of an interpellation.[2] Cochery agreed.

---

[1] [Several such examples are given by M. Ollivier at this point in vol. xiv, pp. 89–92: the famous Don Pacifico case, in 1850, when the relations between France and England became somewhat strained, and the more recent Luxembourg affair, in 1866. He adds]: "All English statesmen, without distinction of party, Palmerston as well as Disraeli, agreed in declaring that in 1853 a more emphatic firmness of language would have halted Nicholas. Lord Derby formally accused the ministry of deceiving the Czar by allowing him to think that England would never oppose with arms the invasion of Turkey."

[2] ["M. Cochery sat on the confines of the Left and the Left Centre, that is to say, in that portion of the Chamber most hostile to the bare idea of war. If we are to believe his subsequent declaration (May 9, 1878), he flattered himself that he could 'bridle' the warlike policy by forcing it to unmask." La Gorce, vol. vi, p. 221.

"M. Cochery was supposed to have M. Thiers as his Egeria." Lehautcourt, vol. i, p. 226. This author (pp. 224–225) refers the genesis of the Cochery interpellation to the unfruitful attempt of the Marquis de Massa to bring about an understanding between the Emperor and Thiers, through the Duchesse de Mouchy, as related by M. Ollivier in a later chapter. See *infra*, pp. 153–155. It will be noticed that M. Ollivier places this incident on July 10–11, whereas Lehautcourt, in order to connect it with the Cochery interpellation, places it about a week earlier — July 4. But he quotes the *Souvenirs* of M. de Massa himself to the effect that, while he took no notes, he thinks that it was not previous to the time when the withdrawal of the candidacy by the candidate's father became known, that is to say, about July 12.

However, before handing it to the President of the Chamber, he sent two of his colleagues, Planat and Genton, to me, to ask if I could see any reason why the notice should not be given.

The interpellation was signed by Cochery and nine others.

"A deputy of the Left Centre, who showed himself that day to be far from circumspect as a politician, offered an interpellation 'concerning the possible candidacy of a prince of the Prussian royal family to the throne of Spain.' This interpellation was responsive to the general trend of public opinion, but it was a serious mistake. By carrying the affair to the tribune for speech-making, M. Cochery and his friends cut short all hope of diplomatic intervention by Europe." Sorel, vol. i, p. 64.

On this subject M. Ollivier has this to say (vol. xiv, pp. 94, 95):] "The enemies of 'fatal parliamentarism' have accused Cochery of helping to create in the country the outburst of public feeling which precipitated the war, and they have, in some sense, held him responsible for it. No accusation could be more puerile. Cochery's conduct was irreproachable, and he is not responsible for the war either proximately or remotely. His interpellation did not disclose a fact that was previously unknown: it was the evidence and the result, not the cause, of the public excitement; it was impossible that Parliament should continue to be indifferent to a matter about which the whole country was talking, and if there had been no Parliament, the government would have had to explain itself by a note in the *Journal Officiel*, as it did in 1856 and 1859. The terms of the interpellation, it is true, by bringing in the 'Prussian royal family,' were not inoffensive. But how could we have found a form of words which would not have betrayed the uneasiness caused by the insolent enterprise? Even if it had been unseasonable, the real culprit would not be Cochery who, before offering it, questioned the government; but the government, which did not decline to receive it, as the rules of 'fatal parliamentarism' authorized it to do. In fact, some old parliamentarians did reproach us for accepting it and applauded Doudan's ebullition on this subject: 'I imagine Désages learning that Marshal Prim puts forward Prince Leopold for the throne of Philip V. He would have put the letter in his pocket and have meditated thrice twenty-four hours, waiting for news to come, before making the Chamber a confidant of his troubles.' We should have kept the unpleasant news in our pocket more than thrice twenty-four hours if everybody had not read it at the same time that we did, in the newspapers of all lands. The Havas Agency had spread it abroad during the 3d, when we ourselves learned of it. How could we have concealed it? When we spoke from the tribune the press of the world had been discussing it for three days." [And see La Gorce, vol. vi, pp. 229, 230.]

OUR INABILITY TO NEGOTIATE 79

Had negotiations been then in progress, or had we had any hope of beginning negotiations in any direction, I should have refused to accept the interpellation and Cochery and his friends would not have insisted. But I had the telegram in which Lesourd advised us of Thile's categorical refusal to enter into explanations, so there was no objection to the interpellation; on the contrary, it afforded us a perfectly natural means of placing a barrier between the Prussian enterprise and the date of July 20, and of making from the tribune the declaration on which we had decided that morning.

Being thus authorized, Cochery rose and declared that he desired to interpellate the government concerning the possible candidacy of a prince of the reigning house of Prussia to the throne of Spain. "Instantly he was surrounded and congratulated and advised to strike firm and hard. It may well be said that the measure is full to overflowing."[1]

Had our preconceived purpose really been to attack Prussia, had our susceptibility been but a farce, and our real aim not to allow this war, that we desired, to escape us, how easy it would have been for us to begin it at that moment! Gramont had only to rise, after Cochery, and read Lesourd's telegram, accompanied by an inflammatory word or two: general acclamations would have greeted his words, and the decisive resolutions would have been adopted on the spot. But we held our peace.

That evening my official reception was more numerously attended than usual. Nothing was talked of but the interpellation. It was strongly approved, and I was urged on all sides to reply to it in vigorous terms.

[1] [*Le Soir*, July 5, 1870.]

Lyons having come, I expressed our ideas to him with a freedom inspired by confidence. That confidence was absolute. The statements of many diplomats are open to suspicion, either because they hear imperfectly, or because they repeat all awry. But Lyons's uprightness and serious-mindedness were superior to every test: if one asked him to forget a conversation, he was dumb; if one authorized him to make use of it, he would repeat it almost word for word. He was, like Walewski, one of those men whose reports could always be regarded as true. I felt bound to no reticence with him.

"You know," I said to him, "how little opposed I am to the movement for the free internal expansion of Germany; on that account, I feel all the more keenly the unexpected affront which she seeks to put upon us, and my indignation is no less than that of the public. Be well assured, and so inform your government, that it is impossible for us to permit a Prussian prince to become king of Spain. Even if we should consent, the nation would not go with us: any cabinet, any government, which should be so weak, would be incontinently overthrown. I am not disturbed, because I have a firm hope that that contingency will be avoided; but be sure that, if it should come to pass, we would not put up with it." [1]

[1] [Lord Lyons reported this interview of July 5 to his chief on July 7. In his despatch the last sentence quoted by M. Ollivier is given as a reply to his (Lyons's) urgent advice that the declaration to be made on the 6th should be moderate in tone. "M. Ollivier assured me that it should be as mild as was compatible with the necessity of satisfying public opinion in France. But, in fact, he said, our language is this: 'We are not uneasy, because we have a firm hope that the thing will not be done; but if it were to be done we would not tolerate it.'" *Blue Book*, p. 6. See Sorel, vol. i, p. 66, for a summary of a conversation between Gramont and Prince Metternich, Austrian Ambassador to France, on the same day.]

CHAPTER VII

DECLARATION OF JULY 6, 1870

IN the morning of the 6th, at the Council of Ministers, Gramont described what had happened. Discussion followed. We inquired first of all concerning our military and diplomatic situation. That was the indispensable preliminary. In truth, there is a sort of pride which is forbidden to him who has not the strength to maintain it, as there are submissions which are disgraceful to him who cannot invoke his weakness of spirit to submit to them. At Olmütz, Bismarck had felt as bitterly as any Prussian the affront put upon Prussia by Schwarzenberg's insolent demand; but when the minister of war informed him that the army was not ready, he had advised temporary humility until Prussia should be in condition to take her revenge, which she did with interest in 1866.[1]

Our first question, then, was: Is our army ready? And we asked the question for form's sake simply, for not one of us had any doubt as to the reply. We had all followed the desultory discussion that had been had on the subject in the Chambers since 1866, renewed at least twice every session. We had in mind all of the

[1] [The Conference of Olmütz, between Prussia, represented by Von Manteuffel, and Austria, represented by Schwarzenberg, was held in November, 1850, under the mediation of Russia. It dealt principally with the affairs of Schleswig and Holstein. At that time Bismarck was simply an unofficial member of the Prussian National Assembly, but his rise from the ranks began very soon thereafter.]

Emperor's words to the Chambers: "Our completed armament, our overflowing magazines and arsenals, our trained reserves, the mobile National Guard now in process of organization, our transformed fleet, our fortifications all in good condition, supply what was indispensable to the solidification of our power. The constant aim of our efforts is attained; the military resources of France are henceforth on a level with her destiny in the world." [1]

We recalled Neil's assertions: "I regard the questions of peace or war, which are being agitated all about us in other lands, very philosophically, because, if war should become necessary, we should be in perfect shape to undergo it. . . . To-day, whether we are at peace or at war is of no consequence to the minister of war; he is always prepared." [2] And those even more significant words before the committees of the Senate and Corps Législatif: "When one has such an army, not to make war is downright virtue." And he had said, too: "In a fortnight, we would have an army of 415,000 men."

Marshal Vaillant, Generals Bourbaki, Frossard, Failly, and many others, expressed a like confidence. Le Bœuf [3] shared it absolutely. Having no vain-

[1] January 18, 1867.

[2] *L'Empire Libéral*, vol. xi, p. 350, and vol. x, p. 376.

[3] [Marshal Le Bœuf (1809–1888) had had an honorable military record; he became Minister of War on the death of Marshal Niel in 1869, and was, with the exception of Admiral Rigault de Genouilly, Minister of Marine, the only member of the Rouher Cabinet who retained his portfolio in the ministry of January 2. "Brave, intelligent, of fine physique, with a frank, hearty manner which made him popular in the Chamber, the new minister combined a large measure of frivolity with a profound love of popularity and all the tastes of the courtier. We have seen him give his assent to an incomprehensible reduction of the contingent force of the army on the very

DECLARATION OF JULY 6, 1870

glory in what concerned himself, he said to me, "I am good for only 60,000 men." On the other hand, he believed the army to be capable of all sorts of miracles, and, without dissembling the inferiority of its effective, to be likely to furnish an additional demonstration of number overmatched by quality. Military affairs concerned the Emperor alone: he had claimed, and we had not denied him, the imperial privilege of regulating and superintending them, except in the exclusively political department relative to fixing the number of troops. Le Bœuf was in error when he spoke of presenting reports to the Council: the Council asked him for none and he submitted none to it.[1] His communications were

eve of the declaration of war. . . . Surely, his share is a heavy one in the blunders which were to be so dearly expiated." Lehautcourt, vol. i, p. 196.

"Marshal Le Bœuf, the Minister of War, — who, perhaps, after the Duc de Gramont, holds the chief responsibility for the great tragedy which was impending —" Walpole, *History of Twenty-five Years*, vol. ii, p. 496.]

[1] [Le Bœuf made the "error" attributed to him, in his deposition before the Committee of Inquiry concerning the 4th of September. He then testified that he said in the Council of July 6: "The mobilization of the active army would cover perhaps 350,000 men; but, in order not to commit myself too far in so serious a matter, I will promise only 300,000. . . . I have strong hopes that within a fortnight we shall have 250,000 sufficiently organized. . . . To assemble 300,000, I think that we shall need at least three weeks." See Sorel, vol. i, p. 73; La Gorce, vol. vi, p. 226.

M. Ollivier supports his statement in the text by a letter from his colleague, M. Segris, dated Feb. 14, 1873:] "Never, to my knowledge, did the marshal read or exhibit to us any figures. . . . But I do say this, that at the last moment, when we abandoned the decision which we had formed at quarter to six in the afternoon of the 12th, and which postponed the declaration of war, the marshal, in reply to a question from me, did not say simply, 'We are ready,' but added that 'France would never have such a chance to settle her quarrel with Prussia.'" *L'Empire Libéral*, vol. xiv, p. 99.

[For Le Bœuf's further testimony before the Committee of Inquiry, etc., as to his reasons for believing in the success of France despite her probable inferiority in numbers, see Sorel, *ubi sup*.

made to the Emperor alone; it was with the Emperor alone that he discussed them; and it was in one of them that he said, "*We are stronger than the Prussians on a peace footing and on a war footing.*" The Council simply asked him: "Marshal, you promised us that if war should come, you would be ready. Are you?" The marshal did not say, like an absurd braggart, and with a show of marking the stages of our march on Berlin,[1] that the war would be simply a military promenade; on the contrary, he said that it would be a hard struggle, but that, being inevitable sooner or later, since they offered us an opportunity, we could face it without fear. The army was in admirable trim: disciplined, well-drilled, and brave; its musket far superior to the Prussian musket; its artillery commanded by a picked corps of officers; and our *mitrailleuses*, of which the Prussians had none, would have as terrible an effect as our muskets. The mobilization and concentration could be effected rapidly according to Marshal Neil's plan. And if we acted with decision and without wasting time, we should surprise the Prussians in the midst of their preparations, by an energetic offensive movement. At the outset we could deal one of these fortunate strokes which exalt the *morale* of an army, double its force, and are a pledge of its ultimate success.

Chevandier, who was quite familiar with the Prussian organization, doubted whether we were in a position to anticipate them in offensive action. Le Bœuf

Lehautcourt, vol. i, p. 231, gives the memorandum of the forces of the Empire, said to have been handed by Le Bœuf to the Emperor, on July 6, at the latter's request.]

[1] This remark has been falsely attributed to him, as have many others.

DECLARATION OF JULY 6, 1870

replied that, thanks to the superiority of our peace footing, it was perfectly possible, and he repeated to us, what he constantly declared to every one who questioned him, as MacMahon bears witness,[1] that "the French army, even though inferior in number, would whip the enemy."

His official staff held the same language. During the stormy sessions of the Chamber, my brother happened to meet Le Bœuf's secretary, Clermont-Tonnerre, in the lobby, and expressed to him his anxiety. "Don't be disturbed," that gallant officer replied; "I was with the Prussian army in 1866"; and he added, outlining a triangle on his palm, "as sure as that's a triangle, we shall whip them."

Admiral Rigault de Genouilly, Minister of the Marine, was no less convinced of the strength of the French army. "Never," he said, "have I believed in any institution as I believe in our army."

The starting-point of our deliberations, therefore, was that our army was ready, and in condition to win. Next we took up the question of alliances. We were all in favor, especially the Emperor and myself, of maintaining a firm friendship with England. But, at that conjuncture, we could expect no material aid from her, because we had nothing to offer her. On the other hand, we had something to offer to Italy, Austria, and Russia. To Italy, evacuation of the Papal States and an opportunity to prove her gratitude to us for services rendered; to Austria, revenge for Sadowa; to Russia, revision of the Treaty of Paris.

We had no doubt of Italy. I knew of Bismarck's manœuvres, his relations with Garibaldi and Mazzini,

---

[1] Unpublished *Souvenirs*, in the Archives of the War Department.

and the hostility of the Italian Left. But that revolutionary faction formed a small minority; power was in the hands of the moderates, who were openly favored by our minister, Malaret, and their assistance seemed to us certain. We relied, moreover, on the King's reminding them of their duty if they should forget it.

The choice to be made was between alliance with Austria and alliance with Russia. The difficulty was born of the strained relations between those two countries. We could not think of forming alliances with both at once; intimate relations with one would imply at least a coolness with the other.[1]

A close connection with Austria aroused in me an insurmountable aversion. She did not seriously desire to be revenged for Sadowa; the military party was still smarting with the humiliation of that defeat, but at the same time it bore a grudge to Napoleon III, who had facilitated the catastrophe. Among the other classes there was little mourning for a disaster to which the nation owed its liberties. The Hungarians rejoiced over it, because from it dated the recognition of their just claims; the Slavs, discontented and engrossed by their national aspirations, were indifferent to the prestige of the Empire, and the Germans were not indifferent to the fulfillment of the Germanic destiny. Despotism had been the sole bond between all these different nationalities, juxtaposed rather than commingled: when that bond was broken, the sheaf had fallen apart — some toward Germany,

---

[1] [The "strained relations" between Russia and Austria grew out of the latest Polish insurrection, of 1862. See Sorel, vol. i, pp. 226, 227; also Rustow (French trans.), vol. i, p. 113.]

others toward Panslavism or Russia, — and the situation of the Austro-Hungarian Empire seemed to me to be depicted to the life by the words of the great John De Witt to Louis XIV, concerning the Germanic Empire: "The Empire is a skeleton, whose bones are fastened together, not with nerves, but with wire, and do not move naturally; so that there is no reliance to be had on her friendship or her assistance."

I felt strongly drawn to the Russian alliance. I had refused to join in the demonstrations in favor of the last Polish insurrection; had I had time to formulate a foreign policy, I should have tried to form a solid alliance with Russia, by bringing about an understanding between her and England. The Emperor was favorable, judging by the insistence with which he urged me to read a pamphlet, attributed to Jomini's son, on the suitability of a Franco-Russian alliance. Consequently I advised going straight to St. Petersburg and offering a complete revision of the Treaty of Paris.

While not denying in principle the value of the Russian alliance, Gramont did not believe that we could secure it at the moment. It was too long a time that Russia had been at odds with us, and united to Prussia both by family ties [1] and by services rendered in the Polish business; we ought to deem ourselves fortunate if she adhered to a policy of neutrality. Moreover, the slightest movement on her part would alienate Hungary from us, without whose consent Austria could not form an alliance with us. Now Austria was very favorably disposed, and she had a

[1] [See *supra*, p. 32 n.]

88 THE FRANCO-PRUSSIAN WAR

fine army, fully prepared, whereas Russia was not in condition to act, so long as her railways were not finished.

These arguments of the former Ambassador to Vienna, the friend of Beust, made a strong impression on us. Nevertheless I was offering some further mild objections, when the Emperor rose, walked to a desk, opened a drawer, took therefrom the letters of the Emperor of Austria and the King of Italy in the autumn of 1869, and read them aloud to us.[1] He did not explain what had led to the letters being written; he interpreted them as a conditional promise of assistance in such a case as that in which we now were, and he was absolutely convinced that Francis Joseph and Victor Emanuel would keep their promises. The

[1] [As to the secret negotiations between the Emperor and the Austrian and Italian governments in 1869, which resulted in this exchange of autograph letters of the sovereigns, see Sorel, vol. i, pp. 39–41; La Gorce, vol. vi, pp. 154–157; Welschinger, vol. i, pp. 25–27. These negotiations were known to very few persons: Beust, Metternich, Vitzthum, for Austria, Vimercati, for Italy, Rouher, for France. (La Gorce, p. 154.) To these should doubtless be added La Valette, then Minister for Foreign Affairs. Even Gramont, then Ambassador to Austria, who had exerted himself to the utmost to bring about an alliance between that country and France, knew nothing of the correspondence until he presented his letters of recall in May, 1870. "On his return to Paris, Gramont reproached the Emperor because he had not given him his full confidence. The Emperor excused himself on the ground that he had not had time to inform him, for his departure from Vienna had been too hurried. The Minister for Foreign Affairs, not concealing his anger, demanded confirmation of the Emperor's protestations, and requested the recall of La Valette and Benedetti, Ambassadors at London and Berlin. Napoleon would have consented to recall Benedetti, but he hesitated about La Valette, who stood high in the Empress's good graces. As it was essential that the two should be recalled at the same time . . . they both remained at their posts." Welschinger, *ubi sup.*, citing *Les Coulisses de la Diplomatie*, by J. Hansen. As to the mission of General Lebrun and the visit of Archduke Albert, see *supra*, p. 39, n. 1.]

Duc de Gramont
1819–1880

report of General Lebrun and the plan of Archduke Albert, which were then in his hands, but which he did not mention to us, certainly contributed to impart a tone of expansive confidence to his language. In fact, those letters did not constitute what is properly called a treaty, but they exhibit that identity of opinions and interests from which treaties naturally flow at the propitious moment. This sort of permanent *moral* alliance often exists without being formally reduced to writing; treaties are signed when the vaguely foreseen contingency of a war is crystallized into an imminent fact; indeed, they are a proof that war is about to begin, and that is why the signature is often postponed, although the parties concerned act upon their provisions. The agreement between Cavour and Napoleon III was reached at Plombières in July, 1858; the treaty of alliance, offensive and defensive, between France and Italy, was not signed until January, 1859, on the eve of hostilities.

The fact that no formal treaty of alliance had been concluded proves that the war took us by surprise and was not premeditated by us. The Emperor had not carried to completion the agreement outlined in 1869 because his thoughts were altogether pacific; but as soon as an unlooked-for aggression seemed to him imminent, he did not doubt for an instant — and we were as confident as he — that Italy and Austria would, without waiting to be asked, convert the letters of 1869 into an offensive and defensive treaty. Our second starting-point, therefore, was that we could rely on those two allies.

Thereupon Gramont read his declaration. A few purely grammatical corrections were made in the first part. Then we all agreed that the last sentence was too elliptical and too halting, and that it must be made more emphatic. The Emperor proposed this form: "To put aside a project which would disturb to our detriment the present equilibrium of Europe and would imperil all the material interests and the honor of France."

Even that phrase seemed insufficient to me; I took the pen, and while listening to the suggestions and criticisms of each of my colleagues, I sought, at the common dictation, so to speak, some better phraseology. This task, which was very carefully done and earnestly discussed, and in which I took the principal part, especially in the last sentence, finally led us to the definitive draft. The text as agreed upon was read twice by me, after which it was put to vote, each man answering to his name, and was unanimously adopted.[1]

It is not true that Gramont brought to the Council a violent screed, which we softened; it was we who gave more sharpness of outline and more emphasis to the somewhat colorless text that he had drawn. It is inexact, therefore, to speak of the declaration of July 6 as "Gramont's declaration": it was the declaration of the Emperor and the Cabinet no less than his; and if the fact of having conceived the idea of it and of having drawn the principal parts confers paternity, I am he to whom it belongs. I do not say this to deprive Gramont of the exclusive credit for an act which I regard as meritorious, but because, by attributing it to him it is possible to see therein an

[1] [The Declaration of July 6. See Appendix G, *infra*.]

DECLARATION OF JULY 6, 1870

act of resentment for Sadowa — a secret motive which no one can attribute to me.

While I was reading it the second time, the Emperor passed to Gramont, who was at my right, the following note: "I think it advisable to send to Fleury in cipher this simple telegram: 'Notify Prince Gortchakoff that if Prussia insists upon the accession of the Prince of Hohenzollern to the throne of Spain, it will mean war.'" Gramont put the note before me. The Emperor, near whom I was sitting, saw him do it. He leaned over to me and said: "The Emperor of Russia does not want war; he will bring about the withdrawal of the candidacy."[1] Thus the word "war" was uttered by the Emperor only as the most efficacious means of preserving peace.

We left Saint-Cloud at half after twelve. Gramont, having returned to the Foreign Office, dictated the declaration to two secretaries. At two o'clock, when the Corps Législatif opened its session, he was not ready, and the session was suspended until his arrival. I went into the Chamber first. Before taking my seat, I went to Cochery and said: "You will be satisfied with our declaration; it is pacific, although

---

[1] This was not the first time that the Emperor, by a declaration of similar force, had forestalled a project the execution of which would certainly have led to war. When it was proposed to force Denmark to enter the Germanic Confederation absolutely, a similar despatch, sent by Drouyn de Lhuys to St. Petersburg and Copenhagen, caused the project to be abandoned.

[The despatch sent by Gramont to Fleury on July 6 reads: "We are convinced . . . that Russia will recognize the impossibility on our part of accepting a combination so evidently aimed against France, and we should be glad to learn that she will consent to exert her influence at Berlin to forestall the grave complications which may arise from a misunderstanding on this subject . . . for . . . if that power insists upon the accession of Prince Leopold, it means war."]

very explicit; support it by a few decided words." He answered that he did not consider himself of sufficient prominence, and he repeated my desire to Daru.[1] The latter agreed with him upon a declaration to be read after ours.

My colleagues came in one by one, and at last Gramont appeared. He went straight to the tribune, and read, without changing a word, the text agreed upon in the morning: —

"I rise to reply to the interpellation addressed to me yesterday by the honorable M. Cochery. It is true that Marshal Prim has offered Prince Leopold of Hohenzollern the crown of Spain, and that that prince has accepted it. But the Spanish people have not yet declared their will, and we do not as yet know the actual details of a negotiation which has been concealed from us. So that a discussion at this time could lead to no practical result. We urge you, Messieurs, to postpone it. We have never ceased to manifest our sympathy with the Spanish nation, and to avoid anything that could possibly have the appearance of meddling in any way with the internal affairs of a great and noble nation in the full exercise of its sovereignty. With respect to the various claimants of the throne, we have never departed from the most rigid neutrality, and we have never manifested preference or aversion for any one of them. We shall continue in that course. But we do not consider that respect for the rights of a neighboring people obliges us to suffer a third power, by placing one of its princes on the throne of Charles V, to disturb to our detriment

[1] [Comte Daru, it will be remembered, was Minister of Foreign Affairs in the Ollivier ministry during the first four months of its existence.]

DECLARATION OF JULY 6, 1870

the existing equilibrium of Europe, and to imperil the material interests and the honor of France. [*Loud applause.*] That contingency, we confidently hope, will not become a reality. To prevent it we rely at once on the wisdom of the German people and on the friendship of the Spanish people. If it should be otherwise, strong in your support, Messieurs, and in that of the nation, we shall perform our duty without hesitation and without faltering." [*Long-continued applause. Acclamations renewed again and again.*] The cheers followed Gramont to his seat.[1]

This declaration is beyond reproach, and I re-read it, after so many years, with satisfaction. It is categorical, no doubt, and includes an ultimatum in the event that its warning should not be heeded.[2] Indeed, that was the secret of its effectiveness. And yet, being restrained in tone, and free from any suggestion of a challenge, it does not go beyond a proper firmness, and refrains from anything like recrimination. It confines itself strictly to the Spanish affair, with no allusion to the occurrences of 1866, to Luxembourg, or to the numerous annoyances already under-

[1] Thiers says in his deposition [before the Committee of Inquiry concerning September 4]: "M. Ollivier came to me; although full of animation with everybody else, he was a little embarrassed with me. He was sure that I would condemn the insane thing that they had just done." That is absolutely false: I never had with Thiers the embarrassed manner that he attributes to me, especially after an act which, far from being insane, seemed to me an act of supreme sanity. [See La Gorce, vol. vi, p. 229.]

[2] Guizot, on March 2, 1843, said much the same thing: "If the Spanish monarchy were overthrown, if the sovereign who reigns in Spain to-day were robbed of her throne, if Spain were handed over to an exclusive influence that threatened peril to us, if there should be an attempt to take the throne of Spain away from the glorious family that has sat upon it since Louis XIV, why, then, I should advise my king and my country to keep watch and to take counsel." [Note of M. Ollivier.]

gone. Not a single word aims at being disagreeable to the King or his minister — still less to their people. Accuse it, if you will, of awkwardness (the effect it was soon to produce will answer that charge), but do not say that it was a challenge. Even if there could be found therein — which there cannot — any arrogant expression, it would have been a legitimate act of defence, as it would have been simply a retort to an undeniable challenge: the parry of a thrust, and in no sense a thrust itself; it was not the cannon-shot that begins a battle, but the alarm-gun which calls for help.

Cochery did not think that the words that he and Daru had prepared met the situation. He went to Gramont and said simply this: "I will not interpellate you any further."

Had our declaration been colorless, the deputies of the Left would have taunted us with cowardice; it was dignified, so they called it bellicose. Garnier-Pagès, with his affectation of a horse-jockey's *bonhomie*, declared that "the princes may hate each other and want war, but the nations love each other and desire peace." Raspail interjected some probably insulting exclamations, which were lost in the uproar. Glais-Bizoin shouted: "It's a declaration of war!" "It is war already declared," added Crémieux.

"No!" I cried energetically.

Thereupon Crémieux rejoined: "I know well enough that you are hesitating; that you want neither peace nor war."

That being so, it was not war already declared. Crémieux concluded nevertheless by insisting upon the necessity of interrupting the discussion of the budget, then under way, until there had been fuller explanations. Were that done, the debate that the government wished to postpone would have been opened. Emmanuel Arago, who very recently had supported Kératry's lamentations concerning our long-suffering in the Saint-Gothard affair, supported Crémieux's demand. "The ministry had been imprudent, involving France against her will. [*No! No!*] In our despite, it had named the King of Spain, then declared war."

Each one of these assertions was interrupted by numerous violent protests.[1] Our declaration being thus distorted, it became my duty to restore its real meaning. I did so.

"I ask the Assembly not to accept the motion of the honorable M. Crémieux, and to resume discussion of the budget.[2] The government desires peace. [*Very good! very good!*] It desires it passionately [*Exclamations on the Left*], but with honor! [*Emphatic tokens of assent and approval.*] I cannot admit that by expressing aloud its sentiments regarding a situation which concerns the security and prestige of France, the government jeopardizes the peace of the world. In my opinion it is employing the sole remaining means of solidifying that peace; for whenever France displays firmness without ostentation in defence of a legitimate right, she is sure to obtain the moral support and the approval of Europe. [*Very good! very good!* — *Applause.*] I beg, therefore, the members of this

---

[1] [Some of these interruptions are given by M. Ollivier in vol. xiv, pp. 112, 113; more by Lehautcourt, vol. i, pp. 233 ff. According to the latter, the sitting had to be twice suspended on account of the confusion and uproar, between Gramont's reading of the declaration and M. Ollivier's speech.]

[2] [A part of the opening paragraph of this speech, omitted here, is given in vol. xiv, p. 113, and by Gramont, pp. 43, 44.]

Assembly to be well assured that they are not assisting at disguised preparations for an act toward which we are proceeding by devious paths. We say all that is in our minds: we do not want war; we are intent only upon maintaining our dignity. If we believed that war is inevitable some day, we would not embark in it until we had asked and obtained your approval. [*Very good! very good!*] Then there will be a discussion, and if you do not concur with our opinion, as we are living under a parliamentary régime, it will not be difficult for you to express your own; you will simply have to overturn us by a vote, and entrust the conduct of affairs to those who seem to you likely to manage them according to your ideas. [*Murmurs on the Left.*] Have no doubt of the absolute sincerity of what we say; I declare upon my honor that there is no reservation in the mind of any one of us when we say that we desire peace. I say further that we hope for it, on one condition: that all differences on matters of detail, all factional differences, shall disappear from among us, and that France and this Assembly shall show themselves to the world unanimous in their purpose." [*Very good! very good!*— *Cordial approbation.*] [1]

Once more the press was a faithful reflection of the

[1] "Imagine that there had been on the opposition benches true patriots and not unmanageable partisans, enlightened friends of peace and not systematic enemies of the government, — they would have followed the advice I had given to Cochery. One of their orators would have expressed his assent to my explanation and would have repelled the Prussian candidacy no less emphatically than we did; he would have taken up and emphasized our hope of a pacific conclusion; thus would have been created about us a patriotic unanimity which would have alarmed our adversaries, increased our power of action, and contributed effectively to preserve the two nations from the calamities of war." *L'Empire Libéral*, vol. xiv, p. 115.

public excitement. "If this last affront had been submitted to," cried the *Gaulois*, " there would not have been a woman in the world who would have accepted a Frenchman's arm. Now our honor is secure!" Paul Dalloz, always so moderate in his tone, was no less outspoken in the *Moniteur Universel:* " The blame for this momentous conflict can never be imputed to the French government. For our own part, being fully convinced that it has public opinion on its side, we can see nothing extreme in the course which it has decided to follow, and which was ratified yesterday by the enthusiasm of the Chamber." The commendatory article in the *Figaro* was the more remarked because that journal at the moment maintained an attitude of almost personal hostility to the Emperor.

The most striking article was that in the *Correspondant*, written by Lavedan. Its effect was considerable. "Prussia has no avowable interest in the Peninsula, and she could not interfere there without being guilty of genuine provocation. So that we are of those who applaud the firm attitude adopted by the government. For too long a time our courtesy has been at the service of other people's aggrandizement; we are relieved to find that we have become Frenchmen once more! Like the Chamber, all patriotic hearts salute the declaration of the powers that be, rejoicing to recognize therein the old-time accent of the national pride!"

Louis Veuillot, little open to suspicion of complaisance toward any one on earth, unless perhaps the Pope, was quite as explicit in the *Univers:* "This declaration was the only subject of conversation last night in all the clubs and public places. The firm language of the government was unanimously approved, and even applauded. The Prussian agents, therefore, will be able to inform His Majesty King William and M. de Bismarck that our ministers were unquestionably, on that occasion, the *restrained* organs of public opinion."

The *Débats*, hitherto so favorable to the Cabinet, had shown some coolness since the beginning of the trouble; but one of the principal editors, Saint-Marc Girardin, expressed approval. "As for us, we think that the government has done well to speak, — we are wrong, — has done well to reply. What would have been said if the government had maintained a silence which the public would have considered cowardly and suspicious? It would have been accused of bending its head a second time before the cannon of Sadowa. It was essential to know that the parliamentary government was prepared and determined to provide for all the requirements of the national grandeur."[1]

[1] [More extracts from the Parisian journals are given in vol. xiv, pp. 118–122; and see La Gorce, vol. vi, p. 230. Says M. Ollivier (p. 121):] "There was no really sensational opposition except in the journal of the old Bonapartist party, the *Public*, edited by Dréolle, the deputy, under the lofty inspiration of M. Rouher [formerly Prime Minister and at this time President of the Senate]: 'We do not share the excitement caused by the acceptance of the Spanish throne by the Prince of Hohenzollern's eldest son. What has taken place between Berlin and Madrid seems to us perfectly natural. . . . Upon whom, then, should the popular emotion, now manifest in France, fall? Upon the ministers. It is the ministers whom we must call to account for their conduct. And when we see that M. Prim is bestirring himself like a Spaniard, and that M. de Bismarck is acting like a Prussian, we must find out whether MM. Ollivier and de Gramont are conducting themselves like Frenchmen. They tell us that the Cabinet proposes to resist M. Prim's project. How will it resist? England approves it, Prussia accepts it, and it is not impossible that Spain, for the very reason that we object to it, will subscribe to it. What will our ministers do then? Make war on Prussia? That would be monstrous. On Spain? That would be insane.' — No intransigeant had dared to speak like that; so that the amaze-

DECLARATION OF JULY 6, 1870

A large number of officers, among them Albert de Mun, who has himself recalled the fact, offered Gramont their congratulations.

Lyons, whose clear judgment was clouded by no preconceived opinion, wrote: "The declaration, however, forcible as it was, did not go beyond the feeling of the country. . . . The wound inflicted by Sadowa on French pride had never been completely healed, — nevertheless, time had begun to produce the effect of reconciling men's minds to what was done and could not be helped, and irritation was subsiding. Now this unhappy affair has revived all the old animosity; the government and the people have alike made it a point of honor to prevent the accession of the Prince, and they have gone too far to recede. I do not, however, believe that *either the Emperor or his ministers either wish for war, or expect it.* At this moment they confidently hope that they shall succeed, without war, in preventing the Prince from wearing the crown of Spain." In another despatch on the same day he said that "the feelings of the French nation would now render it impossible for the government, even if they wished it, to acquiesce in the elevation of Prince Leopold to the Spanish throne." [1]

The declaration which France, by an immense majority, greeted with passionate approval, aroused in

ment was general. The Emperor was aroused and wrote to Gramont: 'I am greatly distressed by the article in the *Public*, and I have let Rouher know it, although I am convinced that he had nothing to do with it.' Dréolle at once ceased his attack: through hatred of the ministers he had declared against war; through servility to the Emperor, he became one of its most frantic supporters."

[1] [Lyons to Granville, July 7; *Blue Book*, pp. 6 and 7 (no. 10), and p. 9 (no. 12).]

Europe neither surprise nor indignation, except in the case of some of those timid diplomatists, who take alarm at everything that rises above the level of their customary tittle-tattle. It was perfectly understood. The *Times* of July 8, in its leading article, criticised severely the policy of Prussia.[1]

The organ of the Conservatives, the *Standard*, expressed the same opinion as the *Times*. The *Daily Telegraph*, a journal with an immense circulation, recognized the justice of our position. "If a Hohenzollern should once become firmly seated on the throne of Spain, by the support of Prussia and in defiance of all French policy, every year would add to his power to play a deadly part in every struggle that might arise on the Rhine. *Immediate humiliation, future peril*, that is what the succession of the Prussian prince would really mean for France." The *Pall Mall Gazette* jeered at the claim of the King of Prussia to be regarded as knowing nothing of the affair.

[1] [The *Times* article is quoted in full by M. Ollivier (vol. xiv, pp. 123, 124), and by Gramont, pp. 33, 34. The passage from the *Daily Telegraph* in the following paragraph is a translation of M. Ollivier's French version, and not a transcript of the original.]

CHAPTER VIII

THE FOUR PACIFIC NEGOTIATIONS

OUR declaration was not inspired by the wish to make a rupture inevitable. It seemed to us the last chance to ensure peace by the commotion that it would cause in the hesitating purposes of the Powers and by the salutary reflections which it would arouse in the moving spirits of the affair. And so the approbation that came to us from all quarters, instead of depriving us of our self-possession, augmented it. Instead of plunging us into extreme measures, it incited us to further pacific efforts, and we resumed our negotiations with the more ardor in that they no longer seemed to us doomed to failure.[1]

Having determined not to depart from the consecrated rules of international courtesy, we could not appeal to Spain. Mercier had urged upon us such abstention as early as June 24. "Our opposition will have all the more weight in the premises, if it be aimed directly at Prussia and consequently inflict no wound on Spanish pride." [2]

---

[1] "The Prussians found at Saint-Cloud and published the confidential telegram that I sent to the Emperor after the session. It proves the sincerity of the sentiments that I had just expressed in the tribune. 'The declaration was greeted by the Chamber with emotion and tremendous applause. The excitement, at first, even went beyond what we expected. One would have said that it was a declaration of war. I took advantage of an interruption by Crémieux to set the thing right. I would not allow ourselves to be represented as premeditating war; we desire only peace with honor.'" *L'Empire Libéral*, vol. xiv, p. 126.

[2] [The question whether the French government chose the more judicious course in making its formal demand for the withdrawal of the candidacy at

102   THE FRANCO-PRUSSIAN WAR

To appeal to Spain was to fall into the snare that Bismarck had set for us. Nevertheless, without entering upon negotiations properly so-called, without a formal note or an ultimatum, we conceived that we

Berlin rather than at Madrid is discussed at greater or less length by all the historians of the war. M. de Gramont, himself, as if conscious that his course in that respect was open to criticism, explains it thus: "The news of the Prussian candidacy for the throne of Spain arrived July 3 by telegraph. The first act of the government was to address itself to Berlin. For there it was that we must look for the *fait accompli* which awoke our legitimate anxiety. At Madrid there was, as yet, only a contingency; for the vote of the Cortes, although very probable, was not yet cast in Prussia's favor. Moreover, the French government could not with propriety place itself athwart a national manifestation of the Spanish people. An intervention of that sort, being contrary to the principles of our constitution, would not have failed to offend Spain, and to further a different result from that which we sought. So that, while at Madrid we confined ourselves to appealing to the justice and the friendly sentiments of which the Spanish statesmen had so often assured us, we gave expression at Berlin to our justifiable surprise and to the hope that the King's government, following the example set, under similar circumstances, by England, by Russia, and by France herself, would consent to put aside a complication which threatened the repose of Europe by destroying the equilibrium of the Powers." *La France et la Prusse avant la Guerre*, pp. 27, 28. And see Sorel, vol. i, p. 62. La Gorce (vol. vi, p. 198) criticizes the failure of the then government to make any representations to Spain when the candidacy of Leopold was being discussed in 1869 (see Appendix C).

"He [Gramont] turned to Prussia," says La Gorce, "less as a statesman who seeks to dissipate a misunderstanding, than as an insulted person seeking reparation. If, at the outset, he proposed to call the cabinet of Berlin into court, prudence counselled a lessening of the danger of direct explanations by an adroit moderation in the matter of form. A contrary preoccupation seems to have inspired the French minister. In the very first communication, the agitated brevity of the language used discloses the mental excitement. One is conscious of long arrears of rancor and evil memories, hitherto held in check and ready to overflow. Behind the haughty words that escape, can be discerned the irreparable words that are still held back. Wrath betrays itself by the very efforts that are made to dissemble it. One would say that it was not a diplomatic negotiation, but the preliminaries of a duel — something like the scene between Don Rodrigue and Gormas in the second act of *Le Cid*," vol. vi, p. 218.]

THE FOUR PACIFIC NEGOTIATIONS 103

ought to try once more to arouse and frighten the Spanish government. Gramont telegraphed to Mercier: —

"You will say to Marshal Prim that this choice is the worst that could be made, and that the national affront to France which results from it is very keenly felt by his Majesty. They who propose it to Spain, and who advise it, assume a very considerable responsibility before their peoples and before Europe. You are thoroughly familiar with the Emperor's opinions; remain on the ground on which you stand. Say that nothing is further from our thoughts than to seek to place any restraint on the liberty of the Spanish people, but that the test is, in very truth, too much for us. We hope that our appeal will be heeded, and that that friendly government, that great nation, being persuaded of the friendly feelings toward them by which we have invariably been actuated, will recognize the justice of our emotion at the thought that they might become the instrument of schemes so opposed to our political interests. And if, despite our legitimate representations, the Prince of Hohenzollern should be chosen, however great our friendship for Spain, we should find ourselves in the painful necessity of not recognizing him." [1]

Mercier talked to no purpose — Prim paid no heed to him and did not pause. He continued his preparations for the election as calmly as if we had not said a word. "There is nothing for us to do but go ahead," he said to a Madrid banker. And he wrote to a friend: "I could never have believed that France would take this matter so much to heart; I never dreamed that

[1] July 6–7.

it could give occasion for European complications which distress me sorely; but, at the point that we have reached, to withdraw would be disgraceful. Before all else we must save the honor of the nation. I conclude therefore by saying, with my hand upon my conscience, and fully persuaded that we have dealt no blow to the warm friendship that unites us to our neighbors the French: 'Forward, and long live Spain!'"[1]

And he sent to us, through Olozaga, a circular note signed by Sagasta, his Minister for Foreign Affairs, which flouted us without concealment: "The wholly favorable conditions surrounding that prince and the cordial reception which his selection has met with in the public opinion of the country, afford the government the gratifying hope that its candidate will soon be chosen King by the Cortes by a great majority, and that thus will be brought to a close the glorious interregnum which began in September, 1868." Lastly, Prim caused Salazar to republish his little book of October, 1869, in which he has the insolence to say that "It is notorious that the defeat of Montpensier and the Republic depends upon Napoleon's veto. . . . The Prussian government did not intervene in this negotiation; the Prince informed the King, at Ems, of his final decision, as an act of courtesy."

Thus Prim defied us more and more openly, hoping to exhaust our patience, and to drive us to the violent measures against Spain which his friend Bismarck

[1] [See La Gorce, vol. vi, p. 220; Lehautcourt, vol. i, pp. 257, 258, citing Darimon, *Histoire d'un Jour*. On July 7 Mercier telegraphed that Prim said to him: "How can I get out of it? I see but one way: let the Prince say that he finds obstacles in the way of the King's consent, and then, instead of persisting, I will facilitate his withdrawal." Gramont, p. 366.]

was awaiting. But our determination not to allow ourselves to be drawn into that course was unshaken, and Gramont, as calmly as if we had not felt the prick of the needle, telegraphed again to Mercier:—

"In spite of Marshal Prim's circular note and the communication which M. Olozaga has just made to me, we have too much confidence in the sentiments of the Spanish nation, to believe that the people at Madrid will persist in the only solution which attacks at once our material interests and our dignity. We shall pursue our friendly course of conduct, therefore, and shall continue to maintain, on the Spanish frontier, the vigilant observation necessary to put a stop to whatever is likely to foment disturbance in the Peninsula. We shall be true to our sympathies until the last; most assuredly we shall not be the first to break bonds which were dear to us, and which we hoped that we had made indissoluble."

Nor had we anything to hope from Bismarck, as represented by his retainer Thile. Gramont determined none the less to point out how pitiful were the grounds upon which Thile refused all discussion. A despatch to Lesourd showed that we were not deceived by his evasions.

"They will never make any one believe that a Prussian prince can accept the Spanish crown unless he has been authorized by the King, the head of his family. Now, if the King has authorized him, what becomes of the alleged ignorance of the Cabinet of Berlin, behind which M. de Thile has taken refuge? In the present case, the King can either permit or forbid; if he has not permitted, let him forbid. A few years ago, under analogous circumstances, the Emperor did not hesitate. His Majesty publicly disavowed Prince Murat when he put forward his candidacy to the throne of Naples. We should regard a similar decision on King William's part as a most friendly act toward us, and we should see therein a powerful guarantee of the desire of Prussia to strengthen the bonds that unite us and to assure their permanence." [1]

This calm refutation had no more effect than our representations to Prim, and we were forced to the conviction that we must definitely abandon negotiation and either submit to the candidacy or have recourse to war. But we were no more desirous of war than of the candidacy, and we persisted more obstinately than ever in our determination to negotiate.

The Emperor, being aware of the secret rivalry between Prim and Serrano, thought that therein lay the means of countermining Prim. Serrano was a friend to France, and was on excellent terms personally with Napoleon III. It occurred to the Emperor to appeal, directly and secretly, to his friendly sentiments. He summoned Bartholdi, Mercier's messenger, to Saint-Cloud, and ordered him to start for Madrid on the following day. On his arrival he was to go to the Regent, and request him as a personal service to the Emperor, for which he would always be in his debt, to make representations at once to Prince Antony of Hohenzollern, to the end that that prince should persuade his son to withdraw his candidacy. Bartholdi asked the Emperor if it would not be more correct for the Ambassador himself to make this request. "No," the Emperor replied; "you may mention it to Mercier; but immediately on your arrival go yourself to

[1] July 7.

THE FOUR PACIFIC NEGOTIATIONS 107

Serrano, as coming on a special mission *from me*. That will have a greater effect. Insist; say to the marshal that I appeal to his friendship for me."

Nor did we give over making a supreme effort in the direction of Prussia. We could not think of seeking out Bismarck at Varzin: he would have shut the door in our face even more roughly than Thile had done. There remained but one means: to have recourse to the King of Prussia, then at Ems. We had not to deal with a constitutional king, in duty bound to hold aloof from public affairs; William both reigned and governed; on all occasions he declared that his ministers were mere instruments, that their acts were simply the carrying out of his personal ideas. So that there was nothing irregular in our proceeding, nor was it the first time that the King had discussed matters directly with sovereigns or their representatives. This method of negotiating was dangerous only to ourselves, since it would all be confidential and by word of mouth, and there could be no exchange of notes which would make it possible to prove later, by irrefragable testimony, the rectitude and prudence of our procedure. We were not unaware that it is not in accordance with etiquette to disturb a sovereign when taking a cure; but the matter was urgent and not by our fault, and as we had no other means of averting the conflict, we were forced to disregard the proprieties to that extent.

To give more weight to his representations to Serrano and King William, Gramont sought the support of all the powers. He telegraphed to Fleury: "We are convinced that the Russian ministry will see the impossibility of our accepting a candidacy so plainly aimed against France, and we should be happy to learn that it will exert its influence at Berlin to forestall the complications on this subject which might ensue between the Emperor and Prussia."[1]

To Malaret, at Florence, he telegraphed: "Request M. Visconti-Venosta to direct the Italian agent at Madrid to exert his influence with the statesmen there, and especially with the Regent, to detach him from an intrigue in which Prim alone has taken the initiative so injurious to our dignity and our interests."[2]

He urged Metternich to ask Beust, "to be good enough to make it clear at Berlin that, in view of the national irritation here, they would be well advised, in the interest of peace, to induce Prince Leopold to decline this candidacy."[3]

Gramont was especially urgent with England, from whom he hoped for most effective assistance. He suggested to Lyons, as a solution of the difficulty, that England might advise the voluntary withdrawal of his candidacy by Leopold himself, which would be less humiliating to Prussia than a withdrawal exacted or advised by the King. Such "a voluntary renunciation on the part of the Prince," said Lyons, "would, M. de Gramont thought, be a most fortunate solution of difficult and intricate questions; and he begged Her Majesty's government to use all their influence to bring it about."[4]

Gramont telegraphed directly to La Valette, our

---

[1] July 6.
[2] July 17 [7?]. [See Granville to Lyons, July 9, *Blue Book*, p. 12.]
[3] Metternich to Beust, July 8.
[4] Lyons to Granville, July 8. [*Blue Book*, p. 11.]

THE FOUR PACIFIC NEGOTIATIONS 109

Ambassador in London: "I have begged Lord Lyons to request Lord Granville that the English government be especially insistent with the Regent, to induce him to divorce his cause from that of Marshal Prim in this matter. If, as we hope, the Cabinets will of their own motion use their influence to enlighten Marshal Serrano concerning the perils of the intrigue of which Marshal Prim is the real author, we are confident that that dangerous intrigue will fail." (July 7.) And on the next day, the 8th, he returned to the charge once more: "It is urgently necessary that the powers which are in a position to make King William listen to the counsels of moderation and wisdom should intervene without loss of time, before the true character of this business has been distorted by national sensitiveness. Neither the dignity of the Spanish people nor that of the German people is at stake; but if the discussion drags on for a few days only, popular passions will inevitably inflame it by rearousing those rivalries between the two countries which will be an additional obstacle to the government bent upon maintaining peace."

He even appealed to the States of the South, in order to show that he had no secret unfriendly design against Germany. He telegraphed to Saint-Vallier [at Würtemberg]: "I have no doubt that the German courts will put forth all their powers of persuasion to dissuade King William from supporting the candidacy of the Prince of Hohenzollern; and I am confident that their efforts, upheld by the patriotic good sense of the German nation, will not be without influence on the conduct of Prussia in this matter." [1]

[1] July 8.

Where in these instructions, so nobly pacific and conciliatory in tone, can one detect the slightest trace of angry impatience, the slightest desire to humiliate the King of Prussia or to seek a rupture with him? Explicitness is never carried to the point of discourtesy, and the desire to have done with the business does not degenerate into an impertinent demand. There is "neither contradiction nor hesitation," as the rhetoricians say, who know not the mental flexibility demanded by the changing aspect of affairs. To be sure, he speaks now of advice, now of orders, now of spontaneous withdrawal, and again of enforced withdrawal, but the gist of the thought never varies for an instant, it is always the same — to obtain without war the disappearance of the candidacy.

In fine, Gramont, the madman, the challenger, was so eager to avoid war, like all of us, that he conceived the idea of telegraphing to Benedetti, to "go to see the Prince of Hohenzollern, in order to induce him to withdraw, and thereby avert the ills which his candidacy made inevitable." [1]

The Emperor, whose sensitive nature was wounded to the quick by the criminal conduct of a family so affectionately distinguished by him, would not consent to this step. It had seemed to him perfectly natural, as Gramont had suggested to Lyons and Metternich, that the neutral powers should, on their own initiative, try to obtain the Prince's withdrawal, and he had himself sent Bartholdi to suggest it to Serrano; he forbade that any request whatever should be made directly of the Hohenzollerns in his name. As soon

[1] July 8, 1 A.M. [M. Benedetti had, meanwhile (July 7), been ordered to Ems to negotiate directly with the King. See Sorel, vol. i, p. 90.]

as the despatch to Benedetti was placed before him he wrote to Gramont: —

"MY DEAR DUKE, — I have received your despatches. I deem it neither advisable nor dignified on my part to write to the King of Prussia or to the princes of Hohenzollern. Moreover, I think that you should not tell Benedetti to go to the Prince. It is with Prussia, and with her alone, that we have to do. It is not consistent with our dignity to implore the Prince to withdraw. I beg you therefore to countermand the instruction to Benedetti on this subject. He must not think that the sentiment of the nation rejects the idea of war."

Gramont at once telegraphed to Benedetti (July 9): "You must not see the Prince of Hohenzollern; the Emperor does not wish any overture made to him."

At this juncture Olozaga came of his own motion to propose that he should himself attempt the mission to the Hohenzollerns which the Emperor regarded as inconsistent with his dignity, but which he would have been overjoyed to see others attempt. Olozaga, offended that so momentous a negotiation should have been carried on without his being concerned in it, could not resign himself to the idea that the destiny of his country should be arranged without his knowledge; he was eager to prove that it was not so simple a matter as they thought to do without his assistance, and he burned to repay Prim in his own coin. Moreover, he had a sincere sympathy for France and the Emperor, and would have been happy to spare them the perils of a terrible war. In his meditations on the subject, it occurred to him that he might be able, through the medium of Strat, the Roumanian agent, an alert, shrewd, intelligent man who stood well with the Hohenzollern family, to bring Leopold to the withdrawal which the whole body of European diplomacy was about to seek, probably in vain. He sent him an urgent summons during the night. At four in the morning Strat found him pacing the floor in extreme agitation.

"If the Hohenzollern candidacy," he said, "is a pretext for war, planned by Bismarck and desired by the Emperor, there is nothing to be done; if, as is possible, it is mainly an ambitious proceeding on the part of the Hohenzollern family, perhaps they might be persuaded not to persist. You have friendly relations with that family; are you willing to undertake a mission to them with the object of securing the withdrawal which would save the whole situation?"[1]

[1] All these details and those which follow were given to me by Strat and by Olozaga. [The text leaves the date of Strat's mission in some uncertainty, but the memoirs of the King of Roumania supply explicit information on this point as well as with regard to the circumstances under which the mission was undertaken. Under date of July 6 we find what follows: —

"Meanwhile the storm aroused by the Spanish question has upset everything, and Prince Charles [he was proclaimed King of Roumania only in 1881] is suspected of having conspired behind the scenes with the alleged foes of France!

"As soon as Strat hears these charges, he goes to the Duc de Gramont, to ask him if it is true that Prince Charles is supposed to be concerned in his brother's candidacy. The duke replies frankly that he cannot deny it, and concludes with these significant words: 'The moment that Prince Charles conspires against French interests, it is no more than fair fighting to do our utmost to overturn him, and indeed to begin right there in case of war with Prussia, in order to satisfy to some extent public opinion which has many a time reproached the Emperor for putting a Hohenzollern on the Danube!'

"In vain did Strat try to convince the Duc de Gramont that Prince Charles had had absolutely no part in Prince Leopold's candidacy. When

THE FOUR PACIFIC NEGOTIATIONS 113

Strat asked for time to reflect; he had not time to communicate with his government, and he was afraid of interfering with its plans.

"In short," said Olozaga, "you do not consent, but neither do you refuse. I will go and talk with the Emperor about it."

He was, in truth, too shrewd to make the venture carelessly. He went, therefore, to the Emperor and asked him whether he did or did not want war; whether the Hohenzollern affair was simply an opportunity to restore the equilibrium that was destroyed in 1866, and whether an inopportune interference on his part would thwart it. If the Emperor desired peace, he thought that he could assure it by getting rid of the candidacy. And he explained how.

The Emperor replied without hesitation that he did desire peace; he had no interest to be subserved by war, and was not seeking a pretext for it. His

he saw that the duke turned a deaf ear to his protestations, he begged him to maintain a neutral attitude with regard to Roumania for five days, agreeing to furnish him within that time proofs of the loyalty of the Prince of Roumania's purposes, and thus to destroy the tissue of falsehoods spread broadcast in the French capital by the subversive faction of the Roumanian opposition. . . .

"*Two hours later*, Strat started for Sigmaringen, in order to inform Prince Antony of the state of affairs."

Lehautcourt (vol. i, p. 259) cites Darimon (*Histoire d'un Jour*) for the statement that before leaving Paris, on July 8, "M. Strat deemed it necessary to have an understanding with M. Olozaga." It will be seen that some of M. Ollivier's statements are inconsistent with the passages quoted, notably as to Olozaga's initiative, and as to the stipulation that Gramont should be kept in ignorance of the affair; but the details are important only because it is evident that this mission of Strat had much to do with the later withdrawal of Prince Leopold's candidacy; so that if, as there was every reason to anticipate, war had been avoided by that withdrawal, it would have been so avoided from no higher motive than the safeguarding of the Hohenzollern interests in Roumania.]

sole preoccupation was that no blow should be dealt at the interests of France. If he were satisfactorily assured of that, he would ask for nothing more. Although he did not believe in the success of Strat's attempt, he would be glad to have it made, provided that his name was not involved in it.

Olozaga at once sent for Strat again and repeated this conversation. As he still hesitated, Olozaga proposed to take him to the Emperor. He agreed, on condition that no one should be informed of the interview, for if it should be made known, the success of the mission it was proposed to entrust to him would become impossible. He went to Saint-Cloud secretly at two in the morning. The Emperor told him how earnestly he desired him to undertake the mission of which Olozaga had spoken to him, and again expressed his pacific opinions in such wise that Strat ceased to doubt their sincerity.

Thereupon Strat said: "Sire, my intervention will not be effective unless I have something to offer in return for the sacrifice that I shall ask. Now there is a group of Roumanians here in Paris, whom M. de Gramont receives and who are conspiring against Prince Charles. The duke [Gramont] himself has expressed himself in very harsh terms concerning the Prince, whom he accuses of being an accomplice in his brother's candidacy, and he threatens to assist at overthrowing him in order to satisfy public opinion, which has many a time reproached the Emperor for placing a Hohenzollern on the Danube. Furthermore, Austria is ill-disposed. Your Majesty must authorize me to assure Prince Antony against this threefold menace, and to promise him, without fear of the promise

THE FOUR PACIFIC NEGOTIATIONS 115

being disavowed, that his son, far from having to fear the ill-will of the French government, can, if occasion arise, rely on its support."

The Emperor made the promises that Strat requested, and the latter accepted the mission, demanding that neither Gramont nor any one else should be informed of it. The Emperor promised secrecy, and his most abundant favor if he should succeed; and, thanking Olozaga anew for his initiative, said to him: "This is the last arrow that we have in our quiver; I shall be very much surprised if it reaches the mark, but it would make me very happy."

Strat started at once for Düsseldorf, to find out where the Hohenzollern princes were.

Thus four pacific efforts — that upon Serrano at Madrid, that upon King William at Ems, that upon the Hohenzollern princes at Sigmaringen, and that upon the friendly cabinets — were about to meet and blend and assist one another, although each was ignorant of the others, — all four tending to the same end: to maintain peace by the withdrawal of the candidacy; all four conceived, encouraged, or guided by the Emperor or his ministers, those so-called quarrel-seekers, on the alert for a pretext for war![1]

[1] [I much regret that M. Ollivier has thought it best to omit here three or four pages of his main work in which he gives some instances of the harrying of the ministry by politicians and the press during the days immediately following the declaration of July 6. I quote, however, one passage characteristic of both the parties concerned. On July 7] "I was just entering the legislative hall, when Jules Favre, taking the floor, asked that the adjourned debate should be assigned for the next day or the day after that. I simply requested the Chamber to postpone the debate. — 'Indefinitely?' cried Jules Favre; 'so that you can have a change to take a flyer on the Bourse?' — I could hardly feel that that vile insinuation was aimed at me, as I had not a share of anything dealt in on the Bourse; but I could not endure it.

According to my habit, I walked straight up to the insulter. 'To whom does M. Jules Favre address the words he just uttered?' My threatening glance and gesture said: 'Is it to those who sit on the ministerial benches?' Thereupon, according to his habit, he beat a retreat under cover of an inoffensive generality. . . . 'To all who speculate,' he replied. I rejoined: 'When the government considers that it is in a position to furnish the Chamber with useful information, it will itself invite discussion; it will allow no one else the privilege of fixing a day for that purpose. Surely, if there is a reproach from which the present government is immune, it is that of concealing anything whatever from this Chamber, since the interpellation of one of its members sufficed to cause it to explain an event which, so far as the government was concerned, was only a day or two old. The Chamber and the country may rest assured that we shall not fail, under the present circumstances, to unite, as always, firmness with moderation; that we shall forget neither what the Chamber wants nor what the country wants; but we refuse to engage prematurely in reckless and unconsidered discussions.'" *L'Empire Libéral*, vol. xiv, pp. 143, 144.

CHAPTER IX

GRAMONT'S NEGOTIATIONS WITH THE POWERS

ALTHOUGH our four negotiations were carried on contemporaneously, it is important to take them up separately, in order to follow them the more readily in their logical interdependence; and as the action of the friendly cabinets was, in some sense, the frame in which the private interventions at Madrid, Ems, and Sigmaringen followed their course, I shall describe that first of all.[1]

The powers had replied to our request, each after its own fashion. Gortchakoff failed to justify the hope that the Emperor had placed in Russia: he sneered at our sensitiveness. "When another Hohenzollern prince procured himself to be proclaimed King by the Roumanians, despite the opposition of Russia, but with the support of France," he said, "you confined yourselves to remonstrances and accepted the accomplished fact. Do as much now. You ask our assistance, but France is Russia's debtor; it would be necessary for her to give conciliatory pledges touching the Orient. Not that there is a question of a revision of the humiliating treaty of 1856, which Russia endures with pain; she under-

[1] [On the subject of this chapter, generally, see Sorel, vol. i, pp. 61–71, 140–148; Welschinger, vol. i, Chap. vi; La Gorce, vol. vi, pp. 148–157, 182–188; Taxile Delord, *Histoire du Second Empire*, vol. vi, pp. 132 ff., 145 ff., 167.]

stands that France is not alone, and that she can act only in concert with England." Later, to Fournier, the attaché of the legation at St. Petersburg, Gortchakoff, admitted the malevolence of his expressions. "France," he said, "needed a lesson."[1]

The Tsar, on the other hand, seemed touched by Napoleon's confidence. He bade Fleury to inform him that he had strong reasons for thinking that the intrigue woven by Marshal Prim would not succeed.[2] He wrote to King William, counselling moderation and abstention. Although William replied that he had nothing to do with the offer made to the Prince of Hohenzollern, and that his government was not a party to the negotiation, the Tsar sent still another despatch, which he read to Fleury, in which he pressingly besought his uncle to order the Prince to withdraw. "By such a command, the King would cease to be interested in the candidacy, which would then become purely a Spanish affair, and would not be long in disappearing in discord, before the disapproval of all Europe." "War would be a European calamity," the Tsar added to Fleury, "of which the Revolution would reap all the profit. Say to your government that I will do all that I can to prevent it, within the limits of my advice and influence. My good-will toward the Emperor cannot be questioned: recently the Duc d'Aumale and some of his people formed the plan of coming here to visit Grand Duke Constantine and making the tour of Russia; I sent word

[1] [See Lehautcourt, vol. i, pp. 196-204, 253-256; Sorel, vol. i, p. 96; La Gorce, vol. vi, pp. 234-235; Welschinger, vol. i, p. 222. See also Sir A. Buchanan to Granville, July 9 and 11, *Blue Book*, p. 49.]

[2] Fleury to Gramont, July 9. And see *La France et la Russie in 1870*, by Comte Fleury.

NEGOTIATIONS WITH THE POWERS

to the Orleans princes that after the recent vote of the Chamber, their journey to Russia seemed to me inopportune." [1]

Beust never refused us his good words. He wrote to his ambassador at Berlin: "The French nation has held in check the sentiments to which the aggrandizement of Prussia in Germany gave birth in its mind; but that suspicion, hardly overcome, would not only be rearoused, but would reach the point of serious disquiet, if an attempt should be made to bring Spain under Prussian influence by placing on the throne a member of the royal family of Prussia. Your Excellency will not conceal from the statesmen of Prussia that we can see danger of genuine agitation in the candidacy of Prince Leopold, and will express our strong desire that love of peace and the King's lofty intelligence may prevent the irruption into European politics of an element of discord so full of menace." [2]

Visconti-Venosta, who was much more circumspect, expressed the same hopes at Berlin, and was more insistent at Madrid, although still with reserve. He instructed his representative, Cerutti, to call attention to the fact that, until the decision of the Cortes, any advice might be tendered; it was therefore proper for the governments friendly to Spain to point out the extreme gravity of a situation, the peaceful outcome of which depended solely on the wisdom and politic

[1] Fleury to Gramont, July 12. This conversation proves how untrue it is that the understanding between the Czar and King William concerning the Hohenzollern candidacy was reached at Ems. He would not have advised the withdrawal of a candidacy to which he had given his approval. [Note of M. Ollivier in vol. xiv, p. 153.]

[2] Beust to von Munch, July 6. [See Sorel, vol. i, p. 71; Lehautcourt, vol. i, p. 248 and n.]

spirit of her representatives. The Italian minister was directed to insist on the tremendous responsibility which the Cortes would assume in raising to the throne a prince whose accession would be the signal for a European war; he was to express, in the name of his government, the fear that a monarchy founded under such auspices, far from giving to Spain the security and repose to which she aspired, would expose her to fresh trials and fresh perils. He was even authorized to support the English Ambassador, and to see how far the two nations could agree upon a common course.[1]

The South German States did not give us the assistance that Gramont expected from them. They showed once more how blind was the policy which exalted defence of their territory into a dogma, and they began to turn their backs on us. The weather-cock of Würtemberg, Varnbühler, whose views Saint-Vallier was too ready to share, began to turn. Although not in a position to judge of the imperative reasons for our declaration of the 6th, he had the assurance to regret that our "confidence in the justice of our cause did not advise more moderation in its form"; and he pretended to be amazed and alarmed.[2]

Bray, with more sincerity and downrightness, was no more encouraging. He said to Cadore: "If war should break out between France and Prussia, our position would be most embarrassing; for while, on the one hand, it is beyond question that the affair is of no interest to Bavaria, we could not, on the other

---

[1] Malaret to Gramont; Layard to Granville [July 10, *Blue Book*, p. 18]; Paget to Granville [July 9 and 12, *Blue Book*, pp. 29, 30. See also Sorel, vol. i, p. 95; Lehautcourt, vol. i, p. 249.]

[2] [Lehautcourt, vol. i, pp. 338 and n., 340 and n.]

NEGOTIATIONS WITH THE POWERS

hand, remain unmoved by the invasion of German territory by a French army, on the pretext that Spain has summoned a Prussian prince to govern her. Prussia denies all participation in the matter of the Prince's candidacy; she says that it is no affair of hers, and people are beginning to think that, if you are not satisfied with that assertion, it must be that your government proposes to seize this opportunity to recur to the events of 1866. The line of conduct followed by your government and the language of its journals give some probability to these suspicions; you make our situation very difficult. I have always maintained that the treaties of alliance are defensive in character; if Prussia could with any show of justice accuse you of being the aggressors, and say that your armies first crossed the frontier, we should be obliged to enter the field against you, which I should deeply regret, for Bavaria has never had reason to do aught but praise France, and of all the German states it is the one where the public feeling is most favorable to you." [1]

The English Cabinet failed to see what a decisive influence it might exert. With a word, if it had chosen, it could have stopped the war; it would have been enough for it to say: "A rule of international law, originated by us in Belgium, and submitted to by us in Greece, forbids every great power to place one of its reigning house on a foreign throne, without the consent of Europe first obtained. We consider that

[1] July 13. [See Lehautcourt, vol. i, p. 339. As to the immediate action of the Bavarian and Würtemberg governments after the declaration of war, see despatches of Sir H. Howard and Mr. Gordon to Earl Granville, July 17, in *Blue Book*, No. 3, p. 1.]

there is occasion, under circumstances which threaten the peace of the world, to summon a conference to inquire into the value of this rule and to determine how far it should be made applicable to the candidacy put forward in Spain."

This proposition, which, if made by us, would have been met with a curt refusal by Prussia and Spain, was, on the contrary, certain of acceptance if England had taken the initiative in it. Our assent would have been immediate, that of Austria and Italy would not have been long delayed, nor that of Russia. Bismarck would have grumbled, but his King would not have listened to him; the conference would have been held, and would have settled the dispute.

The English Cabinet could make up its mind neither to approve nor to blame nor to hold aloof; its conduct was two-faced, sordid, and cowardly. It supported us as if we were in the right, and seemed to contest our claim as if it had not supported us. Granville received in a cold and embarrassed way Gramont's appeal for his assistance: he realized the agitation that must have been aroused in France by news which had surprised himself no little; he thought, however, that we had perhaps taken a little too much to heart a fact the consequences of which did not seem to him of such grave importance as the imperial government attributed to it. He regretted that Gramont had used such forcible language to Werther; he wondered whether the attitude we had felt called upon to assume was not calculated of itself to create more serious complications than those which would be caused by the incident itself. However, coming to the point, he declared that he was ready to "use what influence they [the government] might possess both with Prussia and with Spain; and without any pretension to dictate to either power they would advise them to take into their most serious consideration . . . all the bearings of this question." [1]

Strange language! If dynastic questions in Spain were of so little consequence, why did Palmerston threaten Louis-Philippe with war in case the Duc d'Aumale should become the Queen's husband? and why did he manifest such indignation when Montpensier became the husband of the Infanta? [2] Would Granville himself have remained unmoved and dumb if he had been informed that Prince Napoleon was about to be chosen King of Spain?

Gladstone, to whom La Valette expressed his regret at Granville's lukewarm attitude, replied: "We must begin cautiously. We knew nothing of the question at issue, and we do not as yet know the details." They did in fact begin very cautiously, and with abundance of circumlocution and reservations. They instructed their ambassadors at Berlin and Madrid to counsel prudence, avoiding any discussion of Spain's right

[1] [Granville to Lyons, July 6, *Blue Book*, p. 2.]

[2] [The so-called question of the Spanish Marriages nearly involved France and England in war in 1846. The young Queen Isabella, and her sister, Maria Luisa, were both *à marier*, and Lord Palmerston, then Foreign Minister in the government of Lord John Russell, strove to defeat the endeavors of the government of Louis Philippe to obtain a preponderant influence in Spain by marrying the Queen to the King's fourth son, the Duc d'Aumale. In the end, the Queen married her cousin, and the hand of the younger princess was bestowed on the Duc de Montpensier, fifth son of Louis Philippe, who, as we have seen, was a candidate for the Spanish throne in 1870. See the *Life of Viscount Palmerston*, by Sir Henry Bulwer (Lord Dalling), who was British Minister at Madrid and Palmerston's chief agent in the affair, and Sir Spencer Walpole's *Life of Lord John Russell;* also the *Memoirs* of Charles C. F. Greville, 2d Series.]

to choose her own sovereign, and any appearance of putting pressure on Germany, or any admission that the accession of a Hohenzollern would justify the immediate recourse to arms which France threatened. "Her Majesty's government," Granville wrote to Loftus, "certainly hope, and they cannot but believe, that this project of which they have been hitherto ignorant, has not received any sanction from the King. . . . [I venture, therefore, to hope that] the King [and his advisers] will find it consistent with their own views [of what is best for Spain] effectually to discourage a project fraught with risk to the best interests of that country. . . . The King of Prussia, whose reign has brought about so signal an aggrandizement of that country, has now an opportunity not less signal of exercising a wise and disinterested magnanimity, with the certain effect of conferring an inestimable service on Europe by the maintenance of its peace."[1]

He instructed his ambassador at Madrid, Layard, "while carefully abstaining from employing any language calculated to offend them [the Spanish government], to use every pressure upon them which, in your judgment, may contribute to induce them to abandon the project of conferring the throne of Spain on Prince Leopold of Hohenzollern."[2]

This advice was, in reality, given in the interest of Prussia rather than in ours. Granville, although personally inclined toward France, was swayed by the Queen's German predilections. As for Gladstone, his sympathies were absolutely Prussian. Both alike

[1] [Granville to Loftus, July 6, *Blue Book*, p. 3.]
[2] [Granville to Layard, July 7, *Blue Book*, p. 5.]

NEGOTIATIONS WITH THE POWERS 125

regarded the greatness of Prussia as a British interest. They dreaded war from motives of sincere philanthropy, but also because they feared that it might result too favorably for us. This fact is confirmed by the testimony of the Prussian Ambassador, Bernsdorff. He frequently heard it said, in the most aristocratic and most influential English clubs, that, while they esteemed highly the genius and ability of Bismarck, as well as the valor of the Prussian army, they considered that Napoleon's qualities as a statesman and the valor of the French army should be rated much higher.[1]

The overtures of friendly diplomacy had no success at Berlin. Thile persisted in his sneering reticence, and began, by his telegrams to his agents, the cynical series of Prussian impostures. "Prussia had never interfered in the choice of a monarch in Spain; any confidential discussion of details with France had been prevented by the tone that the French ministry

[1] Bernsdorff, *Im Kampfe für Preussens Ehre*, p. 618. [As to the attitude of England in the early days of July, see La Gorce, vol. vi, p. 234; Sorel, vol. i, pp. 70, 71; Lehautcourt, vol. i, pp. 246–248 and notes; Welschinger, vol. i, pp. 224–228; also Granville to Layard, July 8, *Blue Book*, p. 9; Layard to Granville, July 7 and 10, *Ibid.*, pp. 14, 18. The following passage occurs at this point in M. Ollivier's larger work (vol. xiv, p. 160) : —]

"A hazardous argument on Gramont's part came near arresting the intervention of England. He had said to Lyons [Lyons to Granville, July 8, *Blue Book*, p. 10] that we had begun to prepare for war, although in reality we had done nothing at all; he hoped thus to arouse the apprehensions of the English Cabinet and to make its action more energetic. The contrary result was on the point of being produced. 'The Council considered whether it was worth while to continue to seek an amicable solution when the facts spoke more loudly than pacific exhortations, and whether it would not be well to wait until things had calmed down a little, so that the voices of friends could make themselves heard.' [This seems to be a paraphrase of a passage in Granville to Lyons, July 9, *Blue Book*, p. 12.] La Valette's explanations put an end to this hesitation."

had assumed in its public utterances in the Assembly."[1] Two falsehoods coupled together: the French ministry spoke in the Chamber on the 6th, and a confidential discussion of details had been declined on the 4th.

Nor had European diplomacy any better fortune at Madrid. The skill with which we had avoided offending Spanish sentiment had placed Prim in a difficult position. Neither Serrano nor Sagasta had been admitted to the secret of his plot; indeed, Sagasta had given his word in good faith to Mercier that there had been no letters exchanged between Prim and Bismarck. Prim, being unable to disclose his base performance to them, took refuge definitely in the mystification that he had outlined to Mercier. He played the part of an innocent man, surprised at the excitement he had caused, and shocked by the news he had received from Paris: he had had no evil intention against France or her Emperor; he had had no suspicion that either could take alarm at an arrangement suggested solely by the urgent necessity of putting an end to a disastrous interregnum. It had been kept a secret only to avoid premature discussion, which might have blocked the solution; the purpose of offending the Emperor had been so far from his mind that he expected to go to Vichy

[1] [Under date of July 13, Busch quotes the following as having been dictated to him by Bismarck for publication in "other papers" (than the official *Norddeutsche Zeitung*): "It cannot be denied that a Spanish government disposed to promote the cause of peace, and to abstain from conspiring with France, would be of some value to us. *But if, some fourteen days ago, the Emperor Napoleon had addressed himself confidentially to Berlin*, or indicated that the affair was attracting attention, Prussia, *instead of adopting an indifferent attitude*, would have coöperated in pacifying public opinion in Paris." Bismarck: *Some Secret Papers*, etc., vol. i, p. 35.]

NEGOTIATIONS WITH THE POWERS

and obtain his concurrence at the same time that Prince Leopold was to inform Napoleon III, directly, of his candidacy. He gave an appearance of sincerity to these outrageous but not yet unmasked falsehoods, by feigning to assist us to extricate ourselves from the embarrassment into which he had "unwittingly" led us.

"How are we to get out of it?" he said to Mercier. "I see but one way: let the Prince inform me that he has met with obstacles to the King's consent; then I myself will facilitate his withdrawal."[1]

"Take the initiative," said Mercier.

How could he have taken it? He knew that the King's consent was granted, and he can hardly have thought of obtaining its revocation. He replied that he could not do it, and asked Mercier not to disclose the fact that he had suggested that way out for us. Meanwhile there was no change in his official conduct. Sagasta and he received in a friendly way the well-meant representations of Layard and the other diplomatic agents; they repeated, as often as any one wished, that the Spanish government had never had any idea of forming an alliance with Prussia, or of taking any step hostile to France, and that it was as desirous as possible to find a way out of the difficulty into which it had fallen without suspecting it. But they held out no hope of the withdrawal of the candidacy; they did not go beyond evasions, and did not postpone for a day the meeting of the Cortes, still appointed for July 20.

Prim and his acolytes conceived once more the lofty fantasy of making sport of us, while lulling

[1] [Mercier to Gramont, July 7; see Gramont, pp. 63, 366.]

our suspicions by deceitful assurances. "Why," they said to Mercier, "lay so much stress on this date of the 20th of July? Let the days pass quietly without worrying us and without getting excited yourself. The state of public opinion has changed materially: at the outset the Hohenzollern candidacy seemed sure of unanimous acceptance; to-day it is doubtful if it obtains a majority; our army will not care about fighting for a German prince who is a grandson of Murat; do not you oppose the free expression of the national will. There is no surer way of getting rid of Prince Leopold."

Mercier, from policy, pretended to be taken in by this buncombe. "My rôle, which is not an easy one," he wrote to Gramont, "is, while doing my utmost to influence public opinion, to make it easier for individuals to change sides. Be good enough therefore, I pray you, not to impute to weakness what I may do to that end. A certain amount of careful handling will take nothing from the firmness of my attitude and my language. I am as distrustful as I ought to be, believe me." [1]

Gramont did not take seriously what seemed to be so far from serious, and neither he nor the Cabinet nor the Emperor halted in the measures they were taking.

Thus the intervention of the powers had failed at Berlin and at Madrid. On the other hand, the secret personal negotiation of the Emperor with Serrano was wholly successful. Gramont, knowing that Mercier had been let into the secret by Bartholdi, thought that he should confirm, by his instructions as

[1] From a private letter.

responsible official chief, those of the Emperor. On the 9th, the day following the Regent's return to Madrid, he urged Mercier to call upon him and to say to him that, "at the point which affairs have now reached, he alone can ensure peace to Europe by representations to the King of Prussia and the Prince of Hohenzollern. Add that France, together with the whole world, will be grateful to him, and that the government of the Emperor will never forget so magnanimous an action."[1]

Is this the language of a minister "whose deliberate purpose it was to precipitate a rupture and to make the most of the quarrel instead of putting an end to it?"

Bartholdi reached Madrid in the morning of July 10. Having communicated his instructions to Mercier, he hastened incontinently to Serrano, and laid before him, with adroit earnestness, the Emperor's wish. Serrano, since he had been unable to keep his engagements with Montpensier, had lost interest in the search for a king, and had accepted the Hohenzollern without objection. The news from Paris had roused him from his torpor. He would have been very glad to draw back, but being very careful not to step outside of his constitutional rôle, and having also given his assent, he dared not follow his impulse. He was lavish of friendly words to Mercier, assuring him of his good-will: he had not realized what he was doing. He defended Prim and repeated the cock-and-bull stories that the latter had told him; he even denied that there had been letters exchanged between Prim and the Prince. And after all this

[1] Gramont to Mercier, July 8.

130 THE FRANCO-PRUSSIAN WAR

was said, he added with premeditated candor: "To say, after that, that he is not concerned in it — no, indeed, for one tells many lies in this sort of business." [1] The confidence in him manifested by the Emperor touched him more than all the arguments of Mercier and Layard and the other diplomats, and decided him to venture what his personal inclination prompted. He promised Bartholdi to send some one to Prince Leopold; neither the ministers nor Olozaga were to be informed of a mission which he deemed himself bound to regard as of a mysterious and wholly private nature. He informed Prim alone. That hypocritical confederate of Bismarck was careful not to discourage him; he relied on Leopold's firmness and his loyalty to Bismarck and himself, and had no doubt

---

[1] [Mercier to Gramont, July 9 and 10. See the despatches in full in Benedetti, *Ma Mission en Prusse*, 434–436. The words quoted by M. Ollivier do not appear in either despatch.]

Serrano being in Paris in 1884, I requested Darimon, whom at that time I still regarded as a friend, to see him and to ask him in my name the following questions: 1. Who conceived the idea of the Hohenzollern candidacy? Marshal Serrano declared that he was absolutely ignorant. He did not learn of the candidacy until Prim's return from hunting in the mountains of Toledo; that is to say, July 1, 1870. He was unable to make any opposition to the choice because he had no other to offer; because the character of Prince Leopold had been highly praised to him; and especially because he was assured that that candidacy would give rise to no complications with France. The ex-Regent knew nothing of the steps that had been taken by M. de Rancès at Berlin in March, 1869, and had aroused the suspicion and susceptibility of the Imperial government. 2. What part did Prim play? The marshal was very reserved on this subject. He declared that Prim told him nothing of what he did. The Cortes had given Prim *carte blanche*. It was to that body alone that Prim owed an account of the machinery set to work to discover a candidate. He put forward Prince Leopold, but the Council of Ministers assembled at La Granja under the presidency of the Regent did not ask him how he had set about attaining his end. [Note of M. Ollivier, vol. xiv, p. 165.]

that the Regent's messenger would be met with an immovable refusal. Whereupon, turning upon Serrano, he would have said to him: "Inasmuch as the Prince is determined to go on to the end, the honor of the noble Spanish nation compels us to follow him." But as he preferred not to give his assent to a step of which he desired and anticipated the failure, he got the Regent to agree that he should be supposed to have known nothing about it.

On the 10th, at nine in the evening, Serrano wrote to Mercier: "He started at half after five. Silence!" The messenger whose departure was thus announced was the Regent's nephew and secretary, General Lopez Dominguez, an officer of unusual distinction. He was to go to Sigmaringen, there to lay before the head of the family the weighty reasons which necessitated the withdrawal of Prince Leopold's candidacy. He was also, in the event that it should become necessary, accredited to the King of Prussia and to Bismarck.

By this very act of accrediting his messenger to the King and Bismarck as well as to the Hohenzollerns, Serrano in his turn confirmed what we were hearing on all sides, that both had had a share in the conspiracy.[1]

This step on the Regent's part was an important one: it would become decisive only in case it were not thwarted by the will of the King of Prussia. Thus the negotiation that we had undertaken with him at Ems overshadows the other diplomatic incidents.

[1] [On this whole subject, see Appendix C. Also La Gorce, vol. vi, pp. 251-253; Sorel, vol. i, pp. 106, 107; Lehautcourt, vol. i, pp. 257-259.]

CHAPTER X

THE NEGOTIATIONS WITH THE KING OF PRUSSIA AT EMS [1]

THE idea of a negotiation at Ems once agreed upon, we did not hesitate concerning the plenipotentiary to be sent thither. Public opinion, in its frantic rage, attacked our ambassador at Madrid as well as him at Berlin. Even in the only journal that had an official character, the *Constitutionnel*, there were some sharp criticisms of Benedetti. We were advised to recall both him and Mercier: both alike were blamed for not detecting the Hohenzollern plot, and Benedetti especially for leaving us in ignorance of Prussia's ambitious views, and for not advising us of her understanding with Russia.

It was not true that Benedetti had not warned us of the ambitious views of Bismarck and the Prussian government: he had done so often, and, in particular, in his fine despatch of January, 1870, which I analyzed in its proper place,[2] and he had neglected no opportunity of reminding us that the understanding with Russia was one of the means of action held in readiness by that ambition. But, after he had informed us of it, he had been too reassuring in recent months, representing it to us as postponed and forgotten.

It was true that in 1869 he had advised his government of the Hohenzollern candidacy; but he was en-

---
[1] [On the subject of this chapter, generally, see *infra*, Appendix I.]
[2] [This despatch is given by Benedetti, p. 284.]

Comte Vincent Benedetti
1817 – 1900

THE EMS NEGOTIATION 133

titled to no great credit, as the majority of the German newspapers were full of the scheme. But it was in March, 1870, that Benedetti should have detected the plot; and not only did he fail to do it, but he allowed himself to be deceived concerning the cause of the presence of the Hohenzollern princes at Berlin, although he should have been put on his guard by the alarm of the preceding year.[1]

If we had complied with the demand of public opinion by tossing to it, as scapegoats, the two ambassadors, we should have cast off our own responsibility amid universal applause. We were not even tempted to do it. Urged onward by the course of events, having no time to investigate the conduct of Mercier and Benedetti, we resolved the doubt in their favor. We caused a cessation of the attacks in the *Constitutionnel*, we kept Mercier at his post, and we entrusted the much-abused Benedetti with the negotiation with King William at Ems. Was not this protecting and shielding him more efficaciously than by a declaration from the tribune or in the press, of which we had not at hand the necessary elements, and which would have given rise to irritating and fruitless disputes? Benedetti afterward ill requited this generosity on our part.[2]

If a person has a physical deformity, it is the first thing that one notices in him. Leo XIII had for his Master of the Chamber a certain Monsignor Macchi, who was blessed with an inordinately long nose. The Pope used to say: "*Si vede un naso, poi Macchi.*" (One sees a nose, and then Macchi.) It is the same with

---

[1] [See *supra*, pp. 18, 19.]

[2] [By the publication of his self-exculpatory volume, *Ma Mission en Prusse*, in 1871. See Appendix I.]

moral imperfections; that which first impressed one in Benedetti was an absorption in himself which amounted to a mania. "When he looks upon himself," said Gramont, "he is dazzled." Had he a part in some successful negotiation, its success was due to him alone. If the negotiation did not succeed, the blame belonged to some one else, and he had an inexhaustible stock of wiles and sophistries to denounce that other. Moreover he belonged to the school of his friend Rouher's mandarin J. M. F., and any counsel, so long as it was skilfully supported, seemed to him the best. He said to me one day with a self-satisfied little smile: "Thouvenel has asked me for a report in favor of recognizing Italy; I could just as well have made another of the contrary tenor."

The hereditary diplomats declared that he lacked something because he began his career in the consulates. However that may be, he speedily acquired what was then considered the most useful quality of the diplomat: he knew how to frame a despatch. When one had said, "He can write a despatch," that was the highest praise. Now let me tell what framing a despatch is: it is saying in ten pages what might be said in ten lines; stretching out the unimportant facts to the point of tearing them apart, so that they may reach a respectable length; drowning the important facts in a flood of monotonous rhetoric, in which they lose all color and all sharpness of outline; extending one's self in vapid, sententious platitudes with an air of profundity; and placing in a subordinate clause, beside the opinion or prognostication set forth in the principal clause, a lot of *buts* and *ifs* and *fors*, in such wise that, whatever happens, one can boast

THE EMS NEGOTIATION

of being a true prophet. Whenever, in my investigations in the Archives, I fell in with one of those endless despatches written, worse luck! not with the lasting black ink used by our old diplomats, upon which time can make no impression, but in a pale, already almost invisible ink, I heaved a little sigh; and when I had finished my reading, would say to myself, "How much this abundance of words would have gained by being reduced one half!" And if, after that, I happened on the narrative of a Talleyrand, a Fleury, or a Mercier, who could not "frame a despatch," but who set forth concisely exact facts or words, what a delight it was!

Benedetti was thoughtful, diligent, hard-working, entirely devoted to his duties, but, after the fashion of the majority of the diplomatists of that time, he failed to realize that an ambassador's first care should be to learn, when he is unacquainted with it, the language of the country where he is to reside. Bismarck had no sooner arrived at St. Petersburg than he bought a grammar and began to study Russian; he had done the like at Paris. Benedetti lived several years at Berlin without a thought that it would be useful to him to learn German, and that the best sort of intelligence is that that one picks up on the streets or overhears in a conversation between the natives of the country. He excelled, however, in supplying what he missed in that direction by a peculiar aptitude for spying and surmising and guessing; but there again he was not sufficiently on his guard against another tendency which I will call "the diplomatic failing": an artless credulity, as a result of which, suspicion was succeeded by the most unbounded confidence. For the rest, a man of distinction, with an intelligent, open countenance, agreeable manners, not too effusive, most attractive in conversation, without noisy self-assertion, of a ready wit, skilful in slipping between the crevices of events, trained in the art of exposition and argumentation, able at need to say disagreeable things without being disagreeable himself,— in fine, an excellent diplomat, to whom one could in all confidence entrust a difficult mission.[1]

Bismarck had not been disturbed by the explosion of French wrath: he had foreseen it and wished for it. Our declaration irritated his self-esteem a little, but did not make him depart from his immobility. He did not complain, demanded no explanation, but waited. Until the meeting of the Cortes on July 20, and the election of Leopold, he did not propose to depart from that attitude of expectation. The sending of Benedetti to Ems gave him his first uneasy moment. The King, being at a distance from him and in the neighborhood of his enemy, Queen Augusta, who was at Coblentz, might yield to his aversion from war: his seventy-three years made him afraid of endangering the laurels won in 1866; he had gone into the enterprise only with regret, and did not know the true inwardness of it. Would he not be too conciliatory, and would not his concessions destroy the plan so laboriously constructed? Bismarck wrote at once: "I beg your Majesty not to treat with Benedetti, and if he is persistent, to reply: 'My Minister for Foreign Affairs is at Varzin.'"[2]

---

[1] [As to the difficulties of the mission, see Sorel, vol. i, pp. 100, 101; La Gorce, vol. vi, pp. 238, 239.]

[2] According to Oncken [*Unser helden Kaiser*, pp. 123–125], Bismarck in his wrath first wrote this telegram: "Mobilize at once, declare war, and

THE EMS NEGOTIATION

In fact, the Hohenzollern affair greatly disturbed the King. He had been much vexed by the unforeseen incident which had caused it to be noised abroad too soon. He wrote to the Queen July 5: "The Spanish bomb has exploded all at once, but in an entirely different way from what I had been led to expect. We have not heard a word thereon from our cousin. At Berlin the French chargé d'affaires has already spoken to Thile about it, who naturally replied that the government had nothing whatever to do with the affair, and that such negotiations as had taken place between Prim and the Hohenzollern family had not yet been communicated to us. At Paris, too, the minister questioned Werther, who was able to reply, with a

attack before France is ready." This telegram is regarded by German critics as an unfounded conjecture. Nor should we pay any greater heed to the tales told of Bismarck's amazement and wrath at Varzin when he read Gramont's declaration [of July 6]. He was not indignant until later, when it had produced its effect adverse to him. [Note of M. Ollivier in vol. xiv, p. 173.]

[See La Gorce, vol. vi, pp. 279, 280; Lehautcourt, i, pp. 238, 239 and notes; Sorel, vol i, pp. 102, 103 and note. Lehautcourt refers to Bismarck as "Gramont's German partner." According to Sorel, it "seems clear that, at first, seeing that the success of the affair was endangered, he [Bismarck] advised his master to abandon Prince Leopold and save the honor of Prussia. (He said so in so many words to Jules Favre; see Favre, *Gouvernement de la Defense Nationale*, p. 176.) He was not for war whatever the cost, but only under circumstances favorable to his schemes. He did not abandon the hope of bringing such circumstances into being, but he awaited the opportunity. Believing that war was resolved upon by the French government and forced upon France by her social condition, he waited for the imprudence of his adversary to force the King's hand and sweep public opinion in Germany off its feet. It seemed to him wise to be moderate. . . . The position taken by M. de Bismarck was undoubtedly a very strong one. . . . It was possible to turn it, but it was necessary first of all to reconnoitre it. This is what the French government seems to have entirely neglected to do. It was unable to discover the plan of campaign that M. de Bismarck was pursuing; or if it had any suspicion of it, it paid no heed."]

perfectly clear conscience, that he knew nothing about it."[1]

On July 6, William wrote to Prince Antony that he could not understand how General Prim could have informed the French ambassador of the acceptance of the hereditary prince before the Cortes had been consulted. "I regard it as possible that the excitement aroused in France may yet be quieted, but *none the less I regret that the opinion first expressed by the Prince of Hohenzollern was not followed, namely, that they must make sure of the assent of France.* This was not done because General Prim desired it to be kept secret, and Count von Bismarck argued that every nation is free to choose its king without consulting another nation."[2]

Our declaration produced the salutary effect upon the King that we had anticipated; it wounded his susceptibility, unquestionably, but at the same time it set him face to face with the reality, and convinced him that the public agitation in France would be allayed only by the withdrawal of Prince Leopold. The scruples which had deterred him before embarking on the enterprise reawoke; his conscience, which was honest when it was not blinded by deceitful appearances took account of the equivocal action to which he had given his sanction. The observations of the Tsar and of Queen Victoria intensified those scruples and mental perturbations, and, in obedience to these various motives, he resolved to do what was in him to side-track the candidacy, of which he saw clearly enough the inevitable menace.

[1] [Oncken, *Unser helden Kaiser*, p. 184. This letter is not printed in the collection cited on the next page.]

[2] [Memoirs of the King of Roumania, French trans., vol. i, p. 590.]

THE EMS NEGOTIATION

In a letter to his wife, of the 7th, he approves our action in refusing an interpellation, and explains his point of view: he considered the candidacy as purely a Spanish matter; the honor of France was not involved; and he calculated thus the chances of the election by the Cortes: —

"The French will spend many millions to buy votes, we shall not spend a thaler; but their violent articles have exasperated public opinion, which fact will tend to make the vote more favorable to the Hohenzollern." And that prospect was far from filling him with rapture. "Be it said between ourselves, I would gladly see Leopold fail of election."[1]

With a word he could prevent that election. It was enough for him to let the Prince know that, in view of all the circumstances it would be the wiser course for him to decline; he would have been obeyed on the instant. But that decisive course was offensive to his pride: it would have lowered him in the eyes of Germany and Spain and his own family, and would have exasperated Bismarck. He tried to induce the Hohenzollern princes to extricate him from embarrassment by taking the responsibility of withdrawal. He hinted, impressed upon them the seriousness of the business, urged them to reflect carefully on the inconveniences of obstinacy, and without saying, "Withdraw," he assured them that, if they should decide to do so, it would be with great pleasure that he would bestow upon such withdrawal the sanction that he had lately accorded to their acceptance.

But for the Hohenzollern princes as well, considera-

[1] [*Briefe Kaiser Wilhelms der Erste* (1911), p. 218.]

tions of their dignity were complicated with a question of honor. By accepting the candidacy they had been guilty of a crime against the Emperor Napoleon; by withdrawing their acceptance they would become guilty in respect to Prim and Bismarck, to whom they had bound themselves. They evaded the necessity of replying to the King by pretending not to understand his hints. But the King would not allow that equivocation, and pressed them to explain themselves.

He was awaiting their reply when Benedetti arrived, on July 8 at 11 o'clock at night. He requested an audience forthwith. The King appointed it for the next day at three o'clock, sending word to him that he would keep him to dinner, and apologizing, with good grace, on the ground of his health and the expected arrival of the Queen, for his inability to receive him earlier.

Benedetti's instructions were contained in an official letter of July 7, and in a private letter of the same date at midnight. At Berlin and at Madrid we were assured that the King of Prussia had not given his assent to the candidacy. We were convinced of the contrary, although we had then no proofs. Gramont, being obliged for the nonce, by a diplomatic hypothesis, to take Thile's assertion as a starting point, said in his official letter : —

"If the head of the Hohenzollern family has heretofore been indifferent to this affair, we request that he will no longer be so, and we beg him to intervene, *if not by his command, at least by his counsel*, with the Prince, and to put an end, together with the schemes based by Marshal Prim upon that candidacy, to the profound uneasiness which it has everywhere aroused.

THE EMS NEGOTIATION 141

In King William's intervention to prevent the execution of these schemes we should see first of all the service that it would render to the cause of peace, and a pledge of the strengthening of our friendly relations with Prussia. The Emperor's government would appreciate such a friendly step, which would, there can be no doubt, be greeted at the same time with universal approbation." [1]

In the private letter, written on the same day, at midnight, Gramont is more urgent, because he has received additional information.

"We know from the admissions of the Prince himself that he has carried on the whole affair with the Prussian government, and we cannot accept the evasive reply with which M. de Thile seeks to escape from the dilemma which has been propounded to him; it is absolutely necessary that you obtain a categorical reply, followed by its natural consequences. Now this is the only reply which will satisfy us and prevent war: 'The King's government does not approve the Prince of Hohenzollern's acceptance, and orders him to abandon his decision made without the King's permission.' It will remain for you then to let me know whether the Prince, in obedience to that injunction, abandons his candidacy publicly and officially. We are very much hurried, because we must make the first move in case of an unsatisfactory reply, and must begin on Saturday the movements of troops with a view to taking the field in a fortnight. I insist especially on the importance of allowing no time to be wasted in evasive replies; we must know whether we are to have peace, or whether a plea in abatement will force us to declare

[1] [Benedetti, pp. 316–318; Gramont, pp. 58–60.]

war. If you obtain the King's promise to revoke the Prince's acceptance, it will be a tremendous triumph and a great service. The King, for his part, will have assured the peace of Europe; otherwise, it is war." [1]

In common parlance these two letters may be summarized thus: "You will inform the King that we will not tolerate the enthronement in Spain of the Prussian Prince Leopold of Hohenzollern, and as that Prussian Prince, being a member of his family and subject to his authority, cannot accept a crown without his authorization, we ask him not to grant such authorization, if it has not already been obtained, and to withdraw it if it has been." [2]

Gramont communicated his instructions to Lyons, who was kept informed of our proceedings almost hour by hour. As he seemed to fear that the candidacy was only the beginning of the trouble, Gramont told

[1] [Benedetti, pp. 319, 320; Gramont, pp. 61, 62. The concluding paragraphs of the letter are worth quoting: "As for the Prince, his reign in Spain will not last a month; but the war caused by this intrigue of M. de Bismarck — how long will it last, and what will be its consequences?

"So, no beating about the bush, no dawdling. No mission was ever more important. May you be successful; that is my most earnest wish."]

[2] It is incomprehensible that any one could claim that there is any difference between the instruction sent and the way in which Benedetti interpreted it. He understood that he was to obtain first the withdrawal of the candidacy, then the King's acquiescence therein; whereas Gramont wished the withdrawal to be the result of the King's command or advice. The absurdity of this antithesis does not need to be demonstrated. With whom was Benedetti to negotiate, and from whom could he obtain the withdrawal if not the King? A withdrawal without the King's participation might be obtained by others than him, through negotiations at Madrid or at Sigmaringen, and thereupon would arise the question of the King's acquiescence. But it was impossible to admit the hypothesis of a withdrawal obtained by Benedetti from anybody except the King, because the King was the only person with whom he was negotiating. [Note of M. Ollivier in vol. xiv, p. 179. See Benedetti, p. 322.]

him once more just what we were resolved to obtain, what we were prepared to consider sufficient.

Lyons faithfully sent these declarations to Granville: "M. de Gramont told me that I might report to your Lordship that if the Prince of Hohenzollern should now, on the advice of the King of Prussia, withdraw his acceptance of the Crown, the whole affair would be at an end."[1]

In the morning of the 9th, at Ems, Werther went to Benedetti for information, so that the King, being advised of what Benedetti had come to ask, should not be taken by surprise. Our Ambassador told him our sentiments, our demands, our wish for an immediate solution. Werther did not conceal the fact that "His Majesty, having been consulted by the Prince of Hohenzollern, had deemed it not to be within his power to place obstacles in the way of his desire to accept the crown of Spain, and that it was now very difficult, if not impossible, to request him to abandon it."[2]

[1] [Lyons to Granville, July 10, *Blue Book*, p. 17. This seems to be the first despatch of Lord Lyons in which Benedetti's presence at Ems is mentioned, and the only reference to it is this: "The King of Prussia had told M. Benedetti last evening that he had in fact consented to the Prince of Hohenzollern's accepting the crown of Spain; and that, having given his consent, it would be difficult for him now to withdraw it. His Majesty had added, however, that he would confer with the Prince, and would give a definitive answer to France when he had done so." The paragraph quoted in the text, in which Gramont is reported as practically reiterating the statement previously made by him to Lyons (see *supra*, p. 108), assumed great importance in its effect upon the attitude of England when, the Prince having actually withdrawn, the situation was rendered hopeless by the demand of guaranties.]

[2] [Benedetti to Gramont, July 9; Benedetti, p. 325.] He did not say as Sybel falsely asserts, that *the King was unable to place obstacles in his way,* but that he *had deemed it not to be within his power;* which implied that he

Benedetti thereupon went to the King and set forth, with much tact and with entire respect, in very firm and well-measured words, the object of his mission; he appealed to William's wisdom and his heart, and implored him to advise Prince Leopold to reconsider his acceptance. He described to him the excitement that the candidacy had caused in France, — an excitement shared by other countries, notably England, where the press was unanimous in deploring a combination that was equally disastrous to the repose of Spain and to the maintenance of friendly relations among the great powers. He assured him that the Emperor's government had no other desire than to put an end to that excitement. He conjured the King to give to Europe a testimony of the generosity

might have done it. [Note of M. Ollivier in vol. xiv, p. 180. But Von Sybel's English translator (vol. vii, p. 353) makes Werther say that the King "*felt* he had no right to forbid," etc.

After finishing his private letter of July 7 to Benedetti, Gramont received the telegram from Mercier quoted on page 127, covering Prim's suggestion that the Prince himself should inform him [Prim] that "he had met with obstacles to the King's consent." "I confess," says Gramont, "that on July 8, at one in the morning, I had the idea of forcing the intervention of the Prince of Hohenzollern, and in my desire to avert a conflict whose gravity I foresaw, I telegraphed these words to Comte Benedetti, at the same time repeating to him the despatch from Madrid: 'Say this to the King, and at need go to the Prince himself and say it to him.' I was wrong. The Hohenzollern candidacy was not put forward without the concurrence of the King of Prussia; it was a Prussian candidacy, and it was as such that France rejected it. Being put forward by the King, it was to the King alone that M. Benedetti must address himself. I had allowed myself to be carried away by a very natural desire to leave nothing undone that might facilitate a peaceful solution. But my despatch had no sooner started on its way than I realized its inopportuneness, and after taking the Emperor's orders, I sent the following telegram the next day: 'You must not see the Prince of Hohenzollern. The Emperor wishes no overtures made to him.'" Gramont, pp. 66, 67.]

THE EMS NEGOTIATION 145

of his sentiments: the Emperor's government would see therein a guaranty of the strengthening of its friendly relations with his Majesty's government, and would congratulate itself mightily on a decision which would be welcomed everywhere with no less gratitude than satisfaction.

The King set forth, with calm and courteous decision, the well-considered thesis which he intended to oppose to our demands and from which he never departed. The Prussian government was not a party to the negotiation; appropriating Thile's language, he did not conceive that the Berlin Cabinet could be called to account concerning a matter of which it knew nothing, and for which it was no more responsible than any other cabinet in Europe. He admitted, however, that his prime minister had been kept posted on the various phases of the question. His personal intervention thus avowed, he claimed to have intervened only as the head of the family, not as sovereign; and even as head of the family, his part had been in some sense passive: he had taken no part in the negotiation, he had refused to receive an envoy of the Spanish Cabinet bearing a letter from Prim; he had not encouraged Prince Leopold to accept the Spanish overtures, but had contented himself with not forbidding him to do so, when the Prince, having decided to accept, had solicited his consent on his arrival at Ems. He deemed it incompatible with his royal dignity to demand from the Prince a renunciation of the crown, after he had refrained from forbidding him to accept it. If the Prince should spontaneously withdraw his candidacy, he would abstain from advising him against that step: he proposed to leave him the most entire freedom of action, after no less than before his acceptance. He had placed himself in communication with Prince Antony, who was then at Sigmaringen, and had questioned him as to the effect of the agitation in France upon his mind and his son's; he would make his own course conform to the reply. He deemed it useless to continue the interview; he hoped to be informed soon, but some time must necessarily elapse, for he could not use the telegraph, having no cipher at Ems for that means of correspondence.

Then he proceeded to give his views concerning our action. He approved the first part of our declaration, but had felt keenly the second part. Starting from the premise that Prussia had no part in Leopold's candidacy, he saw an unfounded interpretation, almost an insult, in our words concerning the views of "a third power." Our emotion seemed to him unjustified; we exaggerated the effect of the seating of a prince of his family on the throne of Spain, which, for his part, he had never desired. The present Spanish government was supreme, recognized by all the powers, and he could not conceive how we could place it under guardianship and oppose the choice of a sovereign freely elected by the representatives of the nation; there was nothing to do but await the meeting of the Cortes. "It is at Madrid, and not to me, that you should apply," he said. "You have only to exert your influence to induce the government of the Regent to abandon its project. The honor of France has not been and cannot be assailed by the decision of the Prince of Hohenzollern; it was preceded by negotiations which the Cabinet of Madrid opened of its own will, and in which

THE EMS NEGOTIATION 147

no other government took part; it cannot therefore be a subject either of dissent or of conflict, and war cannot result from an incident in which no one of the powers has intervened."[1]

In fine, the King refused to give either orders or advice to the Hohenzollerns; he had questioned them as to their intentions, and he awaited their reply. He wrote to his wife of the audience: "Yesterday, after you left, Benedetti was with me; he was calm and unexcited except in speaking of the newspapers, 'which are demanding his head and a court to try him.'"[2]

The account of this audience, which reached us July 10, lessened neither our perplexities nor our apprehensions. The King had made therein significant admissions which proved his participation, and that very fact gave more importance to his refusal to compel the disappearance, by direct command, or by advice (which amounted to the same thing), of the scheme which he had known of and approved. He took up, and developed more fully, the inadmissible argument of Thile that the Prussian government knew nothing, although the King and Bismarck knew all about it. Was the Prussian government Thile? Was it not Bismarck and the King? Imagine Louis XIII saying to a foreign government: "I knew that Cardinal Richelieu

---

[1] [See Benedetti's report, of July 9, of which M. Ollivier gives a paraphrase of only a portion, in *Ma Mission en Prusse*, pp. 328–338.]

The Prussian documents give to the King's answers a stiffness which does not appear in Benedetti's report. The *Official Journal* of July 9 says: "The Ambassador of France to the [North German] Confederation, having travelled to Ems, was received by the King and requested His Majesty to forbid the Prince of Hohenzollern to accept the Spanish crown; the King refused." [Note of M. Ollivier in vol. xiv, p. 183.]

[2] [*Briefe des Kaiser Wilhelms der Erste*, pp. 218, 219.]

was fully advised, but still the affair was not known to my government!"

"Was it not rather too subtle an idea," said Scherr, "which ascribed to mankind in general, and to the French in particular, the credulity to put faith in the 'unofficial knowledge' that we had of the candidacy, and in the 'official non-knowledge' in which we still remained with respect thereto?"[1]

It was precisely this fashion of juggling with words which was later to contribute to the currency, in France and elsewhere, of the opinion that the Hohenzollern candidacy was "from *a* to *z* a ruse deliberately devised by the Prussian government." This ruse was peculiarly transparent in Prussia, where King and State are all one.[2]

King and State, they tell us, are in truth the same thing when the King is acting as king. But there is in the King a head of a family who is distinct from the King, and when it is the head of the family who acts, the State is not identified with him. Scherr, whose book on the war is from end to end simply a frantic diatribe against France and the Empire, agrees that "it must be said, out of regard for the truth, that it is impossible to bear the French a grudge because the distinction between King William as head of the house of Hohenzollern and King William as King of Prus-

[1] Johannes Scherr, *1870–1871*, p. 114.
[2] "And it was Bismarck himself who told us so. 'You deny the King,' he said after the Convention of Gastein [1865], 'possession of the Prussian half of the Duchy of Lauenburg, on the theory that it belongs to the State, not to the King. The flaw in this theory is the separating the King from the State — a separation that is impossible in Prussia from the standpoint of law and facts and policy alike.' Speech of Feb. 30, 1866." *L'Empire Libéral*, vol. xiv, p. 185.

sia was too fine — as fine as a hair — for them to heed."[1]

The German writer is mistaken: it did not seem to us too fine, and we understood the distinction, but we considered it amusing. It reminded us of our own Molière's Maître Jacques, now cook, now coachman, according to the costume he wore, and saying to Harpagon: "Is it to your coachman, Monsieur, or to your cook that you intend to speak? for I am both." "To both," Harpagon replies.[2] In like manner we said to the royal Maître Jacques, now head of the family, now king, "It is to both that we intend to speak."

In fact, the King was head of the family only because he was King of Prussia. But even if he were considered solely as head of the family, that did not make him immune from our action. A head of a family cannot give to a prince, a subordinate member thereof, a valid authorization to accept a crown, if he himself is not authorized to that effect by the great powers. And if such authorization has not been secured, his strict duty, as a member of the great European family, is to forbid the prince to take part in an intrigue which has become a cause of disturbance. That is what we asked the King of Prussia to do.

Ottokar Lorenz does not deny, as Sybel had mistakenly done, that the King had the power to forbid. "But," he says, "it was impossible that such a prohibition should be uttered at the demand of a foreign power."[3] And why, pray? Would it have been the first time that such a thing had happened? Was it

---

[1] Scherr, pp. 110, 111.
[2] [In the comedy of *L'Avare*.]
[3] Lorenz, p. 254.

not at the public demand of England that Louis-Philippe refused the Belgians his son de Nemours for their King, and the Spaniards his son d'Aumale for their Queen's husband?[1] Was it not at the demand of Russia and France that the Queen of England declined the offer of the crown of Greece for her son Alfred? Wherein does one offend or humiliate a sovereign by asking him to submit to a general rule of international law to which everybody before him has submitted, and which he himself helped to establish?

What were we to think of the King's communication to the Hohenzollern princes. Was it sincere, or was it a new trick? We were sorely puzzled to decide, on reading Benedetti's interpretations; they perplexed us by their convolutions. "Must we conclude from the King's language to me that he has determined to comply with our wishes, leaving it for the Prince of Hohenzollern to take the initiative instead of advising him to do so, in order to avoid making personally a concession which might be severely criticised in Germany? Or does he simply desire to gain time in order to make his military arrangements in advance of us, and at the same time allow the meeting of the Cortes to draw near, in order to argue that it is proper to await the vote of that body? Considering only his attitude

[1] [Busch notes under date of July 8: "Another communication to Bucher from Varzin runs: 'The precedents furnished by Louis Philippe's refusal of the Belgian throne on behalf of the Duc de Nemours, in 1831, on the ground that it would create uneasiness, and by the protest which England entered against the marriage of the Duc de Montpensier to the sister of Queen Isabella, are neither of them very applicable, as the Prince of Hohenzollern is not a son of King William, but only a remote connection, and Spain does not border on Prussia." *Bismarck: Some Pages*, etc., vol. i, p. 28. — For an elaboration of this theme, see the passages from *L'Empire Libéral*, given in Appendix F.]

THE EMS NEGOTIATION

and what I have gathered in his entourage, I should perhaps incline to think the first of these two hypotheses the more probable, *if it were not that we are justified in being incredulous, or, at least, suspicious.*" [1] In a private letter of the same date he added: "I do not know what we ought to expect from his Majesty's better judgment, and I cannot conceal from you my impression that we may perhaps have to reckon more with his shrewdness and his habit of resorting to expedients."

It was our impression that the King was playing with us. Feeling that we were surrounded by liars, fearing every moment to be surprised by some fresh perfidy, beset by that date of July 20, which was ever before our eyes like a scarecrow, we could not believe in the truth of any word uttered by the authors of the plot that we were trying to foil. And this step on the part of the King, who was sincere and whose intentions were certainly pacific, seemed to us one more incident in the comedy of duplicity in which we were enveloped: the reply of the princes whom he had consulted would be that they would persist in their candidacy; whence it resulted that the King had written to them only to shelter his own responsibility behind theirs. We considered that the negotiation was virtually closed, and that all hope of peace had vanished. I find this feeling expressed in a short note that I wrote to Gramont, after reading Benedetti's despatch which he had sent to me: —

MY DEAR FRIEND, — I am summoning all our colleagues to meet at your office at two o'clock. Bene-

[1] [This is quoted from a telegram sent by Benedetti before his detailed report of his first interview with the King, and the passage following from a private letter sent after the report — all on the same day: July 9. Benedetti, pp. 327, 328, 339.]

detti's despatch is very clear: it confirms all my presentiments, and from this moment war seems to me to be forced upon us: it only remains for us to make up our minds to it fearlessly and with energy."

Our colleagues viewed the situation as we did, and, pending the drafting of resolutions to be adopted the next day by the Council, under the presidency of the Emperor, we requested Gramont to telegraph and write to Benedetti that we were more and more submerged by public opinion, that we were counting the hours, and that he must absolutely insist upon a reply from the King — that we must have it on the following day: the day after that would be too late.[1]

The Emperor, on his side, agreed with Le Bœuf upon a most serious step. He sent Staff-Colonel Gresley to Algiers with orders to MacMahon to embark at the earliest possible moment the troops from Africa which were to serve on the continent, and to inform him that he was summoned home to take command of one army; the most distant troops must be at Algiers on July 18. Furthermore, the generals of artillery and of engineers were sent on a confidential tour of inspection — that is to say, in citizens' clothes — to the forts in the Northeast, so that we might be prepared to supply such deficiencies as should be pointed out; all the generals of brigade were ordered to ascertain whether the recruiting offices were ready to despatch orders of recall forthwith; and Intendant-General Blondeau, Director of Administration of the War Department, was au-

[1] [For the despatches in which Gramont carried out the request of his colleagues, see Benedetti, pp. 342, 343; also *infra*, Appendix I.]

THE EMS NEGOTIATION

thorized to exceed by a million francs the credit assigned for the administrative service.

On July 10, it was the general opinion that, by the suspicious whimpering of the King of Prussia, we were forced to choose between a degrading submission and war. This conviction inspired Thiers to take a signally honorable course. He was present at the sessions of the Chamber, closely attentive, but silent, recommending prudence but without rejecting the possibility of war, for he was too well aware of our interests in Spain to think that we could quietly allow a Prussian prince to be seated on that throne. When the possibility of that result approached, he conceived the patriotic idea of offering the Emperor his assistance. He might well have confided that excellent purpose to me, and I would instantly have escorted him to Saint-Cloud. But that would have seemed to him too compromising; he adopted a roundabout course. He was accustomed to go every Sunday to Madame Roger's on Rue de Morny; she was the sister-in-law of Philippe de Massa, a young officer of brilliant intellect and charmingly distinguished manners and character, an equerry to the Emperor, in high favor at the Tuileries, and on intimate terms with the Duc and Duchesse de Mouchy. On Sunday, July 10, he sent Massa to the duchess to request her to inform the Empress that, if we did not succeed in averting war, the Emperor could rely on his patriotism; that he would support from the tribune the request for military appropriations, so that they might be voted unanimously, as was most desirable; and that he would associate himself with all the efforts of the government. This was not a formal request to be received, but a very plain hint that he would be very glad to be summoned. Such a step was most natural. It was the Emperor who had made the first advances, when he sent to Thiers by Le Bœuf a request to defend the contingent; and Thiers very nobly offered to supplement the service that had been asked of him by an even greater service which was not asked.

Massa went to the Duchesse de Mouchy's on Boulevard de Courcelles. She thought that such a message should be delivered without loss of time, and she started at once for Saint-Cloud. Instead of addressing herself to the Empress, she went to the Emperor, who was walking in the park, gloomy and absorbed. She repeated what she had heard; and, as the Emperor received the communication without warmth, even coldly, she insisted, dwelling upon the strength that such concurrence would give.

"Doubtless," replied Napoleon III, "M. Thiers is very familiar with military questions. But he's a demolisher; he has pulled down all who have trusted him. Besides, we are not at that point yet, and this is not the time to make changes in the government. Send word that the Emperor relies on the patriotism of the author of *Le Consulat et l'Empire*, on the opposition benches no less than in the ministry."[1]

The duchess transmitted these words to Massa, who called upon her at five o'clock. It was not a generous response. It was not the time to characterize Thiers's general conduct: the only one of his acts that there was occasion to recall was his speech of June 30, in which he had so admirably defended the army against his own friends, and had done justice to the Emperor's new policy — a speech for which he was entitled to

[1] [As to the time at which this incident occurred, see *supra*, p. 77, n. 2.]

THE EMS NEGOTIATION

gratitude which had not yet been made manifest to him.[1] A well-turned compliment was not the reception due to that expression of good-will.

"Thank M. Thiers," the Emperor should have replied, "thank him, and say to him that I should be delighted to talk with him on such a day, at such an hour."

The failure to summon Thiers at that moment is as incomprehensible as the failure to offer the portfolio of Public Instruction to Victor Hugo at an earlier date. Unconquerable personal antipathy alone can explain this error on the part of a sovereign usually so careful to hurt the feelings of no one. I would have saved him from it, if he had consulted me. Unluckily his uncle's fatal maxim was deeply graven on his mind: "Never give your full confidence to any one." He did, however, remember this embassy of the Duchesse de Mouchy, when on setting out for the army, he said to Le Bœuf: "Thiers might be your successor." Thiers remembered it too, but to different purpose.

On the 11th we arrived at the Council with the purpose of taking warlike measures. Gramont read two telegrams received that morning which modified our point of view. In one, Benedetti said that the King, meeting him the evening before, as he returned from driving, had accosted him and told him that there was no reply from the Prince, and, at his request, had granted him a second audience. In the second tele-

[1] [The debate in the Corps Legislatif on June 30, 1870, was on the proposition of the government to reduce the regular "contingent" of the army from 100,000 to 90,000 men. Thiers opposed a further reduction, advocated by various deputies, and supported the ministerial measure. See Delord, vol. vi, pp. 139 ff.; Lehautcourt, vol. i, pp. 175-179; Welschinger, vol. i, p. 43; Ollivier, vol. xiii, pp. 602 ff.]

gram he said: "You will allow me to add that, in my opinion, war would become inevitable if we should openly begin military preparations." [1]

Inasmuch as, while facing firmly the possibility of war, we by no means wished to make it inevitable, we decided to postpone all compromising measures: we were ignorant of that already taken by the Emperor in concert with Le Bœuf, which might have had grave results if the negotiations had not come to an end before it was carried out. We simply authorized the creation of the fourth battalions, and the recall of the volunteers. Admiral Rigault, who generally had nothing to say at our deliberations, thereupon asked for authority to recall six thousand seamen. The Council refused, fearing to precipitate a crisis. Whereupon the admiral, taking up his portfolio, said: "You can

[1] [M. Ollivier reverses the order of these telegrams, both sent on the evening of the 10th, which are given by Gramont, pp. 380, 381, and by Benedetti, pp. 343, 344. In the second, the Ambassador refers to the attacks made upon him by the *Constitutionnel* and requests Gramont to inform the Chamber of his despatches relating to the Hohenzollern candidacy in 1869. — It is important to note that on the 10th Gramont had received several despatches from Mercier at Madrid indicating, as Gramont himself says, that a definitive revulsion of feeling had taken place in the Spanish government. The first despatch was as follows: "The Regent has arrived. I have had a very satisfactory conversation with him. He has found the ministers inclined to prudence, and he desires to withdraw from the affair in a dignified manner. He thinks, as does Marshal Prim, that the best way, since Prussia claims to have had no part in the enterprise, would be for the King of Prussia to refuse his consent. He admits that the public opinion is no longer the same as at first."

This was dated at Madrid at 10.20 A.M. on the 9th. On the same day, at 11.55 P.M., Mercier telegraphed: "Have seen the Regent again. He is disposed to do his utmost, but he cannot act independently of Marshal Prim. He had a long interview with him this morning, and he is able to assure me that he (Prim) is more concerned than any one and very desirous to find a way out. He did not realize the full scope of what he did; nor did the Regent either. That is what comes of meddling with what one does not

take it, or leave it where it is." And before that ultimatum, we, with very ill grace, reconsidered our refusal.[1]

understand. He will see him to-morrow morning, and if Prim consents, he asks nothing better than to send a confidential messenger to the Prince to induce him to withdraw. He dwelt strongly on Marshal Prim's regret and his good-will. He told me also that the certainty of having a majority in the Cortes is diminishing from day to day." Again, on the 10th, at 2.30 P.M., Mercier informs Gramont of the determination to send a messenger to the Prince, "who will be authorized also to see the King and Bismarck." As we saw at the end of the last chapter, the messenger was actually sent on the 10th.

Gramont sent at least one of these despatches to Benedetti with his private letter of that date; "That from Madrid," he wrote, "will serve to set the King's conscience at rest if he deems himself bound by the Spanish overtures, to which he yielded with so little consideration for us." Benedetti, pp. 346, 434–436; Gramont, p. 72. In reporting his second audience with the King on the 11th, Benedetti says: "I do not use the information that came to you from Madrid. You know already that the King claims that we have no ground for any step except to request the Spanish government to withdraw voluntarily from the plan it has conceived, and His Majesty would not have failed to make that information a pretext for insisting upon that view." Benedetti, p. 350. As to this change of front on the part of Prim, see Darimon, *Histoire d'un Jour*, pp. 18 ff., cited by Lehautcourt, vol. vi, p. 258; also Sorel, vol. i, p. 107; and the despatches of July 10 and 11 from Layard at Madrid to Lord Granville, *Blue Book*, pp. 18 and 24; and of July 9 and 12 from Paget at Florence to Granville, *Ibid.*, pp. 29 and 30.]

[1] [In Benedetti's first despatch of the 10th, after his first audience of the King, he says: "M. de Werther leads me to hope that the King may summon me again to-morrow, to resume our interview. His Majesty has received despatches to-day from Prince Antony of Hohenzollern; Prince Leopold not being with his father, the information that has reached His Majesty thus far is still incomplete or insufficient. You will allow me to add," etc. (see p. 156).

Commenting thereon, Gramont says: "It was evident that we must, at any cost, await the result of the second interview, which was to take place during the day. . . . On the other hand, the necessity of refraining from open military preparations placed us in a position so much the more disadvantageous in that when nothing could be done *openly*, nothing could be done at all, because our institutions and our administrative regulations did not lend themselves, as those of Prussia did, to secret preparations for mobili-

The audience accorded to Benedetti by the King on July 11 was again of a dilatory character. The King had received a letter from Prince Antony the night before, which was not satisfactory to him. "My cousin," he wrote the Queen, "is much impressed by the turn things are taking at Paris, but he thinks that he cannot draw back, and that I am the one who ought to break off the affair. I have replied that I could do nothing about it, but that I would approve a rupture on his part (with joy)."[1] He found the cousins very slow of comprehension, and he sent a second messenger to Sigmaringen, Colonel Strantz, bearing a letter in which he said: "It is plain that France wants war, but in case Prince Antony should have decided upon the abandonment of the Spanish candidacy by the hereditary prince, the King, as head of the family, would be in accord with him, as when he intimated his assent to his acceptance several weeks since."[2] And he wrote again to the Queen: "God grant that the Hohenzollerns have an understanding mind!"[3]

Disturbed by our insistence, as we ourselves were by his postponements, he had telegraphed to Roon, who had returned to Berlin: "The news from Paris, which has been communicated to your Excellency by the Foreign

zation. So that this recommendation of our ambassador was the subject of a long discussion in the council held that morning; but political considerations carried the day, the government did not propose to endanger the chances of peace on any account, and decided to wait." Gramont, pp. 78, 79. See Sorel, vol. i, pp. 111, 112.]

[1] [*Briefe des Kaiser Wilhelms der Erste*, p 220.]

[2] [See Memoirs of the King of Roumania (French trans.), vol. i, p. 592. Welschinger apparently confuses the King's messenger to Sigmaringen with the Roumanian agent at Paris (*supra*, pp. 112 ff.) and refers to him several times as "Colonel de Stratt "; Welschinger, vol. i, pp. 68, 72, etc.]

[3] [*Briefe*, etc., p. 221.]

Office, requires that you prepare the necessary measures for the safety of the Rhenish provinces, and of Mayence and Saarbrück."

Roon had replied, after consulting such ministers and generals as were at hand, that no special measures were immediately necessary; that Saarbrück could be put in a state of defence in twenty-four hours, and Mayence in forty-eight. If war seemed unavoidable, he would advise mobilization of the army at a stroke.

Thus the second audience, at noon of the 11th, did not improve the state of affairs; rather, it made it worse. The King, being unable to tell the story of his thus far ineffectual *pourparlers* with his cousins at Sigmaringen, invented a fable: "Prince Leopold, expecting that, in accordance with Prim's programme, the Cortes would not be called together for three months, and that the project would not be made public till then, had thought that he might go away without causing inconvenience.[1] But he must have joined his father by now, and a definitive reply from him may be expected to-night or to-morrow."

It is to be observed here that what the King was awaiting was not Prince Antony's decision in his son's name, but that of the son himself. It was the son who had solicited his consent, and it was he, not his father, who was to withdraw if there were occasion.

On Benedetti's remarking that at Paris they would not believe in the hereditary prince's absence, the King

[1] The despatches sent by Salazar after the King's consent, and reproduced by Major Versen, give the lie to this assertion and prove clearly that it was in July that the affair was to come off, and that this journey of the Prince was an invention. [Note of M. Ollivier, vol. xiv, p. 196. Welschinger (vol. i, p. 66) avers that Bismarck devised Leopold's journey in order to get him out of reach of suggestions contrary to his (Bismarck's) plans.]

replied: "If you tell the whole truth, as I tell it to you, they ought to believe you; and if, notwithstanding, they do not, then it must be that they have a reason for it, and I think that I know that reason from Gramont's declarations: it is that he wants war, and the armaments going on in France are well known to me. I ought not to conceal from you that I myself am taking precautions against being surprised." He realized at once the imprudence of such an admission, and tried to take it back, or at least to lessen its force. He still had confidence, he said, in the preservation of peace: it would not be disturbed if the people in Paris would wait until he was in a position to contribute to it, and give him the necessary time. Still amiable, he invited Benedetti to dinner again for the morrow.

Benedetti informed the King of the impatience of the Senate and Corps Législatif, of the necessity on the part of the Emperor's government of paying due heed thereto, and of the peril of such a state of affairs — a peril increased by every day's delay. And he combated the arguments again advanced by the King on the distinction between the sovereign and the head of the family. It was all in vain. The King remained immovable in his formula: "I will neither command nor advise my kinsmen, whom I authorized to accept, to reconsider their decision; but if they do spontaneously, and of their own motion, reconsider it, I will approve their withdrawal as I approved their acceptance." And he asked Benedetti to telegraph in his name, instantly, that he expected to receive "this evening or to-morrow" a communication from Prince Leopold.[1]

[1] [Benedetti's report of his second interview, here summarized by M. Ollivier, is given in *Ma Mission en Prusse*, pp. 349–357; and by Gramont, pp. 381–388.]

THE EMS NEGOTIATION 161

In the afternoon of that same day, the 11th, we were ourselves engaged with the intractable opposition in the Chamber. Although we had no announcement to make, we thought that we ought not to refuse to say a few words in response to the public demand. Gramont went to the tribune and said: "The government appeals to the patriotism and political good sense of the Chamber and asks it to await the reply of the King, on which the government's decision depends." [1]

For the second audience as for the earlier one, the Prussian documents give the King's replies without any of Benedetti's conciliatory expressions. This is the way the *Official Journal* describes this second audience: "July 11 Count Benedetti continues to urge upon the King that His Majesty compel the Prince of Hohenzollern to withdraw his candidacy for the throne; the King rejects this demand." [Note of M. Ollivier, in vol. xiv, p. 197.]

[1] [The whole of Gramont's speech as reported by himself (p. 81), and by M. Ollivier (vol. xiv, p. 198) was as follows: "The government appreciates the impatience of the Chamber and of the country, and shares their anxiety; but it is impossible for it to bring to their knowledge a definite result. It awaits the reply on which all its decisions depend. *All the cabinets to which we have appealed seem to admit the legitimacy of our grievance.* I hope to be very shortly in a position to enlighten the Chamber, but to-day I appeal to its patriotism," etc.

The passage italicized was not allowed to pass unchallenged. "It was strictly true," says Gramont, "and our communications had met everywhere a sympathetic reception, when we had set forth through our representatives the considerations which rendered the withdrawal of the candidacy desirable" (p. 83). On the 12th Lord Lyons sent to Earl Granville an extract from the report in the *Journal Officiel* of the debate of the 11th (*Blue Book*, p. 19); whereupon the English Foreign Minister wrote, on the 13th, after quoting the above passage: "While making every allowance for the generality of statements made in debate, I nevertheless think it right to observe, though without wishing to raise any formal question with his Excellency, that the Duc de Gramont's statement, in the terms in which it is reported, is not applicable to Her Majesty's Government. No such general admission has been made by me in writing to your Excellency or in conversing with M. de Lavalette; and I have no doubt that a reference to M. de Lavalette's reports to his Government will bear me out in what I say.

"I have expressed regret at an occurrence which had, at all events, given

THE FRANCO-PRUSSIAN WAR

Notwithstanding this request, Emmanuel Arago, drowning all the murmurs with his ear-splitting voice, asked whether "the questions addressed to Prussia have reference only to the special episode, to the offer made by Marshal Prim to a Prussian prince; if so," he said, "it seems to me that we should hope for a satisfactory reply, an assurance of peace. But if the questions are complex, and of a nature to arouse discussion upon other subjects than the Hohenzollern incident, then we should be compelled, unhappily, to look upon them as affording other pretexts for a declaration of war."

Our declaration of July 6, relating solely to that particular incident, *was not therefore a declaration of war*, as the same orator had at first vociferously asserted.[1]

Gramont rose with the purpose of stating that we had

rise to great excitement in the Imperial Government and French nation; but I have carefully abstained from admitting that the cause was sufficient to warrant the intentions which had been announced; while I have at the same time deprecated precipitate action, and recommended that no means should be left untried by which any interruption of the general peace could be averted." (*Blue Book*, p. 22.)

"It was not without some surprise," says Gramont (p. 84), "that I learned a few days later from the English Ambassador that Lord Granville denied the accuracy of my words. . . . This tardy disclaimer, which all our information tended to disprove, naturally produced a painful effect, for it was the first indication of the extreme reserve which the government was destined to encounter thenceforth in the assistance rendered by Great Britain. The real cause of this performance was not then known. We should have divined it without difficulty if we had had before us the report of the conversation which took place the same day at Berlin between Lord A. Loftus and Count Bismarck, in which the latter expressed a wish that the English government 'should take some opportunity of bearing public testimony to the calm and wise moderation of the King of Prussia, his Government, and of the public press.'" Complete report of this conversation in Loftus to Granville, July 13, *Blue Book*, pp. 32, 33, reproduced in Appendix L. See Welschinger, vol. i, p. 69.]

[1] [See *supra*, p. 95.]

raised no question unconnected with the Spanish candidacy, and that we should raise no other. A veritable tempest on the benches of the Right prevented him from uttering a word, and he was unwillingly doomed, by a vote of closure, to a silence in which the bad faith of our opponents triumphed. "People will draw such inferences from the minister's silence as it naturally suggests," they said.[1]

Lyons, who was present at the session, drew the only inference from the incident that could honestly be drawn from it. "It is quite true that the nation is exceedingly impatient, and, as time goes on, the war party becomes more exacting. It has, in fact, already raised a cry that the settlement of the Hohenzollern question will not be sufficient, and that France must demand satisfaction on the subject of the Treaty of Prague."[2]

My interpretation did not differ from that of the English ambassador. On leaving the Chamber I

[1] ["A word would have sufficed to banish the anxieties of which M. Arago made himself the mouthpiece," says Gramont (p. 82). "'We have raised no question,' the minister would have said, 'foreign to the Spanish candidacy and shall raise none; we seek, we desire, like yourselves, a solution which will ensure the peace of Europe.' But those words from the minister would have instantly, and in a sense regularly, according to the customs of the Chamber, reopened the field of discussion which the President had had so much difficulty in closing. So that [the uproar] had its advantages; but, on the other hand, it left without reply the serious insinuations of the radical opposition, which at once gave form to them in this final shaft: 'People will draw such inferences,'" etc. See Sorel, vol. i, pp. 113, 114; Lehautcourt, pp. 262, 263.]

[The following sentence occurs at this point in *L'Empire Libéral* (vol. xiv, p. 200):] "So that observers who were unfamiliar with the actual state of affairs could write as Waldersee, the Prussian military attaché, did, imputing to the government manœuvres which were really the ruses of its opponents: 'The situation is as serious as possible. I am thoroughly convinced that the French are bent on war whether Hohenzollern withdraws or not.'"

[2] [Lyons to Granville, July 12, *Blue Book*, p. 19.]

wrote to the Emperor at Saint-Cloud (July 11, 6 P.M.): —

"SIRE, — There is taking place at this moment in the Corps Législatif a movement of which it is important that I advise your Majesty. When, after Gramont's declaration, which was very well received, Emmanuel Arago asked the ministry: 'Have you raised any other questions than that of the Prince of Hohenzollern?' Gramont having risen to reply, the Right, with extraordinary vehemence, demurred. This attitude may be explained by patriotism, doubtless, but also by the ideas which are finding utterance in the lobbies. The Right declares aloud that the Hohenzollern affair should be regarded only as an incident; that, even if it should be favorably concluded, we must not stop at that, but must raise the question of the Treaty of Prague, and resolutely place Prussia between accepting a congress and war. This sort of talk was indulged in by MM. Gambetta and Môntpayroux of the Left, and Jérôme David and Pinard of the Right, and all alike made no secret of their intention to attack the Cabinet if it should halt after the settlement of the Hohenzollern affair. M. Thiers expressed himself with extreme warmth in the opposite sense: he considers that the Prussian retreat, in which he has more faith than I, would be a satisfaction with which we must be content."

However, this goading did not persuade us to widen the discussion as we were urged to do, and we kept it strictly within the limits in which we had entered upon it, — the Hohenzollern candidacy, and nothing more.

THE EMS NEGOTIATION

The King was content with the language we had held in the session of the 11th. He wrote to his wife: "Gramont's calm speech is probably the result of Benedetti's telegram after our interview at ten o'clock yesterday morning, of which I wrote you."[1]

The King was mistaken: the thing that had made Gramont calm was our personal resolution not to cease to be calm, and not the story of Benedetti's second audience, which, on the contrary, had done little to reassure us. We could not make up our minds to believe that the Prince had really taken a trip to the Tyrol, when a Spanish deputation might appear at any moment to offer him the crown. This improbability made us fearful that his alleged trip had been thought of solely to gain time and to get nearer to July 20.

Gramont explained to Benedetti the frame of mind which the King's constant evasions induced in us. "At the point which we have now reached, I cannot hesitate to inform you that your language no longer represents, in respect to firmness of tone, the position assumed by the Emperor's government. You must to-day make it more emphatic. We cannot admit the distinction between the King and his government which has been suggested to you. We demand that the King forbid the Prince to persist in his candidacy."[2]

---

[1] [Oncken, *Unser helden Kaiser*, p. 187; *Briefe Kaiser Wilhelms der Erste*, p. 222. Other passages from the same letter are quoted on pp. 183, 184.]

[2] July 11, 6 P.M. [Benedetti, p. 361; Gramont, p. 88. This despatch was sent, it should be noted, immediately after the session of the Chamber of the 11th, and *before* the receipt of Benedetti's despatches reporting his second interview with the King; Gramont, p. 89. As the Council of that morning had determined to await the report of that interview before taking any further step, Gramont's action was clearly impelled by the scene in the

Thus far Benedetti's negotiation with the King had remained at precisely the same point. It had consisted in conjugating the verb "to await." — "I am awaiting a letter from the princes," William had said. "Has Your Majesty received the letter you were awaiting?" The dialogue between the Ambassador and the King had been reduced to this.

Benedetti wrote to Gramont: "I spare neither my time nor my efforts, and I am in despair at my inability to succeed." Later, in an apologetic and sophistical screed against Gramont, he claimed that, even if he had failed to induce the King to intervene directly, by command or advice, with the Hohenzollern princes, he had, by his shrewd management, led him to sacrifice the political plans of his advisers and to declare that he would put no obstacle in the way of Leopold's withdrawal.[1]

Now, it is clear from the King's letters to the Queen and from the messages despatched to Sigmaringen, that before Benedetti's arrival at Ems, William had thrown over a candidacy of which he had never been a strong partisan; that without commanding or advising its abandonment, he had hinted, in very transparent fashion, that he would be overjoyed if his kinsmen

Chamber following M. Arago's interruption. See Sorel, vol. i, p. 114. For Benedetti's reply to this despatch, see *infra*, Appendix I.]

[1] [M. Ollivier presumably refers to Benedetti's essay on his mission to Ems, printed in his volume of *Essais Diplomatiques*, where this claim is made more precisely, although it is really the burden of the chapter devoted to the same subject in his earlier book, *Ma Mission en Prusse*, published in 1871, which gave great umbrage to the Duc de Gramont and is said by him to have induced the writing and publication of his own volume, *La France et la Prusse avant la Guerre*. As to the controversy between them, see *infra*, Appendix E.]

should take the initiative, and that, in that case, he would immediately approve their decision. At Benedetti's first audience he had informed him of his question to Sigmaringen. Benedetti therefore had no occasion to obtain what was already conceded to him in the King's mind.

This vain braggadocio adds nothing to the merit of his negotiation — which was genuinely meritorious, none the less. To make a most irascible monarch swallow harsh words, without offending him, to be firm without being obsequious or yielding — that is what Benedetti accomplished; and by that feat alone he approved himself the equal of the most skilful diplomatists. But he did well in other respects. Harassed by public opinion and by our own anxieties, we spurred him on, urged him to greater energy, and he was wise enough to withstand our impatience, and to endanger by no imprudent step the object he was pursuing. Thus he had obtained leave to open the negotiation, which was a considerable achievement after Bismarck's prohibition, and had extorted from the King valuable admissions. "If he had laid down an ultimatum, he would have caused us to lose the advantages which were assured to us by the disloyal treatment accorded us at Berlin and Madrid."

He was not content to be prudent himself: he put us on our guard against impulsive action. He knew enough, not only to carry out his instructions tactfully, but not to follow those which he deemed injudicious. For instance, Gramont having sent to him information concerning Serrano's disposition, he took it upon himself not to make use of it, and to call his chief to account for his lapse. "As you know, the King claims that our only remedy is to call upon the Spanish government itself to abandon the project it has conceived; and his Majesty would not have failed to seize upon what I told him as a pretext for insisting upon that view."[1]

This first part of the negotiation at Ems will always be one of the excellent pages in our diplomatic history. It had a result most unpalatable to Bismarck,—the sending of Werther to Paris by the King. Despite his minister's urgent remonstrances the King had discussed affairs with Benedetti in two audiences; by splitting hairs he could claim that it was in the capacity of head of his family, and not as king. By sending his Ambassador to treat with us, he acted as king, and no longer as head of his family, and made the question an affair of state. We were satisfied therefore with the royal decision, more especially because, the discussion being transferred to Paris, between an ambassador and ministers, it would take a freer course.

In a note which I left for Gramont in the evening of the 11th, I urged him not to continue with Werther the mild tone which Benedetti had been compelled to observe with the King; to insist upon the twofold character of threat and insult attributable to the Hohenzollern candidacy; to press Werther hard; to meet with vigorous rejoinders the trickery already exposed to the light; to force an abandonment of the equivocating process which we could endure no longer; to extricate us, in short, from the period of trifling and bring us face to face with a *yes* or a *no*. We had been played with long enough; it was time to abandon the habit.

[1] [*Supra*, p. 156 n. (on p. 157).]

CHAPTER XI

THE NEGOTIATION WITH PRINCE ANTONY — THE WITHDRAWAL

BEFORE Gramont and Werther had met, a sudden *coup de théâtre* upset all anticipations. Strat's mission to Sigmaringen had succeeded even better than Bartholdi's at Madrid, and the affair took on a new aspect.

Strat had gone first to Düsseldorf, to find out where Prince Antony and Prince Leopold were. He had learned from certain old family retainers, to whom he was well known, that Prince Antony was at his country house at Sigmaringen, and that Prince Leopold, after a trip to the Tyrol, had returned and was keeping out of sight in the neighborhood of Sigmaringen, ready to take ship at Genoa as soon as the vote of the Cortes should be brought to him. Thus informed, Strat betook himself to Sigmaringen (July 8); there he found Prince Antony both disturbed and angered by our declaration of the 6th. To Strat's first overtures he replied by a wrathful refusal: his son had ceased to be the master of his own decision; he was bound, he had given his word, he could not withdraw without dishonor. Moreover, what would be gained by such a discreditable retreat? The Emperor was simply seeking a pretext for war; this one being removed, he would stir up another.

Strat demonstrated that the Prince was in error concerning Napoleon III's purpose; he had no such hidden designs, and his desire for a peaceful settlement was earnest and sincere. Then, without wasting his time in futile sentimentalities about the calamities of war and the terrible responsibility of him who is the cause of it, he went straight to the practical arguments. He painted in the gloomiest colors the situation into which Prince Leopold was on the point of plunging; he would have to contend against the plots of Alfonsists and Carlists, encouraged by France, against the intrigues of discarded rivals and especially of Montpensier, and against republican risings; at the announcement of his candidacy there was an enormous majority in his favor in the Cortes, but every day, under the action of fear or of hatred, that majority was diminishing, and the most favorable result that could be looked for was that it would remain large enough to impose upon him the duty of going to Spain, but not large enough to assure him of sufficient strength to maintain himself in power. He would probably not have time to take his seat on that broken-legged throne; he would be hurled back as he climbed the steps, and would be very fortunate if he escaped with his life; he was summoned to a disaster, not to a reign.

Strat next directed the Prince's attention to the situation in Roumania of his son Charles, the object of his anxious solicitude: a formidable conspiracy was being formed against him; its threads were in Paris; it was in the Emperor's power to cut them or to set them at work; he would cut them if Leopold should withdraw; he would set them at work, if he were obdurate. Was it wise to endanger a throne in possession for the sake of a problematical one?

These considerations notwithstanding, the Prince

THE CANDIDACY WITHDRAWN 171

refused to be moved. But the mother was present at those painful interviews: she was perturbed, agitated, alarmed, convinced; and, moved by her twofold maternal anxiety, she came to Strat's aid and strove to overcome her husband's resistance. Despite her tears, she did not succeed for two days, and the Prince replied to the first questioning letter from Ems that he was prepared to obey, but that he would not voluntarily withdraw his son's candidacy.

The mother refused to be discouraged, and at last, on the third day (July 11), she triumphed and the father imposed silence on the Prussian and the ambitious man. "This decision," Strat told me emphatically many times, "was a genuinely spontaneous act, the impulse of a father's heart, which no external influence prompted. Before me no one had advised or requested the withdrawal of the candidacy, and during my stay at the castle of Hohenzollern, no one came to my assistance, directly or indirectly. King William was telling the truth when he said again and again that he had nothing whatever to do with the withdrawal; that it had come about without any pressure from him; that he had neither ordered it nor advised it. I was not aware at that time that he had even desired it." [1]

[1] ["The mission of M. de Stratt to the princes, supported, *without the slightest doubt*, by confidential advices from the King of Prussia, had succeeded." Sorel, vol. i, p. 124. How far the King actively interfered must remain almost entirely a matter of inference. It appears sufficiently in his correspondence with the Queen, as well as in his letter of July 6 to Prince Antony (*supra*, p. 138), that he regretted the turn affairs had taken and would have been glad to know that the candidacy had disappeared; but there seems to be no direct evidence that he urged, far less commanded, Prince Leopold's withdrawal. It is a very different question, however, whether, considering his relation to the affair, and the momentous importance that it had assumed, his kinsmen would have notified everybody else of the with-

172   THE FRANCO-PRUSSIAN WAR

When Prince Antony informed his son of his decision, he refused to adopt it: the same honorable scruples which had caused him to hesitate so long before accepting, because of his relations with Napoleon III, made him reluctant to withdraw because of his agreements with Prim and Bismarck.[1] To persuade the Prince would have taken time, and there was need of haste. Strat induced the father to exert his authority and to take it upon himself to withdraw in his son's name, knowing that Leopold would not dare to disavow him publicly. And that is how the withdrawal, instead of being made, as the acceptance was, by Leopold himself, was made by Prince Antony. He would have preferred at least to notify the head of the family, in conformity with the family statute, before informing the Spaniards and the public, but that course would necessitate more delay, and Strat, unaware of the King's real preference, feared that some opposition might come from him. He got the Prince to agree that the public announcement should not be postponed. Prince· Antony consented the more willingly because, knowing the

drawal by telegraph, and have left him alone to learn it by messenger. So that, even before the publication of his letter to the Queen (p. 173, n. 1), it was a fair assumption that he was already aware of the withdrawal when Benedetti told him of it on the morning of the 13th, that his surprise was feigned, therefore, and that his persistence in waiting for direct advices was due to his desire to give greater plausibility to his claim that the withdrawal was altogether spontaneous on the Prince's part, and that the King, in merely giving his assent, "as he had given his assent to the acceptance," was still acting as head of the family, and not as king. See Benedetti, pp. 367, 368; Gramont, pp. 133, 134.]

[1] "His wife could not make up her mind to put away from her head the superb crown which she coveted, and which she seemed to feel already resting upon it." [Ollivier, vol. xiv, p. 209. The Princess Leopold was sister to the King of Portugal.]

THE CANDIDACY WITHDRAWN

King's secret wishes, he was certain that the head of the family would not take umbrage at that infraction of family discipline.

Without losing a minute, Strat despatched, that same evening, the 11th, a telegram in cipher to Olozaga, advising him of the fortunate result, which telegram arrived at Paris late in the evening. It had already been sent when the King's messenger, Colonel Strantz, arrived, having been delayed by an accident to his carriage.[1] Prince Antony told him the news, and he at once telegraphed to his master the decision already transmitted to Olozaga.

On the morning of the 12th three telegrams, not in cipher, were sent by Prince Antony.[2] This was the first:—

"To MARSHAL PRIM, Madrid:—

"In view of the complications which the candidacy of my son Leopold for the throne of Spain seems to have encountered, and of the painful situation which recent events have created for the Spanish nation, placing it in a dilemma where it can take counsel only of

[1] The time of Strantz's arrival is fixed in a letter from the King to the Queen of the 12th: "As there was an accident to General Strantz's train, he did not reach Sigmaringen until last evening." [Note of M. Ollivier, vol. xiv. p. 210.] This being so, the decision to withdraw would have been reached even before Prince Antony received the King's letter from Strantz. The King's reply to Benedetti is inconsistent with his further statement in the same letter to the Queen, that Strantz had telegraphed that Leopold had withdrawn. *Briefe des Kaiser Wilhelms der Erste*, p. 222.

[2] It is evident what one should think of the fanciful conjecture put forth later by Benedetti, in an outburst of personal excitement, that "this transmission of Prince Antony's despatch had been arranged between Ems and Sigmaringen," and that, on the 12th the King had in his hands the copy of the despatch sent by Prince Antony to Olozaga on the same day. [Note of M. Ollivier, vol. xiv, p. 210. But the author has just stated that Strantz learned the news and repeated it to the King on the night of the 11th.]

its own sentiment of independence; and being persuaded that under such circumstances its choice would not have the sincerity and spontaneity upon which my son counted when he accepted the candidacy, I withdraw it in his name."

The second was addressed to Olozaga: —
"To the Spanish Ambassador at Paris: —
"I deem it my duty to inform you, as Spanish representative at Paris, that I have but now sent to Madrid, to Marshal Prim, the following telegram." Then follows the text given above.

The third telegram was addressed to the principal journals of Berlin and of Germany, notably the *Gazette* of Augsbourg and the *Gazette* of Cologne, and to the German telegraphic agencies: —[1]
"The Hereditary Prince of Hohenzollern, in order to restore to Spain her freedom of initiative, withdraws his candidacy for the throne of Spain, being firmly resolved not to allow a question of war to grow out of a family question of secondary importance in his eyes. — By order of the Prince,
"Lesser, Councillor of his Chamber."

The telegram to Prim returned from Madrid to Paris about five in the evening. The despatch to Olozaga reached Paris at 1.40 p.m. That to the German newspapers reached them in the afternoon, early enough for the agencies to send the news before night

[1] [The *Swabian Mercury* is generally mentioned as the German journal in which the news was first published; and Bismarck is said to have read it there. See Sorel, vol. i, p. 124; Welschinger, p. 72.]

THE CANDIDACY WITHDRAWN 175

to their correspondents, clubs, bankers, journals, etc. The *Gazettes* of Cologne and Augsbourg and other papers published it in their evening editions. Thus the news did not reach Paris from Madrid: it reached Paris and Madrid at the same time, and, soon after, it became known in all the important centres of Europe.

While the telegrams were flying to Paris and Madrid, Strat and Strantz left Sigmaringen, the latter returning to Ems with a letter from Prince Antony setting forth the reasons of his spontaneous decision, the former carrying to Olozaga the original draft of the withdrawal.

There remained at Sigmaringen a gentleman who, like everybody else at that period, was waiting. It was Admiral Polo de Bernabé. He had arrived several days before, with Prim's official letter offering the crown to Prince Leopold. Prince Antony, still deliberating, had told him, as the King of Prussia told Benedetti, that the Prince was travelling in the Tyrol; and the admiral was awaiting his return. The withdrawal being decided upon, Prince Antony so informed him, saying that he might now consider his mission concluded and return to Madrid.

The admiral objected that, despite that assurance, his mission would not be concluded until, the document of which he was the bearer having been delivered to Prince Leopold, that Prince should give him his formal response. It became necessary therefore to summon the Prince from his hiding-place, exhibit him to the Spanish admiral, and obtain from him a formal letter of withdrawal.[1]

[1] Letters from Admiral Polo de Bernabé to E. Ollivier of July 12 and August 2, 1888.

176 THE FRANCO-PRUSSIAN WAR

The Prince refused. Thereupon there were painful scenes between the father and son. Those Hohenzollern princes, under a delightful exterior, concealed a substratum of tyrannical harshness; everything about them bent beneath a discipline as inflexible as steel. The young Prince ended by submitting,[1] and handed the admiral his withdrawal. When General Lopez Dominguez arrived, the admiral informed him that there was nothing for him to do but return with him to Madrid; that it was all over.[2]

[1] Concerning Prince Leopold's disposition in the matter I have the concordant testimony of the two Spanish envoys. Admiral Polo de Bernabé wrote me on August 2, 1888: "Creo tambien la contrarietad del hijo por esa resolucion de su Padre"; and Lopez Dominguez on July 17, 1888: "Ordén que aun contrariendole mucho acatabe il archiduque" (prince).

[2] [In a passage of several pages, omitted here, M. Ollivier insists that the whole credit for Prince Leopold's withdrawal belonged to Strat and Olozaga, although it was claimed by "all those who had labored or felt disposed to labor," to bring it about.] "'My dear friend,' Olozaga wrote me, 'I have read, as you have, in the English despatches certain hints which might induce the belief that it was the cabinet of St. James that obtained Prince Leopold's withdrawal. . . . I am in a position to prove, by the testimony of M. Strat, who was my intermediary with the Sigmaringen Hohenzollerns, that no one before myself suggested the withdrawal directly or indirectly. Nor did any one assist me in any way to obtain it; that is all that I can tell you. I should add that all the steps I have taken to find out something concerning the motives or the pretext of the hints that were calculated to make people believe that the English government obtained the withdrawal were absolutely fruitless. I am so far from desiring for myself the monopoly, so to speak, of having conceived the idea of the withdrawal, and the good fortune of having obtained it, that I should have preferred a thousand times that no one should have known what I had done, and that the government of one of the first powers of Europe should have obtained the wit drawal, because in that case it would have turned it to good account and would have avoided war, which was what I desired with all the force of which I am capable. After I had been so fortunate in what the Emperor regarded as almost an impossibility, I cannot console myself for being so powerless.' (March 14, 1871.)" *L'Empire Libéral*, pp. 213, 214.

[As to the "hints" concerning the credit due to the English government,

THE CANDIDACY WITHDRAWN 177

The way in which Bismarck learned of the collapse of his scheme was almost tragic. From the solitude to which he had betaken himself to await the explosion of his mine, kept informed from hour to hour by Abeken,[1] he followed with close attention, becoming more and more perturbed and at last thoroughly angry, at what was taking place at Ems between Benedetti and the King. He was furious because the King received our Ambassador before he had received reparation for what he (Bismarck) called Gramont's insults; because he avowed his share in the candidacy and in the negotiations with Prince Antony, and promised Benedetti, if Leopold should decide to with-

see especially the despatches of Granville to Lyons of July 13, *Blue Book*, pp. 22, 23 (Nos. 33 and 35).]

"The vengeance of Bismarck and Prim did not fail to light upon the real authors of the withdrawal, and thereby to designate them. The Spanish candidacy was no mere act of family ambition, to which the King of Prussia had assented through condescension for a kinsman; it was a State intrigue of which the family ambition was simply an instrument, and Bismarck did not forgive Prince Antony for forgetting that fact and acting as if only his own interest and his children's were involved. The Prince fell into irreparable disgrace: he had to resign the honorable duties that kept him at Düsseldorf, and to go into retirement at Sigmaringen. . . . Nor did Prim's dissembled wrath spare Olozaga. A newspaper having announced that we proposed to give him the Grand Cross of the Legion of Honor in recognition of the services he had rendered us, Mercier wrote to Gramont (July 18) that 'one of the ministers had come to him to say that that would be very ill-timed, and that the ministry would not permit him to accept it because Prim would be offended.'" [*L'Empire Libéral*, vol. xiv, pp. 213-216. And in a note on p. 216:] A letter from Martin Hernandez, Spanish chargé d'affaires, to E. Ollivier, Nov. 12, 1870, reads: "M. Olozaga instructs me to inform you that for having endeavored to do everything in his power in favor of France, he has found himself under the necessity of giving in his resignation as ambassador, and retiring to the country."

[1] [Busch, *Bismarck: Some Secret Pages of his History*, devotes several pages to an account of the character and services of Heinrich Abeken; vol. i, pp. 440-444.]

draw, to inform him of that decision. These were concessions, and the King should not have granted any one of them, but should have shown the negotiator the door at the first word, and not have taken part in any discussion whatsoever. Did the King propose, under the pacific influence of Queen Augusta, to advise the princes to abandon the game?

Bismarck determined to cut short all compromising proceedings, and to stop William on the incline down which he was slipping. He wrote to him that, as his health would now permit him to travel, he was ready to go to Ems at his Majesty's command. The King sent him such a command, and on the morning of the 12th Bismarck started, with Keudell,[1] in his travelling carriage. He left Lothar Bucher at Varzin with his wife. "He was more taciturn than usual," says Keudell, "although his manner was cheerful."

As they drove through Wussow his friend the old pastor Mullert, standing at the door of his parsonage, waved him a friendly salutation; from the back seat of his open carriage Bismarck replied by a gesture mimicking a thrust in *tierce* and *quarte*, to suggest that he was going into a fight.[2] It was his purpose,

[1] [See Busch, *ubi supra*, vol. ii, pp. 104–111, for an elaborate estimate of Herr von Keudell.]

[2] [Busch, vol. i, p. 303. "Dec. 19, 1870. Abeken then talked about the events at Ems which preceded the war, and related that, on one occasion, after a certain despatch had been sent off, the King said: 'Well, he' (Bismarck) 'will be satisfied with us now!' And Abeken added, 'I believe you were.' 'Well,' replied the Chancellor, laughing, 'you may easily be mistaken. That is to say, I was quite satisfied with you. But not quite so much with our Most Gracious, or rather not at all. He ought to have acted in a more dignified way — and more resolutely. I remember,' he continued, 'how I received the news at Varzin. I had gone out, and on my return the first telegram had been delivered. As I started on my journey, I had to pass our pastor's house at Wussow,'" etc.]

THE CANDIDACY WITHDRAWN 179

after conferring a few moments with Roon, who had just arrived at Berlin, to push on to Ems; there he would put an end to compliments, courtesies, and condescensions; he would show how the honor of the country was being sacrificed and would bring about a peremptory, and perhaps an insulting, notification of refusal to withdraw on the part of the princes and the King. He would repeat Thile's arguments in a brutal tone; he would not allow the King to discuss with us any further his acts as head of his family; lastly, he would dismiss Benedetti and would propose the summoning of the Reichstag with a view to mobilization.[1] As a preliminary to these measures, realizing the conciliatory significance of the sending of Werther to Paris, he telegraphed to stop him, but Werther was already on the way.

Bismarck reached Berlin at six in the evening, expecting to take the 8.30 train for Ems. As he drove along Unter den Linden, he met Prince Gortchakoff; they stopped and shook hands. In the courtyard of his house, among the despatches which were handed him before he left his carriage, he found one from Paris announcing Prince Antony's withdrawal. He was fairly petrified. He had no idea that so well-disciplined a prince would take it upon himself, without the sanction, or rather the encouragement, of the King, to do a thing which, if done on his own initiative,

[1] Bismarck, *Reflections*, etc., English trans., vol. ii, p. 93. M. Matter, in his noteworthy study of Bismarck, was the first writer in France to call attention to this set-back of the Chancellor. "The work of many months, a secret and crafty negotiation, the stirring-up of the press, the irritation of the people, all had come to naught; the King of Prussia had yielded, and for the first time in his political career, Count Bismarck had been brought to a halt." Vol. iii, p. 53. [Note of M. Ollivier, vol. xiv, p. 218.]

would be treason; could it be that a Prussian prince, a friend, a confidant, would allow himself, alone, in obedience to a rash impulse, to undo, without a previous understanding, a work which had been so laboriously planned in common? In a flash, he saw all the disastrous consequences to himself of the incident. He was discomfited, beaten, humbled, deserted by his King and his candidate; he would speedily become the derision of Germany and Europe; his edifice of craft was crumbling about his ears. Let a German writer tell our historians the extent of this catastrophe.

"This withdrawal," says Lenz, "meant peace. His journey had become useless; useless the uprising of the nation which he had instigated with all his strength; useless his attempt, made with scientific craft, to prepare a counter-mine for the efforts of the French. Even if he could still maintain his position externally, the game was lost. Instead of taking France by surprise, as he had hoped, he found his path now blocked by her. The moment to fall back had come; for the first time in his life the great statesman had suffered a defeat." [1]

This crushing result was due in great measure to our declaration of July 6. Olozaga and Strat would not have succeeded in their undertaking, would not even have thought of it, but for the facilities afforded by our bold ultimatum. Nigra recognizes this fact. "The prince's withdrawal," he says, "must be attributed mainly to his wish to save Europe from a conflagration, *as well as to the resolute attitude of the French government.*" [2]

[1] Lenz, *Geschichte,* "Bismarck," pp. 349-350.
[2] March, 1895. ["The Hereditary Prince formally withdraws his candi-

THE CANDIDACY WITHDRAWN 181

The declaration had aroused the European cabinets from their apathy by showing them the peril, had awakened the drowsy conscience of the King, and inspired in Prince Antony a salutary dread; it had not closed the door to negotiation, but had thrown it wide open. Thanks to the adroitness with which we had made use of it, it had secured for us what soft words or the long-spun verbiage of timid *pourparlers* would not have done. We had said, "We will not tolerate a Hohenzollern candidate"; and the Hohenzollern candidate had vanished. We had not fallen into the abyss which Bismarck had dug under our feet; we had thrown him into it himself.

Guizot, on hearing of it, exclaimed: "Those fellows have insolent good luck: it's the greatest diplomatic victory I have ever seen in my life."[1] And Thiers: "To have forced Prussia to draw back from an enterprise which everybody believed to have been deliberately undertaken by her, was an immense advantage. . . . We got out of an embarrassment by a triumph! Sadowa was almost avenged!"[2]

Although Bismarck was one of those stout-hearted men who are not thrown entirely off their balance by an unfortunate accident, this set-back was so pronounced that he was stunned for a moment. He has told about it in his *Reflections:* —

"My first thought was to hand in my resignation.

dacy, in order to deprive France of any pretext for war against Germany." Memoirs of the King of Roumania (French trans.), vol. i, p. 593, under date of July 12.]

[1] ["It was an unhoped-for success after the Duc de Gramont's bluster," says Lehautcourt, vol. i, p. 263; and he quotes the above remark of Guizot on the authority of Darimon, *Histoire d'un Jour*, p. 39.]

[2] In his deposition before the Commission of Inquiry concerning the 4th of September.

"After all the insulting provocations that had theretofore been offered us, I saw in that withdrawal which was forced upon us a humiliation for Germany, and I did not propose to take the official responsibility for it. The feeling that the national honor was wounded by that compulsory retreat so possessed me that I had already decided to send my resignation to Ems. I regarded such humiliation, before France and her gasconading manifestations, as worse than the Olmütz affair. The Olmütz incident can always find its excuse in the earlier transactions in which we were involved, and in the impossibility of our beginning a war at that time. I felt sure that France would make the most of the Prince's withdrawal as of a satisfaction accorded to her. I was very much depressed. The approaching disaster to our national position which our timid policy caused me to fear, I saw no means of averting except by seizing awkwardly upon the first quarrel that might come to hand, or by provoking one out of hand. *For I looked upon war as a necessity which we could no longer avoid with honor.* I telegraphed to my people at Varzin not to pack my trunks, not to start; that I should return in a few days. At that moment I believed in peace. But I did not choose to assume the responsibility of defending the policy by which that peace would have been bought. I abandoned my journey to Ems, therefore, and requested Count Eulenbourg to go thither and lay before his Majesty my point of view." [1]

He instructed Eulenbourg to try the great *coup*, which was ordinarily effectual, of offering his resig-

[1] Bismarck, *Reflections*, etc., English trans., vol. ii, pp. 94, 95. But see, on the other hand, *infra*, p. 187, additional note.

THE CANDIDACY WITHDRAWN 183

nation, and to say to the King that Bismarck regarded war as *necessary*, and that he should return to Varzin if that war were avoided.[1] He anticipated his messenger's arrival by a telegram in which he expressed his determination. "He passed the night without sleep," Keudell adds.[2] One can understand it. To decide upon war was a simple matter; but he was not Frederick, manipulating the state at his sole pleasure. He must needs show his hand, make a provocation to order, and assume the rôle of aggressor, of "seeker after quarrels,"[3] which he had tried to force upon France. But where could he have found his quarrel? Would it have been in what he called the insolent terms of our declaration? That had all been condoned by the negotiation at Ems and by the concessions that the King had made to us. "After the principal question had been settled, to go back to it would have been too ill-advised."[4] If he should find a pretext, he must have the King's assent, and it was almost certain that he could not obtain it.

In truth, when he received Colonel Strantz's message on the 12th, the King was genuinely relieved. "This takes a weight from my heart," he wrote to the Queen;

---

[1] These are Bismarck's own words in a report of Sept. 25, 1888, published in the *Official Journal*. They constitute an admission as important as that concerning the Ems despatch, but they have hitherto passed unnoticed. [Note of M. Ollivier, vol. xiv, p. 222.]

[2] Throughout his narrative Keudell makes his chief play the rôle of a peaceably inclined imbecile, who never pays any heed to what he does; and he explains his stopping at Berlin even more absurdly. "He stopped," he says, "because he was not well." If he means mentally, well and good; but if he means physically, it is idiotic. Bismarck's reminiscences of the Ems despatch restore its proper aspect to the affair. [Note of M. Ollivier, *ibid.*]

[3] Bismarck, *Reflections*, etc., vol. ii, p. 95.

[4] Von Sybel, *Die Begründung*, etc., vol. vii, p. 303.

"but say nothing about it to anybody, so that the news may not come first from us; nor shall I mention it to Benedetti until we have the letter actually in our hands, delivered by Strantz, to-morrow. It is all the more important now that you make a point of emphasizing the fact that I leave everything to the Hohenzollerns so far as their decision is concerned, just as I did with regard to their acceptance."[1]

Gramont, on the other hand, had promised at the very beginning of his negotiations with Lyons that, failing a withdrawal ordered or advised by the King, we would be content with a spontaneous withdrawal by Leopold, provided that the King should take part in it in some fashion.[2] As his participation was now beyond doubt, Benedetti was justified in saying that, even if no definite conclusion had been reached on the 12th, the solution of the difficulty was morally certain; that it was then agreed to by both parties, and that nothing remained save to receive the King's declaration.[3]

Overjoyed at having got rid of the "weight on his heart," the King had accepted an invitation to sup with Prince Albrecht and a few friends in the garden of the Casino. As he was on his way thither Abeken arrived with Bismarck's comminatory despatch. The King went to a light and read it. His face lighted up, he exclaimed: "This is the most important de-

---

[1] [*Briefe des Kaiser Wilhelms*, etc., p. 222. In the same letter the King writes: "Bismarck will be here to-morrow morning; at heart he is still for the candidacy. However, he says that the question has become so serious that we must put the Hohenzollerns by altogether, and leave it to them to make a final decision." See Lehautcourt, vol. i, p. 276 and n.]

[2] [*Supra*, p. 143 n.]

[3] [Benedetti, p. 368.]

THE CANDIDACY WITHDRAWN 185

spatch I have ever received. Say to my brother that I probably shall not have time to come because I must work with Abeken, and that it is understood that, if I do come later, no one is to rise." [1]

The supper had long since begun when the King appeared, alone. He motioned to the guests not to rise, and took the seat reserved for him between two ladies. Chappuis, who was taking the place of the Marshal of the Court, having asked him if he would take champagne, the King replied, "Give me some seltzer, I must keep my mind clear."

The King passed a sleepless night, like Bismarck. Was Bismarck's ultimatum destined to turn him back, and to lead him to retract the friendly assurances given to Benedetti?

The reflections of insomnia were not favorable to the Chancellor. Bismarck could manage the King only within certain limits, and on condition that he did not collide with the impregnable ideas that he had adopted as rules of conduct. One of those rules was, never to take the initiative in a great war, and Bismarck had drawn him into such a war twice, only by persuading him that he had received provocation. Now, in this case the provocation on Prussia's part would have been too manifest. Another of those rules was to listen to advice from every quarter before making up his mind, but when it was once made up, to brook no contradiction. Now, he had during the last few days declared so freely what he would do in case of Leopold's withdrawal, that he could not go back upon a decision so fully considered. He persisted therefore in the pur-

[1] [The telegram referred to is, of course, that in which Bismarck proffered his resignation.]

pose to bring to a peaceful close an adventure which he was in haste to have done with, not to dismiss Benedetti, and to communicate to him personally the voluntary decision of the princes which he was about to receive.

If, therefore, no new complication had arisen, this is what would have happened. On the 13th the King would have communicated to Benedetti the withdrawal he was expecting, He would have added that he approved it, and would have authorized our Ambassador to transmit this twofold assurance to our government. Thus the two conditions laid down by Gramont would have been complied with: the abandonment of the candidacy and the tangible participation of the King therein. Our victory of the evening of the 12th would have been made complete on the 13th, and Bismarck would have been definitively beaten. He would have withdrawn from public affairs, for some time at least, and the cloud heavy with calamity which that barbarian of genius was holding over Europe would have vanished from the European horizon. Our ministry, having given the country liberty, would have assured it the prestige of a glorious peace.[1]

Alas! that I cannot stop here! Why am I compelled to continue? At the very moment when Bismarck was trying to find his bearings amid the tumultuous confusion of perilous or impossible schemes, others were at work in France to help him out of his embarrassment, to raise him from his defeat, to restore him to the position which he had lost through our efforts, and to bring back luck into his game. That is the feat which our Right was about to accomplish, led, although

[1] [See La Gorce, vol. vi, p. 260.]

composed of men beyond reproach, by two villains, Jérôme David and Clement Duvernois.[1]

[1] After taking part in public affairs, Duvernois took a hand in private business. There he was less fortunate than in politics. In the criminal court, Nov. 25, 1874, he was sentenced to two years' imprisonment and a fine of 1000 francs under articles 13–15 of the law of July 24, 1876 [*sic*], and articles 405, 459, 460 of the Penal Code. *Gazette des Tribunaux*, Nov. 26, 1874. Jérôme David ended by disavowing flatly what he had said and done. [Note of M. Ollivier in vol. xiv, p. 226.]

ADDITIONAL NOTE. It is instructive as to Count von Bismarck's methods to compare the quotation from his autobiographical work on page 182 of this volume with his observations to Jules Favre, then Minister of War of the Government of National Defence, on the occasion of that official's surreptitious interview at Ferrières on September 20. "When I learned of the quarrel that France was trying to pick with us apropos of the Prince of Hohenzollern's candidacy, I was worried by your Ambassador's persistence in treating with nobody but the King. He wearied the King, and, knowing that, *I advised adopting a policy which would give you satisfaction*, which was done. When I learned that, *in accordance with my advice*, the King had obtained from his cousin the withdrawal of his candidacy, I wrote to my wife that it was all over, and that I was going to join her in the country. Great was my surprise when I found that, on the contrary, it was all beginning again." Favre, *Gouvernement de la Défense Nationale*, vol. i, pp. 176, 177. And Jules Favre seems to have been glad to believe him.

CHAPTER XII

EFFECT AT PARIS OF THE WITHDRAWAL OF THE CANDIDACY

On the 12th of July, in the morning, the Emperor had come to the Tuileries to preside over the Council of Ministers. We discussed the reply to be made to the request for delay, which had been addressed to us on the preceding day by Benedetti, on the King's behalf, in decidedly emphatic terms. We authorized Gramont to telegraph to Benedetti that it had never been our purpose to provoke a conflict, but simply to defend the legitimate interests of France; and so, while denying the justness of the King's arguments and persisting in our demands, we would not refuse the delay requested, but we hoped that it would not extend beyond a single day.[1]

This matter being arranged, we were giving our attention to current business, when a chamberlain entered and said a few words in an undertone to the Emperor, who at once rose and went out. He returned shortly and took part again in our conversation about business, without a word in explanation of his unwonted action. He did, in fact, go out to receive Olozaga, who, not having been able to take to him during the night the tele-

[1] [This Council resulted apparently in the despatch of the 12th, not referred to by M. Ollivier, in which assent was given to the King's "urgent request" for further delay; "but we hope that this delay will not extend beyond another day." Gramont, p. 102. See *infra*, Appendix I.]

gram in cipher from Strat, had sent in an urgent request to see him at once, in order to give him that important information. That telegram in cipher told of the telegrams not in cipher which Prince Antony had sent on the morning of the 12th. Olozaga requested the Emperor to regard his communication as confidential until the arrival of those telegrams, which alone would impart an irrevocable character to the withdrawal of the candidacy. It is to be regretted that the Emperor consented to bind himself to keep the matter secret temporarily from his ministers. If he had told us at that time of the secret negotiation of which we knew nothing, if he had apprized us of its fortunate result, we should not have been taken by surprise by the news, as we were a few hours later. We could have exchanged our ideas thereupon, at leisure, we could have discussed it and reflected upon it, and should not have been inconsistent or embarrassed in our attitude before the Chamber and the public.

About two o'clock I left the department, to walk to the Chamber across the garden of the Tuileries. I was profoundly depressed; it seemed clear to me that Prussia was determined to force war upon us, and that we were driven to the wall. The prospect drove me to despair. I had taken only a few steps, absorbed by my distressing reflections, when I was as it were abruptly awakened by the voice of a clerk in the Department of the Interior, who handed me a letter from Chevandier. It contained a copy of the despatch, not in cipher, from Prince Antony to Olozaga, which had just arrived, and in which was included the text of the Prince's withdrawal in the name of his son. There was in the Department of the Interior a special detail of clerks whose duty it was to take copies of all despatches passing through the Paris office, whether sent from or received there, which were of such a nature as to concern the public peace. As Prince Antony's despatch came within this description, it had been copied, and Chevandier sent a copy to me, and at the same time to the Emperor and Gramont.

I hastily retraced my steps in order to tell my wife the good news; then resumed my walk. Certain doubts beset me. What was the meaning of this withdrawal falling suddenly from the sky? Was it sincere? Was it not a trick of the stock market? Why had not Olozaga, with whom I was in daily communication, given me a hint of it? The Emperor seemed to have no suspicion of it at the Council; did he know of it, or did he not? had he spoken of it with Gramont? I put aside these suspicions. It seemed to me impossible that a step thus announced should be a trick; I looked upon it as a fact. Thereupon I believed that the whole situation was saved, and so great was my joy at having peace within our grasp, so great my dread of losing it again, that the combative disposition which I had displayed in my note of the evening of the 11th melted away before the warmth of the unhoped-for news. There was no further occasion to appear stiff and unyielding, but rather accommodating and pliant, and to make more certain the result arrived at, instead of endangering it. The incident was certainly at an end, if we were guilty of no imprudence; and I was so overjoyed that at times I could not believe it.

However, it seemed to me that I ought not to make public the document which I held in my hand, and which I read again and again as if I should find therein the secret of what had happened. It was a document secured by the police power of the government, and so not of a character to be officially avowed, and I was bound not to disclose its existence. So I put it in my pocket, where it burned a hole, so to speak.

I had taken only a few steps more when I was overtaken by a messenger, this time from my own office — Boissy. He brought me a report in which it was stated that, at a meeting of the irreconcilable Left, on rue de la Sourdière, Gambetta[1] had just made a magnifi-

[1] [Léon Gambetta had first come prominently into public notice in the autumn of 1868, when he was retained to defend M. Delescluze, proprietor of the radical newspaper *Le Reveil*, in the prosecution instituted by the government against the organizers of the subscription for a monument to the memory of Baudin, a deputy, who was killed on the barricades during the execution of the *coup d'état* of December 2, 1851. Gambetta failed to obtain a verdict, "but he won his cause in the country. His speech, less a defence of his client than an attack on the Second Empire, rang like a challenge to the Emperor, which the whole nation seemed ready to support." Walpole, *History of Twenty-five Years*, vol. ii, p. 476.

When the Corps Législatif resumed its labors after the constitution of the Olliver ministry, the "Irreconcilables" (that is to say, the Extreme Left) disclosed their tactics, which was to consist "in multiplying questions, in inflating to the point of menace the rumble of their voices. Their hope, their sole hope, was that the government would lose patience and yield to some ill-advised temptation to exact reprisals. . . . The most aggressive was Gambetta. He questioned the Minister of War concerning two soldiers who had been sent to Algeria for having frequented public meetings. Then, branching off into more general considerations, he took the whole Cabinet to task, and in terms of studied severity, declared war without quarter upon it. M. Émile Ollivier had just appealed to all his colleagues, even those of the opposition. 'If,' retorted Gambetta, 'you rely on our assistance to lay the foundation for liberty, you must make up your minds never to obtain it. You have prated about universal suffrage. In our eyes universal suffrage is incompatible with the form of government which you propose. . . . Between the form now predominant and universal suffrage there is absolute incompatibility. . . . Between the Republic of 1848 and the republic of the future you are merely a bridge; and that bridge we propose to cross.'" La Gorce, vol. vi, pp. 8, 9. During the debate on the proposed *plebiscite*,

cent speech: its purport was that we should regard the Hohenzollern affair simply as a detail, and should firmly demand the execution of the Treaty of Prague, and the demolition of the fortresses that threatened our frontier. "If he should make this speech in the Chamber," I was told, "the Ministry could not withstand it."

I arrived at the Corps Législatif; some one asked me: "What is there new?" I was very careful not to say what I had just learned. "Nothing as yet," I replied, "but Gramont is to confer with Werther immediately, and by the end of the day we shall know definitively what course we must adopt."

At that moment Olozaga entered the hall; his face glowing with excitement, waving a paper in his hand, he rushed up to me and drew me into a corner. "Is

there was a discussion (on April 4) of an interpellation concerning the *constituent power*. "The discussion was proceeding without great amplitude, with no lofty flights, when Gambetta appeared in the tribune. It was through his participation in the debate that it deserves to be remembered, even to this day. Up to that time the deputy from Belleville had distinguished himself by his noisy violence, and in the eyes of a great number of people was hardly to be differentiated from the mob of 'clubists.' The hour had struck when he was to take his place among political orators." Before his speech the Left had inveighed against the appeal to the people as an additional weapon in the hands of despotism, and the Bonapartists gave indications of delighted satisfaction. "Gambetta alone dared to go to the bottom of the appeal to the people, to confiscate it to the profit of his party, to turn it against the Empire. . . . 'The plebiscite is the knowledge and conscience of the people.' . . . With a singular combination of insinuating argument and fiery vehemence, the orator undertook to define universal suffrage: 'Universal suffrage is the national sovereignty acting constantly; now, there is but a single form of government adequate to universal suffrage; that form you will not allow me to refrain from naming, because it is on my lips, because it is in my heart; *it is the republican form.*' The great word was out, and it had been led up to so skilfully that not a murmur, not an interruption halted the supreme audacity on its passage." *Ibid*, pp. 97, 98.]

Gramont here?" — "No, he is at the Foreign Office in conference with Werther." — "You see, I have good news for you." And he read me the despatch of which I had a copy. "So this news is genuine?" I asked. "Yes, yes, do not doubt it; it's all over." And he left me, to go to Gramont.

The deputies who had noticed Olozaga's entrance, his pantomime, the waving of the paper, crowded about me as soon as he had left me. "Is there anything important?" Thereupon there took place in my mind a deliberation as swift as thought itself. Should I make public the despatch, or should I keep it to myself? The copy, seized on the wing and handed to me by the police service of the government, had become an authentic document, displayed before numerous persons by the ambassador to whom it was addressed. A communication made under such circumstances did not indicate a desire for secrecy; the very character of the despatch excluded such an idea; one does not send a despatch in plain language unless one means to make it public. Why should I have concealed from those deputies, in order to parade my own importance to no useful purpose, a fact which everybody would learn from the evening papers, — which many knew already, at the department, at the telegraph office, at the embassies and chancelleries, at the offices of news agencies and newspapers? The shameless adversaries with whom I was engaged would not have failed to denounce my silence as a concession to speculators. I certainly should not have hesitated to take that risk — although I was much more sensitive to it than to others to which I exposed myself day after day — if any public interest had demanded it. But none did, for I could not regard as a matter of public interest the vain hope of preventing a manifestation in the Chamber on the part of the war-party, — a manifestation which, being postponed to the next day and more fully prepared, would have been only the more violent.[1] And so I read the telegram to those who questioned me. One of my auditors was the celebrated engineer, Paulin Talabot, the creator of French railways, who was an advocate of peace both on principle and by interest. "Prussia is making a fool of you," he whispered in my ear.

There were calls for me in the Salle des Pas-Perdus. A mob rushed at me and questioned me. I could not conceal in one hall what I had just disclosed in another.

[1] [On M. Ollivier's procedure on receipt of the news of the withdrawal, see Sorel, vol. i, pp. 126–128; Welschinger, vol. i, pp. 72–74; Lehautcourt, vol. i, pp. 265, 266; La Gorce, vol. vi, pp. 257, 258; Von Sybel, *Founding of the German Empire* (Eng. trans.), vol. vii, pp. 366–368. The general tone of the comment, that is to say, of those writers who are not influenced by an unalterable prejudice against the ministry and all its works, is to the effect that M. Ollivier's action was impulsive and ill-advised, but was the result of a sincere and earnest desire for peace, which he honestly believed to be ensured by the withdrawal. "At heart," says Sorel (vol. i, p. 126), "he desired peace; without reflection, without consulting his colleagues, he rushed to the Corps Législatif to announce the news. His intentions were good, but that heedless haste compromised everything." And La Gorce (vol. vi, pp. 257, 258): Ollivier's "simple and straightforward mind interpreted the despatch according to its natural meaning, that is to say, as announcing peace. Neither his education nor his disposition had trained him to diplomatic reserve. Overjoyed by the changed aspect of affairs (for no one had a greater horror of war than he), he could not forbear to make his joy public. . . . These expansive communications were characteristic of a good citizen rather than a politician. Calm prudence is not so quick to publish abroad even its joys. Genuine sagacity (easier, it is true, to discover afterward than to work out in the excitement of those feverish days) would have consisted in keeping silent until the expected despatches from Benedetti should bring the King's approval."]

"Yes," I replied, "there is a despatch to Olozaga from Prince Antony, announcing that he withdraws his son's candidacy."

"And what about the Treaty of Prague?" cried a voice.

"We have never mentioned it to Prussia; our pourparlers have dealt solely with the candidacy."

"Does this mean peace?" some one shouted.

I replied by throwing my arms apart in an evasive gesture, which was intended to mean, "I do not propose to answer." But if my lips remained mute, the glow of joy that lighted up my face told of the hope that filled my heart.[1]

Noticing among the listeners Léonce Détroyat, editor-in-chief of the *Liberté*, I went to him and asked him to urge his uncle to strive to avert war, since that course had become possible with honor. Girardin, who was very anxious and too nervous to come to the Salle des Pas-Perdus, was waiting for him on Place de la Concorde, at the end of the bridge. Détroyat hastened to him and repeated what I had just said. Girardin left him abruptly at the first word, with a shrug of the shoulders.[2]

---

[1] The *Rappel* (I cite one of the most hostile papers) described the incident thus: "M. Émile Ollivier came in beaming all over. Being surrounded and questioned, he announced in a loud voice that he had received, through M. Olozaga, a despatch from Prince Antony of Hohenzollern, Duke [*sic*] Leopold's father, declaring that he would order his son to withdraw. M. Émile Ollivier added: 'We have never asked of Prussia anything more than the Prince of Hohenzollern's withdrawal. Now the candidacy may be regarded as withdrawn.' He did not finish, but the conclusion went of itself." [Note of M. Ollivier in vol. xiv, p. 233.]

[2] [See *supra*, p. 68, n. 2. This passage appears in slightly different form in M. Ollivier's larger work. "I went to him and asked him to urge his uncle '*not to write any more articles like those of the last few days,* and to strive,' etc.

At the same time an excited crowd poured forth from the Palais Législatif. There was a grand struggle for the cabs on the stand, which were escaladed, carried by assault. "To the Bourse! the Bourse!" cried the speculators. "We'll pay double price — go at full

'I beg you,' I said, 'to have the courage to refuse to insert his articles; you will do him a great service as well as the country.'" Vol. xiv, p. 233. But Détroyat himself seems to have been among the first to suggest a demand for guaranties. Robert Mitchell having written in the *Constitutionnel* that "we should have nothing further to ask from the Cabinet of Berlin if the Spanish people should spontaneously reject the sovereign whom it was proposed to force upon them," Détroyat replied in the *Liberté*: "We do not agree with the *Constitutionnel*; we think that it would remain for France and for Europe to demand from the Cabinet of Berlin such guaranties as will bind it tight for the future." Lehautcourt, vol. i, p. 261.]

Darimon has placed this anecdote, which he had heard me tell, at the time of my arrival at the Chamber; but that is nonsense, for at that time I was dumb. While I am on the subject, it may be well for me to say a word or two about that gentleman. He was one of the Five, and I had never forgotten it. Although, at the time of my rupture with Rouher, he had declared himself against me, I put myself out to make a place for him in the Cour des Comptes. After the war, I continued to admit him to my intimate circle; he met Gramont there and we talked unsuspectingly before him. On leaving me he would make memoranda of what he had heard. If those memoranda had been a truthful reproduction, they would have made a valuable document, but they were always written down by an idiot or a villain, who either did not understand, or did not choose to understand; so that there is not one of them beside which we may not write "false," or "half-false." To these treacherous memoranda, he added all the fables hostile to the ministry, hawked about by the Imperialist Right, which strove to make us the scapegoat of its errors, and he published it all in a volume entitled: *Notes pour servir à l'Histoire de la Guerre*, in which he has drawn freely from all quarters, frequently without indicating his authorities. When I read that detestable book, I closed my door to the author. Nevertheless, some time after, when he had fallen into destitution, I induced the Académie Française to name him for the place at its disposal in the Asile Galignani, where he died. I say all this simply because every serious historian should regard Darimon's statements as false, unless their truth is proved *aliunde*. [Note of M. Ollivier in vol. xiv, p. 233. Lehautcourt's narrative of this period should be read with this caution in mind, as he cites Darimon very frequently as authority for facts which are not mentioned by other writers.]

speed!" Among the newspaper men there was the same haste, and a concert of the same sort. "To the office of the *Marseillaise!*" they shouted. "To the *Reveil!*" "To the *Siècle!*" "To the *Opinion Nationale!*" "To the *Rappel!*"

And under the incitement of the lash, the sorry jades woke one after another from their repose and darted off as swift as arrows.[1]

In the deputies' lobby Gressier, the ex-minister, a resolute, judicial-minded man, in no wise inclined to war, accosted me. I told him of my determination, if the withdrawal was genuine, not to lend myself to the setting up of any fresh demand on top of the Hohenzollern business — with respect either to the Treaty of Prague or to anything else. "That is right," he replied; "you will do a brave thing; but don't fail to understand this — it means your fall; the country will not be satisfied with this concession."

A large number of deputies grouped about me and questioned me. Being more at liberty to express my thoughts to them than I had been when I was surrounded by newspaper men, I repeated what I had just said to Gressier. There were numerous protests. Among the members of the Right, there was an ebullition of wrath. "Ollivier says that it's all over. It's a shame! Prussia came out to pick a quarrel with us; we must make an end of her."

Several members assembled in one of the offices of the Chamber, decided that there must be no delay in protesting against the pusillanimity of the Cabinet,

[1] [The three per cent consols rose almost instantly some two or three points — from 67 to 70. La Gorce, vol. vi, p. 257; Lehautcourt, vol. i, p. 265 and n. 4; Delord, vol. vi, p. 162.]

and drew up a demand for an interpellation, which Duvernois undertook to announce at once from the tribune.

I entered the Chamber. Clement Duvernois rose, and in a threatening tone, as if in reply to my hopes of peace, announced in his own name and de Leusse's the following interpellation: —

"We ask to interpellate the Cabinet concerning the guaranties for which it has stipulated, or for which it proposes to stipulate, in order to avoid the recurrence of complications with Prussia." He added that he would not insist upon a day being fixed, but would leave that to the Chamber and the Government.[1]

[1] [Clement Duvernois, Napoleon's "favorite," had been the intermediary between him and M. Ollivier at the time of the formation of the liberal ministry. "He had special reasons for animosity against M. Ollivier; he took an active part in the formation of the cabinet; indeed, he was a member of it for two hours, and had to step out for purely personal reasons. On the subject of the law concerning general councils, M. Ollivier raised explicitly the question of his discharge from the Emperor's newspaper, the *Peuple Français*. He carried his point. The next day Duvernois founded the *Volontaire*. He was called at the Tuileries, 'the Emperor's pen.'" Lehautcourt, vol. i, p. 266 n.

"Duvernois, who could not forgive M. Émile Ollivier for having caused him to be excluded from the ministry, had announced that morning, that, if affairs assumed a pacific aspect, he should interpellate the government. It was a deplorable manœuvre, for it was destined to lead the ministry to set up new claims and to place peace in danger a second time." Welschinger, vol. i, p. 76.

It was reported that, in his action at this time, Duvernois was the mouthpiece of the Emperor, and according to La Gorce some members of the Centre groups thought to approve themselves good courtiers by talking in a very bellicose vein. Gramont says, however, that the Emperor greatly regretted the interpellation, "because it compelled his government to hasten the moment of explanations which prudence, on the contrary, bade it defer as long as possible." Gramont, p. 130 and n. See La Gorce, vol. vi, pp. 263, 264; Sorel, vol. i, p. 134. Delord, vol. vi, p. 169. Duvernois himself declared in an article in the *Ordre*, of Sept. 15, 1871, that "the Emperor did not even know of his proposed interpellation, and that, when he learned of it, afterward, he certainly did not approve it."]

"The war-current," said the *Gazette de France*, "seems to carry the day. In the lobby of the Corps Législatif a Vendean deputy said aloud that, if the Cabinet rests content with the withdrawal of Prince Antony in his son's name, the Extreme Right will not rest content. In fact, the majority seems bent upon war; it might well be that the Ministry would be overthrown if it should halt now."

Duvernois had taken his seat; an usher informed me that one of the Emperor's aides-de-camp wished to speak to me. I went out, and the aide-de-camp handed me the following note : —

"DEAR MONSIEUR ÉMILE OLLIVIER, — I would like an opportunity to talk with you a few moments before returning to Saint-Cloud. You know of the Prince of Hohenzollern's despatch to Marshal Prim. If the news is announced to the Chamber, we must at the least make the most that we can of it, and cause it to be clearly understood that it is at the command of the King of Prussia that the candidacy is withdrawn. I have not yet seen Gramont. The country will be disappointed. But what can we do?"

This was the first pacific note that reached me. I divined the wish hidden beneath the words, "If the news is announced." Evidently the Emperor would have liked me to go into the tribune, read the despatch, and hint that the result was due to the imperative intervention of the King of Prussia, and that the incident was closed. It was no longer opportune to read the despatch, as all the deputies had knowledge of it; as for the public, they would learn it more quickly, or as quickly, through the evening papers. Nor would a reading, as indeed the Emperor suggested, be of any value unless accompanied by a commentary or followed by a conclusion. How could I have presumed to make a commentary or a conclusion without having first agreed upon it with my colleagues? I looked about in quest of them. Not one was present, and Gramont was conferring with Werther, just from Ems.

One can judge by the following letter from Chevandier, what would have happened if I had obeyed the Emperor's implied wish: —

"According to what I have learned from our colleagues, the Chamber is very bellicose, and that fact has made some little impression on them. They complain — I care too much for you not to tell you — of your having given information in the lobbies concerning a despatch which was not addressed to you (as to that, you would be absolved by the communication made to you by the Spanish Ambassador), and of which, in any event, they consider the disclosure premature. In my opinion, you made a mistake.[1] You know that, while I do not fear war, I am not an advocate of it through thick and thin. *Let us not plunge headforemost into peace.* It is the goal for which we must now aim, but we must surely attain it."

This language from the most pacifically inclined of my colleagues shows to what a pitch the most moderate spirits had risen. What would he not have said, what would not our other colleagues have said in accord with him, especially Gramont, if, in defiance of all

---

[1] Chevandier was not aware, when he wrote, of the circumstances I have narrated. When he learned of them, later, he considered that I was not to be blamed. [Note of M. Ollivier in vol. xiv, p. 237.]

conventions, I had, on my own authority, declared to the Chamber that I regarded the difficulty as solved by a despatch that still remained an enigma? I was not even tempted to do it, and I went to the Tuileries at three o'clock to confer with the Emperor.

As I passed through the lobby, I met Thiers. "I saw," he himself has said, "M. Ollivier hastening toward me; he said, 'Yes, we have succeeded; we have obtained what we wanted, peace is assured.' M. Ollivier's joy was extreme and was displayed without concealment."

I gave him the despatch to read. He said to me, "Now you must keep calm." — "Never fear," I replied, "we have peace in our grasp, we shall not let it escape."[1]

The Emperor was in the antechamber, surrounded by his officers and chatting familiarly with them; he was saying, with an accent of sincerity which impressed them: "It is a vast relief to me. I am very happy that it has all ended thus. A war is always a great risk."

The usher announced: "M. Émile Ollivier is at his Majesty's service."

"I am coming," said the Emperor; and he came out. He seemed to me, in truth, highly content, but yet a little uneasy: content because he considered the Hohenzollern affair completely adjusted; uneasy be-

[1] Thiers's deposition in the Inquiry concerning the 4th of September. It is not true that it was necessary to run through all the halls of the Palais Législatif to get hold of the despatch, because it had been passed from hand to hand. I did not let it go out of my hand for an instant, and I read it word for word only to those deputies who surrounded me and Thiers. To the others I simply told what it contained. It is impossible for Thiers, even when he tells the truth, not to mingle some inaccuracy with it. [Note of M. Ollivier in vol. xiv, p. 238.]

cause of the disappointment which the country would feel at not fighting out its quarrel with Prussia to the end.

I gave him the reasons for my silence in the Chamber, and asked him if it was really by the King's command, despite his repeated refusals to Benedetti, that the withdrawal had· been obtained. Without entering into details, the Emperor informed me that the withdrawal was due to the initiative of Olozaga *alone*, acting of his own motion, without Prim's knowledge, but with his, the Emperor's, sanction.

"In that case," I replied, "it would be most hazardous to boast, even indirectly, of a concession on the part of the King of Prussia. The satisfaction that we might afford public opinion by such an erroneous assurance would not last long: Bismarck would give us the lie brutally, and the affair, which seems to be at an end, would begin anew. Moreover, if Olozaga has acted without orders from his government, who can say how his initiative will be received at Madrid? And who knows what, in face of this surprise, will be the language of the King of Prussia, who, thus far, has made no reply to our requests?"

The Emperor acknowledged the good sense of these suggestions. I added that I could not present to the Chamber as an official communication what Olozaga had communicated to me: Olozaga was not the ambassador of Prince Antony, but of the Spanish government; nothing from him was official except what he communicated in the name of his government. Prince Antony's telegram was not, strictly speaking, anything more than the act of a private individual; it was without official character. In that state of things, an announcement would be untimely and might become dangerous. We were surrounded by obscurities; we were uninformed as to the intentions of Berlin and those of Madrid; was it not our only prudent course to wait? Sometimes one is suddenly surrounded by a dense fog in a mountain path, on the brink of a precipice. What does one do? One halts until the fog has disappeared. Gramont, as the result of his conference with Werther, might be able to inform us of the purposes of King William; at any moment Olozaga might receive a reply from Madrid. Before we had received and considered those necessary elements of a decision, it would be imprudent to enter into any discussion.

The Emperor adopted this point of view, and it was agreed that *nothing* should be decided before the meeting of the Council at Saint-Cloud at nine o'clock the next morning.[1]

Nigra[2] followed me. The Emperor had sent for him. He handed him the copy of Prince Antony's despatch to Olozaga. Nigra read it and heartily congratulated the sovereign. "It is a great moral victory for France, and the more precious in that it has been won without shedding human blood; and I hope that the Emperor is satisfied with it, and that he has summoned me here in order to announce peace."

"Yes, it is peace," the Emperor replied, "and I sent for you that you might telegraph your government to that effect. I have not had time to write to the King. I am well aware that public opinion in France, in its present excited state, would have preferred another solution — war; but I realize that the with-

[1] [This agreement, as will appear, was broken by one of the parties.]
[2] [Italian Ambassador to France.]

drawal is a satisfactory solution, and that it removes every pretext for war — at least, for the moment."[1]

Thus the Emperor seemed determined to content himself with the withdrawal of the candidacy, pure and simple, and had made no allusion to guaranties to be demanded of the King of Prussia.

Le Bœuf coming up, the Emperor spoke to him to the same effect, and so emphatically that when the marshal returned to his department he assembled his chiefs of bureaus, informed them that peace was assured, and ordered them to put a stop to all extraordinary expenses. Our military attaché at Vienna, Colonel Bouillé, who was then on leave of absence and under orders to return to his post with all speed, on going to the department to take leave of the minister, was informed by him that the affair was settled and that he might defer his departure. Lastly, MacMahon was ordered to suspend the embarkation of troops in Africa.

Gramont, being closeted in his private office, knew nothing of all these agitations and pourparlers and goings and comings. Foreseeing, from the advices he had received, that the candidacy was about to be withdrawn spontaneously, without the King's command or advice, he telegraphed to Benedetti confidentially: —

"Exert all your skill, I will say even your cunning, in arranging to have the Prince's withdrawal announced, communicated, or transmitted to us by the King of Prussia or his government. It is of the utmost importance to us; the King's participation must at any

---

[1] "On receipt of Nigra's telegram reporting this conversation, Victor Emanuel, who had returned to Turin [*Florence?*] from a hunting trip, went back to the mountains." *L'Empire Libéral*, vol. xiv, p. 241.

price be sanctioned by him or else be shown to result from the facts in some tangible way."[1]

He no longer demanded the direct and explicit participation of the King; he would be content with an indirect participation, implied by the King's trans-

[1] [This despatch is given by Gramont (p. 103), as having been sent at 1.40 P.M. on the 12th. Benedetti (p. 365) gives 2.15 P.M. as the hour at which it was sent. Benedetti, too, in his version, omits the phrase, "I will even say your cunning" (*je dirai même votre adresse*), and substitutes "satisfactory" (*suffisante*) for "tangible" (*saissante*) in the last clause. Gramont, while attributing these variances to some unintentional error in deciphering the despatch, considers them of importance. "The omission of the words, *je dirai même votre adresse*, does not change the meaning, it is true, but it lessens the urgency, if I may so express it, for it is evident that a phrase so confidential, so foreign to the regular customs, was used only under the influence of a very earnest desire to reach a pacific solution. . . . The second error in the text as given by Comte Benedetti is more serious, for it tends to modify considerably the sense and the scope of his instructions. . . . By the use of the word *suffisante*, the King's participation, and the extent to which it should be manifested, were made in some measure a matter of opinion, and instructions of that sort left to the agent a certain zone of freedom of action, within which he was at liberty to determine at what point his idea of the dignity of his country and of her legitimate interest should establish the limit of a 'satisfactory participation.' On the other hand, by using the word *saissable*, the government's purpose was clearly enunciated. It was not a question of opinion, but one of fact. Two persons may differ in opinion when it is a question of deciding whether a result is satisfactory or unsatisfactory; there can be no difference of opinion when it is a question of deciding whether a result rests upon facts — whether it is tangible (*saissable*) or not" (pp. 105, 106). He also berates Benedetti for publishing this despatch, which he (Gramont) had marked "Most confidential."

The most interesting question connected with the despatch is, whether it was sent before or after Gramont had learned of the telegram from Sigmaringen announcing Prince Antony's withdrawal of the candidacy in his son's name. Without explicitly so stating, he makes impossible any other inference than that he did not know of the withdrawal when he sent the despatch, because he speaks of it (p. 114) as being rendered useless by the withdrawal. But most of the historians of the war assume that the despatch was sent after he had heard the news. Delord says bluntly, without, however, giving his authority, that he had known it since the morning (vol. vi, p. 165), and wonders why he had not telegraphed it to Benedetti. Lehaut-

mission of the Prince's withdrawal, accompanied by a few gracious words. Such indirect participation on the part of the King was assured, without the necessity of employing either skill or cunning.

This excellent despatch which, had it been the last one sent, would have closed the crisis to our honor, had scarcely gone on its way when Gramont in his turn received, at the hands of a messenger of the Department of the Interior, a copy of the despatch from Prince Antony to Olozaga. He did not welcome the news with delight equal to mine. I had seen therein simply the vanishing of the candidacy, caring but little for the manner of its vanishing; he was particularly impressed by the form, and in the direct notification by Prince Antony to Prim, he detected a purpose to dodge the King's indirect participation. From that moment the complete agreement that had hitherto existed between us came to an end: he continued to attach the greater importance to this participation of the King, which in my eyes was a secondary matter.[1]

court (vol. i, p. 264, n. 1) appeals to the regular practice in relation to political telegrams to prove that Gramont must have had a copy of Prince Antony's despatch at almost the same time that it was handed to Olozaga. Of course, if Gramont sent this despatch, urging Benedetti to exert himself to the utmost to the end that the withdrawal should be announced, transmitted, or communicated by the King, after he knew of the withdrawal, it is perfectly clear that the demand of guaranties was not the result of the withdrawal but of the Duvernois interpellation, in which the subject of guaranties was first mentioned in the Chamber. Both La Gorce (vol. vi, p. 259) and Sorel (vol. i, p. 127) characterize the despatch as wise and judicious, and regret that circumstances soon led Gramont to modify his language.

M. Ollivier, it will be noticed, says that a copy of the telegram had just been handed to Gramont when his interview with Werther began.]

[1] [See Gramont, p. 113, for the meaning which that minister read into Prince Antony's despatch. To say the least, his interpretation is somewhat strained.]

This new fact had just been disclosed to him when Werther appeared for his audience (at a quarter to three). As the interview was beginning, a note from Olozaga was handed to Gramont, urgently requesting to be received at once on a matter of the very greatest importance. Werther was good enough to go into an adjoining room, so that Gramont could receive Olozaga. The Spanish Ambassador, showing Gramont the despatch from Prince Antony, congratulated him on that solution of the difficulty.

Gramont made a cold response to his felicitations. In his judgment, he said, the withdrawal in that form, far from advancing our affairs, complicated them: not a word of France, not a word of Prussia — the whole thing was between the Prince of Hohenzollern and Spain. The text of the despatch would offend public sentiment: it seemed to imply that France by her demands had dealt a blow at the independence of the Spanish people.

Engrossed by these ideas, he resumed the interview with Werther. He tried to obtain from him an admission that the King had not been a stranger to the withdrawal. In that case, the situation would take care of itself; he would be able to make, without contradiction, the declaration that the Emperor felt to be necessary. But Werther would not lend himself to that artifice: he declared, in a tone that admitted of no doubt, that "the withdrawal unquestionably emanated from Prince Leopold on his own initiative." And he repeated that everlasting clap-trap, of which our readers must have had their fill, about the distinction between the King and the head of the family, about the impossibility of the King's refusing his sanction from the moment that the Prince accepted the crown, and about the King's conviction that, considering the ties between the Hohenzollern family and Napoleon III, the candidacy could not be offensive to France.

Gramont patiently refuted the sophistries of Prussian bad faith, mentioned the Belgian and Greek precedents, and so forth, and said emphatically that the Emperor regarded the Hohenzollerns, not as relations more or less distant to whom he had shown kindness, but as Prussian princes, officers, subjects, who had been made use of to disturb and humiliate his country, and that to recall that relationship was to wound him.

"You say that the King has never intended to be offensive and to give umbrage to France; I do not doubt it, since you say so; but why should not the King say so to us himself? Why should he not write a friendly letter to the Emperor, in which, while associating himself with the Prince's withdrawal, he would say that we have mistakenly interpreted the origin and exaggerated the results of the candidacy; that he attaches too much value to friendly relations between our countries not to desire that, with the abandonment of the candidacy, all misunderstanding and every subject of offence may disappear?"

And he developed his ideas in a note, the terms of which, having been hardly considered at all, were simply a rough draft *ad memoriam* and not a diplomatic note to be despatched. "By authorizing Prince Leopold to accept the Spanish crown, the King did not consider that he was dealing a blow at the interests or the dignity of France. His Majesty associates himself with the Prince's withdrawal, and expresses his wish that every cause of misunderstanding be-

EFFECT AT PARIS 209

tween his government and the Emperor's may disappear."[1]

In using this language, Gramont had no purpose to commit the gross impropriety of demanding a letter of apology. One does not demand an apology from a king who is at the same time a gentleman, when one is one's self a gentleman and has honorable instincts. He knew that the King would have replied to such an impertinence by sending to the frontier under escort the ambassador who was instructed to present it, and by ordering his army to be mobilized. His sincerely pacific purpose, the respect with which he spoke of the King while expressing his own sentiments forcibly, made it impossible for Werther to believe for an instant that his suggestion was intended offensively. Werther would have cut the interview short had he been talking with a man bent upon humiliating his sovereign; for while he displayed a most conciliatory disposition, he did not fail to maintain the point of view of his government with invincible dignity.

[1] [See Gramont, pp. 115-127, for his account of the interview, and his refutation of the claim that he demanded that the King write a letter of apology, pp. 122-124. Gramont says that he gave Werther a copy of the proposed letter to be written by the King. Neither Gramont nor his colleague "seems to have realized that kings, especially kings puffed up by recent victories, do not like to have models of letters whispered to them, that an artful interpretation might easily, at Berlin or at Ems, characterize as excuses what were in fact merely conciliatory forms of speech, and that in that way a pretext would be supplied for arousing German susceptibility." La Gorce, vol. vi, pp. 262, 263. This, of course, was exactly what Bismarck did. See his note to Count Bernstorff, Prussian Ambassador to England, dated July 18, in *Further Correspondence respecting the War between France and Prussia*, No. 3 (1870), p. 5 (Appendix H. *infra*). "Both Ministers demanded that His Majesty the King should write an apologetic letter to the Emperor Napoleon, the publication of which might pacify the excited feelings in France."]

Gramont, then, made no demand; he suggested an expedient, for the Ambassador's opinion, and in that expedient there was nothing novel or unusual. The Emperor had himself set the chivalrous example which Gramont would have had the King of Prussia follow: after the insertion in the *Journal Officiel*, at the time of Orsini's assault, of the address of the colonels, did he not authorize the English Ambassador, Cowley, to say to Queen Victoria, that he would send Malakoff, the greatest soldier in the army, to London, to atone for the offence caused by the address of the officers of the army? With the purpose of dissipating the distrust rife on all sides since the Italian War, did he not write a public apologetic letter to Persigny (July 25, 1860), and assert his desire to live in the utmost cordiality with all his neighbors, and especially with Germany? Did he not request an interview with the Regent of Prussia and with the German princes assembled at Baden, and did he not make the proposition — much more weighty than a mere friendly letter — to carry his explanations there in person? At the time of the Luxembourg affair, did not his minister disavow *ad nauseam* "all purpose to offend and anger Prussia"?

At that moment (half-past three) I arrived at the Foreign Office.[1] I was told that the interview with

[1] Gramont seems to fix my arrival at three o'clock [he does not say so]; he erroneously assumes (p. 125) that I came directly from the Chamber, which I had left about three. He forgets that, before going to him, I had had a conference with the Emperor at the Tuileries, which had required at least half an hour. [Note of M. Ollivier in vol. xiv, p. 247. Gramont says that the Ambassador was announced about quarter to three, and that it was about half-past three when he went away. "In less than an hour, M. de Gramont had changed his policy, devised new expedients, conceived the

Werther was still in progress. I sent in my name. Gramont came out to me; we posted each other in a few hasty words, then I followed him into his private office. Thereupon the interview changed its character. It ceased to be official, as it had been before, and became one of those unreserved conversations in which public men indulge when they are not acting in an official rôle, and in which they may exchange ideas, without binding themselves, and, *a fortiori*, without binding their governments: "conversations which could not be forbidden without making impossible the familiar relations which facilitate good understandings between ministers and governments."[1]

Werther seemed to me uneasy, excited, depressed. He let slip this remark, which he was careful not to remember in his report: "Ah, if I had been with the King this unfortunate business wouldn't have been undertaken!" — "Most unfortunate, in very truth," I replied, "in its future consequences even more than in itself, since it seems now to be at an end, or, at least, in a fair way to settlement. It's the state of mind that is certain to endure in this country after the solution is known, that disturbs me. The tranquillization which I was working hard to accomplish is in danger: instead of a public opinion resigned to the result, we shall be confronted by an irritated public opinion; the Hohenzollern question is relegated to the second place, and people are talking about demanding guaranties from Prussia for

idea of a letter from the King of Prussia to the Emperor, made a draft of such a letter — three quarters of an hour had sufficed for him to receive two ambassadors, confer with his colleague, reflect, and decide!" Sorel, vol. i, p. 133.]

[1] Palmerston to his brother, Jan. 22, 1842.

the faithful execution of the Treaty of Prague. Shall we be strong enough to check this movement? Already we are called too conciliatory, and the war party is preparing to take the management of affairs out of our hands. As the duke says, King William would render an inestimable service to our two countries and to the whole world if, by a spontaneous act of friendship, he should reëstablish the cordial relations which he himself has disturbed. By strengthening our hands as ministers, he would afford us the means of pursuing our labors in behalf of peace."

Thus no more after my arrival than before was there question of any demand of a nature to change the character of the negotiation. How could I have allowed myself to make such a demand? How could I have failed to stop Gramont, if he had made it, when I had agreed with the Emperor, only a few moments before, that we would postpone *any decision* until the Council should meet in the morning at nine o'clock? There are certain impossibilities, logical and moral, which are in themselves proofs. I did, it is true, approve Gramont's suggestion; but that suggestion, not having been approved by the Emperor or by the Council, was entirely a personal matter and had no sort of official weight. It is manifest that, if we had demanded a letter of apology from the King, through Werther, we should immediately have renewed our demand through Benedetti, and he would have become the natural conduit of this new requisition, as he already was of the others. Gramont did not communicate this suggestion to our agent, even by way of information, and he would most assuredly not have failed to do so, trained as he was in diplomatic methods, if it had had any real importance.[1] It matters little that Werther, an honorable but dull-witted person, may have made mistakes in repeating, in a hurried report, what he thought that he understood and what he did not understand. I have not to consider that report. Bismarck said many a time, and common sense had said it before he did, that it is impossible to hold a minister responsible for the words, more or less accurate, which a foreign ambassador puts in his mouth. He is bound only by what he has himself said or done.

The fact is that there is no official despatch of our government in existence demanding a letter of apology from the King. Moreover, Gramont formally contradicted Werther's version in a circular note,[2] and I corroborate his contradiction by my own. Will any truly patriotic Frenchman prefer the assertion of an enemy many times convicted of falsehood to those of the ministers of his own country whose veracity has never been impugned? This transformation of a sincere suggestion looking toward peace into an unblushing and insulting machination; this repre-

[1] Gramont did not inform Benedetti. The fair interpretation of his omission is that there was no reason for doing so, since he had put forward no new demand. — "No," certain historians say, "it was from heedlessness." Who, pray, gives you the right to speak thus of a minister who in this very matter adjusted his conduct so vigorously to the rules of the profession by keeping Benedetti posted concerning all the incidents that were likely to be of advantage to him in his negotiation? [Note of M. Ollivier in vol. xiv, p. 251. The balance of this paragraph and the whole of the next one do not appear in *L'Empire Libéral*.

The result of the failure to advise Benedetti of the interview with Werther is referred to in Appendix I, "The Ems Negotiation."]

[2] [For Werther's report of the interview, and for Gramont's circular here referred to, see *infra*, Appendix J.]

senting a suggestion of a friendly letter as a demand for a letter of apology, is one of the most outrageous slanders in the whole legend of falsehood manufactured by low-lived historians. Only malicious imbecility can persist in prating of letters of apology. With creatures of that stamp one does not argue, but confines one's self to the classic retort: *Mentiris impudentissime.*[1]

We left Werther at four o'clock. Gramont started for Saint-Cloud. When we parted it was understood, as it had been with the Emperor, that we would come to no decision until the Council the next morning. As I returned to the department I met, on the bridge, Pessard, editor of the *Gaulois*, distinguished for its virulent articles. I told him that I considered his scolding absurd, and I earnestly requested him, now that there was no longer a Hohenzollern candidacy, not to go on with it. And I used the same language to all the newspaper men whom I met on the road.

[1] See Welschinger, vol. i, pp. 80, 81, for an argument in opposition to M. Ollivier's views as to the character of the Werther interview.

CHAPTER XIII

THE DEMAND OF GUARANTIES

ON leaving the Tuileries the Emperor was calm and composed. Bourbaki, the aide-de-camp on duty, who accompanied him, said to him: "Shall I have my warhorses saddled, Sire?" "Not so fast, general," was the reply. "Suppose that an island suddenly appears between France and Spain; both claim it; it disappears; what is there for them to go on quarrelling about?"[1]

Nevertheless the Emperor was impressed by the extraordinary acclamations which arose as he passed, and which were manifestly a warlike demonstration. At Saint-Cloud he found himself in an even more highly charged atmosphere. At the court, the Right predominated, and the war party; the only protest came from Bachon, the equerry. "I can't understand," he said, "how a man can think of war when he can no longer sit a horse."[2]

The Empress, who also was convinced that France had been sick ever since Sadowa, had taken the course, after the temporary depression mentioned by Marshal Vaillant, of listening eagerly to the party which gave her promises of victory. General Bourbaki, an excellent judge in the matter of warfare and of martial valor,

[1] General Bourbaki, as quoted by one of his orderlies.
[2] [The Emperor's physical condition is discussed at length by M. Ollivier in vol. xv of *L'Empire Libéral*, pp. 136 ff.]

and thoroughly acquainted with the Prussian army, lavished encouraging assurances upon her. "We have eight chances out of ten in our favor," he said.

The plebiscite had placed the solidity of the dynasty beyond attack, but it had not restored the preponderance of France. If war was no longer of importance to the dynasty, it was still of importance to the nation, and the Empress deemed it to be the Emperor's duty to retrieve our prestige, especially as he could no longer be suspected of being influenced by dynastic interests.

On her husband's arrival, she hastened to question him.

"Well," he said, "it seems to be all over."

Faces grew dark. The Emperor explained. They listened to him incredulously, and repeated the current phrase: "The country will not be satisfied." When the news spread among the staff of the château, disappointment burst forth as in the Corps Législatif. "The Empire is lost!" came from all sides. "It's a disgrace!" cried the Empress; "the Empire will fall like a card house!" General Bourbaki, who was the most excited of all, unbuckled his sword, laid it on the billiard table, and said: "If that is true, I refuse to serve."

The text of the Duvernois interpellation was handed to the Emperor: he divined its malevolent purpose and condemned it; nevertheless he recognized therein the expression of a public demand with which it would perhaps be difficult not to comply.[1]

---

[1] [See Gramont, pp. 128 ff.; La Gorce, vol. vi, pp. 264–266; Welschinger, vol. i, p. 81; Sorel, vol. i, p. 134. Such vague references as this in the text to the influence of the Empress at this critical moment are about all that one

Napoléon III
1808–1873

THE DEMAND OF GUARANTIES 217

At this juncture Gramont appeared. He told of Werther's exasperating evasions, of his declaration that the King had absolutely nothing to do with the withdrawal; he pointed out the palpable inadequacy of Prince Antony's act. Thereupon the Emperor forgot that any definite resolution had been postponed to the next day's Council, and, says Gramont, "a conscientious discussion was at once opened."[1]

finds in the various accounts of the preliminaries of the war. La Gorce (see the next note) is rather more explicit than others. The fact that the Empress is still living doubtless counts for much in this reticence.

In his justificatory volume, so frequently cited, Gramont says: "Nevertheless the idea of that interpellation of Duvernois was so clearly responsive to the feeling of the majority in Parliament and to that of the public, of whom almost the entire press made itself the vigorous interpreter, that it was impossible not to heed it." Sorel comments thus on the statement that the majority in Parliament were in sympathy with the substance of the interpellation: "This is a delicate point to handle. M. Thiers and M. de Gramont contradict each other, and both tell the truth. We must not forget that the majority consisted of official candidates, timid, reserved men, accustomed to a halting pace, very deferential to the court, exceedingly ignorant of European affairs and of things military, every one of them having an old-fashioned substratum of Chauvinism, easy to stir up, and above all, a solid foundation of prudence which caused them to dread losing the favors of the master and the public by showing too little patriotism. They were surprised by the declaration of July 6, carried off their feet by the Cabinet, intoxicated by the uproar of the newspapers, terrified by the absolutist Bonapartists; they would have preferred peace but they said so only in the lobbies." Sorel, vol. i, p. 135 n.]

[1] [Gramont's exact words are (p. 130): "I pass over in silence the conscientious discussions which preceded the decision *which the government felt it to be its duty to make.*" This implies, to say the least, that the decision was the decision of the ministry, and not of himself and the Emperor and the Emperor's *entourage*. Gramont's silence "deprives history of the principal source upon which it might have drawn," says La Gorce (vol. vi, p. 265). "Momentous as was the crisis, it is certain that there was no official deliberation.... M. de Gramont remained only a short time at the Château, barely an hour, for we know that at seven o'clock he was back on Quai d'Orsay sending his despatches.... He speaks of 'conscientious discussions which preceded the decision.' In the absence of ministers, who were

Who took part in that discussion? I know only those who were not invited: they were: the Minister of War, who, having been assured of peace, had stopped his preparations, and whose responsibility, none the less, might well become so heavy; the Keeper of the Seals, who bore almost alone the burden of public discussion in the Chambers; the Minister of the Interior, who was especially familiar with the movements of public opinion; the Minister of Finance, who was keeping watch on the fluctuations of the credit of the State; in a word, no member of the Cabinet save the Minister of Foreign Affairs.[1]

The result of the discussion was the following despatch to Benedetti, which Gramont went off at once to send (at seven in the evening):—

"We have received by the hand of the Spanish Ambassador the withdrawal by Prince Antony, in the

the non-official friends admitted to proffer their opinions? A silence, hitherto impenetrable, has shrouded this confabulation, and, although we know the resolutions that resulted from it, we are still unable to apportion the responsibility. All the probabilities authorize us to believe that a preponderating influence was that of the Empress. What other could have been powerful enough to change the Emperor's mind as by a sudden blow? M. de Gramont's absolute reserve of itself leaves one to conjecture a feeling of delicacy toward an august person, whom an honorable loyalty forbids him to unmask and call by name." (But Lord Malmesbury declares that the same Gramont, in conversation with him, threw all the blame on the Empress. *Memoirs of an Ex-Minister*, p. 665.) Lehautcourt, vol. i, p. 274 n., cites several contradictory statements attributed to Gramont, concerning the Emperor's attitude toward the withdrawal, and quotes Beust's comment, that these inconsistencies were due to the duke's mobile imagination.]

[1] [The four ministers referred to are Le Bœuf (War), Ollivier himself (Keeper of the Seals), Chevandier (Interior), and Segris (Finance). "'On July 12, the cabinet was not consulted' (unpublished letter from Segris to Plichon, March 5, 1871). The manuscript correspondence and narratives of Louvet and Plichon agree perfectly with M. Segris's statement." La Gorce, vol. vi, p. 265 n. And see Delord, vol. vi, p. 165; Lehautcourt, vol. i, pp. 277, 278.]

THE DEMAND OF GUARANTIES 219

name of his son Leopold, of the latter's candidacy for the throne of Spain. In order that this withdrawal by Prince Antony may have its full effect, it seems necessary *that the King of Prussia should associate himself with it, and should give us an assurance that he will not again sanction that candidacy.* You will go at once to the King to ask from him a declaration to this effect, which he cannot refuse if he is in truth actuated by no secret motive. Despite the withdrawal, which is now known to all, the public excitement is so great that we do not know whether we shall succeed in controlling it. Make a paraphrase of this despatch which you can communicate to the King. Reply as quickly as possible."[1]

This is what is known as the demand of guaranties.

There was no question therein of the Emperor's consent to write the letter of apology which Gramont is alleged to have demanded of Werther a few moments before. A letter of apology would have implied simply a disavowal of the past, whereas the demand of guaranties exacted a promise for the future.[2]

This ill-advised despatch neutralized the judicious one sent at twenty minutes to two. It was not content with the avowed participation of the King in the present incident, but demanded a promise in view of certain problematic future occurrences, and plunged

[1] [See Gramont, p. 131; Benedetti, p. 370; La Gorce, vol. vi, pp. 267, 268; Sorel, vol. i, pp. 135, 136; Delord, vol. vi, p. 165. Delord reads into the despatch an injunction to Benedetti to be particularly discreet, because Gramont "dreams of an unhoped-for triumph for the Empire, and wishes to take the credit all to himself."]

[2] [The last two sentences were added by M. Ollivier in the present volume. See *infra* p. 235 n., for a probable explanation of the addition.]

us anew into the perils from which, but for it, we were sure of coming safely forth. What need was there to rush matters thus? What danger was to be feared, that we could not await patiently a reply from Madrid and Berlin which was certain to arrive in a few hours, and which would have brought us sufficient satisfaction? But the Right did not propose that the affair should have a peaceful ending.[1] This demand of guaranties was, as we have seen from Duvernois's interpellation, which preceded it, conceived by the Right. At the outset, joining its voice with that which arose from every French heart against the challenging candidacy, it assumed that we could not assent to it and that Prussia would not withdraw it. As soon as the prospect of a withdrawal appeared, it changed its tone, and we heard the same men who had deemed the Hohenzollern candidacy so threatening that its success would have been our ruin, affect to regard it as merely a secondary matter, much exaggerated, at which we had been wrong to take fright, unless we were determined to seek therein a favorable opportunity to settle our permanent quarrel with Prussia. I had called the Emperor's attention to this movement when it began to manifest itself, and I had opposed it with unbending determination.[2]

The Right, not hoping to overcome my opposition, attacked me savagely, tooth and nail. I was accused of lacking courage, patriotism, and foresight. The *Pays* and the *Public* put forth the most offensive in-

[1] ["But this solution [Prince Leopold's withdrawal] upset the schemes of the ambitious courtiers, who recoiled from no folly in order to gratify their passions." Jules Favre, *Gouvernement de la Defénse Nationale*, p. 11.]
[2] [*Supra*, p. 164.]

THE DEMAND OF GUARANTIES

sinuations.[1] But all that outpouring of wrath did not move me. Gramont, by the agreements he had made with Lyons and myself, the Emperor, by his assent to Gramont's promises, were as much bound as I was not to enlarge the field of discussion. Thereupon the

[1] [M. Ollivier omits here some of the details of the journalistic attacks upon him of which he tells in his larger work.] "Forgetting that Olozaga was as ignorant of the Hohenzollern candidacy as I was myself, the *Pays* [Paul de Cassagnac] wrote: 'When M. Olozaga came coquetting about Place Vendôme and offering his Golden Fleeces, he knew doubtless that vanity intoxicates and confuses men's brains. And if the eyes of our rulers were closed and blinded, it was perhaps some *grand cordon* of the order of Noble Dames that served them as a bandage.' Rouher's *Public* was even more venomous. Violent party men are dishonorable men — of course, I do not refer to their private lives. Luckily they are, in general, stupid, which fact corrects and paralyzes their villainy. Thus Dréolle manufactured out of the whole cloth a conversation that I was supposed to have had with a deputy. In the first part he makes me say that I desired peace, that I realized the necessity therefor, and that I knew to what certain disaster a warlike policy would expose the country. And then, abruptly, from these premises, he makes me conclude that, during my brief interim service at the Foreign Office, I had read through our diplomatic files, and that the flush of shame had risen to my brow: I had seen France degraded, the Emperor on his knees before Europe, and I had said to myself: 'We must have a war — war alone can set us up again.' And I added: 'We were awaiting only an excuse or an opportunity: the Hohenzollern affair comes in the nick of time!' It was my custom never to reply to personal attacks, and that course was all the easier for me because I never read any newspaper except the revolutionary sheets, which I was watching very closely. Surely if there ever was a fable to which silent disdain appeared to me to be the only fitting reply, it was Dréolle's. . . . But the press service in the Department of the Interior . . . took alarm at the article and stirred up Chevandier, and the editor of the *Patrie*, who received C.'s confidential communications as Mitchell did mine, came to me and begged me to authorize him to contradict it. I made an exception to my rule and consented, and Dréolle had his shame to show for it." *L'Empire Libéral*, vol. xiv, pp. 256–258.

[See further, concerning the attitude of the press at this moment, Lehautcourt, vol. i, pp. 273, 274 and note; especially a long extract from Paul de Cassagnac's article in the *Pays* of July 13. Also, Gramont, pp. 128, 129, citing Fernand Giraudeau's *La Vérité sur la Campagne de 1870*.]

Right had the infernal adroitness not to meet face to face a resistance which it was sure that it could not overcome: it abandoned all talk of the Treaty of Prague, and set to work to envenom the Hohenzollern question, which we could not refuse to discuss. It shrewdly seized upon what there was open to criticism in the withdrawal: the English newspapers commented on its peculiar form; it was made by the father for the son, and the *Standard* called it "this curious proceeding"; the *Times* was amazed that the name of Prince Leopold himself appeared nowhere, "although he is of age, thirty-five years old, and has taken an active part in the whole affair. It remains to be seen," it added, "how far the young Prince will consider himself bound by his father's action."

"Père Antoine," said the Right, "is fooling us as truly as Prince Augustenbourg did." On November 30, 1852, the head of the Augustenbourg family, in consideration of a million and a half double rix-thalers, had renounced for himself and his son, on his honor and faith as a prince, all his rights in the Duchies; his son none the less laid claim to the succession, at the same time retaining the sum of money received; and when the validity of his claim was contested, he replied: "What! my rights not valid! why, I have already sold them, and they are still good!"[1]

Luckily the members of the Right did not know that Prince Antony had renounced the candidacy in his son's name only because Prince Leopold had at first refused to do it. They invoked some most specious

---

[1] [The claim of the younger Duke of Augustenbourg to the duchies of Schleswig and Holstein was supported by Austria and denied by Prussia in the negotiations and disputes preceding the War of 1866.]

THE DEMAND OF GUARANTIES 223

historical arguments; they quoted that weighty reflection of La Bruyère: "To think only of the present is a source of error in politics." That is why, they argued, serious-minded statesmen could never regard as terminated an affair apt by its very nature to be reopened, so long as the present solution was not supplemented by measures providing against its reopening in the future. They overwhelmed us with examples of cases whose immediate settlement had been made subordinate to a guaranty for the future. After a popular uprising, the Austrians, summoned by the Pope, had occupied the Legations: Casimir Périer at once sent troops to Ancona, and the Pope concluded to recognize this seizure of a city in his dominions on condition that it should be temporary, and that the French should withdraw from Ancona when the Austrians withdrew from Bologna. Nevertheless Thiers, then Minister of Foreign Affairs, subordinated the departure of our troops to *guaranties for the future*, in case of further Austrian intervention based upon new uprisings. His successor, Molé, having evacuated Ancona without obtaining such guaranties, Duchatel, Thiers, Guizot, and Broglie criticised him in Parliament.[1]

Palmerston subordinated the end of the Crimean War to the obtaining of "*guaranties for the future* against possible enterprises on the part of Russia." [2] Prussia and Germany persistently demanded from the Danish government *guaranties for the future* in favor of Germans settled in the Duchies.

If, in 1869, when the Hohenzollern candidacy was

[1] At the session of the Chamber on Jan. 12, 1839.
[2] Letter of Lord Palmerston to Lord John Russell, March 28, 1855.

first mentioned, the Emperor, following the example of sober-minded statesmen, had not looked simply at the present, if he had taken hostages for the future, he would not have been taken by surprise by the Prussian-Spanish intrigue. He was blamed for that lack of foresight. Ought he to repeat that mistake, to leave open the possibility of a third claim? It was necessary, then, to make sure of the future by requesting from the King of Prussia, not only his approval of the withdrawal of the candidacy, but a formal guaranty that he would not authorize the princes to renew it.

These arguments, theoretically, were not devoid of justice. It is undeniable that, when an affair is smoothed over temporarily, it is prudent to forestall by guaranties a possible revival. But such was not the present case. The incident had had consequences so painful to all those who had been involved in it that no one could suspect them of being tempted to reopen it; and the King of Prussia, who had gone into it against his will, would surely never listen to it again.* Moreover, when one is considering whether to do or not to do a certain thing, it is not enough to consider the thing by itself: one must take into account the circumstances amid which it must be done. The King's acquiescence in the Emperor's demand would have produced consequences most unfortunate for him. If, to the withdrawal which, despite all contradictions, was attributed to him, he had added any promise whatsoever, there would have been a universal outcry against his humiliation; the perfidy of the Right consisted precisely in thus putting forth a claim to which it was impossible for our opponent to accede. The demand of guaranties could be interpreted only as a purpose to bring on war.[1]

Most of the leaders of the Right (it is proper always to do justice to the sincere) cared little for Spain or the Hohenzollerns or the future: the present alone interested them. Relying on the triumph which the generals promised them, they wanted a war which we did not want, in order to force us out of the government, to resume it themselves, and to fling the liberal régime into the gutter, like an old rag. They expected from the wrath of the King of Prussia the rejection of the demand of guaranties; they assumed that that rejection would embitter men's minds, and that the dispute, thus envenomed on both sides, would lead them, by that roundabout road, to war.

Between the bellicose propulsion of the Right, and the pacific policy of the Ministry, the Emperor oscillated, yielding by turn to one and the other of those forces. Did peace seem assured — he regretted the gratification that war would have afforded the country, and was conscious of a martial thrill. Did war seem imminent — he recoiled and fell back upon his real preference for peace. This time, by adopting the Right's demand of guaranties, it really seemed as if he had made up his mind for war; and as he was certain that he would obtain neither my assistance nor that of the Cabinet for that policy, he imposed it, by an exercise of his personal authority, upon the only one of his ministers who would lend himself to such a

[1] [This plain statement of the purpose of injecting into the discussion what Benedetti, in the Preface to his book (p. 7), rightly characterizes as "new claims which led us inevitably to war," constitutes as severe an indictment as any even of the most virulent critics of the ministry have presented in more violent language.]

disregard of the self-defensive rules of the parliamentary form of government.

Gramont was not thoroughly imbued with the requirements of that régime; he was still the ambassador accustomed to obey his sovereign's every command; in the utmost good faith, he had no conception that that was not the correct thing to do, and, although a parliamentary minister, he associated himself with an act destructive of parliamentary power.[1] On his part

[1] [In his book, Gramont, while discussing Benedetti's despatches from Ems of July 11, paves the way for the contention which was, so to speak, forced upon him by later developments, that the "demand of guaranties" was new, if at all, in form only, not in substance. "Abandoning," he says (p. 101), "any further requests for an initiative which there was no longer any possibility of obtaining, the government determined to seek in an indirect coöperation on the part of the King, in an apparent oneness of purpose, *the guaranties* which it had failed to obtain by his direct concurrence. Assuming that the Prince of Hohenzollern, without the King's command, without any suggestion from the King, should of his own motion abandon the candidacy and inform His Majesty of his purpose, the King, making himself the direct interpreter of his cousin's spontaneous decision, might himself announce the withdrawal, accompanying the announcement with a gracious word or two. The withdrawal, communicated by the King, would thus become an official act, the act of Prussia, and the French government would have found therein *the shadow of a guaranty* which, for love of peace, it would have magnified to the proportions of a satisfactory assurance. I do not know how far public opinion would have followed us in this direction; but this much is certain, that the government would have accepted it with no mental reservations. We would have said to the Chambers: 'The King of Prussia has informed us of Prince Leopold's withdrawal; it is from him that we learn of it, and we see in this act of the King a *guaranty* of the pacific sentiments of his government and of the importance which he attaches to the removal of all complications of a nature to disturb the peace." — And yet, in his interview with Werther, after he knew of Prince Antony's withdrawal of his son's candidacy, he did not even hint at guaranties for the future, but suggested that the King of Prussia should disclaim any purpose to offend France and express his regret for the misunderstanding. It seems clear enough that the passage quoted above was an afterthought, and that the "demand of guaranties" formulated in the despatch to Benedetti of July 12 at 7 P.M., was due to the influence of

THE DEMAND OF GUARANTIES

it was simply obedience, not warlike premeditation; on the Emperor's part, I am convinced that it was simply the compliant humor of weakness, not a determined stand for war. My familiarity with his mental processes, and with the readiness with which, refusing to be deterred by motives of self-esteem, he often retraced his steps if he had gone too far, convinces me that it was an afterthought that led him to change from the wise resolution of the Tuileries to the hastily conceived folly of Saint-Cloud: he said to himself that, after all, this demand of guaranties, which had not been expressed in the form of an ultimatum, was not of such a character that it could not be abandoned, if it were likely to lead to war. He forgot that, in critical situations, certain acts produce instant and irrevocable effects and drive one whither one does not wish to go.

Gramont was able to satisfy himself, upon his return to the department, of the way in which his despatch from Saint-Cloud was interpreted. Lyons having called upon him, Gramont did not conceal from him his objections to the insufficiency of Prince Antony's action, and the impossibility, in view of the excited state of public feeling, of closing the incident without obtaining some sort of satisfaction from the King of Prussia.

Lyons expressed his surprise. He pointed out that the situation was completely changed. "If war took place now, all Europe would say that it was the fault of

the Emperor's entourage, combined with the natural tendency of men not over-courageous to associate themselves with what seems to be an overwhelming public sentiment. M. de Gramont asserts that it was necessary for the ministers so to associate themselves, "if they would retain a chance of being able to restrain public sentiment on the safe side of a resort to arms " !]

France; that France plunged into it without any substantial cause, merely from pride and resentment. . . . If there should, at the first moment, be some disappointment felt here, in the Chamber and in the country, . . . the Ministry would in a very short time stand better with both if it contented itself with the diplomatic triumph it had achieved and abstained from plunging into war, for which there was certainly no avowable motive."

He dwelt especially on the assurances which he had been officially authorized to give to the Queen's government, that, *if the Prince would withdraw his candidacy, the affair would be at an end.* That was the language of common sense and of friendship.

Gramont admitted that he had authorized him to give that assurance, but on the condition, which Lyons forgot, that Prince Leopold should withdraw his candidacy *by the advice* of the King of Prussia. That advice would imply a tacit engagement that the candidacy would not be renewed; the King of Prussia had refused to proffer it, and caused us to be informed by his ambassador that he had nothing to do with the wholly spontaneous decision of Prince Antony. The result was that the guaranty upon which we relied, and to which we had subordinated the closing of the incident, had not been obtained.

While arguing thus Gramont overlooked his despatch of 1.40 P.M., in which, supposing the case of a withdrawal without the King's command or advice, he said that he would be satisfied with indirect participation in a spontaneous withdrawal; and he had no reason to believe, when he discharged his last despatch, that such participation would not appear. However,

THE DEMAND OF GUARANTIES 229

impressed by the Ambassador's comments, and wishing perhaps to prepare a way of retreat, he said to Lyons that the final decision would be made by the Council the next morning, and announced forthwith to the Chambers.[1]

[1] [In Lyons's report to Granville of this interview, dated July 12 (*Blue Book*, pp. 20, 21), there is no mention of Gramont's having admitted his previous assurance to Lyons, or of the unfulfilled condition that the withdrawal should be brought about by the King's advice; but Lyons had previously (July 10) quoted the minister as attaching such a condition. "M. de Gramont told me that I might report to your Lordship that if the Prince of Hohenzollern should now, on the advice of the King of Prussia, withdraw his acceptance of the Crown, the whole affair would be at an end." *Blue Book*, p. 17. In the despatch of the 12th from which M. Ollivier quotes, Lyons reports further that he pointed out to M. de Gramont that "one of the advantages of the former position of France was that the quarrel rested on a cause in which the feelings of Germany were very little concerned, and German interests not at all. Now Prussia might well expect to rally all Germany to resist an attack which could be attributed to no other motives than ill-will and jealousy on the part of France, and a passionate desire to humiliate her neighbor. In fact, I said, France would have public opinion throughout the world against her, and her antagonist would have all the advantage of being manifestly forced into the war in self-defence to repel an attack." Gramont himself does not mention this interview.

Acknowledging Lord Lyons's despatch, Earl Granville telegraphed on the 13th: "Her Majesty's Government learned with great concern, by your telegram of yesterday evening . . . that . . . the Duc de Gramont intimated to you that the French Government continued to be dissatisfied with the communications which they had received from the King of Prussia. . . . Under these circumstances Her Majesty's Government . . . feel bound to impress upon the Government of the Emperor the immense responsibility that would rest on France if she should seek to enlarge the grounds of quarrel by declining to accept the withdrawal by Prince Leopold of Hohenzollern of his candidature, as a satisfactory solution of the question."

See Lehautcourt, vol. i, pp. 282-284; Sorel, vol. i, pp. 137, 138.]

CHAPTER XIV

THE EMPEROR'S LETTER TO GRAMONT ON THE DEMAND OF GUARANTIES

I WAS not interested in what might come from Berlin or Ems. I was, on the other hand, most anxious concerning what was to arrive from Madrid, and I was in constant dread of some new villainy on the part of Prim. As Gramont very justly observed, Prince Antony's despatch was so conceived as to arouse public sentiment in Spain; one could detect therein a certain purpose to suggest that France was dealing a blow at the independence of that nation; one would have said that it was his intention to establish a close connection between his son's candidacy and the national pride of Spain. He said in effect: "If I should not withdraw my son's candidacy, the Spanish people might well take counsel only of their sentiment of independence, and his election would be assured. I withdraw it in order not to expose Spain to the necessity of defending her rights."[1] Would not the Spanish government, covertly incited by Prim, following the example of the Greeks after the declination of Prince Alfred, decide to disregard his action and proclaim Prince Leopold king, by way of asserting its national independence? And would not the Prince, who had not personally withdrawn, imitate the action of his brother Charles

[1] [This passage, beginning with "Prince Antony's despatch," is taken, substantially *in totidem verbis*, from Gramont, p. 113.]

in Roumania,[1] and land unexpectedly on the Spanish coast. Certain foreign correspondence so affirmed.

In the evening, with my wife on my arm, I walked to Quai d'Orsay, where the Spanish embassy then was. Olozaga was dining out. We waited some time for him, walking up and down the quay. He had received nothing from Madrid as yet, he said, but he encouraged me: he had no doubt that his initiative would be approved; if it should be disavowed, he should cease at once to be ambassador; he had so stated, and they would not dare to subject him to that embarrassment. He confirmed what the Emperor had told me as to the way in which the withdrawal had been brought about. "Despite our intimate relations," he said, "I told you nothing about it because the most absolute secrecy was the first condition of success. At my entreaty the Emperor maintained the same reserve." And he thereupon told me of his visit to the Tuileries during the Council that morning. To these confidences he added the most affectionate and most judicious advice. "Believe me, it's all over so far as we are concerned; the withdrawal will be accepted, the candidacy will not be renewed; do not be disturbed, do not be hasty in your decision, and it will all arrange itself."

Although it was late, after eleven o'clock, we went on to Gramont's office, his department being only a few steps away, so that I might repeat to him what

[1] [Charles of Roumania, by the way, had not once withdrawn; moreover, he was secretly supported in his enterprise by Napoleon III, as Prince Gortchakoff did not fail to remind the French Ambassador when the Spanish business was discussed by them. "At a not very distant date," he said, "another Prince of Hohenzollern was invited to reign over Roumania. Russia protested, but her protest awoke no echo." Fleury to Gramont, July 7; cited by La Gorce, vol. vi, p. 234.]

I had just heard from Olozaga's lips, and might learn if any information had come from Ems.

In reply to my question, Gramont handed me his seven o'clock despatch demanding guaranties. I had not finished reading it when an aide-de-camp was announced, bringing a letter from the Emperor. Gramont read it, then passed it to me. It was thus conceived: —

"PALACE OF SAINT-CLOUD,
"12 July, 1870.

"MY DEAR DUKE, — Upon reflecting on our conversations to-day, and upon rereading the despatch from 'Père Antoine,' as Cassagnac calls him,[1] I think that we must confine ourselves to making more emphatic the despatch which you were to send to Benedetti, bringing out the following facts: (1) We have had to do with Prussia, not with Spain; (2) Prince Antony's despatch addressed to Prim is an unofficial document so far as concerns us, which no one has been formally instructed to transmit to us; (3) Prince Leopold accepted the candidacy for the throne of Spain, and it is his father who renounces it; (4) Benedetti should insist therefore, as he has orders to do, upon a categorical response wherein the King should agree for the future not to allow Prince Leopold, who has made no promise to follow his brother's example and set out for Spain some fine day; (5) So long as we have no official communication from Ems, we are not supposed to have had any reply to our just demands; (6) So long as we have no such reply, we shall continue our armaments; (7) It is impossible, therefore, to make

[1] This clause is omitted in the Emperor's letter as given by Gramont [who has simply "Prince Antoine" (p. 136)]. I supply it because it indicates the inspiration of the letter. [Note of M. Ollivier in vol. xiv, p. 267.]

THE EMPEROR'S LETTER

any announcement to the Chambers until we are more fully informed.

"Accept, my dear Duke, the assurance of my sincere friendship."[1]

The explanation of this letter is as follows. During the evening certain members of the Right, among them Jérôme David and Cassagnac, had gone to Saint-Cloud. They had declared (which was quite true) that "Père Antoine's" withdrawal was the joke of the day in Paris; they had frightened the Emperor by representing the dangers and the ridicule to which he exposed himself by taking his pay in a derisory concession; they had pointed to the dissatisfaction of the army, the grumbling of the people, the hostile sneers of the opposition, our inevitable degradation in Europe; and they had threatened him with Gambetta's savage speech, of which the lobbies were talking. The Emperor, under the influence of their harangues, wrapping himself in his weakness, wrote to Gramont to "make more emphatic" the despatch he was to have sent to Benedetti. The interior impulsion of Saint-Cloud had led to the seven o'clock despatch; the external impulsion of the evening visitors dictated the letter to Gramont.[2]

However high one may have raised one's spirit above vulgar susceptibility, it is impossible not to feel treatment of a certain sort. To have agreed with the Emperor at three o'clock that no decision should be made until the Council of the next day, and to learn after eleven o'clock at night, by a mere chance, that

---

[1] ["To tell the truth," says Gramont (p. 137), "this letter simply summarized, while stating them more concisely, our earlier deliberations."]

[2] [See Von Sybel, English trans., vol. vii, pp. 373 ff.]

a momentous decision had been reached and put in execution without one's being consulted or even notified; to find one's self, when one arrives to finish an interrupted conversation, confronted by an accomplished fact of very great importance — therein was abundant justification for an explosion of harsh words. But I controlled my feelings. That letter of the Emperor — the first one marking out a line of conduct for the Ministry that had not been addressed to me — caused the demand of guaranties to appear to my eyes, not as the prompting of a colleague forgetful of the necessity of ministerial solidarity, but as an exercise of personal power to which Gramont had assented as a matter of professional habit. It was not to him but to the Emperor that I proposed to address my remonstrance.

But what to do at the present moment? I had not the power to demand of Gramont that he recall the seven o'clock despatch, sent in pursuance of an earlier order; nor could I forbid him to carry out the second order, which he had just received. The utmost that I could have done would have been to ask him to go with me to the Emperor, to the end that we might persuade him to withdraw his commands. If it had been in the daytime, I should not have failed to do it. But at midnight I could not think of it. Even if I had succeeded in reaching the Emperor, and had persuaded him to recall his instructions and not to recur to them, a large part of the night would have been employed in the process, and the countermand would not have reached Benedetti until he had executed the order. The thing was done irrevocably; I had but two courses to choose between; either to protest

THE EMPEROR'S LETTER

by resigning, or to exert myself to nullify the consequences of that step, which I was powerless to prevent.[1] Although deeply hurt, I thought it my duty first of all to take the latter course. I said to Gramont in a tone of deep distress: "You will be accused of hav-

[1] [I do not think it necessary to transcribe the comments of M. Welschinger on this portion of *L'Empire Libéral*. They may be found in the first volume of his book on the war on pages 83 ff. He seems to me both unnecessarily and unreasonably severe in his contemptuous strictures, especially in the argument that the alleged "letter of apology" which Gramont suggested to Werther that the King should write, was in fact a demand upon the King for guaranties for the future, and that M. Ollivier therefore, having strongly supported that suggestion, was estopped from objecting to the 7 o'clock despatch to Benedetti, because the latter was no more serious than the other. So far as I have discovered, no other serious writer, not even Taxile Delord, or Von Sybel, is inclined to question the sincerity of M. Ollivier's belief that peace was assured by the withdrawal of the candidacy, and of his chagrin when he discovered that a momentous step had been taken, not only without consultation with him or his colleagues, but in direct contravention of a distinct agreement with the Emperor and Gramont that nothing should be done before the Council to be held on the 13th.

Darimon, *Notes*, etc., pp. 75 ff., quotes M. Ollivier as saying in conversation, in 1879, that there was "a lively altercation" between him and Gramont, which ended only when the latter agreed to send a despatch softening the earlier one. Also that "by entering upon negotiations in that direction without the concurrence of his colleagues, the Foreign Minister was lacking in delicacy toward them, and especially toward me. Since he was giving a different turn to the negotiations, he should have informed me. The Emperor and the Duc de Gramont should have remembered that they were in the presence of a responsible Cabinet." Lehautcourt, vol. i, p. 278. "But I must add," says this author, "that on January 2, the Emperor had expressly reserved for himself the effective presidency of the Council and the appointment of the ministers of War, Marine and Foreign Affairs." *Ibid.*, n. 3.

"Very late in the evening M. Ollivier went to the Foreign Office. On learning of the instructions sent to Benedetti he concealed neither his amazement, nor his displeasure, nor his anxiety. Calmer than his colleagues, and unable to resign himself to throwing away the blessing of peace reëstablished, he tried to soften, at least in form, the demands of his government. . . . The step was a wise one and the intention meritorious; but the blow was struck, and God would not allow anything to check it or to lessen its force." La Gorce, vol. vi, p. 268.]

ing premeditated war, and of having regarded the Hohenzollern incident simply as a pretext for bringing it about. Do not emphasize your first despatch, as the Emperor bids you, but soften it. Benedetti will already have performed his mission when the softened version reaches him; but in the Chamber you will have in it an argument to confirm your pacific views."

Thereupon I sat down at a desk and wrote the two paragraphs following: —

"In order that we may be assured that the son will not disavow his father's withdrawal, and that he will not appear in Spain as his brother did in Roumania, it is indispensable that the King deign to say to us that he will not allow the Prince to disregard the withdrawal transmitted by Prince Antony.

"Do not fail to say to the King that we have no secret motive, that we are not seeking a pretext for war, and that we desire only to come forth with honor from a difficulty which we did not ourselves create."

The difference between this language and the other was considerable. It was rather a transformation than a mere softening; aside from the assurance of our pacific purpose, which did not appear in the first despatch, it contained a narrower demand of guaranties: the seven o'clock despatch called for a general guaranty as against all future contingencies; my language limited the guaranty to the present, and had in view only the event of Leopold's not confirming the

[It is needless to say that Gramont does not refer to any disagreement between himself and his colleague, or to any "softening" of the first despatch. He says simply (p. 137): "The Keeper of the Seals read the Emperor's letter, and we agreed to send to Comte Benedetti a second telegram more explicit than the first." And see Sorel, vol. i, p. 139.]

present withdrawal made by his father. Even if my friendly counsel should be mistakenly called collaboration, it is impossible to argue therefrom that I approved the demand that was hastily despatched without my knowledge. The former demand could not be accepted by the King, whereas it was almost certain that he would not reject the second.[1]

Having written the above lines, I rose, and as I had not as yet clearly discerned what course of action the momentous step that had just been disclosed to me called upon me to follow, I took my leave, perturbed and anxious.

Gramont thought my advice good, but he followed it only halfway. He added my language, which restricted the guaranty to the present case, to his earlier text, which demanded guaranties for the future, and thus the despatch that he sent to Benedetti after I left him contained a contradiction in terms.[2] However, as I had foreseen, the despatch, sent at 11.45 P.M. did not reach Benedetti until 10.30 the next morning, when he had already seen the King.

At my office I found Robert Mitchell. He asked me what he should say as to Prince Antony's withdrawal in the *Constitutionnel* the next morning. As I had not

[1] [The last two sentences are not taken from *L'Empire Libéral*.]
[2] [As finally despatched, the second telegram read thus: "The Emperor instructs me to call your attention to the fact that we cannot regard the withdrawal communicated to us by the Spanish Ambassador, which was not addressed directly to us, as a sufficient response to the just demands presented by us to the King of Prussia; still less can we see therein a guaranty for the future." (Then follows the first paragraph suggested by M. Ollivier word for word.) "If M. de Bismarck comes to Ems, be good enough to remain there until summoned to Paris. And lastly say to Count Bismarck and the King," — and the balance of M. Ollivier's second paragraph. Gramont, pp. 137, 138.]

yet reflected on the course I should follow, I said nothing to him of the demand of guaranties, and simply told him my own opinion, which was one way of beginning the struggle with Saint-Cloud: "Say that we are satisfied, and that it's all over."

Mitchell, who supported the cause of peace with all the vigor of his wonderful mind, and with the courage of a brave heart, almost alone amid the bellicose ardor of the majority of Parisian journalists, welcomed my assurance as a personal victory, and after congratulating me cordially, went off in high spirits to write his pacific article.

Left alone, I debated with myself during a long sleepless night the line of conduct that I should pursue, and I passed in review all the happenings of the day. My first impulse was to resign.

"You are too overburdened with business," one of my colleagues, Parieu, who had known the Right at close quarters for a long time, wrote to me, "to keep an eye on all the intriguing that is going on about you."

In fact, although I had not had time to watch their intrigue, I had divined it. I was conscious of being ill served, betrayed, on all sides; it was absolutely essential to purge the personnel of the administration, and I had not the hardness of heart to undertake it. I felt deeply wounded by this renascence of the sovereign's personal power. I was weary, and I wanted to recover my breath. The mere thought of being forced to give the signal for war tore my heart; the chance to avoid it was most opportune, and I was violently tempted to grasp it.

But, as I dug deep into my thoughts, such a retreat seemed to me reprehensibly selfish. It would have been to go over to the enemy in the midst of the battle, like the Saxons; to offer myself as a witness against my country's cause; to justify Bismarck, and intensify the arrogance of his refusal to comply with our demand; to invite Europe to take sides against us; in a word, to destroy the only hope of peace that was still left to us. I had no doubt as to what would happen. The King of Prussia would approve the withdrawal of the candidacy, but would refuse any promise of guaranties. Immediately on my resignation, a war ministry, which was all prepared in the lobby, would succeed me, and would meet the King's refusal with an overbearing insistence from which war would inevitably result. On the other hand, by remaining in the government, I might hope to secure the abandonment of the demand of guaranties, and persuade the Council and the Emperor himself to accept the King's refusal and not prolong the crisis by fruitless insistence. When Daru sent his memorandum without consulting the Council, I did not withdraw, and I succeeded in emasculating the memorandum.[1]

I was certain of a majority in the Council; would the Chamber follow me? Should I not go down before a coalition of Right and Left? I thought not, so long as the Emperor was with me. In any event, I should fall with dignity, having refrained from sacrificing the interests of my country to my personal sensitiveness, however well justified it might be. And so I did not

[1] [The *Memorandum* of April 6, drawn by Comte Daru and setting forth the views of the government concerning certain matters connected with the supremacy of the church in secular affairs, was written to be handed to the Pope as President of the Vatican Council, then in session. See *L'Empire Libéral*, vol. xiii, pp. 182 ff.; La Gorce, vol. vi, pp. 72-74. On April 6, Comte Daru had actually ceased to belong to the government.]

offer my resignation. Thereby, it is true, I made myself officially responsible for a step which I regretted. To all appearance I associated myself with it, but only as the lightning-rod associates itself with the lightning, in order to turn it aside.

CHAPTER XV

THE MORNING OF JULY 13 AT EMS — THE KING OF PRUSSIA BRUSHES ASIDE THE DEMAND OF GUARANTIES

DURING the night of the 12th and 13th Benedetti received Gramont's seven o'clock despatch. He declared afterward that he considered the demand of guaranties formulated in that despatch useless, ill-timed, and hazardous. "Were such guaranties indispensable, and what reason had we to imagine that the King of Prussia, having once got clear of the dispute, not without injury to his prestige, could ever consent to go into it again? How could one conceive that the King, after he had, in a communication to the French ambassador, approved his nephew's decision, would be either capable or desirous of authorizing him to revive his candidacy?"[1]

That being Benedetti's opinion, he should not, without remonstrance, have taken a step of which he foresaw the disastrous results. Was he constrained to do so by his duties as ambassador? An ambassador is not simply a telephone to transmit the words of his government. Doubtless he is that, but he is much more than that — an intelligencer, an adviser, in duty bound

[1] Benedetti, *Essais Diplomatiques*, p. 385. ["I observed to M. de Gramont," Lord Lyons wrote to Granville on the 13th, "that I could hardly conceive that the French Government could really apprehend that after all that had occurred Prince Leopold would again offer himself as a candidate, or be accepted by the Spanish Government if he did." *Blue Book*, pp. 26, 27.]

THE FRANCO-PRUSSIAN WAR

to be on the alert to take the initiative.[1] Benedetti himself often practised this rule opportunely; he dissuaded the government from demanding that Italy guarantee the Pope's power in 1860, and procured the

[1] [M. Ollivier elaborates this subject in *L'Empire Libéral*, vol. xiv, pp. 276–278, giving several instances of the exercise by ambassadors of their individual discretion.] "There is no doubt as to the strict obligation of an ambassador when he detects serious inconveniences in the instructions sent to him, to advise his government, to point out the objections, to point out the shoals and quicksands which his chiefs seem not to have noticed, but which he has discovered, having scrutinized men's faces, listened to their words, and fathomed their purposes. . . . Nevertheless, if the command is imperatively repeated, and it is no longer possible to doubt the fixed purpose of his government, then only is his implicit obedience quite free from blame. This duty of the ambassador was set forth with a great flourish on a momentous occasion when Thiers was prime minister and Guizot his ambassador at London. The treaty of July 15, 1840, relating to Egypt, brutally shut France out from the European concert. Thiers was forced to leave the ministry; passionate disputations followed, one of Thiers's grievances being that Guizot had imperfectly performed his ambassadorial duty. 'In principle it is quite true that the minister alone is responsible; it is quite true that when there is a division of opinion between the minister and the ambassador, the minister's opinion should prevail; but that this leads to any such consequence as that the ambassador ought not to give advice or even to express an opinion concerning the policy to be pursued, it is impossible to admit. The ambassador's duty is to keep his government posted, to enlighten it, to urge it to act or not to act, and at need to contradict it.' Guizot did not deny Thiers's theoretical point of view; he acknowledged that it is the ambassador's duty to offer advice." [But he claimed that he had performed that duty.] Speech of Nov. 26, 1840.

["The demand of guaranties for the future meant war. What was only half seen at Saint-Cloud through the mist of illusions, appeared at Ems with the clearness of direct evidence. But M. Benedetti, whose laxity the Duc de Gramont had already reproved, was by no means anxious to incur fresh reproofs. Being a reporter of news from day to day rather than a statesman, his credit was not sufficiently assured, or his intelligence sufficiently exalted, or his character strong enough, to venture, even in view of a great public advantage, to discuss his instructions or postpone their execution. Armed with a formal command, he, like a docile subordinate, considered that his duty, his only duty, lay in perfect obedience." La Gorce, vol. vi, p. 269.]

omission of certain clauses from the treaty relative to the conquest of Belgium, in 1866. He had remembered the rule in this very negotiation at Ems: he had employed more temperate language than that which he had been ordered to employ; he had preferred to speak, not of commands, but of advice, and had refused to inform the King of the sending of a messenger by Serrano to Prince Leopold.[1]

Gramont's instructions of seven o'clock on the 12th were, I agree, more imperative than the earlier ones; but they were more momentous as well, and, far from obviating the duty of remonstrance, they imposed that duty the more forcibly because the effects of an ill-advised step were likely, in his opinion, to be irreparable. "I was not in agreement with the Duc de Gramont," he wrote in 1895. But he should not have waited so long before advertising his disagreement, in his *Essais Diplomatiques;* he should have done it on the morning of July 13, by a despatch of warning and remonstrance. By not doing that, he deprived himself of the right to censure Gramont and to consider himself as absolved from all blame. Not only did he carry out his instructions without sending a word of criticism to Paris, but he displayed as much insistence in carrying them out as if they expressed his individual convictions.

On the 13th, at the earliest moment, he called upon the aide-de-camp on duty, Radziwill, and asked him to request an audience. The King had already gone out. However, they were able to inform him of the Ambassador's wish, and he replied that he would receive him on his return. While he was waiting,

[1] [See *supra*, p. 156 n. (on p. 157)].

Benedetti, strolling about in the park, near the Springs, suddenly found himself face to face with the King (at ten minutes after nine).

William was walking with his brother, Prince Albrecht, followed by an adjutant, when he spied Benedetti on the bank of the Sahr, near the Baths. The Ambassador was too courteous to accost the King; it was the King who walked toward him. Those who were walking there, having noticed that movement, looked on with interest, as if trying to fathom the significance of the meeting. Thereupon Prince Albrecht and the adjutant halted a few steps behind, to keep the crowd back so that they should not overhear the conversation.

The King's face was bright with the satisfied expression of one who is about to see the last of an affair which has weighed heavily on his heart. "The post from Sigmaringen hasn't arrived yet," he said, "but here is some good news." And as he spoke, he handed him a supplement of the Cologne *Gazette*, containing the telegram from Sigmaringen. "Thereby," he added joyfully, "all our anxieties and trouble have come to an end."[1]

[1] [M. Ollivier cites Von Sybel (vol. vii, p. 387), as his authority for the incident of the Cologne *Gazette* (which was first mentioned in the so-called "Official Report of what took place at Ems, prepared under the direction of the King," see *infra*, Appendix K); but does not refer to the statement of Benedetti in his report of the audience (p. 378), that the King "seemed surprised" when he (Benedetti) told him of the step taken by Prince Antony, of which he had had no notice. As he certainly had been informed of it by telegram from Colonel Strantz on the 12th (*supra*, p. 173), he can hardly be acquitted of disingenuousness at least. La Gorce (vol. vi, p. 270), mentions the Cologne *Gazette* incident, and Lehautcourt (vol. i, p. 283) says that the King sent the paper to Benedetti before he had requested an audience, and that he replied that he already had the news from Paris.]

WILHELM I, GERMAN EMPEROR
1797–1888

He expected cordial and gratified thanks. Instead, Benedetti said to him in a tone of great gravity: —

"A telegram from the Duc de Gramont informs me of the Prince's declination of the Spanish crown. The Emperor Napoleon has received the information with satisfaction, and he hopes that it will bring the incident to a close; but he wishes to obtain from Your Majesty the assurance that the candidacy which has been withdrawn will not be revived in the future. And I ask Your Majesty to authorize me to inform the Duc de Gramont that you would on occasion forbid the Prince to put forward his candidacy anew."

One can imagine what must have taken place in the King's mind. Being resolved to bring the affair to a peaceful termination, even to risk a rupture with his confidential minister and to subject himself to the criticisms of German public opinion, he received by way of reply to that honest effort an utterly futile demand, which, despite his good-will, it was impossible for him to listen to without self-degradation. He showed a truly royal self-control. With great firmness, but omitting none of the outward forms of his customary courtesy, he expressed his surprise at this unexpected demand, and explained why he rejected it.

"I do not know as yet Prince Leopold's decision; I am expecting momentarily the message which will advise me thereupon. I cannot therefore give you any information, or authorize you to transmit to your government the assurance that you request."

Benedetti persisted, urged the King to act upon hypotheses, to assume that the withdrawal was absolute. He besought him — thereby admitting a distinction which he was not authorized to admit — to consent as head of the family, if not as sovereign.

The King said nothing as to his approval of the Prince's withdrawal, and peremptorily refused to give any guaranty for the future. "I neither can nor will make such an agreement; in such a contingency, as in every other, I must reserve for myself entire liberty to consider the special circumstances. For instance, what would happen if Napoleon himself should hereafter consent to the candidacy? In that case should I be bound to oppose it? I have no hidden purpose, and *this business has given me too much anxiety for me not to desire that it be definitively put aside.* However, you may repeat to the Emperor, your sovereign, what I now say: 'I know my cousins, Prince Antony of Hohenzollern and his son; they are honorable men, and when they withdrew from the candidacy which they had accepted, they certainly did not act with the secret purpose of renewing it hereafter.'"

Benedetti returned to the charge a third time: "I can understand that up to a certain point a sovereign or his government would not be willing to pledge the future; but, keeping to the ground on which the King himself has taken his stand, I appeal to the head of the Hohenzollern family, and in that capacity Your Majesty may assuredly receive, without prejudice of any sort, the request which I have been instructed to make. Our action is without mental reservation; we have no other object in view than to avert any fresh disagreement and to restore fully the confidence of those interests that have taken alarm."

The King lost patience and considered such pertinacity ill-placed. Still courteously, but in a sterner tone, he said: "Monsieur l'Ambassadeur, I have given you my reply, and as I have nothing to add to it, allow me to retire."

He stepped back, bowed, passed through the crowd which drew aside before him, and returned to his quarters, more displeased than he had allowed to appear; in the narrative he sent to the Queen, he called Benedetti "almost impertinent."

Benedetti instantly sent this reply to Paris by telegraph (10.30). A few moments later he received Gramont's second despatch, which softened and narrowed the first. He replied: "I am expecting that the King will send for me to acquaint me with the message from the Prince of Hohenzollern, which is likely to arrive at any moment. I will avail myself of that opportunity to insist upon what I have said to the King this morning, and to execute further the Emperor's command." [1]

[1] [Benedetti's report of the audience is printed by him on pp. 376-382, and by Gramont, pp. 396-401. Von Sybel's account differs little from Benedetti's except in the detail mentioned above.]

CHAPTER XVI

THE MORNING OF JULY 13 AT PARIS

AT Paris the 13th of July opened with Robert Mitchell's article in the *Constitutionnel:* —
"The candidacy of a German prince to the throne of Spain is put aside, and the peace of Europe will not be disturbed. The Emperor's ministers have spoken clearly and firmly, as is fitting when one has the honor to govern a great nation. They have been listened to; their just demand has been satisfied. We are content. Prince Leopold of Hohenzollern had accepted the crown of Spain; France declared that she would resist a political scheme or a family arrangement which she deemed threatening to her interests, and the candidacy has been withdrawn. The Prince of Hohenzollern will not reign in Spain. We asked nothing more; we welcome this peaceful solution with pride — a great triumph which has cost not a tear or a drop of blood."[1]

I found the article to be in conformity with my opinions, and admirable in its optimistic tone; and I went to Saint-Cloud, to the Council, at nine in the morning, resolved to obtain from my colleagues official sanction of what the intelligent editor had so courageously expressed.

[1] [This article was recognized as expressing M. Ollivier's views. La Gorce, vol. vi, 273; Lehautcourt, vol. i, pp. 305, 306. The *Constitutionnel*, in the same issue, denied in an unofficial note that there was any disagreement between MM. Gramont and Ollivier. Welschinger, vol. i, p. 94.]

Le Bœuf, in common with all the other ministers, knew nothing of the despatch of the demand of guaranties. In the lobby of the Council Chamber, he met the Prince Imperial, attended by an aide-de-camp. The aide-de-camp said to him with a haughty air: "It's not all over yet! We are demanding guaranties; we must have them!"

Le Bœuf jumped. "Guaranties! What does that mean? What has happened? Is there anything new?" He rushed into the Council Chamber like a madman, and spying Gramont and myself talking at a window, demanded in a wrathful tone: "What's all this? What are these guaranties? Has the quarrel begun again, and I know nothing of it? Why, I have stopped my preparations! You don't realize what a terrible responsibility rests on me! This state of things cannot go on: I must know absolutely, this morning, whether it's peace or war!"

Hitherto Le Bœuf had sat silent at meetings of the Council and had not advocated war. Indeed, on one occasion, when Chevandier had dwelt upon our duty to neglect no effort to preserve peace, Le Bœuf said to him, patting his leg, "Don't be afraid to insist, that's the Emperor's view." But on this day he entered into the discussion like a gust of wind. Gramont had hardly finished reading the various documents received and sent since the last meeting, and notably the despatches of the previous evening, when Le Bœuf demanded, in fervent words, the immediate assembling of the reserves; after which he would not oppose our dealing in diplomacy as much as we chose. "Every day that you force me to lose," he cried, "endangers the destiny of the country!"

To summon the reserves as he demanded meant immediate war; for Prussia, as Benedetti had warned us, would have retorted at once by the mobilization of her army. At the time of the Luxembourg affair, Niel, having sent MacMahon to Metz to look after certain supplies, had nearly hurried us into hostilities thereby. The summoning of the reserves, then, meant that war was inevitable. Ought we to wish for war? We had not to discuss the question whether it was or was not advisable to emit a demand of guaranties which was in the hands of the King of Prussia at that moment; we could not deliberate as if the telegrams of the previous night had not been sent, and as if the whole question were still open: we were confronted by an accomplished fact by which we were bound, with which we were forced to reckon, and against which there was no possible protest open to us save resignation. No one mentioned resigning, nor was there a word of recrimination on the part of anybody, whether from respect to the Emperor or because of its futility. There was but one practical course to follow: that was, instead of wasting time in recrimination, to prevent the unfortunate step that had been taken from producing the warlike results that those who inspired it had anticipated.[1]

We gave our attention, therefore, solely to the urgent question: What consequences should we allow to result from the demand of guaranties which we were powerless to recall? As yet we had in our hands only the telegram transmitted by Olozaga containing Prince Antony's withdrawal of the candidacy, and we were unanimously of opinion that we could

[1] [This sentence does not appear in *L'Empire Libéral*.]

not regard it as sufficient so long as it was not ratified by Prince Leopold, approved by the King of Prussia, and accepted by Spain. If, as was probable, Prince Leopold should not disavow his father's act, if the King should approve, as he had agreed to do, and if Spain should conclude to abandon her candidate, should we declare ourselves content even though the King should refuse to give us a guaranty for the future? Or, on the contrary, should we insist? Should we give to that insistence the character of an ultimatum, and summon our reserves in order to support our demands? It was under this form alone that the question of peace or war presented itself.

The Council [1] was divided. Mège and Maurice Richard warmly supported Le Bœuf's demands: "Père Antoine's" withdrawal was not sincere; the exasperated country would howl at us if we should be satisfied with it; the offence had come from the King of Prussia, and it was from him that the reparation should come; a guaranty for the future was the least we could claim; we must not back water, and, in order to be ready to exact it, if it were refused, it was essential to accede to the marshal's request and to order the summoning of the reserves.

The Emperor adopted this view; he repeated the various arguments of his letter, and let slip in a bitter tone the remark: "We have many other grievances against Prussia than this Hohenzollern business."

At that moment the discussion was interrupted by the arrival of a letter from Lord Lyons, which the Emperor read to us. It contained a letter from Earl

---

[1] "The Council was divided *for the first and last time.*" *L'Empire Libéral,* vol. xiv, p. 125.

252 THE FRANCO-PRUSSIAN WAR

Granville, pointing out the tremendous responsibility which the Emperor's government would incur if it should enlarge the ground of discussion and should not declare itself to be satisfied with the withdrawal. Referring to the prompt and vigorous support that he had given us, he urged us, in friendly, but at the same time most pressing, terms, to accept the solution offered as satisfactory.[1]

The discussion was renewed — dignified, thoughtful, earnest. Each of the members of the Council was

[1] [Lyons to Granville, July 13, *Blue Book*, p. 25 (No. 39): "Your Lordship's telegram dated at 2.30 A.M. to-day reached me at Paris at half-past nine o'clock this morning. The Council of Ministers assembled at St. Cloud at 9 o'clock. It was impossible, therefore, for me to execute literally your Lordship's instruction to see the Duc de Gramont before the Council, and renew, in the name of Her Majesty's Government, the earnest recommendation to accept the . . . renunciation . . . as a satisfactory settlement of the whole question. I embodied, however, the substance of your Lordship's telegram, as fast as possible, in a letter, which I sent to St. Cloud . . . and which was put into M. de Gramont's hand at the table at which he and the other Ministers were still sitting in Council in the presence of the Emperor."

Lyons's letter to Gramont was in these words: "With reference to our conversation last evening, I think it right not to lose a moment in making your Excellency acquainted with the substance of a telegram which I have just received from Lord Granville. His Lordship desires me to represent to the Government of the Emperor the immense responsibility it will incur if it enlarges the ground of quarrel and does not at once declare itself satisfied with the renunciation of the Prince of Hohenzollern. Lord Granville desires me to remind you that, at the very beginning of the affair, France asked Her Majesty's Government to exert their influence, and that they did so at once, to attain the immediate object — the withdrawal of the candidature of the Prince of Hohenzollern. Her Majesty's Government gave the aid that was asked of them in the promptest and most energetic manner, and allusion was made to this in public by the French Minister. Lord Granville considers, therefore, that Her Majesty's Government is justified, nay bound, to urge the Government of the Emperor, in the most friendly and, at the same time, most pressing manner, to accept the renunciation of the Prince as a satisfactory settlement."—"This advice, which was not followed, was listened to with favor," says La Gorce, vol. vi, p. 274.]

called upon by name to give his views. I opposed summoning the reserves for the reasons that I should have urged against the demand of guaranties had I been consulted before it was sent; and I maintained that, even if the King should refuse to give any sort of guaranty, as he was almost certain to do, we should not insist, but should declare the incident closed and not summon our reserves and so plunge into war at the very moment when it rested with us to assure peace.

Segris and Chevandier supported me, the one with his noble eloquence, the other with his persuasive common sense. Louvet and Plichon were no less urgent. I spoke several times, repeating the same arguments with much vehemence, almost with violence, until the Emperor, who followed the discussion without taking part in it, was shaken at last and came over to my side, and brought Gramont's concurrence with him.

We proceeded to a vote, and my conclusions were adopted by eight votes against four (the admiral, the marshal, Mège, and Maurice Richard), and it was agreed that we would await without interference the result of Benedetti's efforts; but that, if they were not successful in obtaining the guaranties demanded, and brought only the King's approval, we would be content with that. Thus, without withdrawing the demand of guaranties, which was impossible, we annulled its effect in advance. The wicked purpose of those persons who had inspired it was foiled, and I congratulated myself on not having yielded to my wounded pride, and having been able to contribute to this peaceful triumph.

Meanwhile, as it was impossible for us to announce and justify our decision, and to enter upon the debate to which it would give rise until we had received the expected replies from Madrid and Ems, we drew up the following declaration, to be read from the tribune: —

"The Spanish Ambassador informed us officially yesterday of the abandonment by the Prince of Hohenzollern of his candidacy for the throne of Spain; the negotiations which are now in progress with Prussia, *and which have never had any other subject,* are not yet at an end; it is therefore impossible for us to speak of them or to submit to the Chamber and the country to-day a general statement of the affair."

This declaration accepted as official the communication which the Emperor, on the preceding evening, had very properly refused to accept in that light. That was the only inaccuracy that we ventured upon in that crisis; it was inspired by our wish to increase the chances of peace, by giving substance to Prince Antony's much-discussed act. By declaring that the negotiations with Prussia had no other subject than the Hohenzollern candidacy, we brushed aside the demands of the Right, and banished Granville's fear that we might enlarge the ground of discussion; by referring to our demands without specifying them, we indicated that we had not given them the character of an ultimatum; our silence concerning the demand of guaranties paved the way for dropping it.

Suppose that, during our deliberations, we had received a telegram from Benedetti specifying the objections which the demand of guaranties would call forth, and informing us that he would postpone

MORNING OF JULY 13 AT PARIS 255

presenting it until we should repeat our instructions to that effect: in that case, the Council, instead of avoiding the effects of an accomplished fact, would have prevented it from reaching that stage. As may be seen from this truthful account of the first great council that we held on those decisive days, and as will be seen even more clearly soon, in our deliberations everything was well weighed, orderly, and coherent, and our decisions varied only because events themselves varied.[1]

[1] [Gramont has almost nothing to say of this Council of the 13th. "The Council strove to define the character of the instructions sent to our Ambassador. They did not constitute an ultimatum, and were not to be presented as such. . . . The demand of guaranties was susceptible of shadings and concessions. There was no stipulation as to the form, explicit or implicit, in which it might be expressed, and in that respect, the government, as the sequel will prove, was inclined to almost any modification, I will say, even, to any compromise" (p. 148).

M. Welschinger (vol. i, pp. 132, 133) asserts that at this Council M. Ollivier should have seized the opportunity to express his reprobation of the extraordinary performance of the Emperor in forming a most important decision without consulting the Council.

La Gorce (vol. vi, pp. 271–273) gives some details of this Council, taken mainly from the unpublished papers of two of the ministers, MM. Plichon and Louvet. "When the duke [Gramont] had divulged the fatal demand of guaranties which had been grafted upon the original demand, a long silence followed the disclosure. Several of the ministers could not conceal their excited and alarmed surprise. M. de Parieu was one — a clear-sighted, austere man, instinctively disposed to blame a contest which presented itself in the guise of an impulsive and hazardous caprice. Others were MM. Plichon and Louvet — men of lucid intellect, independent and staunch, who saw in war the possibility of defeat, in defeat the imperilling of the dynasty; and they were not of a sort to hold back useful truths. By their side, M. Segris, an excellent soul, but timid and impressionable to excess, was really terrified by the responsibility of which he must bear his part. It was from this little group that objections came. They expressed their surprise that, contrary to all the rules of parliamentary government, instructions of so serious a nature should have been sent to Ems without the previous concurrence of ministers. They laid bare the dangers of this new exploration: the King

The session at an end, all of us had left the Council Chamber and gone into the salon, except Segris, Maurice Richard, and Parieu, who were talking in a corner,

would not consent to give the guaranties; if Count Bismarck wanted war, we were supplying him with a pretext to push his people into it; the recent demands were of little profit and might endanger everything. 'It is war, probably, almost certainly,' said M. Plichon vehemently, 'and who can assure us the victory?'

"Somewhat disturbed at first by these criticisms, M. de Gramont strove to explain his extraordinary performance: if he had not consulted the Cabinet, it was simply to gain time; if he could have suspected any differences of opinion, he would have invited a discussion; the public excitement and the sentiment of the Chambers made an emphatic policy necessary; the demand of guaranties was no new demand, but was simply the logical sequel of the original claim: any other course would allow Prussia to escape. The discussion was continued for some time. 'I am satisfied with the Hohenzollern withdrawal, no matter whence it comes,' said M. Louvet, 'on the single condition that it is certain.'

"Throughout the whole colloquy the Emperor had held his peace. When the discussion was exhausted, he asked his advisers to vote. Was there good ground for being content with the withdrawal of the candidacy and the approval thereof which the King would signify? Or, on the other hand, was it necessary to insist on the demand of guaranties for the future? They proceeded to vote. MM. de Parieu, Plichon, Segris, and Louvet voted in favor of resting content with the satisfaction obtained. The others ratified the instructions sent to Benedetti on the night before."

Perhaps the above account is one of those alluded to in the following passage of *L'Empire Libéral* (vol. xiv, pp. 290, 291), which M. Ollivier omitted in the present volume: —]

"I can understand that those who read the imaginary reports of our Councils in the narrations of so-called 'well-informed' historians, regard us as frantic madmen who knew not what they wanted and deliberated incoherently; the incoherence and terror are not in our acts, but in the narratives of them that are presented. Even what is true is denatured because it is misplaced chronologically, and I wonder how a reader can form any sort of opinion in that chaos, in which there is nothing constant except the well-matured determination to find us bungling or incapable whatever we might do. It must be admitted, however, that some of our colleagues have contributed to lead the historians astray. For example, in accordance with their confidences, surely misunderstood, this Council of the 13th has been described in a truly extraordinary fashion. It was Plichon and Louvet who

and Admiral Rigault, who was standing in a window recess. Le Bœuf, who had followed the Emperor to his apartments for a moment, suddenly rushed back into the Council Chamber, wildly excited and breathing hard, threw his portfolio on a little oaken table near the door, and exclaimed: —

"If it weren't for the Emperor, I wouldn't remain for five minutes a member of such a cabinet, which is endangering the destiny of the country by its idiocies!"

Segris paused, aghast, and Richard went to him to soothe him.

"Come, my dear colleague, —"

Le Bœuf did not let him finish, but waved him aside:

"Let me alone!" and, with his face flushed purple, he entered the salon whither I had preceded him, went up to Pietri and Bachon, and said to them: "The summoning of the reserves was rejected by eight to four. It's a disgrace, and there is nothing left for me but to hand in my resignation. I shall be the most popular man in France. The Emperor is betrayed, and" — pointing to me — "there is the man who has betrayed him!"

led the discussion and urged the vote; I am not even mentioned: I remained dumb and gave my opinion under my hat. Now, although Louvet and Plichon were excellent men, whom we were very fond of and upon whom we bestowed our regard, they had in our councils no influence superior to that of any one of us. Louvet seldom spoke; Plichon talked more, but he had no special gift of persuasion. And who could believe that I was present for several hours, during a discussion concerning peace and war, and confined myself to admiring Plichon's speeches?" [In the *Éclaircissements* to vol. xiv, p. 604, M. Ollivier flatly contradicts Louvet's statement quoted above as to the form and result of the vote. He says that if it had been taken in the alternative form as alleged by Louvet, his own vote and Parieu's would have been added to those of the four advocates of peace.]

He spoke so loud that Bachon said: "Be careful — M. Ollivier will hear you."

My colleagues often blamed that outburst of the marshal's; I never agreed with them. The sensation of finding himself suddenly subjected anew, without warning, to the terrible responsibility from which he had thought that he was delivered, explains the unreflecting impulses of a military spirit.

The news of our pacific decision had reached the salon where the Empress and her suite were awaiting us for luncheon. They vied with one another in turning their backs, or frowning upon us. At table the Emperor had the Prince Imperial on his right and the Empress on his left. I sat at the Empress's left: she ostentatiously refrained from speaking to me, and when I invited her to talk, she barely replied, with brief phrases, seized upon a remark of mine about the withdrawal to sneer at "Père Antoine," and ended by turning her back on me. She was barely polite when we took our leave.[1]

From Saint-Cloud we went to the Chamber, where the dissatisfaction of the court awaited us in a more aggressive form. One was conscious of a subdued quiver of intense feeling passing over the benches — a sure presage of a stormy sitting. In the lobby Gambetta accosted Mitchell, grasped him by the

[1] [Lehautcourt (vol. vi, p. 306) reports an *on dit* to the effect that the Empress supported Le Bœuf in his demand that the reserves should be summoned. Lord Malmesbury quotes Gramont as saying to him in conversation that after a few moments of discussion, the Empress, in great excitement, took the floor and declared vehemently that war was inevitable if they had any regard for the honor of France. She was at once supported by Marshal Le Bœuf, who threw his portfolio violently to the floor and swore that, if they did not go to war, he would not resume it and would give up his marshal's staff. *Memoirs of an Ex-Minister*, p. 373.]

coat, and said angrily: "Your satisfaction is atrocious!" An officer insulted the courageous journalist, accusing him of cowardice. When a minister seems to be in a strong position, people vie with one another in speaking to him, shaking hands with him, smiling on him, and obtaining a word with him; but when he loses strength, there is equal rivalry in avoiding him: men confine themselves to bowing from afar, with an imperceptible nod; only a few faithful friends venture to approach him, perturbed and questioning. On that day, people saluted us from afar, or passed us without stopping, as if in a great hurry; and those who did not step aside shook our hands with an air of condolence.

Gramont went into the tribune and read our declaration. Jérôme David inquired from whom the withdrawal came; he sought to reopen the dispute about "Père Antoine."

Gramont replied: "I have been informed by the Spanish Ambassador that Prince Leopold of Hohenzollern has withdrawn his candidacy for the crown of Spain."

"Yesterday," rejoined David, "there was a report that the withdrawal came, not from the Prince of Hohenzollern, but from his father."

"I am not called upon to deal with rumors that are current in the lobbies," retorted Gramont, dryly.[1]

"That statement," continued Jérôme David, "was made by the Keeper of the Seals publicly in the lobby, not only to deputies, but to newspapermen and to all those who were near him."

---

[1] [Delord (vol. vi, p. 170) says of this reply that it was made "with a disdain which fell with full force on the Keeper of the Seals."]

Gramont made no reply, and Duvernois intervened. He was no longer unprepared, as on the previous day. During the morning he had consulted Rouher as to the guaranties that we ought to demand. Rouher was in fullest agreement with him, and urged him to demand disarmament.[1] There was no surer way of putting a torch to the situation, after the check to our efforts in January, of which Rouher must have been informed by his friend, La Valette.[2] To revive the question of disarmament was to go straight to war by way of a sharp exchange of bitter words, as swiftly as if we had demanded the execution of the Treaty of Prague, or a relocation of the frontier near the Rhine. Thus prompted, Duvernois, in a malicious tone, asked the Chamber to appoint a very early day for the discussion of his interpellation.

Without awaiting our reply, Jérôme David, angered by his failure to drag Gramont into a debate on "Père Antoine," rose once more, and in a sibilant voice read a proposed interpellation — a veritable indictment of the Cabinet : —

"Whereas the firm, concise, patriotic declarations of the Ministry at the session of July 6 were greeted by the Chamber and the country with favor; and whereas those declarations of the ministry are at odds with the derisory sluggishness of the negotiations with Prussia" — (*Loud murmurs on a great number of benches.*) — 'I withdraw the word "derisory" if you prefer' — (*Uproar.*) — "Whereas those declarations of

---

[1] ["According to his confidences to M. Pinard, Duvernois meant that we should call upon Prussia to disarm. In reality, his purpose was to force the Cabinet to resign. Pinard, vol. ii, p. 48." Lehautcourt, vol. i, p. 308 n.]

[2] [See the translator's Introduction, *supra*, p. xxxv.]

the Ministry are at odds with the sluggishness of the negotiations with Prussia, I ask leave to interpellate the Ministry concerning the motives of its foreign policy, which not only arouses perturbation in the various branches of public industry, but also bids fair to impair the national dignity." [1] (*Exclamations and commotion of varying import.*)

To no purpose did he withdraw the word "derisory." His game was already lost, in face of the exclamations and murmurs of the Right itself. One cannot comprehend, unless one has sat in a legislative assembly, those instantaneous impulses which, at critical moments, force the majority from its course, and drive it from the views which it seems to have adopted with passionate earnestness, into the diametrically opposite views: all assemblies are moblike.

Gramont, while protesting against Jérôme David's language, proposed that the debate should be set down for Friday the 15th. Clement Duvernois did not object. David did not venture to intervene further. Kératry alone, putting the seal to the union in process of formation between the Right and a section of the Left, exclaimed: "You sent the King of Prussia an ultimatum, giving him three days in which to reply. Those three days expired day before yesterday; if you postpone discussion till Friday, you are playing into M. de Bismarck's hands, who is simply playing with you. As a Frenchman, I protest in the name of my country!"

[1] ["The name of the interpellator, who was one of the leaders of the Right, the bitter phraseology of the interpellation itself, all proved that the foe was not Prussia alone, whom they wished to fight, but the Cabinet, whom they dreamed of overturning." La Gorce, vol. vi, p. 276.]

Kératry made no mistake in thinking that Bismarck was playing with France, but I do not know where he got the idea that we had given the King of Prussia three days to reply.

The Assembly passed to other business and men's faces became smiling once more. Some members were outspoken. "You owe a debt of gratitude," they told us, "to Jérôme David's bungling brutality; it has saved you: but for it you would have been overthrown to-day." Lyons, however, notwithstanding our victory, was not misled as to the disposition of the majority. "There was no very violent manifestation of opinion in the Chamber," he wrote to Granville on leaving the hall, "but the appearance certainly was that the war party were in the ascendant."[1]

[1] [*Blue Book*, p. 26. At this point M. Ollivier omits a passage of *L'Empire Libéral*, relating to an incident which seems of sufficient importance to be noticed here.]

"As Gramont and I went out after the interpellation, we met Thiers just going in. We exchanged a few brief words; he urged us to be prudent and advised us to invoke the mediation of England. In the inner lobby he found himself in the midst of the hurly-burly of deputies . . . exchanging their views in violent terms, and he realized, as Lyons did, the increasing predominance of the war party. He asked Louvet to collect some of his colleagues in one of the lobbies. Five ministers . . . went at once to the room designated, namely: Mège, Maurice Richard, Louvet, Segris, and Chevandier. Thiers said to them: 'I wanted to talk with you. This is a very serious business. They want to drag us into war, but the time has not come yet. Prussia, it is true, has put herself seriously in the wrong. I am as anxious as you to obtain reparation for the events of 1866. Without the slightest doubt, after Sadowa and the endless provocations of Prussia, it is to be feared that vengeance will become absolutely necessary one day or another. But the present moment would be very ill chosen. We must be wise and await the hour when Germany, driven to the wall by the inordinate appetites and the exactions of Prussia, shall turn to us as liberators. To-day we are without alliances. The cause of the rupture is very trivial. Europe will hold us responsible and it may be that we shall kindle a general conflagration.' The conversation was confined within these limits. These remarks

From the Chamber Gramont went to the Senate. He was greeted there by more clearly defined demonstrations. Senators vied with one another in giving expression to their bellicose impatience. "Why, that is nothing at all!" came the cry from divers directions after he had read his declaration. "It tells us nothing about Prussia's attitude." "And what of article five of the Treaty of Prague?" added Larabit.

"Your declaration mentions a withdrawal," said Hubert Delisle, "but does not tell us whether it comes from the Prince or his father; it does not say whether any sort of assent thereto has resulted from the negotiations entered into with Prussia." He concluded by alleging the necessity of offering some sort of palliative to the public anxiety.

were made and repeated slowly and several times, and were listened to with the attention due to the position of the speaker. There was no discussion. Thiers had no occasion to overheat himself to the point of being bathed in sweat; the interview lasted half an hour at most. Not a word was said by him tending to suggest a suspicion that France was not ready. The universal conflagration seemed to be his only anxiety, and his hearers were rather led to entertain a feeling of confidence, if the conflict was to be confined to Prussia and France. Segris went out with Thiers. 'I thank you,' he said, 'for saying what you did; it agrees entirely with my ideas.'"

[In his deposition at the Inquiry concerning the 4th of September, Thiers testified: "We got them together in one of the offices, and there I passed two hours talking to them. Never, I think, did I exert myself more strenuously to convince men. I spoke with extraordinary vehemence; I was panting, bathed in sweat! I told those ministers that, if they hesitated, they would destroy the dynasty, which did not concern me but did concern them particularly, whose duty it was to defend it; but that they would also destroy France, which was much more serious, and that, for my part, I had no doubt of it." M. Ollivier, in the Appendix to vol. xiv, pp. 592–597, quotes letters from MM. Segris, Maurice Richard and Louvet, absolutely contradicting Thiers's version of the interview. Welschinger (vol. i, p. 135) tries, ineffectually it seems to me, to reconcile them. According to La Gorce (vol. vi, p. 273), Chevandier and Segris *had promised M. Thiers or the 12th to support the cause of peace.*]

"There is no question here of palliatives!" cried Bonjean; "it's a question of the national dignity!"

Brenier went even further: "While maintaining that the right of the Emperor to declare war cannot be impugned, I undertake to prove to you that you ought to do it."

Gramont refused to be drawn into a discussion, and contented himself with replying: "We will go to war on the day that you prove that it is necessary."[1]

The older Senators, who should have been the peacemakers, displayed the greatest ardor. "A bad session," Vaillant wrote in his note-book, "and even worse in the Corps Législatif. There is extreme irritation against Émile Ollivier."

This irritation arose from the fact that they saw in me the obstacle to a war which they were determined to have at all hazards.[2]

[1] [On the debate in the Senate, see Gramont, pp. 164–168.]

[2] [This sentence does not appear in *L'Empire Libéral*. On the other hand there is here an omission of several paragraphs from the larger work, vol. xiv, pp. 299–301, which emphasize still further M. Ollivier's disagreement with Gramont's policy.]

"On his return to the Foreign Office, Gramont found Lyons there. The English Ambassador expressed his regret that he had not confined himself to announcing simply that all trouble with Prussia and Spain was at an end. This criticism was unjust: Gramont could not then make that announcement, because in fact it was not true. Gramont, if we are to judge by Lyons's report, was not, in that interview, quick to make the most of our advantages: he stuck to the fiction of an official withdrawal of the candidacy, to the point of authorizing Lyons to infer the personal confirmation by the son of his father's withdrawal, which . . . did not take place until later. It would have been much the simpler way, speaking to a keen and genuinely loyal ambassador, to tell him the truth without reticences and to explain to him how our ardent desire not to inflame the excitement of men's minds and not to lessen the chances of accommodation had decided us . . . to ascribe an official character to Olozaga's communication, although it would not have that character until assented to at Madrid: the confidence and good-will

MORNING OF JULY 13 AT PARIS

of the English government would certainly not have been weakened thereby. Gramont was even less well inspired when, clinging desperately to the demand of guaranties which the Council had implicitly disavowed, he invoked the mediation of England in its behalf. He set forth that demand, which was becoming hourly more incomprehensible, in the following note which he handed to Lyons: 'We ask the King of Prussia to forbid the Prince of Hohenzollern to reconsider his decision. If he does that, the incident is closed.' Lyons made the reply which sensible men in all the corners of Europe were addressing to Gramont, that he had difficulty in understanding how the French government could seriously apprehend that, after all that had happened, Prince Leopold would ever offer himself as a candidate, or that he could be accepted by the Spanish government. Gramont put himself still more at odds with the opinion of the Council when he added that 'if the King refused to issue the simple prohibition which was proposed, France could only suppose that designs hostile to her were entertained, and must take her measures accordingly.' This was very like an ultimatum and the Council decided that there should be no ultimatum." [See Lyons to Granville, July 13, *Blue Book*, pp. 26, 27. Gramont makes no other reference to this interview with Lyons, than to print the latter's despatch to Granville side by side with Loftus's despatch from Berlin of the same date (*Blue Book*, pp. 32, 33), and invite the reader to decide which of the two governments was the more warlike. He also prints in this connection several extracts from a book published in England, *Who is Responsible for the War?* by "Scrutator" (sometimes alleged to be Mr. Gladstone). He claims, in opposition to M. Ollivier, that his appeal for the mediation of England proved clearly enough that the government had presented no ultimatum. See Gramont, pp. 176–186.]

CHAPTER XVII

THE EVENING OF JULY 13 AT EMS

BISMARCK had been informed forthwith by Abeken of Benedetti's action. He at once telegraphed that, if the King should receive Benedetti once more, he should forward his resignation. Having received no reply, he telegraphed once more that, if His Majesty should again receive the Ambassador, he should regard that act as equivalent to accepting his resignation.[1] This peremptory summons was unnecessary, for, after Benedetti's persistence in putting forward a demand which, on reflection, disgusted the King more and more, he had fully decided not to hold any further conversation with the Ambassador, to whom he had said his last word.

"The scene of the morning, on the promenade at the Springs," says Von Sybel, "had changed the King's feeling with regard to Benedetti; he determined not to receive him again." [2] But he was

[1] These telegrams were disclosed by Moritz Busch in an article printed in the *Times* soon after Bismarck's death under the title "Bismarck and William I." [Note of M. Ollivier in vol. xiv, p. 301.]

[2] Von Sybel (English trans.), vol. vii, p. 389. [But there is no question that at the close of the interview on the promenade the King, notwithstanding his irritation, had promised to receive Benedetti again; and Von Sybel's suggestion is that his anger on receipt of Werther's report was intensified by his remembrance of the Ambassador's persistence in urging the demand of guaranties. Benedetti afterward claimed in his book that it was the perusal of Werther's report which brought about the change in the King's attitude toward him; and this claim was vigorously denied by Gramont. See *infra*, Appendix I.]

EVENING OF JULY 13 AT EMS

equally determined not to allow this interruption in their personal intercourse to assume an offensive character either to France or to the Ambassador.

This determination was not changed by an incident which might well have tempted a sovereign less self-controlled to go beyond what was just and fair. At 8.27 Werther's report of his interview with Gramont and myself had come into Abeken's hands. Before mentioning it to the King, Abeken wished to consult the ministers of the Interior and Finance, Eulenbourg and Camphausen, who were to arrive at quarter past eleven. Their opinion was against handing the document to the King, for they judged that Bismarck, to whom the report had been telegraphed, would be of that opinion. They went to the King, explained to him why the Chancellor had not continued his journey, and repeated with emphasis his advice, already given twice by telegraph, to break off all relations with Benedetti; otherwise, to the serious detriment of his prestige, His Majesty would be held responsible for a withdrawal which would be considered a surrender to France, and Bismarck would lay down his office.

The King having asked whether anything had been heard from Werther, Abeken said that a report had arrived in the morning, which he had transmitted to Berlin; but that the two ministers had thought that the document was not of a nature to be communicated officially to His Majesty.

"Very good," said the King; "but imagine for the moment that we are private individuals, and read it to me."[1]

[1] [La Gorce (vol. vi, p. 277) cites as authority for this detail, Abeken, *Ein Schlichtes Leben in bewegter Zeit*, p. 374.]

Werther's report, especially as read and interpreted by Bismarck's agents, stirred him to violent wrath. "Was ever such insolence heard of!" he wrote to the Queen. "So I must needs appear before the world as a repentant sinner in an affair which it was not I who planned or set in motion, or managed, but Prim, and he is left out of the game! Unfortunately Werther did not leave the room instantly after such a claim was made, and refer his interlocutors to Bismarck. They even went so far as to say that they would place the matter in Benedetti's hands. Unhappily one can but conclude from such inexplicable conduct, that they are resolved to insult us, at whatever cost, and that the Emperor, in his own despite, allows himself to be led by the nose by these inexpert intriguers."[1]

When his first burst of wrath had spent itself, the King was compelled to recognize the fact that there was no question of an official proposition from the French government, but simply of a suggestion of two of the ministers speaking for themselves alone. Indeed, he might have reflected that that very morning Benedetti, whose instructions were later than the conversation with Werther, had not, as Werther mistakenly asserted, received orders to demand a letter of apology. His wrath therefore was really directed against Werther rather than against us: by receiving our expression of our wish, the Ambassador had by implication admitted that his sovereign had something to make reparation for, which fact was indeed in our minds and in his. It is, the King had written, "an affair which I did not plan or set in motion or manage." That was quite true. But it was no less

[1] [*Briefe des Kaiser Wilhelms der Erste*, p. 226.]

true that with a word he could have put a stop to it, and he was the more blameworthy for not uttering that word because he was fully awake to the deplorable consequences of the enterprise. He owed us some reparation, and it was because Werther agreed with us that it was so, that he had listened to us to the end. That is what wounded the King's pride. He wrote to Abeken: "It is absolutely essential, however, to telegraph to Werther in cipher that I am indignant at the Gramont-Ollivier demand, and that I reserve for myself the next step."[1] The next step was never taken, or the "inexpert intriguers" would have shown him that they respected their own dignity too much to offend that of other people.

The incongruities of Werther's report did not in any wise modify the King's attitude toward Benedetti. Even if there had been no such incongruities, our Ambassador would not have been received again, for it was the fact of the demand of guaranties that had offended the King and had changed his sentiments, before Bismarck s telegram, the arrival of the two Prussian ministers, and Werther's report. The formal courtesy of sending an aide-de-camp to our Ambassador was modified so slightly that Benedetti — and this is a significant detail — had no suspicion of this incident. Not until the publication of the diplomatic documents, at a later date, did he learn of that report which he afterward exploited with so little sense of honor.[2]

---

[1] [This despatch was read to the Reichstag by Chancellor von Caprivi, Nov. 23, 1892, in the course of his communication respecting the Ems despatch. Lehautcourt, vol. i, p. 286.]

[2] [See *supra*, p. 266, n. 2; also Appendix I.]

At two o'clock the aide-de-camp, Radziwill, called on Benedetti, not to summon him to the King, as the latter had promised the day before, but to inform him that the expected letter from Prince Antony had arrived at one o'clock. That was the first refusal of an audience. Radziwill told him that Prince Antony's letter informed His Majesty that Prince Leopold had abandoned his candidacy to the crown of Spain; whereby His Majesty regarded the affair as settled.

Thanking the King for this communication, Benedetti observed that he had constantly requested authority to transmit, together with the Prince's withdrawal, His Majesty's explicit approval of that step. He said further that he had received a later despatch which compelled him to insist upon the matter which he had had the honor to mention to the King that morning; that he found himself under the necessity of having a definite understanding upon those two points before transmitting to his chief the information that His Majesty had deigned to send to him, and that he solicited an audience in order to present once more the wishes of the French government.

The King replied through his aide-de-camp — this was at three o'clock — that he had given his approval to the Prince's withdrawal *in the same spirit and with the same purpose* as in the case of his assent to his candidacy, and that he authorized him to transmit this statement to his government; as for the guaranty for the future, he referred to what he had said that very morning.

This was a second refusal of an audience; but in spite of it, Benedetti insisted upon a final interview, "were it only to hear His Majesty repeat what he had said to him." And without awaiting any further reply from the King, he telegraphed to Gramont that which had been previously brought to him (3.45 p.m.).[1]

Convinced as he was that he could obtain no concession, Benedetti should have understood that one does not annoy a king solely to hear him repeat what he has already said in peremptory fashion; that the least insistence to that end would be tactless and would surely result in an unpleasant rebuff. To be sure, Gramont had instructed him to insist; but the minister could not take into account the exact state of the King's mind, and he certainly would not have repeated the instructions if he had been on the spot. On the preceding day Benedetti had remonstrated against his chief's over-eager spurring; he should have done it all the more freely that day because the situation had become more serious.

The consequences of our Ambassador's ill-advised importunity were immediate. The King, wearied by such persecution after repeated refusals couched in the most absolute terms, appealed to Bismarck. He ordered that he should be informed of the condition of affairs, and the whole business placed in his hands. This was done by a telegram of two hundred words from Abeken, despatched to Berlin in cipher at twenty minutes to four.

Ems, July 13, 3.40 p.m.

His Majesty writes to me: "Count Benedetti stopped me on the promenade to ask me finally, in most urgent terms, to authorize him to telegraph

---

[1] [For Benedetti's various despatches, see Benedetti, pp. 372, 375, 376, 377–382.]

forthwith that I would bind myself never to give my consent in the future if the Hohenzollerns should renew their candidacy. I refused in rather a decided tone, because one cannot and should not make such agreements for all time. I told him, naturally, that I had as yet received no information, and, as he was informed before I was, both from Paris and from Madrid, he could see from that that my government was not interested."

His Majesty afterwards received a letter from Prince Charles Antony. As His Majesty had told Count Benedetti that he expected to hear from the Prince, the King decided, at the suggestion of Count Eulenbourg and myself, not to receive Count Benedetti again, because of the demand referred to above, but to send word to him by his adjutant that His Majesty had now received from the Prince confirmation of the intelligence that the count had already received from Paris, and that His Majesty had nothing further to say to the ambassador. His Majesty refers to Your Excellency for decision *the question whether Count Benedetti's latest demand, and the refusal with which it was met, should be communicated at once to our ministers, to foreign nations, and to the press.*

The King dined quietly, and then disposed of Benedetti by sending Radziwill to him a third time (5.30). The aide-de-camp told him, still with perfect courtesy, that the King "could not resume the discussion with him as to assurances to be given for the future; he was glad to give his full and unreserved approval to the Prince's withdrawal; he could do no more." This was a third refusal of an audience, of which

Benedetti might very well have spared us the unpleasantness.[1]

The telegram signed by Abeken was framed in consultation with Eulenbourg and Camphausen, Bismarck's tools. It constitutes the first serious departure from the truth as it is set forth in Radziwill's reports. I have been agreeably surprised to find this most important detail, which our French writers in their carelessness have overlooked, taken up by the German historical critics.

"Abeken's despatch does not give an at all exact representation of what took place," says Rathlef. "It is evidently intended to make things out worse than

---

[1] Benedetti has maintained that Radziwill's visits to him to notify him that the King declined any further discussion, did not constitute a denial of an audience. "The King," he says, "did not refuse to receive me." And he adds, a moment later: "He did not receive me, it is true, but he gave as a reason that we had no occasion to continue our interview on the third point." (Deposition at the Inquiry concerning the 4th of September.) Whatever the King's reason may have been, as a matter of fact he did not receive him. How then could he say that he did not refuse to receive him? Later, in his *Essais Diplomatiques* (p. 391), he repeated: "The King did not close his door to me, he simply declined to examine anew our last proposal. Moreover, he did receive me the next day at the railroad station before his departure." Not to receive, no matter for what reason, a person who persistently seeks permission to talk with you — is not that a closing of your door to him? We shall see what happened on the 14th, but at this moment the question is whether on the 13th the King refused to receive Benedetti. Now, it is undisputed that on that day the King closed his door to him thrice: at two o'clock, at three o'clock, and at half-past five. [Note of M. Ollivier, in vol xiv, p. 308. Several pages (308–313) of the text of *L'Empire Libéral* are omitted here, containing the text of Radziwill's report concerning the events of July 13 and of the Official Report of what took place at Ems, prepared under the direction of the King, and a discussion of the contradictions between the two, and especially between the former and the Abeken telegram. The two reports were appended by Bismarck to his Circular Note of July 18. and are printed as a part of that Note in Appendix H.]

they are, because it does not bring out the friendliness of the King's attitude, because it says nothing of the sending of the aide-de-camp again and again, or of the various propositions that he had to submit; and, above all, because it gives one to understand that the King rejected all the demands of France, *en bloc*, whereas he agreed to two out of three. He rejected only the third, the demand of guaranties, and that without excluding the possibility of subsequent negotiations at Berlin."[1]

Further, the telegram stated falsely that the Ambassador committed the impropriety of *stopping* the King on the promenade, whereas it was the King who accosted the Ambassador.

This first perversion of the truth was the beginning of Bismarck's final manœuvre, for it was advised, obtained, and carried out by his three agents; and the perversion was aggravated by conferring upon Bismarck the power to decide "whether Benedetti's latest demand, and the refusal with which it was met, should be communicated forthwith to the ministers, foreign nations, and the press."

This authorization of publicity was an act of diplomatic disloyalty. It is a universally admitted rule, consecrated by unbroken tradition, that so long as a negotiation is in progress, its various phases should be scrupulously kept secret. We had conformed to this safeguarding rule; we had spoken publicly from the tribune, on July 6, only because at Berlin and Madrid they had refused to negotiate with us; since the King had consented to negotiate at Ems, we had refused to reply

[1] *Jahrbuch* [vol. iii, "Die Emser Depesche"], p. 458. See also Schultze, *Die Thronkandidatur Hohenzollern*.

EVENING OF JULY 13 AT EMS

to the reiterated questions that were asked us in the Chambers.

The King had rejected the demand of guaranties: that was his right. He had refused to receive Benedetti again, because he had already said his last word to him: that too was his right. But all this being done, it was his bounden duty, before taking the public into his confidence, to await our reply to his refusal. If he had obeyed that duty, we should have taken official notice of his refusal, and we should have dropped the demand of guaranties. And it would have meant peace, as on the evening of the 12th; it would not have been so triumphant a peace, for a partial check would have dimmed its brilliancy; but in a certain point of view that would not have been without its advantage, for the King of Prussia, having thus secured some alleviation of his first discomfiture, would not have harbored against us the resentment born of wounded self-esteem. By prematurely making public his refusal, he effectively did away with the possibility of a resumption of the negotiations in Berlin, which, as Rathlef justly remarks, even the language of the telegram left open. One can understand therefore the remark that Busch attributes to the King when he ordered Abeken to send his despatch: "Now Bismarck will be satisfied with us."[1]

[1] [*Bismarck: Some Secret Pages*, etc., English trans., vol. i, p. 303.]

CHAPTER XVIII

THE EVENING OF JULY 13 AT BERLIN — BISMARCK'S SLAP IN THE FACE

BISMARCK had passed the day of the 13th in the same frenzy of rage, anxiety, and despair in which he had been plunged since his arrival at Berlin, roaring like a lion behind the bars of his cage. The more he reflected upon it, the more heavily weighted the episode seemed to be with consequences painful to contemplate. He had planned to be the trapper, and he was trapped; he had shown his hand without advantage; his king was compromised; he had aroused us abruptly from our dreams of peace, and thenceforth we should surely be on our guard; Europe was fully informed as to the value of his reassuring statements, Prussia's prestige in Germany was diminished, and German Unity under the Prussian sceptre postponed. He cried, like Shakespeare:—

> France, I am burn'd up with inflaming wrath;
> A rage whose heat hath this condition,
> That nothing can allay, nothing but blood,—
> The blood, and dearest-valu'd blood of France.[1]

The English Ambassador, Loftus, having called to felicitate him on the passing of the crisis, Bismarck expressed doubt whether the withdrawal would settle the dispute. According to his statement, he had received that morning despatches from Bremen, Königsberg, and other places, expressing strong disapproval

[1] [*King John*, Act III, Scene 2.]

of the King's conciliatory attitude, and demanding that the honor of the country be safeguarded. The English Ambassador, being accustomed to his ways, divined what he had in mind. "Unless," he wrote, "some timely counsel, some friendly hand, can intervene to appease the irritation between the two governments, the breach, in lieu of being closed by the solution of the Spanish difficulty, is likely to become wider. *It is evident to me that Count Bismarck and the Prussian Ministry regret the attitude and disposition of the King towards Count Benedetti, and that, in view of the public opinion of Germany, they feel the necessity of some decided measures to safeguard the honor of the nation.*"[1]

What should those decisive measures be? Sometimes Bismarck thought of demanding an explanation of our alleged armaments; sometimes he was for insisting that France should give some guaranty to the powers, conceding that the present solution of the Spanish question was a satisfactory answer to our demands, and that no further claim should be put forward later. "We must find out," he said, "whether, the Spanish difficulty being out of the way, there is not some other mysterious scheme which may burst upon us like a thunder-clap." *Risum teneatis.*

At last he hit upon the idea of addressing a peremptory demand to us, to which we should be compelled to reply by a challenge, or be dishonored; for it was of more importance to him than ever that we should be forced to take the initiative in the rupture, from a diplomatic standpoint. He would have called upon us to retract or explain Gramont's language in the

[1] [Loftus to Granville, July 13, *Blue Book*, pp. 32, 33. This important despatch is given in full in Appendix L.]

tribune, denouncing it as "a threat and an insult to the nation and to the King." He could no longer "maintain friendly relations with the Ambassador of France, after the language addressed to Prussia by the French Minister for Foreign Affairs in the face of Europe."

This aggressive disposition was not manifested in words alone. The German press raised or lowered its voice at a sign from him. He had imposed upon the journals known to have official connections a sarcastic, almost indifferent, placidity, so long as he had believed that we should not rid ourselves of the Hohenzollern, and that we should be constrained to assume the attitude of assailants. When he was disappointed in that belief, he unmuzzled the press

---

[1] [Loftus to Granville, July 13, *ubi sup.*]

"These recriminations were pitiful [adds M. Ollivier (vol. xiv, pp. 318, 319)] and would not have withstood discussion before the public opinion of Europe. We should have said: 'You claim that our declaration was a threat, an insult. Now, when was it read from the tribune? On the 6th; and not until the 13th do you, your King, your press, your people, discover that you have been threatened, insulted; an insult makes itself felt more quickly. Your King was outraged, on the 6th, your country defied, on the 6th, and you remain quietly at Varzin until the 13th, and your sensibility does not awake until your conspiracy is laid bare and your accomplice has abandoned you. You do not wish, you say, to be aroused by a thunderstorm; it is for you to choose: you have only to go up among the clouds and play with the lightning. You ask us for guaranties. For what? That you will be henceforth loyal and peaceful, attentive to your own business and not to other people's? You have only to give yourselves that guaranty; we shall be overjoyed.' Loftus warned our chargé d'affaires, Lesourd, of Bismarck's intentions. 'If, as I am convinced,' he said, 'the French government is earnestly desirous of peace, let it not make parade, in the tribune at least, of the favorable issue of the dispute; let it do justice to the King's conciliatory spirit, and soothe public opinion by frankly amicable statements. If, on the other hand, the present apprehensions persist, be assured that war is inevitable.' (Lesourd to Gramont, July 13.)"

and made it insulting. He himself published in the *Provincial Correspondence*, an official newspaper, a threatening article; he complained, as we alone were justified in doing, of the deplorable traces which the insulting attitude of France would leave in the relations between the two countries.

In the midst of this vaporing he received Werther's report from Ems. In his frantic quest of a means of making war inevitable, if he could have found any plausible ground for regarding our conversation with the Prussian Ambassador as a demand for a letter of apology, he would have had right at his hand something better than a pretext — a legitimate cause of war — and he would not have let it escape him. But, with all his anger, he was too much the statesman to deem himself justified in finding an excuse for war in an interview *not authenticated by him to whom it was attributed.* He recalled no doubt what he himself had written concerning the inaccuracy of ambassadors' reports.[1]

He telegraphed to Ems not to show the report to the King and to regard it as not having arrived. To Werther himself he telegraphed: "Count Bismarck is convinced that Herr Werther misinterpreted *the oral overtures* of the French minister; overtures of that sort seem to him absolutely impossible; but however that may be, he declines, as a responsible minister, to submit the report to His Majesty *as an official negotiation. If the French government has communications of that sort to make, it should draft them itself and transmit them through the French Ambassador at Berlin.*"

Thus, at Berlin as at Ems Werther's report had not

[1] To Count von Solms, at Paris, March 11, 1869.

the slightest influence on the negotiations and in no wise modified their progress. Keudell, who was at Bismarck's side, so states: —

"*The report had no other consequence than to draw down upon our representative, in addition to his instant dismissal, a severe reprimand* for his readiness to become the medium of transmission of so offensive a proposition. *On the French side, there was never any mention of the report in connection with us.*"[1]

Bismarck did, in fact, recall Werther, but not as a means of informing us of a rupture, for Werther was to explain his departure by alleging the necessity of a water-cure; he recalled him to punish him, because with the ingenuousness of an honorable man, he appeared, by listening to our grievances, to have admitted their justice.[2]

---

[1] Keudell, p. 405.

[2] ["With regard to the departure of our Ambassador, I only remark, as was officially known to the French Cabinet, that it was no recall, but a leave of absence requested by the Ambassador for personal reasons," etc. Bismarck to Bernstorff (communicated to Earl Granville), July 18. See Appendix H. — "He (Bismarck), however, sent Werther orders to quit Paris at once, directing him to take leave of absence on the pretext of ill health; at the same time he delivered a severe rebuke to the Ambassador for the manner in which he had conducted matters." Von Sybel, English trans., vol. vii, p. 393. — "At this juncture," says Gramont, writing of the 14th of July, "the Prussian Ambassador was announced and entered my private office. His face bore visible traces of the anxiety which obsessed us both. Our interview was brief; he informed me without comment that his government had reproved him for the way in which he had received our suggestions at our last interview, on the 12th, and that he had received orders to take a furlough. Consequently he had come to advise me of his immediate departure." And, after quoting the above passage of Count Bismarck's circular letter, he adds: "If it were still possible to be surprised at the lack of restraint with which M. de Bismarck substitutes for the truth fables which momentarily serve his purposes, one would be genuinely stupefied on reading these lines." Gramont, pp. 208, 209.]

Realizing that he had nothing to expect from Paris, Bismarck kept his ears open in the direction of Ems. Thence it was that the pretext for kindling the war that he had determined on was destined to come. How had the King borne himself toward Benedetti after the fulminating telegrams with which he, Bismarck, had assailed him?

Roon and Moltke were at Berlin. Roon had hastened thither on the 10th; Moltke arrived on the 12th. On the following day, the 13th, Bismarck invited them to dinner, that they might be with him to receive the decisive news. The first news came from Paris; it was the report of the session at which Gramont had read our declaration of the 13th. The interpellation had come to an end at half-past two, and the Prussian embassy and the various news-agencies had immediately telegraphed the report in every direction. As it was short and not in cipher, there was no time lost in translating it, and it reached all parts of Europe during the afternoon. Bismarck, with his swift perception, realized its full significance: we did not propose to raise any new question — consequently, no recriminations concerning the disregard of the treaty of Prague, no reservations against German Unity, nothing, in a word, to arouse the national sensitiveness; our mild words about the negotiations then in progress, when placed side by side with the emphatic tone of our ultimatum of July 6, left no doubt that we were ready to settle, and to abandon the only one of our demands that was of a nature to lead to war — that of guaranties for the future.

Thus it was still peace, as in the evening of the 12th. The war that Bismarck needed eluded him once more. His wrath became a sullen depression. It was in that frame of mind that Roon and Moltke found him. He repeated to them his purpose to retire; it seemed plain to him that the King had allowed himself to be hoodwinked; the Hohenzollern withdrawal would soon be a fact, sanctioned by His Majesty; he could not take part in such a back-down.

Roon and Moltke fought against his resolution.

"Your position," he replied, "is not like mine: being ministers in charge of special departments, you are not responsible for what is about to happen; but I, as Minister for Foreign Affairs, cannot assume the responsibility of a peace without honor. The halo that Prussia won in 1866 will fall from her brow if once the notion gains currency among the people that she 'eats crow.'"

They seated themselves at table in melancholy mood. At half-past six Abeken's despatch arrived. Bismarck read that unctuous document, which, to be sure, was not without venom, but which laid no stress on any so-called impertinence, and, above all, by leaving the door of negotiation still ajar, did not drive France into the necessity of declaring war. The two generals were thunderstruck by what they heard, to the point of forgetting to eat and drink.

Bismarck read and re-read the despatch; then, turning to Moltke, he asked abruptly, "Have we any interest in postponing the conflict?"

"We have everything to gain by hastening it," Moltke replied. "Even if we should not be strong enough at the outset to protect the left bank of the Rhine, the speed with which we could take the field would be much superior to that of France."

With that Bismarck rose, took his seat at a small table, and edited Abeken's despatch in this wise: —

Prince von Bismarck
1815 – 1898

EVENING OF JULY 13 AT BERLIN

"When the news of the withdrawal of the hereditary Prince of Hohenzollern was transmitted by the Spanish government to the French government, the French Ambassador requested His Majesty the King, at Ems, to authorize him to telegraph to Paris that His Majesty would bind himself for all time never again to give his sanction if the Hohenzollerns should renew their candidacy. Thereupon His Majesty refused to receive the French Ambassador again, and sent the aide-de-camp on duty to say that His Majesty had nothing more to communicate to him."[1]

This language is a falsification[2] of a document that was in itself falsified. Abeken's falsification was very serious, for it declared, as Rathlef remarks, that Benedetti had made but a single request, that of guaranties for the future, and suppressed his other request, that of approval of the actual withdrawal. But for this suppression, it would have been impossible to say the King refused the request of France; for of the two that were put before him, he had agreed to one.

But Abeken's despatch did mention the exchange of pourparlers; Bismarck omitted all mention of them;

[1] [It is to be understood that this account of the conference between the three great men of Prussia is taken principally from Bismarck's own cynical disclosures of later years, as made public in the various works of Dr. Busch and in his own *Reflections and Reminiscences* (*Gedenken und Erinnerungen*). In *Bismarck: Some Secret Papers*, etc., vol. i, p. 304, Busch quotes the Chancellor, on Abeken's authority, as saying (in Dec., 1870): "As I read it [Abeken's telegram] to them — it must have been about two hundred words — they were both actually terrified, and Moltke's whole being suddenly changed. *It looked as if our Most Gracious might knuckle under after all.*" See *Reflections and Reminiscences*, vol. ii, pp. 96 ff.]

[2] *Falsification*, according to the Dictionary of the Academy: Altering with intent to deceive. "I have taken pains not to falsify the meaning of a single passage." (PASCAL.) [Note of M. Ollivier in vol. xiv, p. 325.]

he ignored the King's discussion with Benedetti on the Promenade at the Springs, the notification to the Ambassador of an expected letter from the Hohenzollerns, the sending of the aide-de-camp to advise him of the arrival of that letter; naught remained save a request and a brutal refusal, with nothing between, without explanation or discussion. Abeken's muddled despatch becomes harsh, brutal, stinging, arrogant, and, as Nigra happily phrases it, discourteously laconic. The shell sent from Ems had only a fuse calculated to explode without effect; Bismarck supplied it with an excellent one which would cause it to burst with a thunderous roar as soon as it should touch the ground.

If Bismarck's manipulation of the despatch had been confined to these suppressions and to this abridgment of its language, the charge of having falsified Abeken's text would be abundantly justified. But he did more: in Abeken's despatch there was, to be sure, a reference to Benedetti's having been denied an audience; but that fact was not put forward prominently; it was mentioned by the way, as the natural consequence of the discussion being exhausted. Bismarck puts it forward as being the essential part, or, to speak more accurately, the whole of the despatch; the Ambassador was not received, not because, the King having said to him all that there was to say, there was nothing left for discussion, but because he did not choose to say to him anything whatsoever. Bismarck's despatch did not lie in stating that the King had refused to receive Benedetti; it placed a false interpretation upon a veritable fact, and transformed a perfectly natural act into a premeditated insult; so that the despatch may be summarized in a word, "The King of Prussia has refused to receive the French Ambassador."

Finally, it contained a third source of aggravation more wicked than the others. According to Abeken's despatch, the King had authorized, but had not ordered, him to make public — what? Weigh well the words: Benedetti's latest demand, and the refusal with which it was met. He had in no wise authorized the making public of the refusal to receive the Ambassador; that is to say, the making known to the world the fact that he had closed his door to the representative of one of his royal brethren; he had not carried to that point his submission to his Chancellor's behests. But Bismarck went a step further, and took especial care to publish the very thing that he had no warrant to disclose.

The telegram being thus doctored and its publication decided upon, there arose the question of the method of discharging it so that it might produce a terrific effect. Bismarck explained to his guests how he proposed to proceed: —

"Success depends above all on the impression which the outbreak of war will cause among our people, and among other peoples. *It is essential that we should be the party attacked.* Gallic presumption and excitability will confer that rôle on us *if we announce publicly to Europe, so far as possible without the interference of the Reichstag, that we accept without apprehension the public insults of France.*"[1]

Why attach so much importance to having the refusal of an audience made known, not in a discussion in the Reichstag, but by making an extraordinary communication to Europe? For the reason that the enforced publicity resulting from the inevitable explanations of a

[1] [*Reflections and Reminiscences*, English trans., vol. ii, p. 101. I have translated M. Ollivier's French version, but the sense is unchanged.]

minister from the tribune has not the insulting character of the voluntary publicity resulting from a communication unusual in form.

It was not enough for the Chancellor to strike us: he proposed that the blow should arouse such an echo that it would be impossible for us to avoid returning it. "If now," he said, "availing myself of His Majesty's permission, I send it at once to the newspapers, and if, in addition, I telegraph it to all our embassies, it will be known in Paris before midnight; not only by what it says, *but also by the way in which it will have been circulated, it will have the effect over yonder of a red flag on the Gallic bull.* We must fight, unless we choose to have the appearance of having been whipped without so much as a battle." [1]

These arguments banished the gloom of the two generals, and imparted to them a lightness of heart which surprised even Bismarck. They returned to their eating and drinking.

"The God of the old days still lives," said Roon, "and he will not let us back down in dishonor."

"Just now," cried Moltke, "I thought I heard the drums beating the retreat — now it's a fanfare. If," he added, looking joyously upward and striking his breast, "I am permitted to live long enough to lead our armies in such a war, then let the devil fly away with this old carcass!" [2]

[1] *Reflections and Reminiscences*, vol. ii, p. 101.
[2] It has been very distasteful to the German Chauvinists to describe this scene, and the explanations of it which are given, notably by Oncken, to lessen its importance and magnitude, are so ridiculous that they do not deserve discussion. Others have conceived the idea of maintaining that this scene, described so often by Bismarck before it was written down in his memoirs, was a pure invention on his part, and for proof thereof they have claimed

EVENING OF JULY 13 AT BERLIN

The judgment expressed by the two generals concerning the meaning, the purpose, and the effect of the falsified despatch has been confirmed since by all honorable and sincere Germans. Even Sybel himself ceases momentarily to be unconquerably partial, and summarizes with the arrogance of a victor, but with the accuracy of an expert historian, this machination, which was quite worthy of that artificer of intrigues who, in 1866, advised the Italians to cause themselves to be attacked by a body of hired Croatians.[1]

"By the utmost concentration in form and the omission of decisive circumstances, the meaning of the despatch was completely transformed. The publication doubled the gravity of the refusal of an audience; its conciseness of phrase multiplied it tenfold; it was for the French now to consider whether they preferred to swallow the bitter pill or to put their threats in execution."[2]

"The despatch," says Rathlef, "appears as a report of what took place at Ems, and as a historical document it is calculated to give a false idea thereof, or to arouse a suspicion that the Ambassador was perhaps subjected to something that he was not subjected to, and that the King perhaps acted as he did not act and as, indeed, he could not act; it may lead one to regard what was in

that a certain letter established the fact that on the 13th he dined with his sister, Madame von Arnim. M. Paul Matter observes that in order to assign that letter to the 13th we must agree that Bismarck passed part of the day with Roon on his estate at Gütergotz, an hour from Berlin, which seems impossible in view of the chancellor's numerous interviews — with Gortchakoff, Loftus, etc. — and the constant exchange of telegrams between Ems and Berlin. [Note of M. Ollivier in vol. xiv, p. 328.]

[1] General Alfonso La Marmora, *A Little More Light* (*Un po più di luce*).
[2] Von Sybel [English trans.], vol. vii, pp. 396, 397.

fact a courteous but firm reply as a brutal dismissal, and to believe that the King is the sort of man to reply to a suggestion that annoys him by an insult, which has never been the case. What is most unpleasant, and indeed in my judgment most distressing for us Germans in the Ems despatch is in the first place the false aspect of affairs that it suggests. But the retort which that despatch contained had in view not only the provocations of the French of that day: it was the retort to all the irritations that Bismarck had been subjected to on the part of France during his ministry — it was the final rejoinder to the acts of the French for two hundred years past. It is altogether unjust not to recognize the fact that the formal and official promulgation of such intelligence, which, for the very reason that it did not give an exact portrayal of the facts, *was looked upon and acclaimed as a challenge to France*, constituted a veritable insult to that country. Bismarck would certainly have regarded such a course of conduct with respect to Germany as an insult. — The German narratives of these events fail entirely to admit this offence on our part. Therein they are unfair." [1]

Karl Bleibtreu judges these facts with praiseworthy fairness; he declares without circumlocution that the telegram unquestionably contained "a premeditated public insult, a public outrage"; he even goes so far as to say that it unquestionably constituted *an unpardonable offence*.[2]

[1] *Jahrbuch* [vol. iii, "Die Emser Depesche"], p. 456.
[2] While seeking to tone down the severity of the judgment pronounced by him upon this act of Bismarck's, in the article from the *Jahrbuch* quoted above (because of the excitement caused in Germany by that judgment and the consequent attacks upon him), Georg Rathlef again acknowledged in a new work, published in 1903 at Dorpat, on *Bismarck's Attitude in the Period*

"That despatch," says Erich Marcks, "completely changed the color of the occurrences at Ems: no exchange of intelligence and of declarations, as Radziwill had transmitted them, was mentioned therein; it was simply a general refusal, and of biting brevity. According to that despatch, the King did what Bismarck and his friends would have done in his place: he passed, without transition, from the defensive *to the least scrupulous and most irrevocable form of the offensive. It was a slap in the face to France*, the consequence of which would be to force her to declare war."[1]

It is this opinion from which I have borrowed the phrase, "slap in the face," at the head of this chapter.

Bismarck at once put his plan in execution. He sent the telegram to his unofficial organ, the *North German Gazette*,[2] to be published at once in a special supplement, and to be posted on the hoardings. At nine o'clock in the evening, great numbers of newsboys appeared in the streets and the most frequented resorts of Berlin,

preceding the Franco-German War, that the opinion that the Ems despatch contained a counter-provocation, a counter-insult to France, albeit it was justified and well-deserved, was becoming more and more general in Germany. Erich Marcks, Kämmel, Horst-Kohl himself, so characterize it, and that opinion can but be confirmed by the fact that, in his *Reflections and Reminiscences*, Bismarck speaks of the despatch as "a red flag waved before the eyes of the French bull." [Note of M. Ollivier in vol. xiv, p. 331.]

[1] Erich Marcks, *Kaiser Wilhelm*, vol. i, p. 280. [A number of comments by German writers, of even greater severity, are quoted by Welschinger, vol. i, pp. 121 ff.]

[2] In a speech on Feb. 9, 1876 [Bismarck said:] "It is natural that governments, for certain things which they do not choose to say in their official gazettes, should reserve as much blank space in some friendly sheet as they require to express their opinion if occasion requires. It was as an auxiliary of this sort that at one time the *North German Gazette* was obligingly placed by its owners at the disposal of the government." [Note of M. Ollivier, in vol. xiv, p. 332.]

distributing *free* the supplement giving the telegram. I have before me the placard which contained that fatal news, and which was speedily pasted on the windows of the cafés, and read and commented on by numerous groups. An enormous crowd thronged the broad Unter den Linden until midnight. "The first sentiment," says an eye-witness, "was a profound amazement, a painful surprise, and the thunderstruck attitude of the crowd reminded me of the vast mute grief of which the poet of the *Pharsalia* speaks: 'Exstat sine voce dolor!' I confess that there was something heartrending to me in the spectacle of that great throng surprised and alarmed by news which presaged bloody battles and shocking disasters." [1]

Another witness was especially impressed by the warlike impulses of the crowd. "The effect," says the *Times* correspondent, "which that bit of printed paper produced upon the city was terrible. It was hailed by old and young alike; it was welcome to fathers of families and to beardless youths; it was read and re-read by women and girls, and, in an outburst of patriotism, turned over finally to the servants. There was but one opinion concerning the manly and dignified conduct of the King; there was a unanimous determination to follow his example and pick up the glove that had been thrown in the face of the nation. At ten o'clock the square before the royal palace was filled by an excited multitude. Hurrahs for the King and shouts of 'To the Rhine!' arose on all sides. Similar demonstrations took place in every quarter of the city. It was the explosion of long-restrained wrath."

[1] Berlin correspondence of the *Gazette de France*, July 16. [See La Gorce, vol. vi, pp. 284, 285.]

"The excitement was tremendous," says Von Sybel; "a shout of joy issued from the depths of the chorus of myriads of voices which formed but a single voice; men embraced with tears of joy; acclamations to the King rent the air."[1]

The fanfare which had inflamed the generals aroused Berlin. The diplomatists did not mistake the significance of the uproarious scene that was enacted before them. Bylandt, Minister of the Low Countries, told a friend of mine that, after reading the supplement of the *North German Gazette*, he rushed to his house, translated it, and telegraphed it to his government with these simple words, "War inevitable now."

At half-past eleven the placarded despatch was sent to the Prussian ministers at Dresden, Hamburg, Munich, and Stuttgart, and at half-past two in the morning to St. Petersburg, Brussels, Florence, and Rome.[2] In the morning of the 14th the *Prussian*

---

[1] [Von Sybel, vol. vii (English trans.), p. 400. This, being a translation of M. Ollivier's French translation, varies slightly from that made directly from the German.]

[2] [The precise times were given by Chancellor von Caprivi (in his address in the Reichstag, Nov. 23, 1892). But Bismarck in his circular letter of the 18th (Appendix H) said: "There exists no note or despatch by which the Prussian Government notified to the Cabinets of Europe a refusal to receive the French Ambassador. There exists nothing but the *newspaper telegram* known to all the world, which was communicated to the German Governments, and to some of our Representatives with non-German Governments . . . in order to inform them of the nature of the French demands, and the impossibility of complying with them, and which, moreover, contains nothing injurious to France." — "By a skilful splitting of hairs," says La Gorce (vol. vi, p. 255), "the communication was made, not officially, but by way of information, so that, if France should protest, they could feign surprise, could affect to be amazed that she should take offence at a simple unofficial communication, and at last could denounce her as the insulter." And see Gramont, pp. 230, 231.]

Monitor published it at the head of its unofficial section. While it was being posted on the hoardings, cried in the streets, and authenticated in the official organ, the telegraphic agencies spread it abroad to every country reached by a newspaper. Lastly, in the principal capitals, the ambassadors or ministers of the North German Confederation called upon the ministers of foreign affairs and officially communicated it to them. To all countries, in all tongues, flew the insulting falsification put forth by Bismarck. The effect of this detestable publication manifested itself at the outset with no less intensity throughout all Germany than in Berlin. "People welcomed joyfully Benedetti's dismissal just because of what it seemed to import of brutality and insult to France."

The newspapers fairly raved. Among the caricatures was this: In the background the outer room of the King's suite; in the foreground Benedetti in full uniform, shamefaced and abashed, detained by an aide-de-camp, who blocked his way with a mocking smile. The legend was to the effect that the King had abruptly turned his back and said to his aide, "Tell this gentleman that I have no reply to give him; I will not see him again."

"Even before the King's order of mobilization the people rose like one man with one mind. This mighty emotion was the work of the Ems despatch. That despatch set free the *furor teutonicus*, the holy wrath of the German 'Ich.'"[1] Since that time it has always been in Germany the synonym of a blow aimed at an adversary. Mommsen put the seal to this now historic meaning of the phrase when, in an open letter,

[1] Oncken [*Unser helden Kaiser*], p. 132.

he advised the Italians to be discreet, for otherwise there was in readiness for them "another Ems despatch."[1]

The King, like his people, felt the effect of his Chancellor's *coup de main*. He was in the Promenade by the Springs at Ems on the 14th in the morning, when the doctored telegram, which bore so little resemblance to the story written by Radziwill, was handed to him. He read it twice, deeply moved, then handed it to Eulenbourg, who was in attendance, and said, "This is war!"[2]

"This is war!" the Prussian minister at Berne exclaimed at the same moment, as if he had heard his sovereign's exclamation. Our minister, Comminges-Guitaud, was on his way to the Federal palace on some current business, when General Count Roeder, the Prussian minister, came out of the residence of the President of the Confederation. As soon as he saw Comminges-Guitaud, he went up to him and said: "Well, my dear count, so we are going to fight; I am fairly aghast. Let us shake hands once before we become enemies."

Comminges-Guitaud, astounded, exclaimed, "Do you mean that war is declared?"

"Why, yes," Roeder replied; "according to a telegram received last night, the King has refused to receive Count Benedetti, and has sent word to him that he rejected the demands of France."

---

[1] [The last two sentences are not in *L'Empire Libéral*.]

[2] This fact was told by Count Eulenbourg to Hans Delbrück (*Preussiche Jahrbücher*, 1895, p. 48), and nothing proves more conclusively Bismarck's falsification than this exclamation of the King. [Note of M. Ollivier, in vol. xiv, p. 335.]

Comminges-Guitaud's first words when he was in President Doubs's presence were, "So war is declared?"

"That is what the Prussian minister just told me," was the reply.[1]

Thus, on the 14th, before our press or our government had uttered a single word, the mob, from one end of Germany to the other, instinctively interpreted the telegram as meaning war. And that terrible word was uttered by Germany when the Cabinet at Paris was still contending, energetically and not without hope, for the maintenance of peace.

[1] "My narrative is a literal transcription of a note which Comminges-Guitaud was good enough to hand me on June 27, 1880, and which was in agreement with the suggestion of Gramont (p. 230), based on the official despatches. This narrative is very favorable to us in that it shows that the words, 'War is declared,' as characterizing Bismarck's act, were first uttered by a Prussian agent." [*L'Empire Libéral*, Appendix to vol. xiv, pp. 601, 603. And M. Ollivier proceeds to demolish a story told by Darimon (*Notes*, etc., p. 118) to the effect that he had learned from Comminges-Guitaud's own lips that he overheard the Prussian minister reading the telegram to the Swiss President, and received no direct communication of it.]

CHAPTER XIX

THE EVENING OF JULY 13 AT PARIS — PACIFIC MEASURES PREVAIL

FROM the adjournment of the Chamber until a late hour of the night of the 13th, in the absence of definite news from Ems and Berlin, the agitation of men's minds became momentarily more violent at Paris. Our reply to the interpellation called forth almost universal reprobation. The *Pays* said, in an article that men fought for a chance to read: —

"We are in the situation of those officers who are hopeless of their leaders and, having broken their swords, throw away the pieces. It is with a feeling of melancholy, almost with disgust, that we consent to take our pen in hand once more — that pen which is powerless to avert the shame that threatens France. The fact is that, with unparalleled ingenuousness, the Prime Minister sincerely believed that everything could and would be settled by Prince Antony's despatch. Now, what has this grotesque, run-to-seed old man, this Père Ducantal, this 'Père Antoine' as people already call him — what has he to do in all this business, — this old man to whom no one has applied, whom nobody knows, and who has nothing to say about it? His son, Prince Leopold, is more than of age, as he is thirty-five years old and has nothing to do with his father's drivel. He did not consult him about accepting, nor has he consulted him about declining.

It is to Prussia that M. de Gramont addresses himself, and it is Père Antoine who replies. Why, nothing could be more comic, that is to say, if there can be anything comic in the degradation of our country. And it is this sort of a peace, without guaranty, without surety, resting solely on an old man's despatch, that they propose to offer to France aroused by a national outburst of feeling? Prussia holds her peace, Prussia refuses to reply, and maintains a contemptuous silence. And the lawyers who govern us, content with their arguments of the other day, abandon their client, France, concerning themselves no further about her honor, her dignity, her interests!

"Ah! if events were destined to take this course definitively, then we must needs blush to be Frenchmen and ask to be naturalized as Prussians! But it is impossible, and the Emperor cannot leave us longer with our heads in the dust. Last evening the boulevards swarmed with an anxious crowd, and bands of students paraded the streets singing the *Chant du Départ*. It is five days now since France decided to fight; the people are murmuring and asking if we are to retreat forever. France is in revolt against ministers who know how neither to defend her, nor to protect her, nor to shelter her, and she makes a last supreme appeal to the Emperor. Let him sweep away all these babblers, these manufacturers of vain and empty words, and let us come at last to deeds! — PAUL DE CASSAGNAC.

"*Latest News.* — Three o'clock. — The back-down is consummated. The ministry, through M. le duc de Gramont as its mouthpiece, announces that France is content with the despatch of Prince Antony of

Hohenzollern. This ministry will henceforth have a name — *The Ministry of Shame!* — P. DE C." [1]

Now that it is agreed that everybody was opposed to the war, I should dumbfound certain persons if I should remind them of the language they used that

[1] [The following additional sentences from this article are given in vol. xiv, pp. 238, 339: —] "'They propose to give us a new edition of the Empire, revised, corrected, and shorn of all its glory, of a sort that an Orleanist can allow his son to read.'" [And in the postscript: —] "'The ministry thinks that it has strengthened itself and proclaimed peace, but it is mistaken. Everywhere, in the Chamber and on the street, people are saying: "This is the downfall of the Cabinet, and it is war!"'"

In April, 1880, this same Cassagnac said, in the *Pays:* "You should have been content with what was strictly necessary with regard to the national dignity. Now, what was strictly necessary was Prince Antony's withdrawal. Nothing more was needed. The honor of France was satisfied; her interests were no longer impaired. Even with a formidable armament, you would have been blameworthy to resist." — Of what use is it to offer any comment? [Note of M. Ollivier in vol. xiv, p. 339. On pages 339–341 he gives extracts from other journals, in the same sense. The *Constitutionnel* was torn to pieces and thrown into the gutter. See also pp. 624, 625. No other papers except the *Temps* and the *Débats* escaped the infection. Organs of the Right and Left and the Legitimists joined in the attack, which was supplemented by the exhortations of individuals.] "Girardin came to me and urged me not to resist the bellicose excitement of public feeling. The same considerations were presented with much greater authority by the Duc d'Albuféra. Being President of the Right Centre, he was really the leader of my majority; I had always found him loyal in my support. I was compelled to give great heed to his opinion and to listen to him with deference. He came, accompanied by Maurice Richard, to beg me not to stiffen myself against necessity and to remain, by submitting to the war, a minister of public opinion. He warned me that, if I did not decide to do it, the Left and Right would combine and overturn us. Buette, the young mechanic at whose marriage I first met Gambetta and Jules Ferry, came and told me of the impassioned speeches at La Sourdière, and in the name of that democracy which was not ill-disposed to us, he conjured me not to oppose what public opinion demanded of me. In April, 1874, he wrote to me: 'At the moment when there was doubt whether you were inclined to peace, I heard the speech that Gambetta delivered in favor of war; and I expressed his thought when I came to see you in order to urge you in that direction.'"

afternoon. "You are incomprehensible," some said to me. "You are the minister of the plebiscite; you might be the minister of victory, and you will not!"

"Whenever I shall believe," I replied, "that France is threatened in her dignity and her honor, I shall be the first to utter the cry of war, and I should not have hesitated to do it, had not the candidacy been withdrawn; but it is on the point of disappearing, and you would have my government, taking advantage of a momentary excitement, engage in a bloody undertaking for the sole purpose of exalting my own personality or my policy? You are in error as to the consequences of a war. Victory is certain — to that I agree: all military men, great and small, promise it. But what shall we do with our victory? Shall we take the Rhine? According to our French theory of nationalities, conquest no longer affords a just claim to acquisition of territory. Do you imagine that Germany would leave you in peaceful possession of your prey? Her children, forcibly separated from her, would always have their hands stretched out to her, and war would break out again and again so long as their deliverance had not been achieved. And, to consider moral results alone, what a calamity a war between two such highly civilized nations would be! Doubtless there does exist a barbarian Germany, greedy of fighting and of conquest — the Germany of the clodhoppers, a Germany pharisaical and godless, the Germany of the unintelligible pedants whose empty lucubrations and microscopical investigations have been vaunted to us overmuch. But these two are not the great Germany, the Germany of the artists, poets, and thinkers; that Germany is kindly, generous, humane, charming, and peace-loving; it is portrayed in the touching remark of Goethe, who, being asked to write against us, replied that he could not find it in his heart to hate the French. If we do not oppose the natural movement toward German Unity, but allow it to work itself out quietly through its successive stages, it will not give the supremacy to the barbarian, sophisticated Germany, but will insure the triumph of intellectual, civilizing Germany. War, on the other hand, would establish the domination, for a period impossible to estimate, of the Germany of the clodhoppers and pedants, for it would be the rallying-point of the struggle to return to the Rhine."[1]

How many times in a few hours I repeated these arguments,[2] until I was worn out, to the men who crowded about me, hoping to persuade me! The other members of the Ministry, being in constant communication with the press, fought no less manfully. Gramont alone continued his dialogue aside with Benedetti, paying no heed to the decision of the Cabinet that morning. At half-past eight he telegraphed: —

"As I have already informed you, public opinion is so overexcited, that we succeeded only with the greatest difficulty in postponing our explanation until Friday. Make one last effort with the King; tell him that we confine ourselves to requesting him to forbid the Prince of Hohenzollern to reconsider his withdrawal; let him say to you: 'I will forbid it,' and authorize you

---

[1] [This passage, as printed in *L'Empire Libéral*, is considerably shortened here.]

[2] "Breathing much harder than M. Thiers did in his conference with my colleagues." *L'Empire Libéral*, vol. xiv, p. 344.

to write us to that effect; or let him instruct his minister or his ambassador to convey that information to me — that will be enough for us. I have reason to believe that the other European cabinets consider us fair and moderate in our demands. The Emperor Alexander gives us his hearty support. In any event, leave Ems and come to Paris with the reply, whether affirmative or negative." [1]

A few moments after he had written this despatch, there came into Gramont's hands proof that he was deluding himself concerning the favorable sentiments of Europe, of which he assured Benedetti. At half-past eight he received a courageous warning from Saint-Vallier: [2] —

"Any further insistence with Prussia on our part would be *now* regarded, in Southern Germany, as proof of warlike intent, and would confirm the current opinion that the Hohenzollern affair is a pretext, so far as we are concerned, and that we want war. The withdrawal reverses the situation; those who approved of our attitude blame us, and we shall be in a bad position if we demand further guaranties."

Friend Beust himself sent word to Gramont that he would make a mistake if he should force matters to extremities; that no one was in a better position than he to judge of the disposition of the states of the South, and that he was convinced that, if France were relying

---

[1] [Part of the despatch, dated July 13, 9.45 P.M., is omitted. See Benedetti, pp. 384, 385; also Gramont, pp. 189–191.]

[2] [Minister to Würtemberg]; it was dated Stuttgart, July 13, 1 P.M.; received at 8.30 P.M. [The whole despatch is given in vol. xiv, p. 346.] "'We might have hoped for the neutrality of the South in this conflict (what an error !); it is impossible to count upon it to-day,'" etc.

EVENING OF JULY 13 AT PARIS 301

on the sympathy of those states, she was making a great mistake.[1]

Fleury, at St. Petersburg, was no less outspoken. In the absence of Gortchakoff, he had seen the Czar. Before he had shown him the text of the demand of guaranties, Alexander flew into a veritable passion. "I have taken much trouble to avert war, but you will have it, eh?" And when Fleury mentioned our honor, he retorted quickly: "Your honor! And what about others' honor?" When he had read Gramont's despatch carefully, he calmed down, but he refused to intervene again with his uncle. Being persuaded, quite mistakenly, that the withdrawal was due to the King's personal influence, he did not choose to exert any further pressure on him, for "his pride had been wounded, and he also found himself face to face with German national sentiment, already offended by Prince Leopold's withdrawal."

At the same time with these salutary warnings, more favorable news reached us. Olozaga came during the evening to inform me that his government had sent him its approval, and that after he had informed Prince Antony thereof, he should pay no further attention to the candidacy. But, in reality, matters were not so far advanced. Serrano admitted the authenticity of the withdrawal; but Sagasta did not at all understand what had taken place, and was awaiting confirmation by the Spanish Ambassador at Berlin; furthermore, he did not regard a withdrawal not emanating from the Prince himself as intended to be taken seriously. Statesmen like Silvela proposed to the ministers to go ahead despite the withdrawal, and to cause Leopold to

[1] Bloomfield to Granville, July 13 [*Blue Book*, p. 50].

be proclaimed by the Cortes.¹ "He can withdraw again if such is his pleasure, when he has been chosen," they said.

We, knowing nothing of these circumstances, accepted the Ambassador's assurances and regarded the incident as closed so far as Spain was concerned. I thanked Olozaga from my heart and said to him: "The King's approval has not reached us, but I have no doubt that it will be forthcoming and I have made up my mind to not obtaining the rest. So that we have peace in our grasp. To-morrow morning, before the Council, I shall prepare a statement to the Chambers to that effect. I shall speak of Spain and of you, and I propose that you shall be satisfied with what I say. So come to see me early to-morrow, and I will submit my draft to you."

He promised to come. I went then to the Foreign Office to see the only document that I still lacked — the King of Prussia's reply — if it had finally arrived.

Gramont was not there. He had received, in addition to Olozaga's communication, a third and fourth despatch from Benedetti, between half-past ten and eleven o'clock. The third (dated 3.45 P.M.) said: "The King has received the reply of the Prince of Hohenzollern. It is from Prince Antony, and informs His

¹ This was told me in May, 1882, by Del Mazo, Ambassador at Rome. [On the 14th Mr. Layard at Madrid telegraphed to Lord Granville: "I received a note from General Prim *yesterday morning*, informing me that the father of Prince Leopold . . . had withdrawn the acceptance of his son to become a candidate for the Throne of Spain, and the cause of the misunderstanding with France might, consequently, be considered at an end." *Blue Book*, p. 43. The candidacy was formally abandoned by the Spanish government, on the 15th. Rances to Granville, July 16, *Blue Book*, p. 55.]

Majesty that Prince Leopold, his son, has withdrawn his candidacy for the Spanish crown. The King authorizes me to make it known to the Emperor's government that he approves this decision. The King sent one of his aides-de-camp to make this communication to me, and I reproduce its exact terms. His Majesty having sent me no message on the subject of the assurances for the future that we desired, I have requested a last audience in order to submit to him anew, and to enlarge upon, the suggestions that I made to him this morning. I have strong reasons to believe that I shall obtain no concession in that respect."

The fourth despatch (from Ems, 7 P.M.) said: "In reply to my request for a further audience the King sent word to me that it was impossible for him to resume our discussion relative to the assurances which, in our opinion, should be given for the future. His Majesty caused me to be informed that on that subject he referred to the considerations that he set before me this morning. The King consents, so his emissary informed me in His Majesty's name, to give his full and unconditional approval to the Prince's withdrawal; he can do no more. I shall await your orders before leaving Ems. Count Bismarck will not come here; I note the arrival of the ministers of Finance and of the Interior."[1]

Gramont had lost no time in taking these important documents to the Emperor at Saint-Cloud.

On returning home after a long walk, I found this note which had been waiting for me some time: —

"MY DEAR FRIEND, — I am going to Saint-Cloud. More news. He (the King) has communicated the

[1] [Benedetti, pp. 375, 376.]

Hohenzollern letter to us, and has *approved* it; but that's not much." [1]

Copies of Benedetti's telegrams were not enclosed with the note. I replied at once: —

"MY DEAR FRIEND, — It does not seem to me that the approval is 'not much,' especially in connection with the despatch Olozaga showed you. Don't bind yourself, even in your own mind, until we have talked matters over. Ever yours."

At Saint-Cloud Gramont fell in with Jérôme David, who had dined there. In truth, one would have thought that he had gone there to make his report of some mission and to receive congratulations. Gramont suggested to the Emperor that that dinner, only a few hours after the session of the Chamber, would produce a bad impression; and as it turned out, the warlike newspapers announced it triumphantly the next day.

The Emperor replied that the invitation came from the Empress, and that he could not have sent David away.

On his return to Paris, at a very late hour, Gramont made haste to inform me of the result of his visit by the following note: —

"MY DEAR FRIEND, — I am just back from Saint-Cloud. There is great indecision there. At first, war.

[1] [M Ollivier here omits part of this note, which is given in full in vol. xiv, p. 350.] — "'Believe that I cannot forgive myself for that *mot* in my reply to-day. It distresses me to think that any one could believe that I had intended to injure you. It is so far from my heart and thought.' He alluded to the contemptuous words concerning reports current in the lobby, which some people had considered as aimed at me." [See *supra*, p. 259 n.]

Later, hesitation because of the King's approval. It may be that the Spanish despatch will make the balance incline toward peace. The Emperor bade me request you to let all our colleagues know that he expects us to dinner at seven o'clock to-morrow, to hold a Council during the evening. Ever yours."

Here again Gramont spoke as an ambassador rather than as a responsible minister. Doubtless the opinion of Saint-Cloud was of some importance, but my opinion and my colleagues' were no less so, and at that hour, and throughout that whole night of the 13th, there was no sort of uncertainty in my mind: King William had answered with a conciseness that left nothing to be desired; he had communicated the withdrawal of the candidacy to us, through Benedetti, declaring that he approved it; Olozaga advised us of unconditional acceptance of the situation by Spain; unless they were not acting in good faith, no one could deny that the twofold acceptance, by Prussia and by Spain, implied a more than sufficient guaranty of the future. We had reached the goal that we had set before ourselves. There was but one way left to bring on war, — that was to go outside of the question that was now settled as we desired, and to resurrect the dispute concerning our general grievances against Prussia; to that I was determined not to consent.

And so when Mitchell, according to his wont, came to learn the news, I summed up the situation at the end of that day in a word: "Prim and the King of Prussia accept the withdrawal, and we shall not insist on the guaranties, nor shall we raise any other question; the thing is really settled now."

Mitchell took his leave with that assurance. He met Paul de Cassagnac.

"Well, what's the news?"

"I have just come from Émile Ollivier's; peace is assured, thank God!"

"Are you quite sure? My father saw the Emperor this morning, and war is determined on, thank God!"[1]

Père Cassagnac was mistaken. Of course, the Empress and her cabal were for war; but the Emperor, as we have seen from Gramont's letter, was only at the stage of indecision. Under the pressure of the bellicose spirits he had seemed to go over to them; in the Council, under the influence of his ministers, he would have adhered definitely to our opinion, and his momentary hesitation would have been changed into a decision in favor of peace. Would the Chamber follow us or overturn us? I am persuaded that, in spite of everything, if the Emperor had declared himself unreservedly, the Chamber would have followed us.[2] Believing that we

[1] [Told by M. Mitchell in an article in the *Courrier de France* of Sept. 24, 1872, as having taken place in the morning of the 14th; Lehautcourt, vol. i, p. 318 n.]

[2] "Meanwhile the Right was organizing a coalition with the Left to make an end of us. Clément Duvernois still kept up an old friendship with Gambetta; they passed the evening together; Gambetta promised to support the order of the day in favor of disarmament, which Duvernois would defend, and the result of which, if the Chamber should adopt it, would be war. Duvernois, returning to the office of the *Volontaire*, found one of his editors there — Castanet. He went up to him, with a beaming face, and held out his hands. 'This time,' he said, speaking of me, 'this time we've got him; he won't escape us . . . a few hours more, and it will be all over with him. I have agreed with Gambetta to propose to the Chamber that the ministry be instructed to inform Prussia that we are ready to disarm and reduce our military force, on condition that she disbands her army and does it first. Gambetta is sure of his friends' support; I have with me all the cowards of the Right, and they are numerous. What a door I am opening

EVENING OF JULY 13 AT PARIS

had seen the end of our agonies, I slept peacefully for the first time in many days, having no suspicion of the cyclone that was destined to burst upon us on our waking.

for them, and how they will plunge through head first and with eyes closed! My order of the day will pass by a large majority. You can judge whether the ministry can hold out against this double blow. Left and Right!' he added, laughing. . . . 'What a face that poor Ollivier will make!' And when Castanet asked him what he thought Prussia would do in the face of such a suggestion, 'Prussia,' he replied, . . . 'Prussia will tell us to go to the devil, and then we shall declare war; you'll see how prettily we'll bring this thing off!'" *L'Empire Libéral*, vol. xiv, pp. 353, 354. [M. Ollivier says that Castanet wrote him this in May, 1880.]

CHAPTER XX

EXASPERATION AT PARIS CAUSED BY THE EMS DESPATCH

ON the morning of the 14th, with my mind at rest at last, after much distress, I sat down to draw the declaration which I proposed to submit to the Council of Ministers at Saint-Cloud in the evening. I have kept what I wrote : —

"A week since, the French Government declared from this tribune that, however sincere its desire to preserve the peace of the world, it would not suffer a foreign prince" (here quote our words of the 6th). "To-day we are certain that a foreign prince will not ascend the Spanish throne. This victory is the more valuable to us in that it has been won by force of reason and justice alone, and not by bloody sacrifices. In presence of the patriotic enthusiasm which our attitude aroused, it would have been easy to complicate one question with another and to manufacture some pretext for dragging the country into a great war. Such conduct would have seemed to us worthy neither of you nor of ourselves; it would have alienated the sympathy of Europe, and, eventually, of our own country. When we are advancing toward a definite goal, we will not conceal it from you. We will point it out to you unmistakably. We requested your support against a Prussian candidacy to the throne of Spain. That candidacy is eliminated; it only remains for us now to resume with confidence the works of peace."

I was going on to speak of the part played by Olozaga and by Spain, when the door opened and an usher announced "His Excellency the Minister for Foreign Affairs." As soon as he had crossed the threshold, even before he had reached the middle of the room, Gramont cried : —

"My dear fellow, you see before you a man who has received a knockdown blow!"

I rose. "I don't understand; explain yourself."

Thereupon he handed me a small sheet of yellow paper, which I shall see before my eyes as long as I live. It was a telegram from Lesourd, sent from Berlin after midnight of the 13th, and thus conceived : —

"A supplement of the *North-German Gazette*, which appeared at ten o'clock this evening, contains in substance what follows: 'The French Ambassador, at Ems, having requested His Majesty the King to authorize him to telegraph to Paris that he would undertake not to give his consent hereafter to the Hohenzollern candidacy, if it should be revived, the King refused to receive the Ambassador and sent word to him by the aide-de-camp on duty that he had no further communication to make to him.' This news, published by the official journal, has caused intense excitement in the city."

"Had not Benedetti advised you?" I asked Gramont.

"Here is what he telegraphed me yesterday afternoon," he replied. "These four despatches came in quick succession during the evening, and I didn't think it necessary to enclose them with my note."

After reading Benedetti's despatches, I re-read Lesourd's. I understood Gramont's exclamation. No one ever foundered nearer port. For a few moments I stood silent, dumfounded. "We can delude ourselves no longer," I said. "They propose to force us into war."

We agreed that I should assemble our colleagues at once, in order to acquaint them with this unforeseen blow, while he returned to the Foreign Office, Werther having called there.

Thereupon Olozaga arrived, as calm as I myself had been a few moments earlier, to hear me read my pacific statement. I told him of Benedetti's despatches and Lesourd's. He was no less horrified than myself. Obliging and eager to be of service, he offered to go to see Werther, in order to obtain an explanation, if that were possible. I accepted his offer, but he did not find the Prussian Ambassador.

Our colleagues soon made their appearance, greatly disturbed; they deemed it impossible to postpone till evening a full Council, and they instructed me to telegraph to the Emperor, begging him to come to the Tuileries in the afternoon, to preside over it.[1]

At half-past twelve the Emperor arrived at the Tuileries, and summoned us to join him. He had, like ourselves, passed through an impatient, wrathful mob, from which arose hoarse cries, incitements to disorder, and protests against diplomatic delays.[2]

[1] "At the same time a very urgent message from Lyons arrived, 'begging Gramont, in the name of Her Majesty's Government, not to commit the Government by a premature declaration to the Chambers,' and representing that 'it would be more prudent, and at the same time more dignified,' to wait 'at least until the time originally fixed' (the following day, Friday)." *L'Empire Libéral*, p. 357. [Lyons to Granville, July 14, *Blue Book*, p. 36.]

[2] [See Gramont, p. 211. "I had some difficulty in reaching the Chamber, for the agitation there had already extended to the masses, and the approaches to the ministry as well as to the Corps Législatif were crowded by an impatient and angry multitude. Hoarse cries, inflammatory and disorderly harangues, protests against any sort of negotiation were shouted and acclaimed by the crowd all along the quays and even to the Tuileries."]

PARIS EXASPERATED 311

Our deliberations lasted nearly six hours. At the opening of the session Gramont dropped his portfolio on the table and said as he took his seat: "After what has happened, a Minister for Foreign Affairs who would not make up his mind for war would not be worthy to retain his portfolio."

Le Bœuf did not tell us, as the newsmongers declared, that the Prussian army was mobilized and marching toward our frontier: if mobilization had been ordered, we should have been informed by Benedetti and Stoffel.[1] He said simply that, according to his secret intelligence, preparations had begun; that they were buying horses in Belgium, and that, unless we wanted to be forestalled, we had not a moment to lose.

[1] [As to Colonel Stoffel, military attaché of the French embassy at Berlin, and his reports from 1866 to 1870, see Welschinger, vol. i, pp. 10–12; La Gorce, vol. vi, pp. 129, 130. — In the Preface to *Ma Mission en Prusse*, p. 9, Benedetti says: "Among our troops, even among some of our officers who are seeking excuses for our defeats, it is assumed as a fact that Prussia mobilized her army in time, that is to say, several weeks before the declaration of war; that she succeeded in concealing from my scrutiny the execution of that manœuvre, and that I gave no information of it at Paris; that thus we were forestalled by the enemy in the midst of the arrangements we were making to take the field. That is absurd, because it is false and impossible. You know, indeed, that Prussia did not summon her reserves until we had announced, in our session of the 15th, our purpose to obtain by arms the guaranties they refused to give us voluntarily, and that it is idiotic to suppose hundreds of thousands of men can be called to the colors at one time, and the measure be hidden from the ken of the public and especially of the press." The reports of the Prussian general staff have shown since that the order for mobilization was issued on the night of the 15th and 16th; but Gramont, writing in 1872 in defence of his action, declares (pp. 232, 233) that "the armies of Prussia were actively beginning their mobilization" — on the 14th — "and everything was proceeding on the other side of the Rhine as if war were declared. *The sequel proved that these preparations had been begun more than a week earlier;* but for twenty-four hours they had been going forward openly." See La Gorce, vol. vi, p. 290; Sorel, vol. i, pp. 169 n., 175, 176.]

Despite the impression made upon us by these remarks of our two colleagues and the indisputable reasons that inspired them, our perplexity was of long duration. Refusing to yield to the bidding of our first impulse, we scrutinized the conduct of Bismarck and the King from a diplomatic and a judicial standpoint. We inquired first what was the nature of the document printed in the *North German Gazette*. If it had been simply a newspaper item, we should have paid no heed to it; we should have taken no more notice of it than of so many others which we had let pass without comment. But this was a special supplement in the shape of a white poster in large type (I have it before me now), which could be pasted on walls and shop-windows. The information it gave was not in the form of a newspaper article, but the exact text of an official document, which could not have been supplied except by the ministers who drew it, and with the deliberate purpose of throwing it to the public. We regarded that publication, therefore, as an intentional insult.

And yet, having reached that conclusion, we could not make up our minds to take the decisive step. We clung desperately to peace, although we knew that it no longer existed. We struggled long between two impossibilities, seeking palliatives and rejecting them, recoiling from the decisive step, and irresistibly drawn back to it. "Hesitation," said they who never knew the torture of heavy responsibilities. "No," replies the great Frederick, "the uncertainty that precedes all great events."[1]

We were compelled at last to admit that submission

---

[1] Frederick II to his brother Henry, June 17, 1778.

PARIS EXASPERATED

would be degrading, that what had taken place at Berlin constituted a declaration of war, and that the only question for us was whether we should bend our necks under the affront, or should hold our heads erect like honorable men. On this question there could be no hesitation, and we ordered the recall of the reserves (four o'clock).

The marshal (Le Bœuf) rose at once, to go to the department and put our decree in execution. He had hardly closed the door when he was attacked by a scruple. He returned and said: "Gentlemen, this that we have decided is a very serious matter, but we did not vote. Before signing the recall of the reserves, I demand a yea-and-nay vote."

He himself asked us the question, one after another, beginning with me and ending with the Emperor. Our response was unanimous.[1] "Now," said the marshal, "I have no further interest in what you may do." And he went off to the department, and had the orders prepared for the recall of the reserves (4.40 P.M.).

Thereupon I laid before the Emperor one last means of placing his desire for peace beyond all suspicion. "Let Your Majesty authorize me to insist in the Corps Législatif that, in spite of everything, the affair is ended and that we attach no importance to the Prussian pronouncement. The cause is a weak one; I shall defend it without conviction and I shall not win it; we shall fall under a crushing vote; but we shall at least have sheltered Your Majesty completely. Forced by the Chamber to dismiss a peace ministry and to name a ministry bent upon war, Your Majesty

[1] ["Almost unanimous," says La Gorce, vol. vi, p. 291, quoting Le Bœuf's testimony at the Inquiry concerning the 4th of September.]

cannot be accused by your enemies of having sought war in your own personal interest."

The Emperor did not relish my suggestion. "I cannot part with you," he said, "just when you are most necessary to me." And he begged me not to insist.

How differently would matters have turned out if I had brought the Emperor over to my opinion!

We had begun to settle the terms of our declaration to the Chambers, when Gramont was advised of the arrival of a despatch in cipher from Benedetti. We suspended our deliberations.[1] The despatch, when translated, proved to be simply an expansion of the latest telegrams. But the language which it attributed to the King, while it was still negative, seemed unbending. There was nothing in it to cause us to retrace our steps. And yet, as if terror-stricken by our decision, we grasped madly at that faint hope; and thereupon a fresh discussion ensued — pusillanimous now, and, above all, devoid of sense. A savage

[1] *L'Empire Libéral*, vol. xiv, pp. 363, 364: "The Chamber was in session, effervescent, anxious; to pacify it and to obtain information we sent Maurice Richard to the Palais-Bourbon. On his return he described the aspect of the assemblage as About's newspaper did a few hours later: 'The enthusiasm is immense. If there is a declaration to-day the Corps Législatif will crumble under the applause. If the declaration does not come, it will be more than a disappointment, more than a disillusionment; there will be a tremendous burst of laughter and the Cabinet will be drowned in its own silence. Yesterday, when it looked like peace, people called that peace by a very pretty name. Historians called it "halting," like that which preceded the St. Bartholomew; but the ignorant folk called it a — No, it is impossible to tell you what they called it. It's a very wicked word which is current in country markets, but which is not used in the Chamber except in a small company, in a very small company, and in the lobbies. — Enters M. Maurice Richard; he is questioned, and he questions. Evidently he wishes to see with his own eyes what is going on. If he reports exactly what he saw, he can tell the Emperor that the Chamber is a huge Leyden jar.' *Le Soir* of July 14."

had struck us with such force that the whole world shuddered, and that Germany, even before the summons of her King, was up in arms; and we were wondering whether that resounding blow might not be wiped from our cheek by a conference!

Gramont started the idea. We approved it, myself among the rest, aye, even more strongly than the rest; for, according to my colleagues, it would seem that I soared to the loftiest heights of eloquence.[1] Louvet and Plichon, taking advantage of a moment's respite, implored the Emperor not to subject the solidity of his throne to the hazards of war, and all of us, without exception, agreed upon an appeal to a European Congress.

I blush as I write of this eclipse of our courage, which does us little credit, but I have promised myself to be absolutely frank. The expedient of a congress was well worn: whenever he found himself in a predicament the Emperor had tried it, and always in vain. We strove to make it presentable once more without absurdity by refurbishing it as to form. We tried a great number of drafts, until at last I suggested orally a form of words which seemed apt. "Go at once to my study and put that in writing," said the Emperor, putting his hand on my arm. And, as he spoke, tears were rolling down his cheeks.

---

[1] [La Gorce, vol. vi, p. 291, quotes "one member of the Council" to this effect, but does not name him. — According to the unpublished papers of M. Louvet, cited by La Gorce (p. 289), Plichon said to the Emperor: " 'Sire, the game is not an even one between King William and you. The King can afford to lose several battles; for Your Majesty, defeat means revolution.' The sovereign seemed neither surprised nor offended by this outspokenness. 'Ah! Monsieur Plichon,' he said, 'what you say is very sad, but I thank you for your frankness.'" And see Sorel, vol. i, p. 170.]

I returned with my draft; we made a few changes in it, and adopted it.[1] The Emperor would have liked us to read it to the Chambers forthwith, but it was too late; neither the Senate nor the Corps Législatif would be in session; moreover, we were worn out, in no condition to face the fierce storm that would have greeted us. So we postponed our declaration until the morrow. However, before leaving the Tuileries the Emperor wrote Le Bœuf a note, which, although it did not countermand the order to recall the reserves, hinted at some doubt concerning the urgency of that measure.[2]

When I emerged from the species of confinement in which we had been deliberating so many hours, I felt what a man feels on coming out into the fresh air from a stifling atmosphere: the phantoms of the brain vanish, and the mind resumes the consciousness of realities. The plan upon which we had agreed appeared to me as what it really was, a mysterious failure of courage. I was able very speedily to convince myself of the interpretation that the public would have placed upon it. On my return to the chancellery, I assembled my family and my secretaries

---

[1] [Gramont (p. 212) gives the following as the substance, if not the exact words, of the communication to be made to the Chambers: "We believe that the principle tacitly sanctioned by Europe has been to prevent a prince belonging to the reigning family of any of the great powers from ascending a foreign throne without a previous agreement to that effect, and we ask the great powers of Europe, assembled in Congress, to affirm this rule of international law." But M. Ollivier says that these few lines were simply an outline, which was not used.] "My draft was oratorical in form and pathetic in tone; I have been unable to find it among my papers." [Note in vol. xiv, p. 336.]

[2] The order for the recall of the reserves was not withdrawn. Gramont (p. 220) is mistaken in saying that it was. [Note of M. Ollivier, *ibid.*]

PARIS EXASPERATED 317

and read to them the declaration agreed upon. My brothers, my wife, my general secretary, Philis, one and all, even the partisans of peace, exploded in angry exclamations. There was a universal chorus of amazement and reproach.

Nor was our appeal to Europe more favorably received at Saint-Cloud. "Well!" said the Empress to the Emperor, "so it seems that we are to have war?"

"No, we have agreed upon an expedient that may enable us to avoid it."

"In that case," said the Empress, handing him a copy of *Le Peuple Français*, "why does your paper say that war is declared?"

"In the first place," rejoined the Emperor, "that is not my paper, as you call it, and I know nothing about that item. Moreover, this is what was drawn up at the Council." And he gave her the declaration to read.

"I doubt," said she, "whether this accords with the sentiment of the Chambers and the country." Only she did not say it calmly, as one would suppose from the Emperor's story to Gramont; she expressed her feelings in impetuous terms.[1]

---

[1] ["At Saint-Cloud, the result of the deliberations at the Tuileries was awaited with anxiety. There the most deplorable passions held sway: those born of presumption, anger, and ignorance. At nightfall the Emperor returned, bringing with him the faint hope of a congress. . . . There can be no doubt that the Empress encouraged, if she did not inspire this chorus of reprobation. `A most honorable reserve, born of pity for misfortune combined with loyalty to an august sovereign, has veiled or softened most of the public testimony which might accuse her. But from all the unpublished correspondence and private papers, one fact stands out very clearly; and that is that she was, on the side of France, the principal author of the war." La Gorce, vol. vi, pp. 293, 294. And see Welschinger, vol. i, pp. 147–151, for an elaborate discussion of the subject.]

Le Bœuf, who, despite the Emperor's note, had despatched the orders for mobilization at eight hours and forty minutes post meridian, went to Saint-Cloud after dinner and urged the Emperor to assemble the Council that evening, in order to decide whether the recall of the reserves should be revoked or confirmed.

The Emperor telegraphed to me to summon the ministers to Saint-Cloud on urgent business. He then informed the marshal of our plan for a congress, resolved upon after he had left the Council.

"Well! what do you think of it?" inquired the Empress.

Le Bœuf replied that war would certainly have been preferable, but that, since that idea was abandoned, the declaration in question seemed to him the next best thing.

"What! so you too approve this dastardly thing?" she cried. "If you are willing to disgrace yourself, do not disgrace the Emperor!"

"Oh!" said the Emperor, "how can you speak so to a man who has given us so many proofs of devotion?"

She realized her mistake, and as impulsive in her regret as she had been in her harshness, she embraced the marshal and begged him to forget her warmth. She had intended especially to attack, over the marshal's head, the middle course at which we had arrived. In that respect her words were not too strong. That evening she felt, thought, and spoke justly. Her wrath was legitimate, and she did well to employ her influence in putting aside an expedient which, without preserving peace, would have discredited the Emperor forever.[1]

[1] [In his larger work, M. Ollivier has this to say of a last attempt of the English government to save the situation.] "It is fortunate, if I may say

When I set out for Saint-Cloud it was one of those delicious evenings that we sometimes have in Paris before August has burned everything and withered the foliage. The air was warm without being oppressive; the sparkle of the stars was less bright than in

so, that we were prevented from displaying our poor solution of the difficulty in the tribune. That very day Bismarck, at Berlin, showed us how he would have accepted it. Granville had conceived the idea of a compromise. He caused a memorandum containing the following suggestion to be placed before the King of Prussia: 'As His Majesty had consented to the acceptance by Prince Leopold of the Spanish crown, and had thereby, in a certain sense, become a party to the arrangement, so he might with perfect dignity communicate to the French Government his consent to the withdrawal of the acceptance, if France shall waive her demand for an engagement covering the future.' [Granville to Lyons, July 24, *Blue Book*, p. 28. Gramont, pp. 198-201, discussing this English proposal, declares that it was substantially identical with the request of France that the King should 'announce, communicate, or transmit' the withdrawal of Prince Leopold.] . . . We should have accepted this suggestion, since, in the Council of the 13th, we had impliedly abandoned the demand of guaranties; but Bismarck did not give us time. He received with very ill grace a proposal which, just as his trumpet was resounding through the world, would bring the King and Prussia into court. He did not disguise his ill humor and assumed a very lofty tone. 'He expressed his regret that Her Majesty's Government should have made a proposal which it would be impossible for him to recommend to the King for His Majesty's acceptance. Prussia had shown, under a public menace from France, a calmness and moderation which would render any further concession on her part equivalent to a submission to the arbitrary will of France, and would be viewed in the light of a humiliation which the national feeling throughout Germany would certainly repudiate as a fresh insult. . . . The Prussian Government, as such, has nothing to do with the acceptance of the candidature . . . and had not even been cognizant of it. They could not, therefore, balance their assent to such acceptance by their assent to its withdrawal. A demand for interference on the part of a sovereign in a matter of purely private character could not, his Excellency considered, be made the subject of public communication between Governments, and that, as the original pretext for such a demand was to be found in the candidature itself, it could no longer be necessary now that the candidature had been renounced.' [Granville to Loftus, July 15, *Blue Book*, p. 30. Both the proposal and its rejection were made through Bernstorff, Prussian Ambassador to England.] . . . One may judge from this of the fate in

our South — it was softer; the Seine flowed gently, with a languid current; along the quays and in the avenues of the Bois de Boulogne, where the violent excitement of the city did not make itself felt, an infectious serenity reigned; care-free youths and maidens walked hither and thither, talking and laughing. The council of Nature was for peace, the source of life and of joy, peace, sister of the Muses and Graces, lovable and fruitful peace, — and not for war, the terrible reaper. I heard her voice, and I was like one overwhelmed. What would I not have given to lay aside authority, and lose myself in that heedless throng!

store for our appeal for a congress. England . . . would not again have risked drawing upon herself a personal rebuff and a certain refusal. Russia would have been even less likely to do it, and Bismarck would have seized the opportunity to give us a second slap in the face, as the first had not sufficed. Then, indeed, we should have deserved the epithet, 'Ministry of Shame,' which Cassagnac had unjustly applied to us the day before." *L'Empire Libéral*, pp. 367–369.

[A different view of the probable result of the suggestion of a congress is held by Sorel. "For a moment," he says (vol. i, p. 171), "it seemed as if the ministry were going to be clever, as if the Empire were going to abstain from making a mistake, and for once at least to defeat the schemes of its foes. This suggestion of a congress would have been a master-stroke. England would have subscribed to it; Russia, which had just proposed a conference [on the 13th: see Granville to Buchanan, July 20, *Blue Book*, p. 66], would undoubtedly have done the same; France could rely on Austria, Italy, and the Turkish Empire. As for Prussia, she would have found herself in the greatest embarrassment. M. de Bismarck considering himself now as sure to be challenged was rushing toward war; at the moment that the ministry were deliberating in Paris, he was rejecting an attempt at intervention by England. This congress would have surprised Prussia and upset her plans; it would have compromised her before Europe and would have forced her to accept the arbitrament of the powers or to lose their moral support." And see to the same effect, La Gorce, vol. vi, p. 193. Welschinger, vol. i, pp. 145, 146, is rather more doubtful of the result, because the congress would have exacted some things to which the ultra-Bonapartists might not have assented. "Still, anything was preferable to blind precipitation."]

Under the influence of this emotion I reviewed the question once more from the beginning. I set the arguments on one side and the other face to face once more, dwelling especially on the arguments for peace. Drops of sweat born of my inward anguish moistened my brow. *Et in agonia ego.* But to no purpose did I argue and quibble and contend against common sense — it seized me, crushed me, vanquished me, and I came back always to the same conclusion: France had been wilfully, grossly insulted, and we should be faithless guardians of her honor if we tolerated it. When a saint is struck, he kneels and offers the other cheek. Could we propose to the French nation to assume that attitude? There is something noble and triumphant, I know, in a fearless insensibility to insults, "whereby they turn and fall in their full force upon the insulters." But is it not true that such disdain, which is a virtue in the individual, is the degradation of a nation?

At last my carriage stopped at the entrance of the Château of Saint-Cloud. I was the first to arrive. I found the Emperor alone. He explained in a few words the reason for the unexpected summons; then he said: "Upon reflection, the declaration that we agreed upon this afternoon seems to me far from satisfactory."

"I agree with you, Sire; if we should offer it to the Chambers, the people would throw mud at our carriages and hoot us."

After a few moments' silence, the Emperor added: "Just see in what a position a government may sometimes find itself: even if we had no admissible excuse for war, we should be obliged none the less to make up our minds to it, in order to comply with the will of the country."

Our colleagues arrived one after another — all save Segris, Louvet, and Plichon, whom the summons did not reach.[1] The Empress was present at the Council, for the first time. Le Bœuf explained the object of the meeting. The Emperor's note had disturbed him; then he had been informed of the new scheme upon which the Council had determined; he wanted the Council to decide whether this new policy could be reconciled with the recall of the reserves; he had despatched orders to that end as the result of our earlier decision but that fact need not influence our deliberations: if we thought it necessary to revoke the order, he alone would assume the responsibility therefor before the country, and would resign.

Gramont did not give us time to discuss that contingency. He placed before us the despatches that had arrived since we had left the Tuileries, as well as Lesourd's report on the attitude of Bismarck at Berlin during the 13th, the last telegram from Ems, and telegrams from Berne and Munich.

Lesourd informed us that, after the news of the withdrawal of the candidacy, there had been a change in Berlin from the tranquillity that he had noted during the past week and that composure had suddenly given place to irritation. He told us of the pessimistic impressions that Loftus had brought away from his interview with Bismarck.

Benedetti, in an embarrassed tone, put us *au courant* of the events which we already know of the last day at Ems.

But far more serious and significant was the telegram from Berne! This telegram (sent at half-past four)

[1] ["M. Louvet seems to have been forgotten." La Gorce, vol. vi, p. 297.]

from Comminges-Guitaud, our minister, was in these words: —

"General de Roeder this morning transmitted to the President a telegram from Count Bismarck announcing King William's refusal to bind himself, as King of Prussia, never again to give his assent to the candidacy of the Hohenzollern prince, if it should be brought forward again; and also the King's refusal, as a result of that demand, to receive our Ambassador."

Cadore, our minister at Munich, said: —

"I think it my duty to transmit to you an almost literal copy of the despatch sent by Count Bismarck: 'After the Prince of Hohenzollern's withdrawal was officially communicated to the French government by the Spanish government, the Ambassador of France demanded of His Majesty the King, at Ems, authority to telegraph to Paris that His Majesty would bind himself to refuse his assent for all time if the princes should reconsider their decision. His Majesty refused to receive the Ambassador again, and sent word to him by an aide-de-camp that he had no further communication to make to him.'"[1]

The *official* character of the two telegrams was evident. Comminges-Guitaud and Cadore had not heard of them through the confidential communications of colleagues, but from the lips of the Presidents of the Swiss Confederation and of the Bavarian Council of Ministers, to whom the Prussian ministers had

[1] "The despatch added that 'The King of Bavaria would doubtless be impressed by the fact that M. Benedetti had accosted the King on the promenade in an insulting manner.'" *L'Empire Libéral*, vol. xiv, p. 375. ["This calumny was suggested," says Gramont (p. 232 n.), "by the desire to strike the impressionable imagination of the young King of Bavaria, and to overcome, with the aid of that romantic prince, the hesitation of his people."]

presented them at official audiences. If the communication had been confined to Munich, we might have thought that it was simply a matter of an isolated notification to an ally who was interested to know the status of an affair of common concern; but the communication at Berne, to a neutral government, could be explained only on the assumption that general instructions had been transmitted to all the legations of the North-German government.[1]

It was as certain therefore as any diplomatic fact can be that the Prussian government had officially informed all the foreign cabinets of the refusal of the King of Prussia to receive our Ambassador and to consider our demands. Had we, in our haste, fallen into a trap by ascribing an official character to that which was only informal? A most foolish supposition. To no purpose should we have cudgelled our brains for whole days and nights — we could never have succeeded in understanding that a communication by a diplomatic agent to a foreign minister is not an official act. Between diplomatic agents and foreign ministers everything is official. There

[1] One of those diplomatists who, with a certain affectation of impartiality, have most distorted the acts of his government, Rothan, has said (in *Allemagne et Italie*, vol. i, p. 17 n.): "The Prussian despatch aroused great excitement in all the diplomatic centres, but nowhere else was the same official character attributed to it as at Berne and Munich!" It is incomprehensible that a diplomatist could write such claptrap. The communication made at Berne and Munich, which he recognizes as undeniably official, was so made by virtue of general instructions sent to all Prussian agents. So that one cannot understand how it could have been of one character in one country and of a different character in another. And finally, how could a diplomatist be ignorant of the fact that a communication made by one government to all other governments is necessarily official? [Note of M. Ollivier, vol. xiv, p. 375.]

PARIS EXASPERATED

can be nothing informal between them except conversations, when, both having first laid aside their diplomatic functions, they exchange their opinions freely, without binding their governments or themselves. The very form of official documents is different: there are despatches of which one leaves copies, others which one reads only, and, lastly, there are some which one summarizes orally, without reading or leaving copies. Among these last are the so-called despatches of information, which advise diplomatic agents of certain facts, to the end that they may communicate them to the governments to which they are accredited without asking them for explanations.[1] Such was the telegram communicated by Bismarck,

[1] [M. Ollivier elaborates his argument by illustrative notes on pp. 377, 378. And on pp. 378–380, is the following passage, which he might well have included in the present volume, in view of the fact that the bitterest critics of his administration have made light both of the Ems despatch itself, and of Bismarck's mis-handling of it.]

"It was not long before we acquired superabundant proof that we had not erred in inferring from the telegrams from Berne and Munich that all the Prussian Ambassadors had *officially* informed the foreign cabinets of the King's refusal to receive our Ambassador. Thus, our minister at Dresden wrote us on July 15: 'This telegram, which has every appearance of being official, is published by the Dresden *Journal;* M de Nostitz admits that it comes from the Prussian government.' Bismarck himself was not slow to dissipate all doubt. In his circular letter of July 18, he enclosed the text of the telegram with this title: 'Telegram of the Prussian Government.' The telegram of a government is manifestly an official act. He had at first maintained that his information had been sent to a few German governments only; but he rejected that fiction, and, in instructing his Ambassador to place the text before the English ministry, he gave it a title which the *Blue Book* translated thus: 'Telegram addressed by the Prussian Government to Foreign Governments.' [*Blue Book*, No. 3, p. 7.] . . . This much from love of accuracy; for the information sent out on the evening of the 13th, even if it had been unofficial, combined with the spreading broadcast of the *North German Gazette*, would have seemed to us as intolerable an insult as if it had been official." [See Appendix K.]

first to his official newspapers, then to his agents in foreign countries.

I was beaten in my fight for peace. In the most pacific of my speeches, I had said: "We, too, are hungry for peace, but we desire peace with honor, peace with dignity, peace with strength! If peace lay in weakness, in humiliation, in debasement, I would say without hesitation, 'Better war, a thousand times!'"

After this slap in the face from Bismarck peace was no longer possible save in weakness, in humiliation, in debasement, for "if a blow does not hurt, it kills!" Thenceforth we were no longer justified in wasting time in fruitless and dangerous sentimentality; we had only to accept the meeting to which we were driven.

We confirmed the recall of the reserves, already under way since forty minutes past four, and it was agreed that Gramont and I should prepare the draft of a declaration to be considered on the morrow at a Council which none of my colleagues would fail to attend. In this meeting at Saint-Cloud there had been no discussion properly so called, but only a conversation in which all had expressed substantially the same opinions. The Empress alone listened without uttering a word. We did not vote by name and *viva voce*, as our custom was on serious questions. In truth we could not adopt a definite course in the absence of three of our colleagues, for whose opinions we all had great respect. Plichon arrived at the end of the session. We told him of what we had done.

At half-past eleven we returned to Paris. Thus ended that evening, which has been represented as

PARIS EXASPERATED

a fatal night during which the fate of France and the dynasty was decided, and when peace, after triumphing for half an hour, was cast aside by the power of I know not what mysterious legerdemain whose nature is not disclosed. There was an exchange of ideas, whence came the conclusion that war could not be avoided; but nothing was decided. No final resolution was reached, no irrevocable step was taken. The recall of the reserves was confirmed, but it had been decreed in the afternoon session of the Council at the Tuileries. A new declaration was deemed necessary, but its preparation was postponed till the morrow.[1]

[1] [There is much confusion in the various accounts of these Councils of the 14th, not only as to just what was done at each of them, and in what order the different measures were adopted and rescinded and adopted anew, but as to how many times the Council actually met. M. Ollivier mentions only two meetings — in the afternoon and evening; but Gramont seems to imply that there was one in the morning (p. 206), and other writers state without comment that the Council met at nine o'clock. Lehautcourt, vol. i, p. 314; La Gorce, vol. vi, p. 286. In 1886, M. Plichon being then a member of the National Assembly, M. Ollivier took exception to a statement made by him in debate, to the effect that he was not present at the sitting of the Council, when war was decided upon, and a long correspondence ensued between them, all of which is printed by M. Ollivier in the *éclaircissements* to vol. xiv, pp. 605–620. M. Plichon claimed that the decisive action was taken at the meeting on the evening of the 14th, in his absence; whereas M. Ollivier maintained that the actual decision was not reached until the meeting on the morning of the 15th. Incidentally, the question as to the number of councils on the 14th was raised by M. Plichon, who stood out for three, while his correspondent declared the one in the morning to have been simply a conversation between ministers at the Chancellery. The correspondence is mainly interesting, however, in the light it throws upon the reasons which actuated some at least of the ministers who were opposed to the war in accepting the accomplished fact and maintaining the solidarity of the Cabinet. See Welschinger, vol. i, pp. 159–165. See also a passage from the *Considerations sur l'Histoire du Second Empire*, by M. Parieu, quoted by Welschinger, p. 158.

In his deposition at the Inquiry concerning the 4th of September, Marshal Le Bœuf testified that, at eleven o'clock in the evening, it was about decided

A former minister, Grivard, told the story, as told to him by MacMahon, who learned it from de Piennes the chamberlain, that, in the midst of our deliberations, the Emperor was suddenly taken with a syncope and hurriedly withdrew. The Empress, instead of

to postpone mobilization, when a despatch was handed to M. de Gramont. "That despatch was read to the Council. It was of such a nature that there was a reaction; we decided that the order for mobilization should be confirmed." Which despatch this was of those which, as Gramont says (p. 220), "destroyed one after another, during the day, or, rather, the night, the hopes of the Cabinet for peace," has never been disclosed; but M. Sorel, by a process of exclusion, reaches the conviction that it was that one by which the Foreign Minister "received, through an unofficial source, a very exact account of the language held by M. de Bismarck on the preceding day, to the English Ambassador, and of the attitude taken up on the 13th by the Cabinet of Berlin. . . . I could not for an instant doubt the accuracy of my information, and I soon had tangible proof thereof." Gramont, p. 223. (See Appendix L.) For an account of the duke's apparently irreconcilable statements as to the time at which he first learned of this momentous interview, see Sorel, vol. i, p. 177 n.

By way of refutation of this reasoning, perhaps, M. Ollivier in the Appendix to vol. xiv, pp. 618–619, denies Le Bœuf's story of the despatch handed to M. de Gramont and the consequent reaction in the Council. He says that from the first moment to the last of the Council in the evening all the members present were agreed that in view of the slap in the face they had received, there was no room for further deliberation, and war was inevitable. The only despatch handed to Gramont during the session was that from Cadore [at Munich.] "That despatch did not change peaceable to warlike dispositions, but simply confirmed the warlike dispositions which we had adopted without variation or dissent from the first moment of our meeting. . . . Nor were we influenced by a report which Gramont received from Vienna, by an indirect channel, of the language held on the 14th by M. de Bismarck to the English Ambassador. . . . What he read was Lesourd's despatches telling us what Loftus had told him of Bismarck's language. But there was nothing in that to surprise us," etc. [And see Von Sybel, English trans., vol. vii, p. 413 n.]

"The whole day of the 14th," says La Gorce, "is summed up in this tragic contrast: on the one side, France hesitating before supreme measures; on the other, Prussia pressing imperiously upon her adversary and compelling her to complete the aggression" (vol. vi, p. 286).]

going with him to look to his needs, is said to have remained with us and to have taken advantage of her husband's absence to change our views, so that the Emperor, having recovered and returned to the Council, found the ministers in warlike mood whom he had left, a few moments before, peacefully inclined. If persons who were not present witnessed this incident, I declare that none of those who were present witnessed it.[1]

[1] [This story is told by Welschinger (vol. i, pp. 154–156), from "an unpublished note of the former minister and senator, Grivart, who got it from Marshal MacMahon and from M. de Piennes, the Empress's chamberlain." According to this version the Emperor, having entered the Council Chamber with the Empress, read a speech tending to pacific measures. He was about to take a vote, when he was taken ill, and was obliged to leave the room. "What impelled the Empress to intervene . . . was the despatches that had arrived during the evening" — those from Ems and Berlin; and the telegrams from Berne and Munich. "The Council believed that those two telegrams were official. . . . Allowing themselves to be misled by appearances, and fancying that they must reply on the spot to the provocation, the ministers who were present realized that war could not be avoided. They confirmed the recall of the reserves, and decided that the Duc de Gramont and M. Émile Ollivier should prepare a draft of a declaration of war. The Empress had proved to the Council that there was nothing left to do but to accept the meeting to which Prussia was driving us." It is incredible, as M. Ollivier suggests, that so extraordinary an incident should never have been mentioned by any of those present at the Council.

It is probable that the paragraph in the text owes its being to the above-quoted passage in Welschinger, as it does not appear in *L'Empire Libéral;* on the other hand, there is at this point in vol. xiv, pp. 381, 382, the following paragraph. "At the close of this day, begun with such comforting hope and ending with so tragic a prospect, I found Mitchell at my house. I told him the decision we had formed and the profound grief that I felt at being compelled to declare war, I who had not ceased to struggle to forfend any war whatsoever, and especially a war with Germany! He shared my affliction. 'Well!' he said, 'hand in your resignation.' — 'I can't do it; the country has confidence in me; I am the guaranty of the compact that binds the Empire to France. If I should retire, the accession of a Rouher ministry would be regarded as a sort of coup d'état against the parliamentary reforms; the situation, already so grave, would be complicated by internal

That morning Lyons, with his usual perspicacity, had foreseen the effect that would be produced by the blow from Ems when the public should be apprized of it. "The language of influential members of the Cabinet," he wrote to Granville, "was more pacific, and it was thought possible that some conciliatory intelligence might arrive from Prussia and *enable the Government to pronounce the whole question to be at an end*. . . . The intelligence of the publication of this article [from the *North-German Gazette*]completely changed the view taken by the French government of the state of the question. . . . Although the . . . article in the *North-German Gazette* had not become generally known, the public excitement was so great and so much irritation existed in the army, that *it became doubtful whether the Government could withstand the cry for war, even if it were able to announce a decided diplomatic success*. It was felt when the Prussian article appeared in the Paris evening papers, it would be very difficult to restrain the anger of the people, and . . . that the Government would feel bound to appease the public impatience by formally declaring its intention to resent the conduct of Prussia." [1]

difficulties. And then,' I added, 'war is decided upon, it is legitimate, it is inevitable; no human power could avert it to-day. Since we cannot prevent it, it is our duty to make it popular. By retiring we should discourage the country, we should demoralize the army, we should contest the righteousness and justice of the cause of France.' — 'What do you hope for, pray ?' — 'For myself, nothing. After the victory' (of which I was certain, like everybody else) 'the military spirit will try to steal my work. If we are victorious, God save our liberties ! if we are beaten, may God help France !' " [This conversation was printed by M. Mitchell, in substantially the same words, in an article in the *Courrier de France* of Sept. 24, 1872. See Lehautcourt, vol. i, p. 318; Welschinger, vol. i, pp. 157, 158.]

[1] [July 14, *Blue Book*, p. 36.]

The explosion of public feeling surpassed what Lyons had anticipated. *Clamor belli ascendit ad coelum ut tuba.* The cry for war arose on all sides. The journals favorable to peace hardly dared whisper a word or two. The others went beyond all bounds.

"It is all war," Marshal Vaillant wrote in his notebook. The boulevards wore the aspect of public holidays. The police report told us: "The same crowds, the same curiosity, the same effervescence; the movement of carriages was impossible; the omnibuses had to change their routes. On all sides there were shouts of '*Vive la guerre!*' 'To Berlin!' In proportion as the possibility of an adjustment had caused disappointment, the rupture of the negotiations was welcomed with feverish excitement. All breathed freely, as if delivered from a burdensome uncertainty."

The *Liberté*, by the pen of Albert Duruy, declared triumphantly the next morning: "The declaration, which the Senate and Corps Législatif awaited with patriotic anxiety, did not appear. But in compensation Paris yesterday made its declaration of war on Prussia. Paris replied with the *Marseillaise* to M. de Bismarck's latest defiance."[1]

While the *furor teutonicus* and the *furor gallicus* were thus unleashed, Benedetti continued imperturbably to solicit audiences. On the morning of

[1] [Other extracts from various Parisian papers are given in *L'Empire Libéral*, vol. xiv, pp. 383–387, together with more details concerning the scenes of excitement in the streets. It was charged in some quarters that the manifestations were started and subsidized by the police. But they "embarrassed the government more than they assisted it. . . . A single act was of a nature to make us appear as if we were stirring up public excitement, and that was the giving permission to sing the *Marseillaise* at the Opera. Maurice Richard obtained the permission directly from the Emperor. The Council, who were not consulted, were not pleased."]

July 14 he had read in the *Cologne Gazette* the Ems telegram; he made no mistake either as to its source or its scope. He had said nothing to any one concerning the events of the previous day, so that the despatch could have emanated only from the King's cabinet; it gave an insulting turn to the last incidents of the negotiations at Ems. In common with nations and statesmen he had heard the word war that issued from that despatch. "The government," he said, "might have hesitated on the 12th, it could hardly do so on the 15th."

There was nothing left for him to do, therefore, but to return to Paris, whither Gramont had summoned him, and, since he had been dismissed, to accept his dismissal and take his departure proudly, without a word to any one. But he had not had enough rebuffs on the previous days; he must needs invite more, and they were lavishly bestowed.

The first came from Eulenbourg, Minister of the Interior. It occurred to Benedetti to go to him and urge the pacific subtleties invented by Gramont, in order to take upon himself the appearance of having secured the King's approval; they were quite out of fashion at that moment. The Minister expressed his intention to submit them to His Majesty, and even promised to see him again; but he speedily sent word to him, in his turn, that he "had no further communication to make to him." Thus our Ambassador, having been thrice refused an audience by the King, completed his collection by adding to it a refusal of audience by a minister. Even that did not exhaust the zeal of his humility.

The King, realizing that that was not the time to continue a water-cure, determined to start that same day for Coblentz, so as to reach Berlin the next day and

PARIS EXASPERATED 333

make the military dispositions which the situation of affairs would certainly demand. Benedetti, informed of his proposed departure, felt called upon, in order not to disregard the proprieties, to request an aide-de-camp to tell the King of his desire to take his leave of His Majesty. This step brought him one more refusal of an audience. His Majesty continued to keep his apartments closed to him, but admitted him to a railroad station, that is to say, to an antechamber, to salute him as he passed.

And so, apparently with no conception that he represented France and the Emperor, Benedetti went to wish a pleasant journey to the sovereign who was leaving Ems in order to hurl his armies of invasion against France and the Emperor. "The King," he said, "confined himself to saying that he had no further communication to make to me, and that the negotiations that might still be carried on would be continued by his government." [1]

Radziwill's memorandum is even more concise: "Count Benedetti's wish to take leave of His Majesty on his departure was gratified, for the King, on starting for Coblentz, July 14, saluted the count in the railway station as he passed." [2]

---

[1] [See Benedetti's despatches of July 14, 12.30 P.M., in Benedetti, 385–387; Gramont, 221–223.]

[2] [See Appendix K. M. Ollivier adds at this point in *L'Empire Libéral* some details of the comments in German newspapers on the King's amiability to Benedetti at the station, with the reflection that] "amiability to the person of an ambassador, whose sovereign one has abused, is simply adding insult to injury" (p. 389). "That same evening the unofficial *North German Gazette* published in huge letters a short notice to the effect that Benedetti had lost sight of the rules of diplomatic relations to the point of not refraining from disturbing the King at his water-cure, of questioning him on the promenade, and of extorting explanations from him."

CHAPTER XXI

OUR REPLY TO BISMARCK'S SLAP IN THE FACE: THE DECLARATION OF JULY 15

ON Friday, July 15, at nine in the morning, the Council met at Saint-Cloud.[1] The Empress was present, as were all the ministers, perfectly free to decide and vote as they chose, no irrevocable public act having been done. Even those among them who, in the conversation of the previous evening, had believed war to be inevitable, might, after a night's reflection, express different views, and, rejecting the declaration which we had prepared, revert either to the proposed appeal to Europe, or to any other solution.

Gramont read the draft that we had prepared in concert. I had looked to it that the grounds of our decision should be stated in such wise that no one could misunderstand them, and that it should be beyond question that we had obstinately refused, at the last moment as at the outset, to extend the discussion beyond the Hohenzollern candidacy; that we invoked neither the Treaty of Prague nor the breach of faith in respect to Luxembourg, nor the constant double-dealing, nor the

[1] [In a note on p. 391 of vol. xiv, M. Ollivier quotes the *Journal Officiel* to prove that the council of the 15th was held at Saint-Cloud and not at the Tuileries, "as some persons, relying upon the accuracy of their memories, persist in asserting." He evidently refers to M. Plichon, who made that mistaken assertion confidently in the correspondence alluded to above, p. 325 n. See vol. xiv, p. 609.]

incessant provocation, nor the impatience to have done with it all and to escape from an enervating and intolerable tension, nor the necessity of wiping out the memory of Sadowa; and that, even in the Hohenzollern affair, everything was not equally a subject of complaint: that we alleged, as the decisive reason for our action, neither the refusal to guarantee the future by a simple promise, nor the refusal to give official form to a private approval, nor even the refusal to receive and listen to our ambassador. We were outraged by that refusal of an audience solely because it had become a palpable insult by virtue of the promulgation of the telegram placarded in the streets and transmitted to the legations and newspapers. In other words our declaration was simply a reply to the blow inflicted by the Ems despatch — a reply which Germany herself seemed to advise by awaiting it as inevitable.

At the words with which it concluded the Emperor clapped his hands. Chevandier took the floor and said: "Having been to this day one of those who have expressed themselves most forcibly in favor of peace, I ask to be allowed to give my opinion first. When any one strikes me, without stopping to consider whether I am more or less able to fight, I return the blow. I vote for war."

When Segris's turn came, he turned to Le Bœuf and said in a voice trembling with emotion: "Marshal, you see my distress; I do not ask you if we are ready, but if we have a fair chance to win."

The marshal replied that we were ready, and that we should never be in a better position to settle our quarrel with Prussia; that we could be perfectly confident.

No one raised any objections or maintained the possibility of peace. Later, certain writers of the Right[1] asserted that the Emperor opened the discussion by saying that, being a constitutional sovereign, he did not wish to influence in any way the decisions of his Cabinet; that he would even abstain from voting, and that war was decided on by the votes of a majority only. The Emperor did not make that ridiculous remark, and war was voted unanimously, his vote included. The Empress alone expressed no opinion and did not vote.

At that last moment of the crisis the Emperor was in the same position that he had occupied from the beginning: sighing for the glories of war as soon as peace was in the ascendant, and rushing back toward peace in dismay when war seemed necessary. While we were on our way to the Corps Législatif he received Vitzthum, the Austrian minister at Brussels, and asked him to prevail upon his sovereign to take the initiative in calling a congress, so that war might be avoided.[2]

Although the Constitution of 1870, like all monarchical constitutions, had reserved to the Emperor alone the right to declare war, I had promised, in the name of the Cabinet, that if at any time we should consider war inevitable, we would not engage in it until we had asked and obtained the consent of the Chambers; thereupon there would be a discussion, and if they did not share our opinion, it would not be difficult for them to enforce their own by turning us out. True to our promise, we

---

[1] [Lehautcourt (vol. i, p. 319) is the only writer who makes the statement, so far as I have discovered, and his confusion of the various councils is apparent from the fact that he makes Segris and Plichon absent from this one of the 15th, at which it is certain that all of the ministers were present. See *supra*, p. 322.]

[2] [Von Sybel (English trans.), vol. vii, pp. 423, 424; based upon information derived from unpublished memoirs.]

did not propose to commit any act of war — beyond recalling the reserves, a measure easily countermanded — until the Chambers had discussed and approved our policy. We accompanied our declaration with a request for a credit of fifty million francs, — a quite inadequate sum, but in granting or refusing it the Corps Législatif and the Senate could express their will by a formal vote, the testimony of which would endure, better than by fleeting expressions of approval or dissent. Hitherto war had been an act of the sovereign's personal power.[1] We proposed that it should be this time the free act of the representatives of the Nation.

In addition to the request for fifty millions we offered the draft of a law authorizing voluntary enlistments limited to the duration of the war. In this way the young men who loved the battlefield and hated the barracks would not be discouraged in their patriotic impulses by the fear of remaining under the flag two years after the peace. A second proposed law called into active service all the *garde mobile*. The marshal, in order to keep down the expenses and to avoid complicating his preparations, had confined the summons to the *garde mobile* of the departments directly threatened. Plichon insisted that it should extend to all of the *garde* in all the departments, and the Council agreed with him.

---

[1] Even under Louis-Philippe, Lamartine complained that such was the fact. Apropos of the complications of 1840 [concerning the affairs of Mehemet Ali], he wrote: "You, a free nation, a democratic nation, the nation of '89 and 1830 — you have sunk so low that you open your newspaper anxiously every morning, to find out whether it has or has not suited seven men, closeted in their office at Paris, to set war loose upon the world. And you still call yourself, in face of such a scandal, a representative nation!" *France Parlementaire*, vol. ii. [Note of M. Ollivier, in vol. xiv, p. 395.]

Before entering the Chamber I stopped at Gramont's quarters at the Foreign Office. There I found Benedetti, who had arrived that morning. We questioned him minutely; he told us nothing new as to what had taken place at Ems, and confirmed, without adding to them, the circumstantial details of his despatches and reports. As to what had taken place at Berlin, as to Bismarck's plotting, he knew absolutely nothing. So that it would have served no useful purpose to defer action in order to hear him in Council.[1] Indeed, he was much more disturbed than by the prospect of war, by an article in the *Constitutionnel* by Léonce Dupont (Renal), already several days old, which blamed him for not having warned his government of the Hohenzollern candidacy.

[1] [Delord, on what authority I cannot guess, says that Benedetti was before the Council that forenoon, where "he completed the report of his negotiations by the story of his interview with Eulenbourg, regarding the fresh attempt that he proposed to make to reach the King. He concluded by telling of the King's refusal to add anything to what he had said on the 13th, his departure for Coblentz, the amiable greeting which he (Benedetti) had received at the station, and, finally, the declaration of William I that, if further discussions should become necessary, they would be carried on by his government. As there had been no other words exchanged between the King of Prussia and himself, M. Benedetti's surprise was great on learning that he had been insulted, and France with him, in the few minutes passed in the station at Ems. No one was in a better position then he to point out to the Cabinet its error and the risk it was running; but the Empress wanted war, the Emperor submitted to the Empress's wish, and — M. Benedetti held his peace. This was, perhaps, his way of avenging himself for the desertion of the ministry, which had delivered him over to the sarcasm of its own newspapers, when it would have been so easy to exculpate him." Delord, vol. vi, p. 178. — Welschinger, an equally bitter and uncompromising opponent and critic of the government, condemns the failure of Gramont and Ollivier to summon Benedetti before the Council, where his testimony would have been singularly useful (vol. i, p. 169). "Certain ministers . . . did not want war, and hearing what Benedetti had to say would have suggested pertinent questions, called forth illuminating replies, dissipated obscurities, and perhaps led to a different decision." *Ibid.*, p. 173.]

In the midst of the negotiations at Ems, he had employed half of a telegram in asking us "to say in a few words that he had several times called attention to the steps that were being taken with that candidacy in view." [1] We were unable to gratify him, for if he had warned us in 1869, he had suspected nothing in 1870, at the decisive moment, and had not even been put on the alert by the presence of the Hohenzollern family at Berlin in March. Having no regard for the thoughts by which my mind was besieged, he recurred to his theme with wearisome importunity, and I had to give over my reflections on the coming struggle, as I walked to the Chamber with him, in order to try to make him understand that, as I paid no heed to attacks directed against myself, — and surely his friends were not sparing of them, — he could not justly demand that I should give my attention to refuting those of which he was the object, whether they were just or unjust.

The Chamber was full; the tribunes were crowded; all the ambassadors were present. Amid an impressive silence, I read our Declaration: —

[1] From Ems, dated July 10, 11.30 P.M. [See Benedetti, p. 345. In connection with this despatch, Gramont says (p. 382 n.): "Count Benedetti's demand was just; but to defend him at that moment against the papers that were attacking him, we should have had to disclose all the pourparlers of 1869, and such disclosure would inevitably have inflamed considerably the excitement of men's minds by proving that . . . the Prussian government knew to what point it would offend French opinion and French interests by recurring to the Hohenzollern candidacy. The government considered therefore that it was in duty bound to keep silent, and supposed that Comte Benedetti would consent to sacrifice his self-esteem a little longer, justly wounded as it was by the undeserved attacks of certain journals. Baron Mercier had voluntarily responded to that thought, and had asked us, of his own motion, not to think of justifying him until the proper time."]

"The manner in which you received our declaration of July 6 having given us the assurance that you approve our policy and that we could prevail with your support, we at once entered into negotiations with the foreign powers, to obtain their good offices with Prussia, to the end that she might acknowledge the justice of our complaints. In these negotiations we asked nothing of Spain, as we do not wish to arouse her susceptibility or to offend her independence. We did not approach the Hohenzollern princes, whom we considered as protected by the King; we also declined to introduce any acrimony in our discussion, or to extend it beyond the single object to which we ourselves limited it.

"Most of the foreign powers answered our appeal with ardor, and, with more or less warmth, they admitted the justice of our demand. The Prussian Minister of Foreign Affairs met us with a plea of not guilty, claiming that he knew nothing of the affair, and that the Berlin Cabinet had always been a stranger to it. [*Murmurs on various benches.*] We were obliged therefore to address ourselves to the King in person, and we ordered our Ambassador to go to Ems, where His Majesty then was.

"While admitting that he had authorized the Prince of Hohenzollern to accept the candidacy that had been proffered to him, the King of Prussia maintained that he had had nothing to do with the negotiations between the Spanish government and the Prince of Hohenzollern; that he had intervened only as head of the family, in no wise as sovereign, and that he had neither convoked nor consulted his Council of Ministers thereon. His Majesty admitted, however, that he had informed Count Bismarck of these different incidents.

"We could not regard this reply as satisfactory. We could not admit the subtle distinction between the sovereign and the head of the family, and we insisted that the King should advise and at need compel Prince Leopold to abandon his candidacy.

"While we were engaged in discussion with Prussia, news of the Prince's withdrawal reached us from a quarter from which we were not expecting it; it was handed to us on July 12 by the Spanish Ambassador. The King having determined to remain a stranger to it, we demanded that he associate himself with it, and that he declare that if, in one of those fluctuations of purpose which are always possible in a country just emerging from a revolution, the crown should be again offered by Spain to Prince Leopold, he would not authorize him to accept it, so that the discussion might be considered to be definitively closed.

"Our demand was a moderate one; the terms in which we expressed it were not less so. 'Say to the King,' we wrote to M. Benedetti on July 12, at midnight, 'that we have no secret motive, that we do not seek a pretext for war, and that we ask only to reach an honorable solution of a difficulty that we did not create.'

"The King consented to approve the withdrawal of Prince Leopold, but he refused to declare that he would not authorize the renewal of his candidacy hereafter.

"'I asked the King,' M. Benedetti wrote to us on July 13 at midnight, 'to consent to allow me to inform you, in his name, that if the Prince of Hohenzollern should revert to his project, His Majesty would interpose his authority, and would forbid him. The King absolutely refused to authorize me to transmit to you such a declaration. I persisted, but without success in modifying His Majesty's position. The King put an end to our interview by saying that he neither could nor would make such an agreement, and that he must, in respect to that as to all other contingencies, reserve to himself liberty to consult the circumstances.'

"Although this refusal seemed regrettable to us, our wish to conserve the blessings of peace for Europe was so great that we did not break off negotiations, but, despite our just impatience, fearing that discussion would carry us too far, we asked your permission to postpone our explanations. So that our surprise was profound when we learned, yesterday, that the King of Prussia had informed our Ambassador, through an aide-de-camp, that he would not receive him again, and that, in order to give to that refusal an unequivocal character, his government had communicated it to all the cabinets of Europe. [*Murmurs.*] We learned at the same time that Baron Werther had been ordered to take a leave of absence, and that armaments were under way in Prussia.[1]

"Under these circumstances, to make further attempts at conciliation would have been a disregard of dignity and an imprudence. We have omitted nothing to avoid war; we propose to prepare to carry on the war that is offered us, leaving to each nation that share of the responsibility which belongs to it."[2]

[1] We did not say that Werther had been recalled, and therein we were inaccurate. [Nor was the statement true that armaments were under way in Prussia.] Le Bœuf had been misinformed; the armaments did not begin until the 16th. [Notes of M. Ollivier in vol. xiv, p. 400. See on the last point, Gramont, pp. 262-264.]

[2] [The concluding sentence is omitted: "Yesterday we called in our reserves, and, with your concurrence, we propose immediately to take the necessary measures to safeguard the interests, the safety, and the honor of France." — The same declaration was read in the Senate by M. de Gramont.]

DECLARATION OF JULY 15

The final sentences were drowned by bravos, renewed plaudits, and shouts of "Vive la France! Vive l'Empereur!" Then there were loud cries of "Vote! vote!" We proceeded at once to vote. A very great majority of the deputies were so excited that when the "noes" were called for, a few members of the Left having risen, the others turned upon them, pointed at them, and cried: "Oh, stand up! stand up! There are only sixteen of them! They're Prussians!"

Urgency being voted, Thiers spoke from his place.[1] After rambling endlessly on personal matters, he said in substance: —

"Is it or is it not true that, on the main issue, that is to say, on the candidacy of the Prince of Hohenzollern, your demand was listened to, and that it was complied with? Is it true that you are going to war on a question of sensitiveness, — most honorable, I agree, — but that you are going to war on a question of sensitiveness? [*Murmurs.*] Well, gentlemen, do you want people to say, do you want all Europe to say that, the main point being granted, you have resolved, for a mere question of form, to shed torrents of blood? [*Noisy remonstrances.*] As for me, let me tell you in two words, to explain both my actions and my language, let me tell you that I look upon this war as supremely imprudent.

[1] ["He had no sooner risen than from the Right there came a great explosion of murmurs. It was the protest of all those who, far from holding ministers in check, considered them too circumspect. In this league there were acting together the most diverse opinions: the credulous ignorance of belated Chauvinists, the hoodwinked good faith of sincere patriots, the ambitious violence of absolutists in quest of change. The rest followed from weakness, from that confused excitement which is sometimes born of fear, and likewise from a conviction that the best way to pay their court was to lack sang-froid." La Gorce, vol. vi, p. 301. Thiers had voted among the sixteen against urgency.]

This declaration offends you, but I surely am entitled to have an opinion on such a question. I love my country; I was more grievously affected than any one else by the events of 1866, and more earnestly than any one else I desire reparation for them; but in my deep-rooted conviction, and, if I may venture to say so, in my experience, the occasion is ill-chosen." [1]

Each of the orator's assertions offended the overexcited feelings of the assembly to such a degree that they were greeted with incessant contradictions and impatient mutterings. However, the number of those who demanded silence was much greater than that of the interrupters. Among the latter, his friends of the Left were almost as numerous as his opponents of the Right. In the interruptions there was no insult, no personal abuse. The only offensive exclamations were Piré's; now, it was a notorious fact that that brilliant man was in a state of excitement bordering on madness. On the other hand,

[1] [Thiers's speech is reported at much greater length, with much detail of interruptions, etc., in *L'Empire Libéral*, vol. xiv, pp. 401–409. See also La Gorce, vol. vi, pp. 301–303; Sorel, vol. i, pp. 182, 183; Gramont, pp. 241–245; Lehautcourt, vol. i, pp. 323, 324; Von Sybel, English trans., vol. vii, pp. 417, 418; Favre, vol. i, pp. 13–25. — "As the uproar drowned his voice, M. Thiers recalled those days of 1866 when the Chamber, having listened to him once, had, at the most critical moment, refused to hear him again. 'To-day,' he added, 'I have decided to listen to your murmurs, and, if necessary, to defy them.' The uproar redoubled, and through the hall rang the voices of incoherent or frantic interrupters, whom no warning could put down. Such were the Marquis de Piré, M. Dugué de la Fanconnerie, and others even more obscure, but eager to pass into history by inscribing their names in the stenographic report of that imperishable session. The Left, too, by its applause, heightened the tumult; those who would have hesitated to interrupt M. Thiers, repudiated Jules Favre and his friends. At last, at the cost of a long struggle against passion, the orator succeeded in approaching the subject of the debate. 'Is it or is it not true,' " etc. La Gorce, vi, 302.]

DECLARATION OF JULY 15

all the interruptions from the Left hostile to the ministry were of an insulting character, which was not to be found, Piré aside, in any of those addressed to Thiers. So that he had not to make any notable display of heroism in order to gain a hearing.[1]

If any one man in France can be accused of having brought on the war, that man is Thiers. By his persistence in talking about the degradation of France, in representing Sadowa as a national calamity, he had created that uneasy, sensitive, jealous, excitable frame of mind which was fatally certain to end in war.[2] I had predicted the consequences of his irritating language as early as 1867. "You acclaim peace at every opportunity, you declare for it at every opportunity, and in reality you vote every day for war. It is necessary that this Chamber, that this nation, not only resign themselves to what is actually done, but accept it without reservation and face man-fashion the necessity of a war that is inevitable sooner or later, a serious war, a terrible war, with Germany."

To be sure, while lamenting over our degradation, Thiers always concluded with counsels of peace. He

[1] [At this point in vol. xiv, pp. 410-412, M. Ollivier cites several cases both before and after 1870 in which M. Thiers's action seems inconsistent with the stand taken by him in the debate of July 15. "How different would his speech have been on that day, if the Emperor had received him at Saint-Cloud on the 10th!" See *supra*, pp. 153-155.]

[2] ["Hardly had the reading of the Cabinet programme been concluded, when, first and foremost of them all, the veteran Thiers took up the battle, in seeming contradiction to his entire past, and to the utter surprise of his hearers; for, in truth, it had been he who more than any one else in France had spread the doctrine that the growing strength of Prussia was a serious menace to the vital interests of France, and that Napoleon ought long ago to have interposed." Von Sybel, English trans., vol. vii, p. 147.]

resembled a joker who should call out to a coachman having a struggle with spirited horses: "Hold them in; if they get away, they'll break your neck!" and who should at the same moment put briers under their tails.[1]

I might have recalled that fact, I might have taken advantage of the agitation of the Assembly, which, with a word of incitement, I could have led on to the most ill-considered measures. On the contrary, I protested against the demonstrations which I had been unable to prevent. I began my reply by saying: "The more unanimous and vehement the current of public opinion is, the more greatness of soul there is in confronting it, when one deems it mistaken, and in trying to check it by saying what one believes to be the truth."

An almost universal assent accentuated this tribute to freedom of contradiction. I continued: —

"And so, after listening respectfully to the honorable M. Thiers, I should, according to my custom, refrain from taking the floor to reply to him, were it not that there are assertions in his speech which I cannot accept."

Every one will agree that that is not the language of a minister who incites his majority to intolerance. I did not depart for one instant from that attitude, and I maintained the greater restraint the more earnestly I was urged to lay it aside. While he was

[1] "'Point out,' the Emperor wrote to me from Wilhelmshöhe [where he was residing as a prisoner of war after Sedan], 'that it is Thiers and Favre who, ever since 1866, have so often repeated in every tone that France's prestige was impaired by Prussia's success, and that we must have revenge, that the first thing that happened was enough to make public opinion explode. They had piled up the inflammable matter and only a spark was needed to start a conflagration.'" *L'Empire Libéral*, vol. xiv, p. 413.

DECLARATION OF JULY 15

speaking I had done my utmost to pacify the Assembly and obtain order; having nothing to conceal, I had the most sincere desire to start an exhaustive debate and to let the light in upon the smallest details of the negotiations; and I felt that those who made participation in the debate difficult for Thiers virtually defeated my purpose.

"We too," I continued, "have a realizing sense of our duty; we too know that this is a momentous day, and that every man of those who have contributed to the decision about to be adopted assumes a grave responsibility before his country and before history. We too, during our six hours of deliberation yesterday, had constantly in our thoughts all the bitterness and pain of giving the signal, in this enlightened age of ours, for a bloody conflict between two great civilized states. We too declare them to be culpable who, yielding to factional passions or unreflecting impulses, engage their countries in such adventures. We too believe that useless wars are criminal wars, and if, *with grief-stricken hearts* [*l'âme désolée*], we resolve upon this war, to which Prussia summons us, it is because there never was a more necessary one." [*Numerous lively tokens of approval.*]

Thereupon I detailed the stages of the negotiations, and I gave prominence to the fact that in the very midst of our pourparlers we had learned that throughout Europe the Prussian representatives were announcing and causing to be announced in the newspapers that the King of Prussia had sent an aide-de-camp to our Ambassador, to inform him that he refused to receive him. [*Bravos and applause from the Centre and Right. Interruptions from the Left.*]

"The honorable M. Thiers has dubbed this sentiment sensitiveness. I do not recognize in that term the customary accuracy of his language. Sensitiveness is not the fitting word, but honor, and in France the safeguarding of the national honor is the highest of interests. [*Warm approval from Centre and Right.*] We have not considered whether this is an opportune or inopportune moment to attack Prussia; we have no purpose to attack either Germany or Prussia; we found ourselves confronted by an insult to which we could not submit, by a threat which, if we had allowed it to be carried out, would have reduced us to the lowest order of states." [*"Very good!"*][1]

[1] [In this volume M. Ollivier's speech is largely abbreviated and the order of sentences changed from the form in which it is given in *L'Empire Libéral*, pp. 413-421, 425-432, with the interruptions and interpolations, notably of MM. Favre and Gambetta.

"Such words demanded a reply. Among all the members of the cabinet, M. Ollivier alone would be a worthy champion. He went up into the tribune. If the momentousness of the occasion had left any room for surprise, it would have been a sufficient cause thereof to see in what positions destiny had placed the two adversaries. M. Thiers had constantly deplored Sadowa, had never stopped denouncing Prussia, and he was the one who was doing his utmost to smooth over the controversy. M. Ollivier had taken for his hobby the cause of nationalities, had preached union with Germany, at least, if not with Prussia, and behold, he was standing forth as the herald of war. His speech, eloquent as always, bore witness to the singularity of his position. He began by asserting his love of peace, and, speaking in that vein, he voiced the oldest, the most sincere thoughts of his soul. With infectious emotion, he described his long hesitation, that of his colleagues, and the eight-hours' deliberation of the preceding night. He recalled — and nothing is more undeniable — the persevering efforts he had put forth as a deputy to banish the misunderstandings between two great civilized nations. What he had tried as a simple representative, he had followed up as minister, and had exerted himself to rearouse no disputed questions, but to establish relations of confidence between Paris and Berlin. At this point in his discourse M. Ollivier turned a sharp corner and showed himself an entirely different man, albeit no less sincere, who appropriated to himself, clothing

DECLARATION OF JULY 15 349

My demonstration concluded, I fell into one of those oratorical abstractions with which public speakers are familiar. I forgot Thiers and the Assembly, the time, and the place; I imagined myself face to face with the brave hearts who were soon to fall on the battlefield, face to face with the fatherland and with posterity; I felt rising to my lips a cry of adjuration to those heroes of duty, to our beloved France, to the impartial future, and, on the threshold of the tragic decision, I could not restrain one last supreme assertion of my integrity of conscience. I deemed myself bound to bear that witness to my colleagues and myself, and, seeking strong words with which to express the violent emotion that agitated me, I remembered the scriptural maledictions upon the impious heavily burdened hearts.[1] I paraphrased them and said: "Yes, with this day there begins, for the ministers my colleagues, and for myself, an immense responsibility. We accept it with light hearts!"

Was there the slightest possible uncertainty as to my meaning when I had said a few moments earlier that *my heart was grief-stricken?* Nevertheless, before

them in his own eloquence, the arguments of M. de Gramont. . . . Strangely enough, throughout the negotiations, no guiding influence had been apparent; there had been no president of the Council, gathering up all the threads and holding them tight in his hands. When everything was consummated, lo! the Keeper of the Seals stood forth as the real head of the Cabinet and assumed responsibility for a crisis that he had not guided, and for acts which had been in part concealed from him. Was this courage or generosity? Was it the mobility of a mind no less impressionable than brilliant? despair of restraining public opinion? conviction that war was inevitable? or eagerness not to complicate such terrible problems by a ministerial crisis?" La Gorce, vol. vi, pp. 303, 304.]

[1] Psalms, iv, 3; St. Luke, xxiv, 25, 26. [Note of M. Ollivier, vol. xiv, p. 422.]

I could finish my sentence and add the words which would have made any quibble impossible, I was recalled to the melancholy surroundings, above which I had risen, by a malicious snarl: "Say saddened hearts! Your heart is light, yet the blood of the nations is about to flow!"

I resumed with an indignant emotion which carried the Assembly with me: "Yes, with light hearts; and do not quibble over that phrase, nor believe that I mean to say, with joy. I have told you myself of my distress at being forced into war: I mean, *with a heart that is not made heavy by remorse, with a confident heart*, because the war that we shall wage we are forced into, because we have done all that it was humanly and honorably possible to do to avoid it, and, lastly, because our cause is just and is entrusted to the French army!" [*Numerous lively marks of approval. Renewed applause.*]

How often have my enemies pursued me, before the ignorant mob of high and low alike, with that phrase, "light hearts"! It has become a stereotyped formula when any one wishes to attack me. Even if it were true that at that moment, worn out by mental anguish, fatigue, and insomnia, obliged to reply unassisted to powerful orators, having had no leisure to reflect for a moment on the ordering and wording of my speech, I had allowed an improper expression to escape me, the explanation which I instantly gave forbade any honest misunderstanding of the meaning of my words, and no one had the right, without ceasing to be a man of honor, to extort therefrom a revolting avowal of hardness of heart or of indifference. At the worst, judges of oratorical talent

DECLARATION OF JULY 15   351

might have criticised therein a fault of the orator or the man of letters. But my expression was as irreproachable as the sentiment which it described, and its literary correction is no more open to question than its moral rectitude. I stand by it.[1]

The speech in which Thiers replied to me was a hodge-podge of truths and errors.[2] He blamed us for

[1] [The foolish pertinacity with which this unfortunate phrase has been and is to this day (see Welschinger, vol. i, p. 174), harped upon by critics of the ministry would seem to suggest a consciousness of the weakness of their case, as against M. Ollivier at least. By charging, directly or by innuendo, that he used the phrase in any other sense than that in which he claims to have used it, — which is surely the sense which it naturally bears, taking the surrounding circumstances into account, — they contradict their own previous admissions of the sincerity of his desire for peace and of his grief at the outcome. Welschinger, *ubi sup.*, discusses it with absurd gravity. Even Sir Spencer Walpole says that M. Ollivier "will live in history as the Minister who accepted *with a light heart* the responsibility of the policy which produced the greatest tragedy of the nineteenth century." *History of Twenty-Five Years*, vol. ii, p. 479. La Gorce, almost alone, treats the subject as it should be treated. "The phrase stuck," he says, "and, being removed from the explanation which accompanied it, was repeated later with more puerile malice than justice" (vol. vi, pp. 304, 305). And see Lehautcourt, vol. i, p. 326.

M. Ollivier has thought it worth while to place in the Appendix to vol. xiv, pp. 620–622, two pages of citations, in which the word *léger* is used in the sense in which he claims to have used it, beginning with Littré's definition: "That which does not depress by a *moral* weight." His examples cover all literature, ancient and modern, and call forth a sneering allusion from M. Welschinger. The labor of collecting them seems to me to have been supererogatory. "Even if I had not used that phrase," says the author, "they would have invented another and persecuted me with it just the same."]

[2] [Thiers's second speech is reported at length by M. Ollivier, in vol. xiv, pp. 433–442. — "Never did citizen honor himself more and better deserve the gratitude of his country than did M. Thiers on that day," exclaims Delord (vol. vi, p. 189), "when after proving the Empire to have been the dupe and accomplice of Sadowa, he strove vainly to preserve France from the fate that awaited her." M. Jules Favre (vol. i, pp. 14, 85) is fairly dithyrambic in his laudation of M. Thiers, that "dear former colleague," in whom he was to find such efficient support of the "Government of Na-

not giving Europe time to intervene. European mediation had been attempted July 14 by England, and surlily rejected by Prussia.[1] One seeks mediation in disputes concerning material questions, one takes counsel only of one's self when honor is at stake. What patriot ever taught us that a nation should adjust its susceptibility according to the advice of strangers? Surely not de Tocqueville. "One has no right," he says, "to express an opinion as to what accords with national interest and honor except when speaking of one's own country."[2] If, as Thiers said, ministers had cherished the wish to obtain reparation for Sadowa, it would have been proper to discuss the question whether they had chosen the opportunity well or ill. But not one of them dreamed of reparation for Sadowa, which they considered irreparable; they had no thought save for protecting the national honor, and such emergencies one deals with as they come — one does not select them.

tional Defence," although he (Thiers) claimed not to approve of the methods by which it rose to power. Lehautcourt, while admitting that he displayed rare moral courage "by defying unpopularity in order to say aloud what he believed to be the truth, — a rare thing among us," — thinks that his declarations and those of his colleagues of the Left, Gambetta and the rest, "came too late, and since war was inevitable, it was better to accept it with the sobriety and resolution which it requires. Protests like those of Thiers and Gambetta, uttered in public session, could not but impair our energy and even blaze out a path to internal discord." And he quotes from the *Opinion National* of July 16, these words: "The Left — I must say it, much as I regret to do so — the Left, yesterday, forgot itself. It gave its grudges and its apprehensions precedence over the sentiment of nationality, over the prudence which was enjoined upon it by the duty of not deadening the French impetus. . . . As for M. Thiers, it would have been better for his memory, if his career had ended before the close of that day."]

[1] [See *supra*, p. 318 n. (on p. 319).]
[2] Tocqueville to Henry Reeve, May, 1853.

DECLARATION OF JULY 15

On the other hand, that speech contained two indictments which history will ratify: that of the attempt of Prussia, in the face of the least disputed principles and of immemorial tradition, to seat a German prince on the throne of Spain; and that of the demand of guaranties, which was defensible as a matter of pure logic, but unjustifiable under the actual circumstances. Thiers's whole argument on that subject was irrefutable: he was right in calling the demand of guaranties a mistake; although the mistake was not made by the Cabinet, I could not shift the responsibility from our shoulders, because, as we did not resign, we associated ourselves with it.

But Thiers became an unfair partisan once more, — and here history will not follow him, — when he declared the war to be a necessary result of the demand of guaranties. That demand was not submitted to the King until July 13, at nine o'clock; it was not known to Bismarck until some time that day; consequently it was not that which induced the Chancellor to form a bellicose resolution which he had imperiously communicated to the King on the evening of the 12th.

Unquestionably the demand of guaranties did furnish Bismarck with facilities for putting an affront upon us, which he would have had difficulty in finding elsewhere if we had not proffered them to him by reopening a negotiation already happily closed. Nevertheless, the demand of guaranties did not necessarily lead to war. In its modified form it was not of the sort that must perforce be answered by an insult; if Bismarck had rejected it in accordance with the ordinary forms of diplomacy, courteously, even curtly, the crisis would not have recurred; we had resolved not to convert it into an ultimatum. It was rejected with contumely; it was that fact alone which brought on the war. If Thiers had been animated by patriotic sentiments, he would, after criticising our error, have reproved much more vigorously the insolence of Prussia, and would have declared it, as we did, intolerable. To be sure, he did not dare to justify it; he admitted that our sensitiveness was honorable, but he said that two nations do not rush at each other's throats "for such absurd reasons."

To have been slapped in the face before all Europe was an absurdity, a mere matter of form! Such monstrous ideas are not to be discussed. Gramont reproved them with the haughty accent of a gentleman and a man of heart, which electrified the Assembly.

"After all that you have just heard, this one *fact* is enough — that the Prussian government has informed all the Cabinets of Europe that it had refused to receive our Ambassador or to continue negotiations with him. That is an insult to the Emperor and to France, and if, which is impossible, there should be found to be, in my country, a Chamber which would submit to it or tolerate it, I would not remain Minister of Foreign Affairs for five minutes!"

Enthusiastic applause drowned those dignified words.

Buffet and Jules Favre demanded the production of the Prussian despatch to foreign courts.[1] How could I

[1] [In the course of his speech, M. Ollivier had read to the Chamber the despatches from Berne and Munich, without naming the places from which they came, or their senders. After Gramont's brief address,] "Jules Favre rose, more livid than ever, his lip more contorted, emphasizing more than ever his words, envenomed by his strident snarl of hatred. He had advised the Emperor to make war on Austria, he would have liked a war over Poland and one over Denmark, and yet he raved against the only war in which France was really interested! . . . The war had no avowable motive: the despatch to foreign governments was fictitious. He demanded

DECLARATION OF JULY 15

produce a despatch sent to third parties and not addressed to me? The very cabinets to which it was sent could not have procured it for us, since it had been *read* to them, no copy being left. Bismarck alone could have given us the original text, as he did later. At that moment we could produce only the despatches from our ministers, who transmitted the message to us according to the reports of those to whom it had been officially read. And those despatches from our ministers we did not refuse to read.

I was preparing to make this explanation, and to say to Buffet: Draw your motion properly; modify it to a request for despatches sent by the French government or received by it, and we will accept it, when an outburst of shouts of "Don't answer! don't answer!" prevented me from uttering a word, and Jules Favre's motion was lost by 159 votes against 84.[1]

that it be laid before the Chamber." *L'Empire Libéral*, vol. xiv, pp. 446, 447. [After M. Thiers, Jules Favre went to the tribune; "foreseeing and concise that day, but too much suspected of hatred not to arouse distrust, he pressed the government with his questions. 'Where is the official despatch?' ... Among the members of the Corps Législatif M. Buffet was one of those most heeded. ... He tried in his turn to restrain his colleagues and to make the ministers speak. ... He appropriated Jules Favre's motion, and demanded the production of documents." La Gorce, vol. vi, 305. Favre himself wrote later, notwithstanding the evidence then accessible, that the alleged despatch to foreign governments *never existed*, and that Bismarck's despatch to the Cabinets of the South contained simply information which was of the deepest interest to them, "conveyed in terms which could not lead to a conflict, since they were an exact reproduction of facts at which our Ambassador had taken no offence." *Gouvernement de la Défense Nationale*, vol. i, p. 27.]

[1] [The names of the 84 are given by Lehautcourt, vol. i, p. 328, n. 1. Among them are those of M. Buffet and Comte Daru, the two men who had resigned from the ministry; also M. Thiers. Some members of the Left, notably M. de Kératry, refused to go with their colleagues.]

Certain deputies, even former ministers of the Empire, have tried to give

The bureaus, upon naming the Commission, instructed it to demand all documents; and we ourselves, as soon as the Commission was organized, under the presidency of Albuféra, and even before they were asked for, carried them before that body.[1]

I arrived first;[2] I explained what the impatience of the Chamber had not allowed me to say, and I announced that Gramont would produce all the documents in our possession: namely, (1) The telegraphic despatches between Gramont and Benedetti, from the 7th to the 13th inclusive; (2) The despatches from Comminges-Guitaud, Cadore, and one or two others of our agents, notably the one at Dresden, which had reached us since. Then I asked leave to withdraw; urgent affairs to be attended to demanded my presence.

Gramont arrived at this juncture; he produced all

to the vote of the 84 the significance of a protest against the war. One of them, Cochery, did it in 1873. . . . A deputy, Haëntjens, who had voted with him on that occasion, recalled him to the truth. . . . "I am one of the 84 who voted with M. Cochery, and do you deny that I know the meaning of my vote? I declare that we did not intend to vote against the war; we simply wanted the production of papers which were denied us . . . and I think now that they were right to refuse to produce them." [Note of M. Ollivier in vol. xiv, p. 449.]

[1] [The Commission consisted of the following: Duc d'Albuféra, President, MM. de Talhouët, de Kératry, Dréolle, de Lagrange, Pinard, Sénéca, Chadenet, and Millon.]

[2] "I arrived first *with Le Bœuf:*" vol xiv, p. 451. [And M. Ollivier (pp. 452, 453) gives a résumé of the Marshal's statements to the Commission, including his oft-repeated assurance] " that we should be ready before the Prussians, whose mobilization would not be so rapid as was supposed; and since war was likely to be forced upon us sooner or later, it was better that it should come before the Prussians had changed their muskets and secured good *mitrailleuses*, and before the opposition had finished demolishing our army. Having given these explanations, he took Talhouët into a corner, and said to him: 'We have a few days' start; don't make us lose it.'"

the documents that I had mentioned. They were most carefully arranged by numbers, that is to say, chronologically, because that order was fixed by the date written at the head of each despatch. He read and explained the principal ones. In this way the Commission was able to verify the accuracy of those that I had read, and to assure themselves that they were not contradicted by those that I had not read.[1]

Next, Albuféra asked if we had any alliances.

"My reason for keeping the Commission waiting," Gramont replied, "is that I had the Austrian Ambassador and the Italian minister with me at the Foreign Office. I hope that the Commission will not interrogate me further."

Talhouët, against his own remonstrance, was appointed reporter. This choice was very significant: Talhouët not only enjoyed general esteem, but was known to be a prudent man, not fond of compromising himself in hazardous affairs, and his presence signified that this one was safe and could be entered into without danger.[2]

On the reopening of the session of the Chamber,

[1] [Here again M. Ollivier has omitted a large part of what he has to say in *L'Empire Libéral* concerning the investigations of the Commission and its report, and the debate thereon. The omitted portions will be found on pp. 452 ff.; as they deal largely with a question of some importance which has been made the subject of much discussion, but which is not mentioned in this volume, I have thought best to consider it by itself in an appendix. See *infra*, Appendix M: The Commission of July 15 and the Ems Correspondence. The question whether Comte Benedetti should have been heard by the Commission, which apparently did not think of summoning him, is argued affirmatively by La Gorce, vol. vi, p. 309; Sorel, vol. i, p. 186.]

[2] ["Talhouët was one of the most honorable men of a Chamber of which almost all the members were men of honor. He took fright at the task and demanded that others be joined with him. M. de Kératry, a fiery partisan of the war, and M. Dréolle, who, as he himself said, yielded only reluctantly to the current, were appointed to assist him." La Gorce, vi, pp. 309, 310.]

Dréolle, a member of the Commission, came to my bench and said to me, "I have drawn the report; you will be satisfied with it."

I was surprised at this confidential communication from a journalist who was constantly abusing me.

Talhouët read Dréolle's report, which unanimously recommended assent to the government's plan. It was greeted by bravos and prolonged applause, blended with cries of "Vive l'Empereur!" This report set forth the capital fact that *the diplomatic papers had been produced.*

Gambetta delivered an artificial harangue which, while apparently against war, was none the less in favor of it. His purpose to differentiate himself from Thiers was manifest in every sentence. In fact, he declared that "no word should come from his mouth which could serve the cause of the foreigner" — "as M. Thiers has just done," understood. Thiers had deemed it quite natural that the King of Prussia should be unwilling to make any agreement concerning the future; Gambetta understood that "that must have disturbed us," and agreed that "it was our duty to insist upon having satisfaction." Thiers had regarded as exaggerated susceptibility the emotion that the public refusal to receive our Ambassador had aroused in us; Gambetta was able to understand that we found "that conduct irregular and offensive." He was quite willing to have war, but a war of revenge for Sadowa, which he had lauded in his speech on rue de la Sourdière; the ministry gave insufficient reasons for its war; it sought "in wretched pretexts the decisive reasons for its conduct; it did not appeal to the veritable grievances, but rested the whole *casus belli* on the base performances at Ems, instead of justifying its decisions by the necessity of atoning for a policy which he deplored and detested — the policy of 1866." Like the deputies of the Right, he blamed me for not making of the war a premeditated revenge for that discomfiture. And still, he associated himself with the demands of his colleagues, from whom he had not the courage to set himself free, and strove to prove that the cause which we assigned for our susceptibility was not adequate; he would wait until the document upon which we wrongfully rested the whole *casus belli* should be communicated directly and in full to the Commission. "You have not given us all the elements of certainty that we are entitled to." [1]

Albuféra, President of the Commission, interrupted to say: "*The Commission has received them all. I so state upon my honor.*"

Gambetta insisted.

Albuféra interrupted him again. "The Commission has read the despatch."

Gramont added: "I declare that I handed the document to the Commission, and that it was read by them."

The members of the Commission confirmed this statement: "Yes! yes!"

Albuféra continued: "We declare that we have read it, and if you do not believe us, you must name other commissioners."

It was impossible not to be convinced and silenced

---

[1] [As to Gambetta's speech, see Sorel, vol. i, p. 193; La Gorce, vol. vi, pp. 312, 313; Welschinger, vol. i, p. 186. "Gambetta's language was very shrewd," says Sorel: "he attacked M. Ollivier in his past opinions — the indulgent contemplation of the policy of 1866; and in his present conduct — a declaration of war without sufficient justification. Therein he conformed to the principles of that faction of the revolutionary school which desired both 'revenge for Sadowa,' and 'abasement of the Empire.'"]

by such emphatic statements made by such men. So that for the time Gambetta stopped short, and, forgetting that he had just been content to call for communication of the documents to the Commission, he said: "If it is true that that despatch is of sufficient importance to have caused you to make this decision, you have a plain duty, and that is to communicate it not only to the members of the Commission and to the Chamber, but to France and to Europe; and if you do not do it, your war is simply a veiled pretext, and it will not be a national war." [*Numerous protests. Demonstrations of approval from several benches on the Left.*]

Talhouët protested: "We have had before us despatches from four or five of our representatives at different European courts, which reproduce this document in almost exactly the same words." [*Numerous voices*: "*Very good! very good!* " — "*Go on! go on!* " — "*Vote! vote!*") The Chamber had had enough. It would scarcely allow me to say a few indignant words in reply, before it proceeded to vote.[1]

While the votes were being counted, I met Gambetta in the lobby.

"How," I said to him, "can you deny the existence

[1] [The "few indignant words" cover several pages of *L'Empire Libéral* (vol. xiv, pp. 466-471), with many interruptions toward the end, when M. de Talhouët made the statement first repeated, not in reply to Gambetta.

The limits of this volume make it impossible to expand M. Ollivier's greatly condensed account of the events of the memorable 15th of July. I can do no more than supply a few references which will enable the reader who desires to do so to obtain a more connected idea of the course of affairs from somewhat different points of view. Besides M. Ollivier's *L'Empire Libéral*, vol. xiv, chapter 6, see La Gorce, vol. vi, pp. 298-313; Gramont, chapter 12; Sorel, vol. i, chapter 5; Welschinger, vol, i, chapter 5; Lehautcourt, vol. i, book 4, chapter 8; Delord, vol. vi, pp. 177-200; Von Sybel, English trans., vol. vii, pp. 415-422; Jules Favre, vol. i, pp.15 ff.]

of the despatches that I read to you? I will show them to you if you wish."

"I don't deny them," he said, "but you didn't read everything."

"That is true: Gramont showed the Commission everything; but I did not read the end of Cadore's despatch from Munich, to the effect that the King of Bavaria was informed that Benedetti had disrespectfully accosted the King on the promenade."

"Very good! that is the very thing that I sought to compel you to read."

"I could not do it without making Cadore's position at Munich impossible; the additional light that that would have thrown on the discussion was not important enough to convince me that I ought to run that risk."

Let us determine the significance of that vote, which furnished us with a credit of fifty million francs. It was not a question of carrying on a war that had begun; we were in no wise compromised or bound; there had been no declaration of war, no irrevocable step had been taken; not a single army was assembled; a vote refusing us the credit we asked would have been sufficient to turn the scale in favor of peace. Throughout the debate this vote was treated as destined to decide the question of peace or war.

"From the decision that you are about to make," said Thiers, "there may result the death of thousands."

"The Cabinet," said Gambetta, "proposes to you to take upon yourselves the responsibility of a vote, an attitude, a parliamentary decision which will allow it to engage in war." And, at the outset of his remarks, he said: "*Before war is declared.*"

Thus the Chamber had the power to prevent us from

declaring war. The duty of those who wanted peace was to deny us the funds and to turn us out. Under the Restoration the members of the opposition would not vote the necessary credit even after the Spanish expedition had been undertaken. If the imperial government, before sending troops to Mexico, had gone to the Corps Législatif to ask for subsidies, would the Five have granted them? To vote the credit was to vote for war. And so the deputies who had declared themselves resolutely against war did not hesitate, but voted *No*.

The votes of those who voted *Yes* meant, "March against the enemy; the Chamber, the mouthpiece of the country, is with you." Two hundred and forty-five deputies held this view, among whom were Gambetta, Jules Simon, Jules Ferry, Ernest Picard, Barthélemy Saint-Hilaire, etc. Only six voted *No:* Emmanuel Arago, Grévy, Desseaux, Esquiros, Glais-Bizoin, Ordinaire. Thiers, more prudent in his acts than in his words, abstained, with Crémieux, Girault, and Raspail. Jules Favre was absent.

Even if one should prefer to exclude from the count all the official candidates and to regard as representing the nation only the fifty or sixty deputies chosen without the patronage of the administration, the war would still have commanded an imposing majority.

It is not legitimate therefore to represent the War of 1870 as an arbitrary enterprise of despotism, forced upon the nation in its own despite. As the Emperor often said afterwards, the responsibility should be divided equally between himself, his ministers, and Parliament. "If I had been against the war," he would say, "I should have dismissed my ministers; if they had not deemed it necessary, they would have resigned; if

DECLARATION OF JULY 15

Parliament had disapproved, it would not have voted for it." [1]

Emperor, ministers, Parliament, all made their decision with entire liberty and with full knowledge of the circumstances, neither of them having been deceived, or having deceived the others. The vote of the fifty millions settled the question.

The Chamber proceeded, without discussion, to vote a credit of fifteen millions for the navy, the law authorizing the limitation of voluntary enlistments to the duration of the war, and that calling the whole of the national *garde mobile* into active service. This session, which began at one in the afternoon of the 15th, was adjourned a few minutes after midnight.[2]

In the Senate the declaration was greeted with cheers

---

[1] Émile Ollivier to Prince Napoleon: — "Saint Tropez, March 18, 1876. My dear Prince: When I came to you in 1871, I complained vigorously of the Bonapartist polemic which aimed to hold me alone responsible for our disasters. You transmitted my complaint to the Emperor, who replied to you: 'In truth the responsibility can not be concentrated on E. O.'s head. It must be divided equally between the ministry, the Chamber, and myself. If I had not wanted the war, I would have dismissed my ministers; if the opposition had come from them, they would have resigned; finally, if the Chamber had been forced into the enterprise against its will, it would have voted against it.' It may be of very great importance to me, in view of certain eventualities, to have a copy of that letter. To send it to me could not, in any case, cause you any embarrassment. That is why I ask it of your friendship."

Prince Napoleon to Émile Ollivier: — "Paris, March 21, 1876. My dear Ollivier: What you remind me of, as coming from the Emperor, was *said*, not *written*. My memory is perfectly clear on that subject. On my next visit to Prangins I will reread and search among my cousin's letters, but I am almost certain that he did not write the sentence that you recall: he repeated it to me *several times*." [Note of M. Ollivier in vol. xiv, p, 474.]

[2] [Here M. Ollivier devotes three pages (475–478) to a refutation of the charge that the Chamber acted with undue haste, comparing it with the action of the Legislative on August 20, 1792, when it decreed the beginning of the great war of the Revolution.]

and prolonged applause, mingled with shouts of "Vive la France! Vive l'Empereur!" The public galleries joined in the enthusiasm of the Senate and intensified it. President Rouher having asked, "Does any one desire to speak?" shouts of "No! no! Vive l'Empereur!" arose on all sides.

Rouher continued: "The Senate, by its enthusiastic cheers, has given its full approval to the conduct of the government. I propose to the Senate to adjourn as a token of our cordial sympathy with the decision of the Emperor."

Shouts of "Vive l'Empereur!" broke out afresh, and the session was adjourned. On leaving the building the senators, popular for the first time, were applauded by the crowd.

The next day the Commission of the Senate met. Gramont was summoned before it. He laid before the commissioners the despatches that he had exhibited to the Corps Législatif on the preceding day. Rouher's report finally disproved the charge against Gramont of having kept from the Commission of the Corps Législatif the despatches prior to the 12th. It stated that the Commission had been supplied *with all the important despatches since July 6*.[1]

[1] [See Appendix M. President Rouher's report is given in full in *L'Empire Libéral*, vol. xiv, pp. 479, 480, followed by an account of the "demonstration" arranged by him, the Senate going in a body to Saint-Cloud to felicitate the Emperor. Rouher made a speech which M. Ollivier describes as] "the speech which the Right had failed to obtain from me on the 15th: a counter-declaration opposed to ours; the programme of the war-party set up against our programme. . . . Very different was the Emperor's reply. No bluster: 'We are beginning a serious struggle.' And he discreetly aligns himself with the ideas of his Cabinet and not with Rouher's, in thanking the Senate for 'the keen enthusiasm with which it had received the declaration that the Foreign Minister had been instructed to make.'

DECLARATION OF JULY 15 365

Our declaration was equivalent to a declaration of war. King William so understood it, for as soon as he was informed of it, during that same night of the 15th, he ordered the mobilization of his army. Nevertheless, most inopportunely, in response to the obstinate persistence of Admiral Rigault, with a view of regularizing the prizes that we never took, we declared, by a note awkwardly drawn by the Foreign Office and handed to Bismarck on July 19, that we considered ourselves to be in a state of war.[1]

But this attitude was so discreetly assumed and so concealed that the public did not take it in. It remembered only Rouher's swaggering and compromising assertions. . . . The speech-making at an end, the sovereigns circulated among the senators. The difference in their attitudes was very marked. The Empress was most expansive, animated by triumphant confidence; she said: 'We are beginning with all the chances in our favor that one can have; all will go well.' The Emperor was melancholy; he said: 'It will be a long and hard struggle; we shall have to make a violent effort.'"

[1] "A declaration of war was a superfluity. . . . But there are, in addition to the belligerents, neutral powers. Neutrality, being a special condition in a legal point of view, can result only from a visible, regular state of things, as to the existence and nature of which there can be no doubt. Hence arises, even after the regularly constituted governing powers of a nation have publicly decided upon war, the necessity of an official notification to the enemy. Ministers did not deny their obigation to comply with the formality; but they would have preferred not to take the initiative. 'We should leave it to the enemy,' said Le Bœuf. But Rigault, whose rare intervention was always overbearing and regrettable, appealed to the provisions of the treaty of Paris concerning naval prizes, as if our fleet were likely to be over-supplied with them. He was so insistent that, fearing to bring about a dislocation of the ministry, we conceded the declaration of war. . . . It was not even read to the Council. It was laid before the Chambers solely as a matter of form and without discussion. . . . In reality it did not give us the initiative in attack: we had taken that in the tribune on the 15th." *L'Empire Libéral*, vol. xiv, pp. 499, 500.

CHAPTER XXII

UPON WHOM SHOULD THE RESPONSIBILITY FOR THE
WAR FALL — FRANCE OR GERMANY?

IN his speech of July 16 in the Bundesrath, and in his circular note of the 18th, Bismarck cast upon France the responsibility of having desired, sought, and provoked the war. As to the origin of the business, he repeated the language that he had placed in the mouths of Thile and the King. He exerted himself particularly to modify the real character of the Ems despatch, which, as he justly said, was, in the last analysis, so far as the French ministry was concerned, *the sole ground of war.* According to him that despatch was simply a newspaper telegram sent to the representatives of Prussia and to other governments regarded as friendly, to keep them informed as to the new phase which the affair had assumed; it was not an official document. "As the determining causes of this deplorable phenomenon of war," he said, "we shall be unable unfortunately to discover nothing more than the basest instincts of hatred and jealousy on the subject of the autonomy and welfare of Germany, conjoined with the desire to keep liberty bound hand and foot at home by rushing the country into war with foreign nations."

The paltry arguments so artfully woven by Bismarck produced at the time a tremendous effect upon a fanatical people, and upon an international opinion always suspicious of Napoleon III. Von Sybel lent them the

WHOSE THE RESPONSIBILITY

authority of his talent. There was no German who did not assent to them and repeat them. Germany's renown gained nothing by this system of imposture, and impartial judges recalled the remark of Velleius Paterculus on the Germans, *Natum ad mendacium genus.*

Bismarck himself was degraded by this vulgar equivocation. He was not slow to perceive how absurd, puerile, and unworthy of him was the rôle of hypocrite which his panegyrists attributed to him, and to which he seemed at first to give his assent. Little by little he cast aside all these false appearances, and ended by avowing: *Ego nominor leo!*

An English correspondent with the Prussian army accosted him one day, saying: "You must be very angry with those Frenchmen who have forced you into this war."

"Angry!" he retorted; "why, it was I who forced them to fight!"[1]

Later, he authorized Busch to divulge the mystery of the insulting despatch. His confidant did not confine himself to that, but, probably without authority, he exhibited the Mephistopheles of the State, in the grip of remorse, at the moment when an awakened conscience tortures the man who has tortured others, admitting that, *but for him, three great wars would not have been undertaken, eighty thousand men would not have died, and so many families, so many fathers and mothers and brothers and sisters, would not be left desolate.*

Bismarck's fondness for expatiating, in his speeches, on the War of 1866, was equalled by his reticence concerning that of 1870. Except on the day when,

[1] Correspondence of the *Standard*, Feb. 10, 1873.

in the heat of the Kulturkampf, he maundered about the effect of Ultramontane influences, he seldom went beyond a few hasty assertions. Finally the truth was told officially by himself. After the brief reign of Frederick III [1888], a German review, the *Deutsche Rundschau*, published extracts from that Emperor's journal, written when he was Crown Prince. A note dated July 13 said that "Bismarck confided to him that he regarded peace as certain, and that he proposed to return to Varzin." A statement so manifestly false would hardly have disturbed Bismarck, had he not been denounced in other extracts as having been far from solicitous to establish German Unity. Now, inasmuch as, but for the War of 1870, that unity would not have advanced beyond the stage of a utopian dream, and as it became a reality solely by virtue of that war, Bismarck placed his renown as the founder of the new Germany beyond attack by claiming the initiative in that war. He declared, in the report whereby he called upon the Emperor to prosecute the authors of that publication (September 28, 1888), that the documents proved that "His Royal Highness was already aware on the 13th *that I looked upon the war as necessary*, and that I should not have returned to Varzin without giving in my resignation, *if war had been averted*."

The most effective blow that he dealt to his mendacious legend was the restoring to the Ems despatch the official and wilfully provocative character which he had at first denied to it, and thus admitting that we were in the right as to the *sole grievance* upon which we justified the war. In his *Reflections and Reminiscences*, he describes the scene of the Ems despatch, and draws

WHOSE THE RESPONSIBILITY 369

a picture of it equal to the most terrific passages of *Macbeth*, a picture so impressively dramatic beneath the simplicity of the words, that it will remain forever in the memory of posterity.[1]

"Vanity!" some one has said of these solemn assertions so deliberately multiplied. No; they were due to the just reasoning of a mind in full control of itself, tired of seeing others appropriate the reward when they had had none of the labor. Perhaps there was involuntarily mingled therewith some impatience with the public folly. It is not altogether certain that, weary of hearing so many fools or knaves repeat consequentially, despite the evidence to the contrary, that the war was engineered and sought by France, he did not take a sort of malicious pleasure in crying out to them: "Well! as you persist in ignoring the fact, let me tell you that that war was my own work!"

But there is one point on which he insists upon not being truthful. That is, the origin and development of the Hohenzollern candidacy. He clings to his fable of the first moment, doubtless because the truth would be too villanous to disclose. There is, in fact, an agreement between him and his accomplices to keep History always in ignorance of the truth. Bernhardi's *Memoirs* would have unveiled the secret; the published portion contains nothing about his mission to Spain except picturesque anecdotical details; the political portion has been suppressed, and, it is said, will never see the light. On the other hand, the papers of Lothar Bucher, another confidant, were burned. We should have been doomed therefore to remain in ignorance of the beginnings of that ambuscade, had not Prince Charles

[1] [See Appendix K.]

of Roumania, by publishing his *Memoirs*, rendered to the truth the service of illuminating with a light which will never again be put out, the only dark corner of that dark affair. I have been told that he was earnestly urged to publish them by Queen Augusta.

Some historians of unconquerable lack of candor, like Oncken, cling obstinately to the outworn legends. But serious critics, like Ottokar Lorenz, Delbrück, Rathlef, Lenz, Johannes Scherr, and Schultze, have had the laudable courage to free themselves from the conventional falsehood. Concerning the origin of the conflict, Lorenz says: —

"Viewed from the standpoint of international law, Herr von Bismarck's theory could hardly be sustained. All the candidacies for the throne which have arisen during the nineteenth century in Spain and Portugal have been invariably subjects of international negotiation, and the Coburgs in Belgium, as well as the Danes in Greece and the Hohenzollerns in Roumania, furnish unquestionable examples of the fact that such dynastic arrangements have always been preceded by an understanding between the powers interested in the negotiations. . . . No one can deny that the pretension of the Prussian government that it was not called upon to concern itself with such a matter, clearly was, and was certain to be considered, a novel principle in diplomatic history. The refusal of the Prussian government to make known its views on this question, on the pretext that it did not concern the State, added to the difficulties of Benedetti's task, because he was certain to conceive from Herr von Thile's assertions the suspicion that there was some scheme in progress on the part of Prussia, which they wished to conceal."[1]

He characterizes no less justly the sudden changes of July 13.

"But on the 13th, God be praised! a spirit worthy of the great Frederick had already come to life in the German nation. They were not only determined to fight, but they longed to crush the French and wipe them out. It was the spirit of 1813. The great statesman did everything to assure a swift, decisive, radical contest, and to forestall the intervention of a halting peace. Timid historians are accustomed to say nothing, or to mention only in the most casual way, the decisive diplomatic skill exerted by Bismarck to fan the warlike excitement in France. While he was proving by his audacious plans that the traditions of Prussian politics, and those of the 'Great Fritz,' who knew enough to cross the Rubicon at need, had not fallen into oblivion, these timid historians represent him as still playing the part of the lamb who threatens the wolf on the bank of the stream. But luckily the cast is materially changed on the 13th of July, and it is Bismarck who plays the wolf on the bank of the stream."[2]

Hans Delbrück has very fittingly characterized Bismarck's sophistical plea of not guilty. "Bismarck," he says, "thought to cover his act with the veil of a private affair of the Hohenzollern family. Von Sybel simply accepted this fiction in his history and sharply reproved the French for not accepting it in the same way. I fear that with that method of narrating facts

[1] Lorenz, *Kaiser Wilhelm und die Begrundung des Reichs*, pp. 238, 239.
[2] Lorenz, *op. cit.*, pp. 270, 271.

we should not cut a good figure in the history of the world, and that the French are simply laughing at us." [1]

Rathlef passes judgment on the Ems despatch without hypocrisy. "They who agree that the affairs of their country shall be managed by a Bismarck, must also accept, with the great things that Germany received from him, those things which they cannot justify and which, it may be, in the depths of their hearts, they reprobate. But in such circumstances there is always more or less injustice done to the adversary. Even for the sake of Germany's noble cause, we cannot fail to deplore immensely the shadow that the Ems despatch casts upon her; we cannot deny it, nor do we wish to do so; and the more momentous that hour is in the history of Germany, the more importance that both Germans and French ascribe to it, the more reasons have we for attenuating by an honorable confession such fault as is attributable to us, not only because we owe it to our opponents, but because we owe it to ourselves." [2]

Johannes Scherr does not consider that the responsibility for the war should be charged to the French alone. "Only those persons," he says, "whom their patriotism petrifies in ignorance, or whose narrow-mindedness prevents them from understanding anything, can believe that France alone, or the Emperor of the French, is responsible for the war. Doubtless the Bonapartist faction desired it for several reasons, and Gallic vanity, as well as the chauvinistic delusion of grandeur, drove in the same direction; but Prussia,

---

[1] In *Preussische Jahrbucher*, Oct., 1895, p. 34.
[2] Georg Rathlef, "Die Emse Depesche," *Jahrbuch*, 1896, p. 453.

WHOSE THE RESPONSIBILITY 373

extended to the Main, had no less need of it, and desired it no less earnestly. Except for the action of Herr von Bismarck, and in spite of Abeken's despatch, the negotiations would have come to a friendly conclusion, not only because of what happened at Ems, but because in many quarters, in France, there were signs of a disposition to leave the sword in the scabbard." [1]

Schultze, in a noteworthy work that reveals the honest man and the true historian, discussing step by step the uncontested facts and documents, demonstrates more clearly than any one "that the Hohenzollern candidacy always had the anti-French character that Bismarck denied that it had; and that, while it was in any event unfriendly to France to follow up the affair, the way in which Bismarck did it disclosed a premeditated design to hasten the catastrophe, and that, in those days of July, Bismarck worked determinedly and persistently to bring on war — that the Hohenzollern business was a trap set for Napoleon, to humble him. The Hohenzollern scheme was to Bismarck one method of pursuing a policy of action adverse to France. In the conception of the Hohenzollern candidacy, Bismarck was the aggressor, who was well aware at the outset, that, so far as any one could foresee, it would lead to a rupture, and who, in the last stage of the affair, brought that rupture to pass in an altogether deliberate way, and knowing full well what he was about." [2]

But it would not be fair to make the German historians and critics say more than they have said. They have declared that Bismarck wanted war, not to blame

[1] Johannes Scherr, *1870–1871*, p. 72.
[2] Walter Schultze, *Die Thronkandidatur Hohenzollern und Graf Bismarck*, pp. 54, 55.

him for it, but to glorify him: to be sure, he planned it all and provoked it all, but that was where his genius shone forth; his offensive tactics were simply the means of forestalling the offensive strategy prepared by Napoleon III. He knew by the disclosures of Bernhardi, and by those, even more reliable, of his Austrian and Italian agents, the plans for a triple alliance that had been discussed since 1869 by the cabinets of Paris, Vienna, and Florence.

"To each step forward in the formation of this alliance," says Schultze, "there was a corresponding step taken by him in the preparation of the candidacy. And it was because the visit of Archduke Albert to Paris, in March, 1870, convinced him that Prussia would be attacked the next spring, that he sent Lothar Bucher to Madrid, in order to hurry forward the crisis, and to disconcert by his sudden attack the premeditated attack for which everything was ready both in a diplomatic and in a military way." [1]

Not one of Schultze's conjectures has the slightest foundation. Bismarck knew better than any other man what to expect. He was fully informed of the Emperor's pacific disposition, especially since the plebiscite; and the interview in the Cologne *Gazette* had apprized him and all Germany that mine was even more certain.[2] However ardent the bellicose sentiments that were attributed, justly or unjustly, to the Empress, there was

[1] Schultze, *ubi sup.*

[2] [The resignation of Comte Daru in April was ostensibly due to the decision of the government to resort to the plebiscite, although he did not at first oppose it. M. Ollivier's article in the Cologne *Gazette*, in March, had shown its author to be not inimical to German unity, — an attitude practically in direct opposition to that recently announced by Comte Daru. See Welschinger, vol. i, pp. 18 ff.]

no occasion to take them into account, for the Emperor could not decide to make war without the assent of his Council, and the Empress possessed no influence over the members of that body, all of whom were notoriously devoted to peace.

The plans for a triple alliance were of a deterrent nature only, — academic, so to speak — and were never reduced to practicable, effective shape.

The Archduke Albert's visit to Paris could not seriously have disturbed Bismarck, for he was well aware how slender that gentleman's influence was on the course of political affairs. Even if he had attached any importance to the friendly professions of Beust, whom he never took seriously, he was protected against them by his understanding with Andrassy and the Hungarians, without whose concurrence no war was possible.

Nor did Victor Emmanuel's inclination toward the Emperor arouse his displeasure. "The alliance of Italy and France," he said, according to Hohenlohe, "is of no importance for the moment. The Italians would not take the field, even if Victor Emmanuel, who is capable of anything for money and women, wished to conclude a treaty." [1] Moreover, it was not enough to warrant undertaking a campaign against Prussia, that an alliance should be formed by Paris, Vienna, and Florence, — it must include Munich and Stuttgart as well. Now, there exists no trace of any negotiations with these two last-named cabinets, for we were well aware that, although the ministers of the Southern kingdoms were defending their states against absorption by Prussia, no one of them would have consented to

[1] See the *Memoirs of Hohenlohe.*

plot an aggression against their powerful neighbor. So that this theory of offensive tactics made necessary by our threats, however specious it may appear, neither explains nor justifies Bismarck's undeniable challenge. The true explanation is quite different; my readers already know it, but I must recur to it one last time.

William and Bismarck, assisted by two military organizers of the first rank, had resolved to complete the conquest of Germany begun by Frederick. The first step was the breaking up of the Germanic Confederation and the exclusion of Austria from Germany. The victory of Sadowa achieved this first result, but only by endangering the final object: Germans had beaten Germans, which fact was not of a nature to facilitate their reunion in the same Empire; the only means of reconciling them was to associate them in a common triumph over the hereditary foe. "This war," said William in July, 1866, "will be followed by another." From that moment, the ravisher of the Duchies and Hanover accepted that other war as a historic necessity as inevitable as the war against Austria had been.

"I was convinced," says Bismarck in his memoirs, "that the gulf between the Northern and Southern sections of the Fatherland, which had been dug in the course of centuries by difference of sentiments, race, dynasty, and mode of life, could be happily bridged only by a national war against the near-by nation, our aggressor for ages past. These political considerations regarding the states of Southern Germany might also be applied, *mutatis mutandis*, to our relations with the people of Hanover, Hesse, and Schleswig-Holstein."[1] After his triumph, he reverted many times to the same

[1] Bismarck, *Reflections and Reminiscences*, English trans., vol. ii, pp. 99, 100.

assertion. "The War of 1870–1871 was also a necessity," he said at Jena in 1892; "unless we had beaten France, we could not have completed peaceably the formation of the German Empire. France would have found, later, allies to help her to prevent us." [1]

After words so explicit as these, how can any intelligent mortal still seek the causes of the War of 1870, or impute them to Napoleon III and his ministers? Neither the King nor Bismarck had the wish or the power to annex the states of the South by force, and they were sincere when they denied having such a thought. Sooner or later the cause of Unity must prevail. But when? For the moment the resistance of the people was so vehement that it was impossible to foresee when it would cease.

A diversion was of no advantage to Napoleon III, who had just learned how deeply the roots of his dynasty were buried in national soil, or to his ministers, who were amply content with the glory of having achieved the transformation of their country into a liberal empire. On the other hand, it was indispensable to Prussia: the peoples of the South, overspent, exhausted by incessant military alarums, were praying for mercy; if no war should break out, a lightening of the burden of militarism would be unavoidable; a conflict between the crown, the parliament, and the nation would inevitably ensue, and under more difficult conditions than the last, as universal suffrage had come upon the stage. A victory over France would solve the difficulty in an instant. Hence, under pain of marking time indefinitely, and leaving the partly built bridge over the Main unfinished, war was a necessity.

[1] Speech of Bismarck at Jena, July 31, 1892.

In 1867, at the time of the Luxembourg difficulty, Bismarck was inclined to push the affair to a conclusion, and to strike, as he said. But he did not find himself sufficiently prepared; he was sure neither of the coöperation of the states of the South, nor of the connivance of Russia. In December, 1869, the Czar's good-will was assured, and Moltke's military arrangements perfected; so war was resolved upon. The difficulty was to produce the appearance of aggression on our part, in order to draw the King on. Bismarck waited, so long as he hoped for an attack from us; as soon as he considered that to be absolutely excluded by my accession to power (in that sense I contributed indirectly to the outbreak of the war), he devised his challenge. All the early months of the year 1870 were devoted to that conspiracy. He thought at first of proclaiming the King German Emperor, which he supposed could not be submitted to by France; but the governments of the South did not lend themselves to that plan. Then, in March, he fixed upon the Prussian candidacy in Spain, which, he knew, was likely to irritate our people more than the assumption of the title of German Emperor. Thus this was an *offensive* war, strategically as well as tactically.

This whole controversy between the Germans and ourselves concerning the responsibility for the war is controlled and solved by two general considerations. From what cause did the war arise? From the Hohenzollern candidacy in the first place, and then from Bismarck's disclosure of the King's refusal to receive our Ambassador. No Hohenzollern candidacy, no war. Even after the Hohenzollern candidacy, no disclosure of the King's refusal, no war. Now, was it the Emperor's government that instigated the Hohenzollern candidacy? Was it the Emperor's government that spread broadcast the occurrence at Ems?

Even if it be true that we showed ourselves to be unskilful diplomatists, that at the beginning we were too stiff and at the end too exacting, still, it is true that we did not suggest the Hohenzollern candidacy; that, if it had not been secretly hatched by Prussia, our bungling and our exactions would have had neither pretext nor opportunity to manifest themselves, and peace would not have been disturbed.

There is not a thinking person in Europe so uncandid as to maintain that, face to face with a German candidacy in Spain, we should have held aloof, submitted, and said nothing. Now, every word exchanged between Prussia and ourselves was a danger, because every word that was not uttered aloud would have lacked dignity. Let us admit that we mispronounced that word which, as everybody admits, we were bound to utter, or else to abdicate: it is still an undeniable fact that it was Prussia who forced us to speak; that but for her conspiracy with Prim, we should not have broken our peaceful silence.

Let us admit further that we were wrong to feel offended by the official insulting promulgation of the refusal to receive our Ambassador; the fact remains that, if Bismarck had not proclaimed that refusal throughout Europe, the Emperor not having put the demand of guarantees in the form of an ultimatum, French susceptibility would have had no occasion to run riot and to rush headlong into extreme measures.

Thus, the primary fact, the candidacy; the final fact, the advertisement of the refusal to receive our Ambassador — these two facts of which the conflict was born, these two facts, without which there would have been no war, are chargeable to Prussia, not to France.

If the French ministers had been on the watch for a pretext for war, they had not to await this Hohenzollern candidacy, which it was not in their power to instigate, and which might never have been put forward. They had only to put out their hand to cause an immediate explosion; they had only to demand, in slightly urgent terms, as the Cabinet of St. Petersburg suggested their doing, the execution of the Treaty of Prague with respect to the Danes of Northern Schleswig. "If France was determined to resent by a war against Prussia the accession of a Prince of Hohenzollern to the Crown of Spain," said Westmann, Gortchakoff's assistant, to the English Ambassador, "she might unfortunately find a pretext for so doing by calling upon the Prussian government to fulfil the stipulations in the Treaty of Prague with respect to Schleswig." [1]

On June 28, Fleury, still harping upon his idea, wrote to Gramont: "I do not despair, on the return of the hereditary Grand Duke and the Czarevitch from their visit to Copenhagen, of seeing the question of the Duchies enter upon a new phase. It will be easy for me, whenever you shall order me to do so, to take up the thread of that affair which I had carried well along, and which I abandoned, when it was very near a conclusion, only in obedience to the formal commands of one of your predecessors."

And, in refusing to support our demand of guaranties, did not the Czar say, "On the question of the Treaty of Prague, I would have followed you"?

[1] Buchanan to Granville, July 11 [*Blue Book*, p. 49].

WHOSE THE RESPONSIBILITY 381

What did the French government do? It abstained, and ordered its Ambassador at St. Petersburg to abstain, from any conversation about Schleswig. It stamped upon the lighted brand and put aside the pretext for war which was always at its command.

The very suddenness of the outbreak of the war shows that it was neither desired nor sought nor premeditated by us. Again, Bismarck shall be our authority. He was blamed for having, long before, planned the persecution of the Catholics known as the Kulturkampf. He replied: "From the suddenness of the change the orator infers that the purpose to change has already been long in existence. I do not understand how it is possible to reach that backward conclusion, so to speak. To my mind it is the very suddenness of the change that attests the love of peace by which the government is inspired. The change is explained simply by the principles of self-defence. When, in the midst of peaceful labors, I am suddenly attacked by an opponent with whom I hoped to be able to live in peace, then I really must defend myself. In every defensive measure there is something unforeseen and sudden."[1]

This theory sums up the whole discussion. The war was unexpected and sudden because it was altogether self-defensive on our part.

It is true that our formal declaration of war from the tribune preceded Bismarck's. The explanation is simple; to induce an attack upon one's self when necessary is one of the secrets of statecraft. Certain diplomatists have owed their renown to their dexterity in provoking opportune quarrels. Thus Charles II of England had in his service one Downing, whom he

[1] Speech of April 24, 1873.

would send as ambassador to The Hague whenever he wanted the United Provinces to attack him; and that famous wrangler always attained his object. Bismarck at all times gave himself credit for that accomplishment. In the midst of Prussia's dispute with the Elector of Hesse, the Minister of Foreign Affairs, Bernstoff, asked him: "What am I to do?" — "If you want war," Bismarck replied, "appoint me your undersecretary, and I will undertake to provide you within four weeks with a German civil war of the first quality." [1]

By his Ems despatch he approved himself superior even to the illustrious wrangler Downing: he drove us to take the offensive, as he wished; for it is the offended and not the offending party who sends the challenge, and we were not the aggressors, although we began hostilities. As Louis XIV wrote to Saint-Géran, his ambassador at Berlin (February 13, 1672), "The aggression, according to the accepted usage of the nations, is not determined by the attack, but by the affronts which have necessitated making it." Now, the affronts that necessitated the war were not inflicted by us. "War is declared," wrote the *Dagblad* at The Hague, "it was Prussia that would have it."

No one has the right to accuse our government of having deliberately, without cause, in the interest of an individual, to gratify its passions, to prop up a dynasty, to popularize a child,[2] torn two nations, unexpectedly

---

[1] See *L'Empire Libéral*, vol. v, p. 548.

[2] "Or even from terror of Rochefort." *L'Empire Libéral*, vol. xiv, p. 541. [Henri Rochefort was imprisoned in the spring on conviction of being concerned in the disturbances following the killing of Victor Noir by Prince Pierre Bonaparte. He says in his *Mémoires:* —] "I will add that at the Tuileries, it was the conviction of the Empress, then all powerful, that

and by intrigue, from their peaceful firesides, and hurled them at each other. The war surprised the Emperor and his ministers in works and thoughts of peace; the Hohenzollern candidacy was neither a pretext nor an opportunity; it was the sole cause of the conflict, and if Bismarck had not avenged himself by a deadly insult for a withdrawal brought about without his knowledge and in his despite, if he had not placed us between dishonor and the battle-field, we should never have begun hostilities.[1]

my release from Ste-Pélagie would be the signal for a revolution that would sweep away the Empire, and that that fear was the principal cause of the declaration of a foreign war, which *alone,* by creating a diversion and restoring the imperial prestige, then decayed to the marrow, could delay the smash."

[1] "The real author of the war, the man who wanted it, sought it, premeditated it, paved the way for it, made it inevitable when the hour struck, was Bismarck. The Empress has often been credited with the remark: 'This is my war.' (Gambetta claimed that Lesourd repeated this remark of the Empress. Lesourd denies that he ever heard it. [See Appendix to vol. xiv, pp. 622, 623.]) If she ever said it, she boasted unduly, for the war was not hers but the Prussian Chancellor's. He had succeeded, as he did in 1866, in forcing his opponent to attack him, in drawing on his hesitant King, and, as he himself expressed it, 'in making his old nag leap the ditch.' He brought upon the battle-field two peace-loving sovereigns, neither of whom wanted war. It is a case in which one can well exclaim: 'See what a determined will can do!'" *L'Empire Libéral,* vol. xiv, pp. 542, 543.

["No man who dispassionately examines this melancholy history will doubt that the war was the war of Count von Bismarck. Germany — so he had determined — had to be founded on blood and iron, and war with France was only the concluding act of the bloody drama, which had been inaugurated in Schleswig and repealed at Sadowa. The Hohenzollern candidature might not have been a thing of his own devising; but it was employed by him to irritate France into hostility; and when the withdrawal of the Prince removed the pretext, which his acceptance of the throne had afforded, his King's message was published in a shape which he anticipated would goad his opponent into madness." Walpole, *History of Twenty-Five Years,* vol. ii, p. 492.]

CHAPTER XXIII

SUMMARY AND JUDGMENTS

Now that we have examined in their smallest details all the individual facts and overturned the legend of falsehood which has enveloped or distorted them, it remains for us to rise above these details, to take a bird's-eye view of the whole affair, and to review the conduct of our Cabinet in that tremendous crisis.

The plot was marvellously well laid. No one of our agents having divined it, it wakened us with a start in the midst of our dreams of peace. All parties were unanimous, the Imperialists with the rest, in the determination not to have a Hohenzollern in Spain at any price, even though war should result. There was a single point of difference in their desires: the warlike souls hoped that the candidacy would endure, so that war might follow; the peacefully inclined did their best to turn aside both the candidacy and the war.

Conformably to the unbroken international tradition, we ask nothing of the people who are to elect; we address ourselves to the head of the family to which the candidate belongs; we question Prussia quietly and by word of mouth. Bismarck having shut himself up at Varzin in order to be out of reach, his deputy, Thile, replies ironically, "The Prussian government knows nothing of this affair; apply to Spain."

We scent the trap; they propose to keep us amused until the election by the Cortes, appointed for July 20,

SUMMARY AND JUDGMENTS 385

shall have brought us face to face with an accomplished fact and embroiled us with Spain. We defeat this ruse by the conciseness and firmness of a public declaration from the tribune on July 6. As our declaration is destined to receive no official reply from Bismarck, we send Benedetti to Ems, to the King of Prussia; we support him by skilful negotiations, and to put ourselves absolutely out of danger from Spain, we detach Serrano from the conspiracy. Finally, we do more and better than this: we annihilate the candidacy by suppressing the candidate. Prince Antony, unknown to Bismarck, under the impulsion of Olozaga and Strat, and encouraged by the Emperor, withdraws his son's candidacy.

Bismarck, having left Varzin for Ems, in order to persuade the King to summon Parliament and mobilize his army, is staggered by the unexpected news and stops at Berlin. All his knaveries have become of no avail, the *casus belli* is eluding him, it is a tremendous set-back which will make him the laughing-stock of Europe. Blood alone can save him from the disaster. He notifies the King that, unless he decides for war, he will resign. The King declines to associate himself with his ravings and to break off his pacific conversations with Benedetti. Bismarck has no choice but to retire to Varzin; the world can breathe freely again.

But behold Napoleon III, to whom this victory of peace was due, has suffered a weakening of the will, and, under pressure from the court and the Right, without taking time to reflect, without consulting his ministers, he reopens the affair, and orders Gramont to submit to the King a demand of guaranties for the future. The ministers, being informed of this demand, are ill at ease; being unable to withdraw it because it is already consummated, they believe that they can avert the danger by deciding that, whatever the King of Prussia's reply may be, they will accept it and will deem the incident closed. The Emperor and Gramont give their assent to this step backward, and it seems that peace is saved!

French historians, all more or less blindly partisan, agree in pouring scorn and insult systematically upon the ministry of January 2. Impelled by no foolish vainglory, but by a sentiment of legitimate pride, which raises its head under injustice and abuse, I deem myself justified in saying that, in that crisis, that ministry gave proof of superior capacity, at once determined and moderate, yielding and firm, conscious of the public excitement but not giving way to it, and ready to ward off unforeseen accidents with vigilant rapidity. And it was its very ability which brought about the final catastrophe: Bismarck, driven to the wall, beaten once by Leopold's withdrawal and on the point of being beaten a second time by our abandonment of the demand of guaranties; forced to submit to a peace which involved his personal extinction; in order to escape from the circle in which we had imprisoned him, threw off the shackles of the rules of international probity and resorted to one of those commonplace brutalities which are within the reach of the most mediocre of men. We were arguing our cause; he struck us in the face, by announcing *urbi et orbi*, to the newspapers and foreign governments, that the King had refused to receive our Ambassador and had rejected the demands of France.

Why, it is said, did you fall into the snare? A brutal

act like that is not a snare into which one is free to fall or not to fall, and from which one can protect one's self by skilful diplomacy. One either submits to it or retaliates. We retaliated, and without delaying for diplomatic palavering, which would have been either idiotic or platitudinous, we, being the insulted party, sent the challenge.

Upon what traditions could we have relied to support a different course? Upon the monarchical tradition? We had not forgotten the remark of Louis XIV: "Everything is as nothing to me compared with honor." Upon the memories of the Revolution? The men of those heroic times inherited that sentiment of the Grand Monarque. The minister Delessart was accused by the Legislative Assembly of having compromised the nation by an undignified correspondence. One of the most forcible motives of the decree by which the same Assembly declared war against Francis I, King of Hungary and Bohemia, in accordance with a report by Condorcet, — "an invaluable monument of common sense and moderation," says Thiers, — was that, "the refusal to reply to the last despatches of the King of the French, leaving no hope of obtaining by friendly negotiations satisfaction for the grievances of France, was equivalent to a declaration of war."

The same Assembly taught us how a proud people responds to a refusal to receive its ambassador. Dumouriez, calling upon the King of Piedmont, Victor Amadeus, to espouse the cause of France, sends Sémonville, our diplomatic agent to the Republic of Genoa, to him with the mission to propose an offensive and defensive alliance in consideration of the promise of Lombardy. The King, being allied with the Coalition and the *émigrés*, despatches Count Solara to meet Sémonville at Alexandria, with orders to prevent him from going any farther, but to employ only friendly means. The count, a man well fitted for delicate missions, carries out his instructions with urbanity: he invites Sémonville to dinner, and as it was a Friday and he did not suppose that a Jacobin ever fasts, he has the delicacy to offer him a dinner of flesh; but he does not allow him to continue his journey to Turin, denies him post-horses, and compels him to return to Genoa.

"The insult offered to France, in the person of her representative," says Nicomède Bianchi, "was too plain to be palliated." Dumouriez in his wrath complains to the Assembly and concludes in favor of a declaration of war. Acclamations arise on all sides. War is solemnly declared (September 15, 1792). Later, when peace was made between the Republic and Victor Amadeus (May 15, 1796), one of the principal conditions was that the King should disavow the insult offered to the Ambassador at Alexandria.

Bismarck's conduct, and the King's, toward us was no less impertinent and much more public than Victor Amadeus's toward Sémonville; it demanded a signal reparation.

The criticism of enterprises which end in failure would be much less listened to if it were possible to determine what the result would have been of the opposite course. We see the results of defeat: have we reflected upon those which humiliation would have involved? Could we forget the lesson of 1840? In the midst of the negotiations in progress between

SUMMARY AND JUDGMENTS

the five great powers in London, the English Foreign Minister, Palmerston, suddenly informs our Ambassador Guizot, that a treaty of coöperation against Mehemet Ali, our protégé, has been signed, without our knowledge, by the other four powers, and is being carried into effect as hurriedly as it was concluded.

France feels that she has been insulted. Rémusat writes to Guizot: "Such as it is, even when reduced to a mere hasty decision, the performance is intolerable, and the only way to avoid being humiliated is to show that we feel outraged." The ministry, presided over by Thiers, prepares for war and summons the Chambers; it proposes to the King that he embody a declaration in a high tone in the speech from the throne. The King declines, because the declaration is drawn with a view to war. "Unquestionably," he says, with Guizot, "they set very little store by the friendship of France; she is wounded, but the offence is not one of those which impose war and justify it; *if there had been a real insult, we must have sacrificed everything;* but there was simply a lack of consideration, not a political insult; there was indifference, rudeness, but no downright affront; the taking of Syria from Mehemet Ali is not a legitimate cause of war." [1]

Listen to the terms in which Thiers, after his retirement, passed judgment upon this submission of Guizot and the King: —

"I cannot discuss this question coolly; I cannot inquire, — I should blush for very shame, — whether

[1] Guizot, *Mémoires*, vol. v, p. 390, and his speeches in the debate on the Address at the close of 1850, in the Chamber of Peers and Chamber of Deputies.

there was rudeness, or affront — I make no distinction.[1] . . . If France backs down, she descends from her rank; this monarchy which we have reared with our hands — I could not again face the men who accuse us of having taken office only to debase her. What shall I be able to reply to those enemies — you know who they are — when they say: 'We do not know what this government may have done, but it is contributing to the greatest humiliation we have ever undergone.' My colleagues and myself retired on the day when we were no longer able to carry to its natural and necessary conclusion the firm determination that we formed, not to make war on Europe, but to demand, in language which would have given no offence, the modification of the treaty, or — I admit that it is a serious thing to say — to declare war. The English minister had said that France, after a display of ill-humor, would hold her peace and yield. When I see my country humiliated, I cannot restrain the sentiment that strangles me, and I cry: 'Come what come may, let us aim to be what our fathers were, and let not France descend from the rank she has always held in Europe.'" [*Warm approval from the Left. Prolonged applause.*] [2]

Even the heir-apparent, the Duc d'Orléans, said, "It is much better to surrender on the shores of the Danube or the Rhine than in a gutter on rue Saint-Denis."

The consequences of this prudence, or this pusillanimity — choose which word you will — of Louis Philippe were fatal to him. He still stood on his

---
[1] Speech of Nov. 25, 1840.
[2] Speech of Nov. 27, 1840.

SUMMARY AND JUDGMENTS 391

feet, but like a tree whose roots are decayed, and at the first gust of wind he was overthrown. The irritated nation thought that he had derogated from his rank, and was "ripe for those desperate steps which such convictions suggest to a proud, restless, sensitive nation like ours." Then was fulfilled Tocqueville's prediction: "A peace without glory is one of the roads leading to revolution." [1] All political relations with England became difficult (it is Guizot who admits it), "because of the burning, bitter memory which these incidents have left in the hearts of the people and the army." [2] The most trivial event was exaggerated, distorted, poisoned; a dispute so microscopical as that about the Pritchard indemnity, an arrangement so beyond criticism as that concerning the right of search, caused outbursts of wrath which amaze us to-day; the government was not hated, for hatred is a form of homage: it was spat upon. "Louis-Philippe," said Chateaubriand, "has no need of honor; he is a policeman: Europe may spit in his face; he wipes it off, thanks her, and shows his commission as king."

The national triumph in the matter of the Spanish marriages did not rehabilitate him. At the last moment he dared not even defend himself, which would have been easy enough in a material way, and he fell because of an incident which, considered in itself, should not have gone beyond the proportions of an ordinary police-court prosecution.

Proudhon, the socialist, states the case thus: "One of the causes that destroyed the last monarchy was

[1] Tocqueville to Reeve, Nov. 7, 1840.
[2] Speech of Nov. 30, 1840.

the having opposed the bellicose instinct of the country. The people have never yet forgiven Louis-Phillippe his policy of peace at any price; he did not want to die on a battle-field, so he dies in a sewer."[1]

The ultra-pacific Victor Hugo also reproaches him for not caring even a little for glory, for having been too modest for France. "Hence an excessive timidity, most intolerable to the nation that has July 14 in its civil tradition and Austerlitz in its military tradition."[2]

"The usurpers," said Louis Veuillot, "did not want glory, because they wanted no trouble. They died out because they sought to avoid trouble of any sort, that is to say, because they evaded all their duties."[3]

Berryer considered the humiliation inflicted on France in 1840 as "the greatest affront possible to receive."[4] What would he have thought if our Ambassador had been shown the door during the negotiations, and if that pleasant performance had been announced to all Europe? What indignant apostrophes would he not have uttered, had there been at that time an Ems despatch!

In our case it was no longer possible to split hairs, to take shelter behind "a lack of consideration that was not an affront." The insult was direct, palpable, stinging, deliberate. Palmerston had certain excuses to put forward to justify his act, notably that it had been preceded by a year of fruitless negotiations, and that, if the signatures were appended secretly,

[1] *Paix et Guerre*, vol. i, p. 97.
[2] *Les Misérables*.
[3] In the *Univers* of May 18, 1873.
[4] Speech of Jan. 20, 1841.

SUMMARY AND JUDGMENTS 393

the preparation of the treaty, its possibility, its imminence, were not unknown to the French government. For Bismarck's deed there was no excuse. Palmerston never ceased to deny that he had intended to affront France or her government; Bismarck said explicitly to Loftus that that was what he proposed. If a Napoleon, in the face of so gross an insult, had displayed a resignation for which the nation had not forgiven Louis-Philippe in the case of a problematical insult, it would have blown him into the air.

The Empire had reached the end of the account for faint-heartedness which our mania for peace had opened to it. It had undergone two bitter humiliations: in Mexico it had fallen back before the American challenge; in the affair of Luxembourg before that of the victors of Sadowa. The challenge of the government at Washington was drowned by the uproarious abuse of the opposition in France. The Luxembourg retreat, although covered by the screen of a secret negotiation, was much more keenly felt by the national pride. It had created that grumbling irritation which we had so much difficulty in restraining at the time of the Saint-Gothard incident, and which burst out so explosively on the announcement of the Hohenzollern candidacy. A second repetition — more degrading because this time everything took place in public — of such a discomfiture would have brought the Empire nearer to the impossibility of a longer life than the Monarchy of July was after 1840.

If the Empire had swallowed the affront, the opposition would have taken up Berryer's apostrophe which brought the whole Assembly to its feet: "What, gentlemen! can it be that there is a country on earth where ambassadors listen to such words and write them down! No, it was not of France that that was said. Whatever you may have done, no one has said that of France! and they who, in the days of our greatest disasters, they even who at Waterloo saw how our soldiers fell, have not said that of France! It was not France that was meant!"

Thiers himself, who had not allowed a session to pass without evoking the memory of Sadowa against the Empire, would have repeated his own speeches against a deadly blow to our honor beside which 1840 would have seemed a triumph; Gambetta would have fulminated in harangues more inflammatory than those of the Baudin trial; Jules Favre would have spat upon us with superb disdain; Jules Simon would have rent us with honeyed words, and one and all would have played variations on the theme attributed to Gortchakoff: "The man on the Seine is kept erect only by the blows that Bismarck gives him on both cheeks at once." No obstacle would have held back the inundation: the irreconcilables, transformed into the heroes of public wrath, would have made the State their prey, and the army, if we had tried to employ it against them, would have confirmed the words of one of its most illustrious leaders, Marshal Niel: "Our people are extremely sensitive to insult, and the greatest misfortune that could befall them would be to receive an insult if they were disarmed. They would overthrow everything in their neighborhood and take the government upon themselves, and they would do right." [1]

Our critics assumed as a starting-point that defeat

[1] Speech of March 20, 1860.

SUMMARY AND JUDGMENTS 395

was inevitable. To-day it is demonstrated that our chances of victory were considerable, and that our magnificent army disappointed our expectations because, passing from the command of one leader who had a stone in his bladder to another who had one in his heart,[1] it was left without guidance, floating at the mercy of chance encounters — a ship without a pilot amid the heavy seas of battle.

On the morrow of our reverses, the generals who caused them by their blunders found it convenient to relieve themselves of all criticism by attributing those reverses to lack of preparation and to our numerical inferiority. This falsehood is confounded to-day by the military men themselves: they have proved that we were sufficiently prepared to win, and that numerical inferiority was not the cause of our disasters.

Until August 5 we had an undeniable superiority in the matter of concentration, and if we had crossed the Sarre and established ourselves between that river and the wooded zone of the Palatinate, we could have thrown back the inferior Prussian forces and upset all of Moltke's plans. At Woerth, it is true, we did yield to numbers, despite a heroism worthy of the troops of Leonidas; but it depended only on MacMahon to lessen that inferiority by postponing the battle until the Fifth and Seventh corps were up. At Spicheren we had the superiority in numbers during most of the day, and it was in Bazaine's power, by going himself to the field and sending two or three divisions thither, to turn what was not a defeat into a signal victory. On August 16, at Rezonville, we had the superiority in numbers and position, we were actually

[1] [Marshal Bazaine.]

victorious, and if Bazaine, with a blindness deserving of never-ending tears, had not given the order to retreat to an army which he should have thrown forward upon an enemy poorly placed and entangled in gorges and ravines, we should have scored one of those triumphs which put an end to wars. Again on August 18, at Saint-Privat, if the Guard and the artillery reserve had been thrown in by Bazaine and Bourbaki, to cut through the centre the insane enveloping movement of the Germans, or to wipe out the Prussian Guard already decimated by Canrobert, we should have found again on that day the good fortune that we were unable to grasp on the 16th. And even after all these mistakes, if our army had been sent back toward Paris, and not to the North into the net of Sedan, France would have been saved, as Thiers often said. To the very end we had opportunities to retrieve our fortunes. Yes, we could have and should have won. And we were justified in believing it. No impartial judge doubts it to-day.

But even if our chances had been less, we had no choice. Placed between a doubtful war and a dishonorable peace, we were compelled to pronounce for the war. "For nations as for individuals," said Thiers in his good moments, "there are circumstances in which the voice of honor speaks more loudly than that of prudence. There are things which, though one must die the next moment, one should never endure."[1] Governments succumb not to reverses alone — dishonor as well destroys them; there are revolutions born of defeat, but those born of contempt are much more to be dreaded. *Intuta quæ inde cora* — there

[1] *Histoire du Consulat et de l'Empire*, vol. xii, p. 219.

SUMMARY AND JUDGMENTS 397

is no safety in ignominy. A military disaster is an accident which may be repaired. What nation has not undergone such? Loss of honor, accepted, is a death from which there is no return.

Since 1870 I have often imagined myself in the tribune on July 15, counselling submission to the insult, and I have wondered how I could have induced a nation so sensitive on the point of honor, confident in the invincibility of its army, to swallow an act without precedent and so manifestly insulting; how I should have replied to the outcries of the Assembly and to the contempt of all men of heart; and I have found no answer. It was not humanly possible, under the circumstances in which we were deliberating, to act otherwise than we did.

On the very morrow of the fall of the Empire, the publicists of the Right conceived the scheme of exonerating the Emperor by casting all the responsibility on the Ministry.[1] In a pamphlet signed by Gricourt, one of his chamberlains, in default of Persigny, who refused to put his name to it, the Emperor himself seemed to look with favor on this manœuvre. In the pamphlet in question, we read: "The Ministry com-

[1] [See *L'Empire Libéral*, vol. xiv, p. 457 and note.] "The Bonapartist party, under the guidance of its former leaders, adopted the tactics of casting all the responsibility on the liberal ministry, which was denounced as the real artisan of all our misfortunes. . . . This programme . . . was very clearly disclosed by Paul de Cassagnac in an article in the *Pays* of Jan. 12, 1876: 'It was necessary that some one, either Emperor or Ministry, should be and remain responsible for a war too recklessly undertaken. Very good; it did not suit us that it should be the Emperor, because the Emperor had nothing to do with it, and the only culprits are the vainglorious liberals of the first parliamentary cabinet. Whoever excuses M. Émile Ollivier should remember that he thereby condemns the Emperor."

mitted the grave error of pronouncing from the tribune a sort of defiance which made any political adjustment difficult."[1]

Although I had no desire to add to the sufferings of the noble captive, I could not remain silent under an undeserved repudiation. I wrote to him at Wilhelmshöhe on December 28, 1870: —

"SIRE, —

"I have received the pamphlet which you were kind enough to send me, and I have read it with the liveliest interest. I find it excellent except in the last part, where it is sought to separate you from your ministers and to throw upon them the burden of a common decision. I am sure that this is the system which certain of your friends propose to adopt. This theory, in addition to being contrary to the truth, lacks generosity; it is unworthy of Your Majesty. Nor do I like it any better that we should assume the attitude of apologizing to Prussia for making war on her. To defend ourselves from the charge of having provoked or sought it — nothing can be better; that is true, and in that respect I shall always bear emphatic testimony for Your Majesty; but we have no occasion to defend ourselves for having accepted it, submitted to it. Suppose that one day your government should have had placarded on the walls of Paris (as King William did at Ems and Berlin) the statement that, the English proposals concerning the denouncing of the treaty of commerce having displeased Your Majesty, you had refused to receive Lord Lyons:

[1] *Les Relations de la France avec l'Allemagne sous Napoléon III* (Brussels, 1871).

not only Gladstone and Bright, but the English cotton nightcaps themselves would have demanded war. If France had not made this war, she would have fallen into the mire; it is much better that she should have been beaten on the battle-field."

An eclipse of equity was never of long duration with the Emperor; he replied: —

["Wilhelmshöhe] *January* 18, 1871.
"MY DEAR MONSIEUR É. OLLIVIER, —
"In reply to your letter I will say to you that *I do not propose to separate my responsibility from that of my ministers in the declaration of the ill-fated war that recently broke out;* Gricourt's pamphlet has no other purpose than to prove that it was not to further a dynastic interest that I declared war, but in response to the justly offended sentiment of the country."

CHAPTER XXIV

CONCLUSION

THIS was a justifiable war — was it inevitable? Mommsen thought that it was, and, after defending the Emperor for having insisted upon it, he adds that, if he had not fought it, it would have been forced on his son. I do not believe it. There have always been, and there are still, between certain nations which seem especially typical of certain forms of civilization, fundamental differences, engendering irreconcilable rivalries, which can be settled only on the battle-field. There was not between Germany and France one of those unadjustable differences Whatever any one may say, we are not the incarnation of the Latin genius at odds with the Germanic genius. There is some Latin in us, but with how many other elements added — and among them the Germanic element itself! And there is no greater difference between us and Germany than between Provence and Brittany, between Gascony and Normandy, or even between certain individuals of those provinces. Kant, Hegel, Goethe, Beethoven, Heine, and Frederick are as fully understood and as much admired in France as Descartes, Molière, Voltaire, Balzac, Renan, and Napoleon are in Germany — a phenomenon which implies a sort of mental similarity.

The cause of the conflict between Germany and France was only one of those "artificial fatalities," born of the false conceptions or unhealthy ambitions of

CONCLUSION

statesmen, which with lapse of time become worn out, transformed, and often extinguished. If France had but resolutely made up her mind not to meddle in the affairs of Germany, not to regard German Unity as a menace or as a lessening of her own importance, it would have seemed perfectly natural to her that a nation so powerful in every way — in intelligence, imagination, poetry, science, and arms — should shape herself as she chose, with full liberty of spontaneous action.

On the other hand, if the German professors, content with the memories of 1814 and of Waterloo, could but have made up their minds to forget the Palatinate and Jena, on the instant this alleged fatality of war would have vanished, and the only relation between the two nations, established by mutual consent, would have been one of friendly coöperation in the common task of spreading light and of emancipation from real fatalities. That was the hope to which I devoted my conduct in international matters, and which, as minister, I would have brought to fruition had my power endured.

But there was a man to whom it was important that that artificial fatality should exist and should end in war. It was that powerful genius, who, not choosing to abandon to time the glory of achieving slowly the work of Unity, whose hour of triumph was inevitable, determined to hasten the evolution, to force upon the present what the future would have accomplished freely, and to retain for himself alone the glory which his successors would otherwise have shared. With him out of the way, war between France and Germany would have ceased to be predestined, and the son of Napoleon III would have escaped it as well as his father.

Napoleon III wanted peace, but with a vacillating

will; Bismarck wanted war, with an inflexible will: the inflexible will overcame the vacillating will. A fresh proof, as that profound thinker Gustave Le Bon so forcibly says, that "the faith that raises mountains is named the will. It is the true creator of things."

So that it is a pitiful thing to read these labored dissertations of our trumpery historians, searching for what they call responsibilities, and struggling to incriminate, some the statesmen of the opposition, others those of the government. Unquestionably the opposition were so short-sighted as to keep alive an irritable agitation in men's minds; unquestionably the Emperor should not have reopened, by a fruitless demand of guaranties, a question already closed by a triumphant solution. But neither the declamations of the opposition, nor the mistake of Napoleon III, were the decisive cause of the war. No Frenchman was responsible for it. The only man who will have the glory or the shame of it, whichever posterity may adjudge it to be, is the man of iron, whose indomitable and heroic will controlled events and made them serve his ambition.

Demosthenes said to the Athenians: "Let an orator rise and say to you: 'It is Diopithus who causes all your ills; it is Chares, or Aristophon,' or any other that it pleases him to name, and instantly you applaud and exclaim loudly, 'Oh! how truly he speaks!' But let a plain-spoken man say to you: 'O Athenians! the sole author of your ills is Philip' — that truth angers you; it is even as an arrow that wounds you." And I say to our Athenians: "The war was let loose upon us neither by Diopithus, nor by Chares, nor by Aristophon, but by Philip, and in 1870 Philip's name was Bismarck."

CONCLUSION

One of Bismarck's panegyrists, Johannes Scherr, has described most excellently the character that should be attributed to the creator of German Unity. "After producing so many giants of thought, Germany was destined to produce, at last, a hero of deeds. In the age of the Reformation, and later, we had had an abundance of idealists, but not a politician. We lacked the practical genius, the genius unhampered by schedules. Yes, just that, in very truth! For reflecting and experienced men must needs leave where it deserves to be, that is to say, in the child's primer, the worn-out commonplace which declares that 'the most honest politician is the best.' There has never been such a thing as an honest politician, in the ordinary sense of the phrase, and there ought never to be. The creative statesman should perform his allotted task without taking pains to find out whether his adversaries consider it 'dishonest,' or whether it is unpleasant or harmful to them. It is not the ethereal arguments of a subjective idealism, but stern realities, super-prosaic material interests, as well as commonplace and exalted passions, which in combination make the science of statecraft."

Thus would Bismarck have liked to be praised — in such terms it is fitting to speak of that extraordinary man, the craftiest of foxes, the boldest of lions, who had the art of fascinating and of terrifying, of making of truth itself an instrument of falsehood; to whom gratitude, forgiveness of injuries, and respect for the vanquished were as entirely unknown as all other noble sentiments save that of devotion to his country's ambition; who deemed legitimate everything that contributes to success and who, by his contempt for the importunities of morality, dazzled the imagination of mankind.

After the affair of the Duchies, as our Ambassador, Talleyrand, was seeking some roundabout phrase by which to express a certain degree of disapproval, "Don't put yourself out," said Bismarck, "nobody but my King thinks that I acted honorably."

Æsthetically, I like him thus. So long as he denies the evidence, plays the virtuous, the guileless man, outdoes himself in tartufferie, he lowers himself to the point of making himself contemptible. As soon as he reveals his true self and boasts of his audacious knaveries which raised his Germany, until then divided and impotent, to the first rank among the nations, then he is as great as Satan — a Satan beautiful to look upon. Bismarck hatching in the dark the Hohenzollern candidacy, without a suspicion that war will inevitably be the result, would be a zany to be hooted at; Bismarck devising that same plot because it is the sole means of causing the outbreak of the war which he must have in order to achieve the unity of his fatherland, is a mighty statesman, of sinister but impressive grandeur. He will not thereby have opened for himself the gates of any Paradise; he will have won forever one of the most exalted places in the German Pantheon of terrestrial apotheoses.

APPENDICES

APPENDIX A

LETTER FROM EMILE OLLIVIER TO PROFESSOR HANS DELBRÜCK OF BERLIN [1]

ILLUSTRIOUS PROFESSOR, — I never argue with those who criticise me, because most of the time I should have to contend with hatred, bad faith, ignorance, or idiocy; but you have examined my story of the Liberal Empire [2] with such elevation of mind, such scrupulous care, such a sincere purpose to be just, and such courteous moderation, and the authority of your judgment is so great, that, for the first time, I feel impelled to argue with one who contradicts me. And I will do it, despite the ever-bleeding wound in my heart, as impartially as if it were a matter of giving judgment on the dispute between the Athenians and Philip.

We are far from the time when Bismarck was represented as an Arcadian shepherd suddenly attacked by the Gallic wolf, what time he was dreaming beneath the stars and learned by mere chance that there was a vacant throne of Spain and a Hohenzollern ready to seat himself thereon, which had seemed to him a perfectly natural thing since he was equally unaware of the existence of a France to which such a neighbor would not be agreeable. You are no longer, monsieur le professeur, in the bucolic stage of the early days of the controversy. You admit that the Hohenzollern candidacy was the work of Bismarck; you admit that it was not only "a provocation" but an act of "astute hostility" against France (pages 320–322). Thus far we travel together, but here we part.

---

[1] From *L'Empire Libéral*, vol. xv, pp. 533–545.
[2] In the *Preussische Jahrbücher*, August, 1909, vol. cxxxvii, part 2, pp. 305 ff.: "Ollivier über den Krieg 1870."

You admit that Bismarck knew that the announcement of a Prussian candidacy in Spain would make the buzzing of the Spanish fly, in which Moltke took such delight, too strident, and would arouse intense excitement in France; but you think that that excitement would have been ephemeral, and that, brought face to face with an accomplished fact, we should have submitted after crying aloud a bit, should have turned our thoughts to something else, and should have allowed the Hohenzollern to establish himself peacefully in Spain, ready to fall upon our rear whenever war should break out on the Rhine. You consider that it is slanderous to attribute to the peace-loving Chancellor the prevision that our transitory excitement would find expression in an act of war.

In support of these theories you invoke three documents which you consider of indisputable force. First, a letter of July 12, from the King of Prussia to the Queen, from which, you think, it is impossible not to infer the abandonment of the candidacy. Let us read over together the letter as it is given by Oncken. I begin with the German text: "Bismarck ist innerlich gewiss *noch* fur den Candidaten," which I translate: "Bismarck is certainly at heart *still* for the candidate." So that he had not abandoned him. The letter continues: "That, however, the question has become so serious that we must put the Hohenzollerns aside altogether, and leave the final decision to them." From these words it would be inferred (such is your claim) that Bismarck, while still at heart loyal to the candidacy, nevertheless abandons it. I draw precisely the contrary inference: He does not wish the King to meddle with it, because, if he does, he will make a mess of it, and, under the pacific influence of the Queen, will advise a withdrawal; whereas, if left to themselves, the Hohenzollern princes, who have given their word and of whom he is absolutely sure, will hold fast.

Secondly, you invoke the Spanish letter which I have

APPENDIX 409

printed.[1] This letter was certainly not an instruction to Lothar Bucher. That envoy extraordinary of the Chancellor was not despatched to Madrid without being supplied with complete instructions, which did not require to be repeated to him a few days later in a jumbled-up form. Bismarck knew that in negotiations of a certain sort, genuine conspiracies, one does not, unless one chances to be a Benedetti, write what one can say. The addressee of the letter is Bernhardi, or some other person of Prim's *entourage*. It does in fact express the belief that the excitement in France will not result in an act of war. In recommending to his accomplices a step which will lead to war, Bismarck gives him to understand that he does not anticipate it. Can such language be taken seriously? Is it not the commonplace trick of those who are laying plans for a war, to abound in pacific protestations? Their purpose is of the sort that one does not avow even to one's shadow, and *a fortiori*, to one's agents: one maintains their illusion, so that they may, with the more assurance, put to sleep the suspicions of the person on whom one is preparing to pounce.

"If you would deceive a prince," says Guicciardini, "deceive your ambassador to him." The hypocrisy of the Spanish letter is simply a ruse prepared beforehand for the day when its author will have to defend himself from the charge of having provoked the quarrel.

Equally a mere ruse is the third fact which you put forward as decisive: namely, the visit which Prim announces his intention to pay to Napoleon III. He would not have announced that visit, you say, unless he had believed that by that time the excitement in France would have subsided. Quite the contrary was Prim's purpose: he wished to lull the Emperor's suspicions, so that he would not prevent

[1] *L'Empire Libéral*, vol. xiii, p. 564. [The letter referred to is printed in Appendix C, *infra*.]

the fact from being consummated. I have demonstrated it with mathematical precision.

But after all, of what avail is it to take the pains to seek for Bismarck's intentions in presumptions more or less forced? He himself disclosed them to Busch, one of those intimate coadjutors before whom one lets one's self go without restraint, and Busch tells us the story in his *Unser Reichskanzler*[1]: —

"In 1867 Bismarck had avoided war, because he considered that Prussia was not strong enough. In 1870 that difficulty was removed, Germany was sufficiently armed. The Arcadians wished for war, the Ultramontanes, with the Empress at their head, clamored ardently for it. France was visibly strengthening her army and arranging alliances. If hitherto we had been able to place our hopes on delay, *that delay was now becoming a danger, and hence resulted, for the statesman, the duty of substituting for a policy which postponed decisive action, the policy which precipitated what was absolutely inevitable. In the interest of Germany, and no less in the interest of Europe, it was imperative to find some way to seize* (fassen), *to surprise the French, who were not entirely ready for the contest, — in such wise as to force them to lay aside their reserve.*"

Such unqualified testimony as this scatters all doubts; and yet it seems not without profit to support it by what I shall call the psychological proof. Since the days of Louis XIV, — under Napoleon I, under the Restoration, under Louis XVIII, under Louis-Philippe, — at all times we have considered that our security was dependent, if not on the friendship, at least on the benevolent neutrality, of Spain, and that the first care of whosoever may be jealous of the grandeur of France will be to stir up trouble for us on the other side of the Pyrenees — to fasten a ball and chain to our leg, so to speak, and to place us between two fires.[2] When Palmerston conceived the perfidious idea

[1] Vol. ii, chap. 1, p. 53.   [2] *L'Empire Libéral*, vol. xiv, p, 64.

APPENDIX 411

of substituting for the Duc d'Aumale (who was excluded from consideration by England) a Coburg as husband to the Queen, Bresson, our Ambassador to Spain, wrote: "I regard a German prince in Spain as the most piercing, the most humiliating blow to the honor of France, and to the pride, perhaps to the very existence, of our dynasty." (September 21, 1844.) Foreigners, knowing how deeply interested we were in union with Spain, exerted themselves to prevent her from becoming our friend; but we, on our part, would not allow them to make her our foe.

If Bismarck had been ignorant of this historical truth, you would have denied him a certificate of scholarship, for the dullest of your students knew it. If, knowing it, as I have no doubt that he did, he believed that we should be so stupid, so heedless, so improvident, so careless of our interest, as not to suspect the purpose of aggression which his German prince would bring with him, and to tolerate it; if he supposed that France, a volcanic nation according to her critics, — France, restless, suspicious, dissatisfied with a change in the European status which weakened her — that France would not emerge from her state of peaceable resignation and suddenly cry out to his government: "Never! rather war!" — if he did not see these things, which were as visible as human things can be, he must needs have been the most imbecile of statesmen.

Ah, well! although I have every reason to curse that man, I cannot make up my mind to call him an imbecile, who let loose upon the world a ghastly war without knowing what he was doing. It is distasteful to me to degrade to that point a personality wherein were united in a very rare degree all the superior qualities of the statesman, and who would have been without a rival, if he had not lacked that generosity and that grace of heart which round out the truly great man.

And lastly, — the final psychological proof of his warlike purpose, — he selected for the weaving of his candidacy

— a precaution, say you, against a threat of war — the precise moment when that threat was fading away. Even before the advent of the liberal ministry, he had no aggression to apprehend on the part of France. When informed by his agents at Vienna of the projects of an alliance in 1869, he did not take alarm; he said to Bernhardi, — it is you who tell me so, on page 333, — "Against an attack from Austria he was absolutely protected by the friendship of Russia and by the determination of Hungary not to allow it." As he was not disturbed on that score during the reign of ministers who deemed themselves to have been conquered at Sadowa, how could he have been under my ministry — mine, who had maintained for four years that Sadowa was not a French defeat for which we ought to seek revenge?

You do not question my sincerity, and you recur to it several times in terms which I appreciate, but you think that my strength was not equal to my sincerity, and you represent the Emperor as making ready behind my back, and without my knowledge, for the unavoidable war. You are mistaken.

The Emperor's personal confidence in me was absolute, and my daily proofs of devotion constantly intensified it. Once when I was insisting upon some measure, I forget what, as to which we did not agree, he said to me affectionately: "I am well aware that I can't do without you; don't take undue advantage of me." The fact that he did not inform me of his military conversations with Archduke Albert and of General Lebrun's mission does not prove that he proposed to get up a war without my knowledge, but simply that he attached no importance to those proceedings. If you had been in frequent intercourse with the Emperor at that time, you would not doubt my statement, for he was incapable then of any vigorous determination, and it would have required very great energy to invite a war with that Germany of whose strength he was not unaware.

APPENDIX 413

Aggression on our part was no more to be dreaded in one year than in two. We had no need of it. It was to him, Bismarck, that war was indispensable. Standing at bay; caught between the impatience of the National Liberals and the growing distrust of the Conservatives; threatened with a fresh conflict over the military law; assured that the States of the South would draw away rather than draw near, and that, without a war waged in common against us, they would not be absorbed; ambitious not to leave to time alone the consummation of German Unity but to be himself its triumphant architect, he saw in war an actual essential of existence.

He would not have set out on this affair, he would not have put compulsion upon his King and the Hohenzollern princes and declared it a duty imposed on Leopold by the honor of Prussia to accept a crown that he did not want, he would not have devoted all his ardor to overcoming the numerous difficulties mentioned in his Spanish letter, if he had not desired to obtain an immediate result — war. And as he no longer expected any provocation from us, he had to make himself the provoker, taking care at the same time to compel us to assume that position in appearance, in order that he might coerce his King and his people. Hence the Hohenzollern machination, which is a masterpiece of ability.

With the candidacy and the candidate thrust aside, the imprudent demand of guaranties waived, the war was slipping through Bismarck's fingers. He seized it again by an act of sheer brutality, wherein there was no ability at all, but simply an energetic resolution — the Ems despatch.

The genuine Ems despatch, the one drawn by Abeken, was in itself an initial Bismarckian falsification of what had happened during the day; for it had been extorted from the King by the imperious telegrams sent by Bismarck throughout the morning, and by the obsession of the two ministers who arrived from Berlin at noon to reinforce those telegrams. Bismarck deemed that falsification insufficient; he emphasized it. Some of his admirers deny his Shakespearean story of the dinner with Roon and Moltke. There seems to me to be no serious argument to cast doubt on its accuracy; Busch and others had told it before Bismarck authenticated it; and although in the different versions one can discover some divergences due doubtless to the carelessness of the narrators, the essential facts remain unchanged.

However, though the scene were imaginary, it is none the less unanimously proved that he made the toilet of the Ems despatch, and every one knows how he set about it. He added nothing, but he struck out all the explanatory and softening details which would show that, if the King did reject our demands, he at least listened to them, discussed them, and complied with them in part. He imputed an insultingly laconic form to the principal, the real fact — the refusal of an audience. Lastly, he altered the source of the despatch. Having been redrafted at Berlin, it was from Berlin that he despatched it to the foreign cabinets, and he represented it as transmitted from Ems. This manœuvring transformed Abeken's ponderous despatch into a strident, stinging message which sank into the flesh.

You do not deny that in making these changes Bismarck had the purpose of inciting war. You are not surprised that I called my chapter on that despatch "Bismarck's Slap in the Face"; but you blame me for forgetting that that slap was simply the *riposte* to one dealt to Germany by our demand of guaranties; that that blow was the reply to another blow; that that thrust, which, as you yourself agree, we could not tolerate, was simply a parry. Be good enough, I pray you, to reflect again.

The demand of guaranties did not in itself contain anything insulting; it was, in fact, defensible, and it became inopportune, offensive if you choose, only because it was addressed to the King of Prussia under circumstances which

APPENDIX 415

made it impossible for him to accept it with honor. That demand was secret, absolutely unknown to the public; it had not the form of an ultimatum; if the King deemed it to be unjustifiable, it was sufficient for him to reject it by a refusal, reserving the right if, upon that refusal, we ventured to make a disturbance, to strike back accordingly. The demand of guaranties was a word said in the ear, in a closed room; the Ems despatch was an outcry on the public square. It did not constitute a simple contradiction, which one can put aside by a *no;* it was an irrevocable moral assault, which we could not meet with dishonorable submission or with an angry retort. What logical similarity is there between two acts so unlike? One of our old proverbs says: *Un soufflet par un stylet* (Answer a blow with a dagger). The French do not answer with a dagger but by sending seconds, and that is what we did.

It displeases you that this manœuvre of Bismarck's, as to the purpose and character of which we are in accord, should be called a falsification. In our language it is impossible to qualify it otherwise. To falsify does not necessarily imply that one adds something to a document, or even that one omits something from it; but simply that one so represents it that one changes its real meaning and gives it an aspect which it would not have had without that handling. A dictionary of eminent authority, Littré's, notes this meaning of the word *falsify:* "IV. Not to represent, not to report things as they are." Some persons in Germany seem to have adopted a different definition. They maintain that we must not say *falsify*, but *edit.* With them the difference is reduced to a trifle. We call that battle Woerth, which you call Reichshoffen, but everybody knows that they mean the same thing. It may be understood then that so to "arrange" a despatch that it will produce an insulting effect which it would not have produced without that arrangement, will be called *falsifying* in France, and *editing* in Germany.

Your objection (page 315) is at once subtler and stronger. Bismarck did not change the truth — he simply showed it as it was. His despatch is not to be measured by the scale of an objective historical exposition, it should be considered as a political act. At Ems was being discussed the claim of France to stand above all others as a great nation and to deny Germany that privilege. The King inwardly thought Benedetti "importunate" and "impertinent," but as he was most courteous, he showed his feeling only with perfect self-control and all the polite forms of a man of the world. Bismarck believed that the common multitude would see in those forms a submission to humiliation. He reconstituted the situation in accordance with the awful, terrifying truth. It was the King who had placed a false aspect on it at Ems by the courtesy of his manners, which, according to the strait sect, were but "vain deception and hypocrisy" (*eitel Trug und Heuchelei*).

I should never have ventured to characterize thus the King's conduct, or not to consider him sincere; but I am not conscious of possessing any qualification to contest your judgment and I bow to it.

You are the stronger, but that is not enough for you, — you are determined also to have been the more just. That feeling does you honor and imparts some respectability to nonsense which would otherwise be pitiable. But the truth has been set free, the history of that epoch is made up. It will attribute the responsibility for the War of 1870 neither to the Emperor of the French nor to the King of Prussia, neither to the French people nor to the German people, but to the man of iron who drove them both to the battle-field which his ambition had prepared. He is the author of the war against France, as he was the author of that against Denmark and of that against Austria.

Who has said it more plainly than he on that pathetic evening when, seated at the foot of the laurel-crowned

Victory, at that half-veiled hour when the melancholy of a closing day intensifies the sadness of a fading life, he exclaimed before his agitated familiar friends: "But for me three great wars would not have taken place; eighty thousand men would not have perished; their fathers, mothers, sisters would not have been plunged into sorrow. Now, I have that account to adjust with God." [1]

If he had not succeeded, the old women, he said, would have done him to death with broomsticks. He did succeed, thanks to Roon and Moltke; no one denies him a glorious place among the dominators of the world. But a political act is not to be judged by its immediate results. There are far-distant ones which change into disaster what had at first seemed good fortune, and render bitter the victory wherein one had rejoiced. At this day the careful thinker can discover the sombre aftermath of the policy which led you to success. Have you profited by conquering peoples whom you cause to suffer, who detest you and curse you, and await only a favorable opportunity to rise against you? Was not the increase of territory which your Unity did not need dearly bought by the impossibility, which you thereby created, of a complete, unreserved understanding with us? Has your security increased since you crushed a nation whose abasement is never more than temporary, and which may of a sudden, on the morrow of a Soubise or a Bazaine, see a Turenne or a Pélissier arise in its midst?

France and Germany living in a state of mutual distrust are a permanent source of disturbance in Europe. Joined in a friendly alliance they would have bestowed upon the world, reassured and grouped about their united power, a new *pax Romana*, as it were, more fruitful than the earlier one. That was the dream that I dreamed in opposition and that I hoped to realize in the ministry. I was beaten in that undertaking to draw our two great countries together.

[1] Moritz Busch; *Unser Reichskanzler*, vol. i, p. 115.

But I regard it as the signal honor of my life that I conceived it and followed it to the farthest limit of my power. Overthrown by a contrary fate, I shall say to my last hour:—

"That way lay common sense, prudence, humanity, mutual advantage, and the interest of civilization."

APPENDIX B

THE SPANISH REVOLUTION OF 1868

ISABELLA II, daughter of Ferdinand VII and Maria Christina, was born in 1830, and was but three years old when her father died. Queen Maria Christina acted as Regent of the Kingdom from 1833–1840, being engaged practically all the time in war with Don Carlos, the claimant of the throne. In 1840 she was deserted by the army and compelled to flee to France, being succeeded in the Regency by Espartero, Duke of Vittoria, who became military dictator. Isabella was declared of age in 1843, and for the next quarter century her reign was simply a record of revolution and counter-revolution, the various parties — Moderates, Progressists, Republicans — succeeding each other in predominance with confusing rapidity. The best brief epitome of Spanish history during those years is given by M. Ch. Seignobos in his *Political History of Europe since 1814*, chapter 10 (translated by Professor S. M. Macvane).

In 1864, the Queen, yielding to her natural inclinations, had sought to restore the absolutist régime, and had revived the tradition of Catholic absolutism and government by the *camarilla*, or junta of favorites. The Liberal parties became revolutionary, and finally attacked the dynasty itself. The Progressists endeavored to excite the army against the dynasty. Various unsuccessful insurrections were organized by General Prim, then in exile. The government dissolved the Cortes and exiled Marshal Serrano, President of the Senate.

After the death of Narvaez, who had been the principal instrument of the restoration of despotism, "the three persecuted parties — Liberal Union, Progressists, and Democrats — agreed to make a joint revolution. . . . It began with the *pronunciamento* of Admiral Topete, commander of the Cadiz fleet; followed by a *pronunciamento* signed by the principal generals of the opposition, Prim and Serrano. . . . There was but one small battle, at Alcolea, near Cordova, on September 29. After this, Madrid, then all Spain, joined the insurgents. Isabella was deserted and fled to France." Seignobos (Macvane's edition), pp. 309, 310.

"The uprising was the work of three parties acting in common: the Unionists, who represented the moderate views of the liberal middle class; the Progressists, who desired more ample reforms; the Democrats, who, for the most part, inclined toward a federalist republic. From the revolution three personages emerged: Marshal Serrano, Admiral Topete, and Marshal Prim. The first two belonged to the Liberal Union; the third, who was to play the most important part, was the leader of the Progressists. A provisional government was organized. Serrano was President of the Council; Prim, Minister of War. The most urgent need was to reëstablish tranquillity. The new authorities did not spare themselves, and Prim, who during his life had led four or five insurrections, incontinently set about preaching discipline. . . . In January, 1869, the elections for the Cortes took place. The only republicans were among the Democrats: Unionists and Progressists remained loyal to the monarchical principle. The ballots reflected these tendencies, and as soon as the names of all those chosen were known, it was manifest that Spain would simply change sovereigns." La Gorce, vol. vi, pp. 189, 190.

In 1869, "the Provisional Government, which was installed at Madrid, and in which Marshal Prim rapidly acquired a predominating influence, decided on framing a constitution, in which a new king, chosen by the nation, should be surrounded with democratic institutions. The adoption of this Constitution forced the men who framed it to commence the painful and difficult task of searching for a

APPENDIX 421

fitting sovereign." Walpole, *History of Twenty-five Years*, vol. ii, p. 483.

Finally, in November, 1870, Amadeus, second son of Victor Emanuel, was chosen King of Spain. He arrived at Madrid just as Prim was assassinated, in December. After a troubled reign of two years, he abdicated in February, 1873, whereupon the Cortes proclaimed a republic. Eventually, in December, 1874, Isabella's son, who had just attained his majority, was recognized as King of Spain — Alfonso XII.

APPENDIX C

THE HOHENZOLLERN CANDIDACY FOR THE SPANISH THRONE

NOTE. — The greater part of what follows is taken bodily from the article by M. H. Leonardon in the *Revue Historique* for 1900, vol. lxxxiv, pp. 287–310. I allow this statement to take the place of quotation marks.

SERRANO, Topete, and with them the majority of the Liberal Union, wished to give the crown either to the Duc de Montpensier, to his wife, the Infante Dona Maria Luisa Fernanda (sister of Isabella), or to their oldest son, then nine years of age. Some of the Unionists, being satisfied by the fall of Isabella, desired the restoration of the dynasty in the person of her son Alfonso, the Prince of Asturias, under the guardianship of Montpensier.

The Progressists and those Democrats who had not pronounced for a republic had an entirely different idea. Long before arriving at power, they dreamed of uniting beneath the same sceptre the two nations of the Iberian peninsula. The revolution accomplished, they seemed to be on the point of realizing that dream, either by inducing the reigning King of Portugal, Dom Luiz, to accept the crown of Spain, or by offering it to his father, the widowed King Consort, Ferdinand of Coburg.

These names were not the only ones put forward on the morrow of the *pronunciamento* of Cadiz: in political circles men mentioned those of Amadeus, Duke of Aosta, of Espartero, the old champion of the Progressist party, of Prince Philip of Coburg, of Prince Frederick Charles of Prussia, of Archduke Charles of Austria, of a son of the Queen of England. Lastly, less than a month after the revolution, and prior to mid-October, 1868, there was already talk of the

APPENDIX 423

Hereditary Prince of Hohenzollern-Sigmaringen, Leopold; for the moment, however, it was simply an unsubstantial rumor, and no overtures were made to the Hohenzollern family.

On October 14, 1868, Prince Antony wrote to his son Charles of Roumania: "In Spain, Prim and Serrano are working together to hasten the election of a new king. Among the candidates other than the King of Portugal are mentioned the Hereditary Prince of Hohenzollern, Philip of Coburg, and the Duc de Montpensier." And on December 9 following: "The candidacy for the throne of Spain is thus far only a phantom stirred up by the newspapers. We do not know the slightest thing about it, and if the idea were to be submitted to us more definitely, I should never advise accepting that risky position, which has only the gleam of false gold. Moreover, France would never permit, considering our relations with Prussia, the enthronement of a Hohenzollern across the Pyrenees. She is already frantic with envy at the sight of a Hohenzollern reigning on the Lower Danube." — Memoirs of the King of Roumania, French translation, vol. i, pp. 458, 473.

"At the outset of the Spanish crisis, it is not without interest to note what ideas were exchanged in Germany. Many thought that a revolution at so great a distance could have no influence on the destinies of the Prussian monarchy. 'It's a matter of indifference to us, and we can await the result in peace, thank God!' said Abeken (*Ein schlichtes Leben in bewegter Zeit*, p. 363). In other circles a certain apprehension manifests itself, lest the Cabinet of the Tuileries should seek to profit by the event. On October 30, 1868, in a letter to the Crown Prince of Prussia, allusion is made to the future fate of the Spanish peninsula. 'Above all things, no regent under the ægis of France!' But a rumor of which it is hard to discover the source is already beginning to circulate in Germany. Vaguely, in veiled words, people are talking of Prince Leopold's son, oldest son of Prince Antony of Hohenzollern-Sigmaringen, and brother of that Prince

Charles who had been called two years earlier to rule over Roumania. The news is reported by the *Journal des Débats* (November 13, 1868), on the word of a Vienna correspondent. At Berlin, Queen Victoria's representative, Lord A. Loftus, picks up the rumor. In a private letter to the head of the Foreign Office he transmits the information, and adds this sentence: 'I observe that if the Prince should be elected, the choice would be looked upon with jealousy and disfavor at Paris.' (*Diplomatic Reminiscences*, 2d Series, vol. i, p. 236.)" La Gorce, vol. i, pp. 190, 191.

Two months passed with no mention of that candidacy in Spain. In February, 1869, a deputy belonging to the Liberal Union, Salazar de Mazarredo, published a short pamphlet in which he shows himself to be a very decided partisan of Ferdinand of Portugal; but, in case that prince should not accept the crown, he points out to his fellow citizens, as second choice, Leopold of Hohenzollern.

About a month later, M. Rances y Villaneuva, Spanish Ambassador to Prussia under Isabella II and transferred to Austria by the Provisional Government, paid a brief visit to Berlin, ostensibly to pay his respects to King William on his birthday, March 22. His visit, coinciding in a general way with the revival of rumors favorable to the Hohenzollern candidacy, aroused the attention of our Ambassador, Comte Benedetti. Count Bismarck being absent at the moment, M. Benedetti applied to the Under-Secretary for Foreign Affairs, Herr von Thile, and took up the question with him. Von Thile replied by "a most explicit assurance that he has never at any time had knowledge of any fact authorizing such a conjecture." He denied that Señor Rances had referred to the Hohenzollern candidacy, and declared that he had expressed the belief that Montpensier would be the final choice.

It is a fair question (says M. Leonardon) whether Benedetti had serious reasons to justify this step, or whether, on the other hand, he did not risk it on the strength of mere pre-

APPENDIX 425

sumptions, thereby carelessly giving Count Bismarck a chance to detect a sensitive spot in the Imperial government, on which it would be possible some day to wound it to the quick. (For Benedetti's report of his conversation with Von Thile, see *Ma Mission en Prusse*, pp. 304–306.)

No document has ever come to light tending to prove that Señor Rances's visit had any relation to the Hohenzollern candidacy. On the other hand, certain things give reason to believe that Count Bismarck, very soon after Benedetti's interview with Von Thile, managed to work upon the Spanish government, either by causing the idea of the Hohenzollern candidacy to be suggested to them, if they had not already entertained it; or if they had entertained it, but without giving it serious thought, by bringing it to their attention anew. The fact is that, in April, 1869, a confidential agent of Prim, Fernandez de los Rios, who had been sent by him to the widowed King Ferdinand in January, received a letter from a Portuguese gentleman, a friend of Prim, the Marquis of Niza, telling him of a conversation he had recently had with Oldoini, Italian Ambassador at Lisbon, who urged him (Niza) to take advantage of his friendly relations with Prim to suggest to him the idea of applying to Leopold. In other letters, Niza quotes Oldoini as suggesting that secret overtures be made, first to Bismarck, then to the Hohenzollern family at Düsseldorf; and the Portugal minister at Brussels also urges the choice of Leopold. Prussia, he says, will be glad to see it; as for Napoleon III, he will prefer this choice to that of Montpensier, and, in any event, he will not dare to oppose it.

These suggestions had, for the moment, no result, but one cannot find their traces without wondering if we should not ascribe their origin to Count Bismarck. It is to be noted also that the intermediary, the Marquis of Niza, was of the immediate suite of King Ferdinand, whose son-in-law was Leopold of Hohenzollern, husband of his daughter the Infanta Antonia.

In April, Benedetti was summoned to Paris by the Emperor. During his absence, on April 26, 1869, the Augsbourg *Gazette* published a letter, said to be from Paris, which, alluding to Leopold, announced that the Spaniards congratulated themselves on having found a young and intelligent prince, related to the Imperial House of France. M. Leonardon does not hesitate to see in this letter a document inspired by the Prussian minister, and intended to sound public opinion as to the impression which that candidacy would produce on France.

The reply was not slow in coming. The *La France* newspaper hastened to sound the alarm. This was an indication, and it was confirmed to Count Bismarck by an interview that Benedetti had with him early in May.

M. Leonardon dismisses as unimportant and unworthy of credence certain unconfirmed reports of views favorable to the candidacy of Leopold or his brother Fritz being held by the Empress and by Princess Mathilde, especially because they are in flat contradiction of the Emperor's remark to Benedetti: "The candidacy of the Duc de Montpensier is purely anti-dynastic, it affects nobody but myself, and I can accept it; the candidacy of the Prince of Hohenzollern is essentially anti-national; the country will not tolerate it and it must be prevented."

He regards it as the capital error of the Imperial government to have tried to prevent the candidacy in Prussia. Benedetti's effort in that direction with Bismarck, as reported in his despatch of May 11, 1869 (Benedetti, pp. 307–311), was simply an attempt to intimidate. But Bismarck not only was not intimidated, but carried away from that interview the conviction that that candidacy was sufficiently distasteful to the Emperor to enable him (Bismarck) to extract a *casus belli* from it, at his pleasure.

It would have been much more adroit for the French government to address itself to Spain. It could easily have broached the subject with Prim in a friendly tone. The gen-

APPENDIX 427

eral's conduct, his persistent hostility to the Montpensier candidacy, tend to prove that he wished to please the Emperor, and he would doubtless have heeded all the more willingly a discreetly worded warning against the Hohenzollern candidacy, because he had not as yet thought seriously of it, or bound himself by any overt act. M. Leonardon disposes of the report that Salazar first sounded the Hohenzollerns in April, but he agrees with La Gorce (vol. vi, pp. 197, 198) that the letter of a Berlin banker to the Regent Serrano, in July, dwelling upon the advantages of the Hohenzollern candidacy, was inspired by Bismarck, to keep the thing alive.

Not until mid-September, 1869, is the first overture made to the Hohenzollerns on the part of Spain. Baron von Werthern, Prussian Ambassador at Munich, an acquaintance of Salazar, asks Prince Antony's permission to present the Spanish deputy, who wishes to offer the crown to his son. The presentation takes place on September 17. Salazar comes direct from Vichy, sent by Prim. In this first interview he pleads his country's cause with warmth. Two days later, a second meeting is arranged between him and the old Prince and his son Charles of Roumania. It is plain that Salazar's purpose was to induce some Hohenzollern, no matter which one, to come forward as a candidate; for on this occasion he hints that the eyes of Spain are turned upon Prince Charles, who, however, categorically declines. In the afternoon of the same day, Salazar is received by Leopold, the oldest son, who, while he does not in terms refuse the crown, imposes conditions almost equivalent to a refusal: he must be chosen unanimously, and must be assured that he will not be dragged into a policy contrary to the interest of Portugal, because of his close connection with the reigning family there. (These details were made known only when the Memoirs of the King of Roumania were published: see vol. i of the French translation, pp. 525, 526.) Whatever Prim's connection with this overture of Salazar's, it is certain that about this time he made another unsuccessful attempt upon King Ferdinand; and then turned his attention to the Duke of Genoa, whose name was actually proposed to the Cortes in October; his mother, however, was greatly opposed to his acceptance, and Victor Emanuel finally declined the offer in his nephew's name.

On October 28 Salazar published a letter in which he passed in review the principal candidacies, arguing against them one after another, until he came to Prince Leopold, whom he extolled as a Catholic, well educated, father of three sons, rich, related through his late sister and his wife to the House of Braganza and through his grandmother and mother to the Imperial family of France (see Appendix D), while his connection with the reigning branch of the Hohenzollerns assured him of the good-will of Prussia, and was at the same time too distant to bind him to its policies.

After the final declination of the Duke of Genoa, Prim determined to address himself unofficially to Leopold. He sent Salazar directly to Berlin, with letters, dated February 17, 1870, for the King of Prussia, Count Bismarck, and Prince Leopold. The negotiations took place at Berlin, Leopold being present, in the last days of February and the early days of March. Bismarck pleaded earnestly for acceptance. In a memorial addressed to William he showed how advantageous it would be, politically, to be able to rely on the friendly disposition of a nation posted on the flank of France; he also dwelt upon the economic advantage which German commerce might well hope to derive from the presence of a Prussian prince on the throne of Spain. King William replied by raising objections and left it to Leopold alone to decide upon his course. The Crown Prince, Frederick, was very lukewarm and urged Leopold especially to make sure that the Prussian government, which perhaps had a special object in view at the moment, would always be disposed to give him effective support. (See Von Sybel, English trans., vol. vii, pp. 305 ff.; Memoirs of the King of Roumania, French trans., vol. i, p. 569, under date of March 2.)

APPENDIX 429

We have already heard of the council of March 15, 1870, which first became known to the world through the memoirs of the King of Roumania (see *supra*, pp. 18 ff. and notes). It may be said here that it would have been advantageous to Von Sybel's accuracy in dealing with this portion of his history, if he had had the benefit of those memoirs. Under date of April 3, 1870, "the Prince (Charles of Roumania) learns from Berlin that Bismarck has declared categorically, several times, that the acceptance of the Spanish crown by one of the Hohenzollern princes is a political necessity. Prince Antony has imposed three conditions: that his son shall obtain two thirds to three fourths of the votes in the Cortes; that the State shall be assured against bankruptcy; that the anti-clerical laws shall be passed before Prince Leopold's election." Memoirs, vol. i, pp. 573, 574.

On the same 3d of April Bismarck despatched Bucher and Versen to Madrid, and their journey thither and its results are described with sufficient detail in the first chapter of this book, pp. 23 ff. Meanwhile Prim demands a categorical reply forthwith. Prince Antony is summoned to Berlin on April 20. Bismarck is ill at Varzin. The King refuses to force Leopold or Fritz, and on the 22d a telegram is sent to Prim through Bucher, conveying Prince Leopold's declination.

Versen returns to Berlin on May 6. He finds that the affair is well-nigh abandoned. Bismarck is still sick, and Versen takes it upon himself to act in his place. He addresses himself to the Crown Prince, causes him to waver in his opinion, and obtains from him a letter with which he joins the old Prince at Nauheim on May 20. He argues insistently in favor of the candidacy, and with so much success that Prince Antony and his son decide to write to the Crown Prince letters in which it is clearly manifest that Leopold, being attacked by scruples, is inclined to reconsider his refusal. The Crown Prince informs the King and Bismarck of this change of attitude; the latter loses no time in despatching to Prince Antony a memorial in which he passes in review the considerations that militate in favor of a revival of the candidacy.

Meanwhile Prim, on receipt of the telegram of April 22, entered into negotiations for the third time with Ferdinand of Portugal, and was again met by a refusal. He seemed then to become discouraged, and being unaware of the change of heart that had taken place in Prussia, he informed the Cortes on June 11 of his unsuccessful overtures to King Ferdinand, the Duke of Aosta, and the Duke of Genoa. In veiled terms he alluded to unfruitful negotiations with a fourth candidate. "I may be permitted," he said, "not to mention his name: that would show a lack of tact; complications might ensue, and, moreover, I have given my word of honor to that effect." This anonymous candidate was Leopold. (See *supra*, p. 40, note.)

On the following day, Prim was informed by a letter from Bismarck, said to be in reply to his letter of February 17, that affairs were looking well for a resumption of negotiations. On June 14 the marshal sent Salazar to Sigmaringen with full powers.

He arrived there, with a secretary, on the 19th. Major von Versen was there and acted as interpreter. They quickly came to an agreement. For the glory of his family and the welfare of his country, Leopold is resigned to the sacrifice of his personal inclinations. A letter is sent to King William, then at Ems, to ask his approval. Awaiting the reply at Sigmaringen, Salazar sends, through Versen, two despatches to Madrid, one to Prim, the other to Zorrilla, President of the Cortes: in the first he announces that Prince Leopold will accept the crown, subject to the King's approval; in the second he tells Zorrilla that he expects to return to Madrid on June 26. Thereupon the election will take place and a deputation of fifteen members of the Cortes will travel to Sigmaringen to offer the crown formally to the Prince. (With regard to the premature adjournment of the Cortes and the doubtful explanation thereof, see *supra*, p. 42, and note.)

APPENDIX 431

It may be, says M. Leonardon, that Prim had suddenly an intuition of the rôle of irritating agent that Bismarck proposed to make him play. There has been published in Spain a confidential document which discloses with singular distinctness the thesis which Prussian policy had prepared, to answer any observations that might be made by France. It is a letter of Count Bismarck quoted in Señor Pirala's *Historia Contemporanea*, but with no indication of the person to whom it was addressed and with no date. The text, however, indicates that the addressee was at Madrid, and that the letter was written at the time when Bismarck replied to Prim's letter of February 17. This long-delayed reply of Bismarck was designed to suggest to Prim the resumption of the Hohenzollern candidacy. M. Leonardon concludes that it, as well as the undated letter which follows, was written about June 11.

"It is possible," Count Bismarck writes, "that we should see a transitory effervescence in France, and doubtless it is necessary to avoid whatever would help to arouse it and add to it. This being so, would it be wise to introduce my name in the story of these negotiations? I think not, but that, on the contrary, we should put my personality entirely outside of the whole thing. In fact, I have taken no part officially. It is simply a question of an expression of the will of the Spanish people on the one side, and, on the other, of a prince who is of age, master of his acts, and a private individual. Whether he had or had not reasons for securing the consent of his father and of the head of his family — that is a private matter, not an affair of state. To give the King advice on such matters is the duty of the minister of the royal household. But I have not aided him with my advice in the capacity of President of the Council of Ministers, but simply as being in charge of foreign affairs, and as a confidential servitor, like the other servants of the state who are in the secret.

"For my own part, I think that the Spanish government

will do better to publish only General Prim's letter of February 17 and the reply. We shall then have an unassailable position before the European public. If they make a noise in France, we shall ask quietly: 'What do you want? Do you propose to dictate the decision of the Spanish nation and a German private citizen?' In that case, doctor, there will be an opportunity to utilize your suggestion. Doubtless they will shriek about intrigue, and they will be furious against me, but unable to localize the point of attack. So far as my reply is concerned, it is simply a question of policy with regard to the general.

"I have answered his letter. I hope that he will have no doubt of my respectful sentiments for him, or of my concurrence in the project the realization of which depends only on him and the Cortes. I have not brought the affair to the point it has now reached without considerable difficulty, which M. Gama, with his knowledge of the ground, will be able to imagine and to explain to the general."

This letter was first published by Pirala in his *Historia Contemporanea*. He seems to have had access to documents in the Department of Foreign Affairs, and one wonders whether this letter may not, through somebody's indiscretion, have come to Prim's knowledge and have given him food for reflection.

Prim's return to Madrid on July 1 (as described by Victor Balaguer in *Memorias de un cónstituante*) and his subsequent interview with Mercier are told at sufficient length in the text, pp. 44 ff. On July 4 the ministers met at La Granja and resolved to submit the candidacy of Leopold to the permanent committee of the Cortes. A few days later that body was summoned to meet in extraordinary session on the 20th.

Meanwhile, says M. Leonardon, one feels that the Spanish government is anxious to clear its skirts of all purpose of complicity with Prussia. In a circular note dated July 7, Sagasta, Foreign Minister, while instructing his representa-

APPENDIX 433

tives abroad to announce the candidacy officially to the powers, took pains to say that the government "has acted solely on its own account and treated directly with Prince Leopold, without for a moment counting upon, or even supposing that its dignity would permit it to count upon, the slightest influence of a foreign Cabinet." This statement is further elaborated and emphasized in later paragraphs of the note, which is printed in full in *Blue Book*, pp. 15, 16.

Prim, for his part, seemed to be seeking a way out of the scrape in which he had involved himself. Luckily, Gramont's declaration of July 6 was sufficiently moderate in tone so far as Spain was concerned, not to overexcite popular sentiment. On the 7th Prim took the first backward step with his suggestion to Mercier that the Prince should find obstacles in the way of the King's consent (*supra*, pp. 126, 127). Mercier's despatches of the 9th and the sending of a special messenger to Sigmaringen on the 10th (*supra*, pp. 131, 156 n.) exhibit the growing determination of the Spanish government, probably under pressure from England and Austria, to rid themselves of Prince Leopold, by inducing him to withdraw his candidacy, if possible. Only let M. de Gramont declare that in the declaration of July 6 the word "suffer" was not addressed to Spain.

Then came the mission of Strat, first conceived by Olozaga, whose loyal efforts to adjust the difficulty are the more noteworthy and creditable in view of the shabby way in which he had been treated by his government. At about the same time, Olozaga telegraphed (July 8) to Saldanha, prime minister of Portugal, endeavoring once more to revive the candidacy of Ferdinand, to which Prim turned in desperation on the same day.

The letter of Prince Antony withdrawing his son's name (July 12) was followed on the 15th by Sagasta's officially informing the diplomatic agents of Spain of the withdrawal of the candidacy. In October, after the Prussian victories, there was again some talk of putting Prince Leopold forward;

but how much reality there was to it is uncertain, as negotiations were then pending with Victor Emanuel concerning the candidacy of the Duke of Aosta.

M. Leonardon concludes his exhaustive review of the Hohenzollern affair with a discussion of Prim's real attitude therein. His judgment, much less severe than M. Ollivier's is that if Prim had been the conscious and determined confederate of Bismarck against France, he would not have slunk away at the last moment. If he had desired, if, as was claimed, he had sought doggedly the gratification of an old grudge against France, going back to the Mexican expedition, it was in his power to carry the vote in favor of Leopold and draw Spain into war. His responsibility, weighty as it is, is limited then to a lack of clearsightedness and to an excess of self-confidence. He was guilty of a mistake, not of a crime.

APPENDIX D

PRINCE LEOPOLD OF HOHENZOLLERN

THE following particulars are taken from a pamphlet by Don Francisco Vila,[1] who declares himself to be in principle a republican. Bowing, however, to the will of the nation as represented by a majority of the Cortes, he passes in review the various candidates proposed and comes forth an enthusiastic partisan of Prince Leopold, in whom he finds all desirable qualifications, both as an individual and by virtue of his birth and connections; whereas, "in our humble opinion he is entirely lacking in defects." It is a significant fact that this author refers to the current remark that France will take umbrage at the candidacy.

"If," he concludes, "monarchy must be our form of government, if all the other candidates officially and extra-officially presented offer such undesirable conditions, then around the altars of the fatherland, which is always desirous of more peace and security, let us all unite and exclaim: Long live Leopold the First, King of Spain! Maledictions on his head if he betrays our hopes!"

Prince Leopold Stephen Charles Antony Gustavus of Hohenzollern-Sigmaringen was born September 22, 1835, and was therefore 35 years old in 1870. His father, Charles Antony Joaquin Frederick, Prince of Hohenzollern-Sigmaringen, Burgrave of Nuremberg, etc., etc., was born September 7, 1811, and succeeded his father in the principality on August 27, 1848. On December 7, 1849, he abdicated in favor of his very distant kinsman, King William of Prussia, and received, in March, 1850, the title of Highness, with the

[1] *El Principe Leopoldo: Juicio é Historia de Este Nuevo Candidato.* Madrid, 1870.

prerogatives of a royal prince; in October, 1861, by royal decree he was given the title of Royal Highness, and was made military governor of the Rhine provinces and Westphalia.

Prince Antony was the son of Charles Antony Frederick (born February 20, 1785), who married in February, 1808, Marie Antoinette Murat, niece of Joachim Murat, King of Naples.

Prince Antony's wife, and Leopold's mother, was Josephine Frederica Louisa (born October 21, 1813), daughter of Charles Louis, Grand Duke of Baden and of Stéphanie Louise, Vicomtesse de Beauharnais, adopted daughter of Napoleon I.

Prince Antony's other children, Leopold's brothers and sisters, were Charles Eitel Frederick, born April 20, 1839, chosen Prince of Roumania, April 20, 1866, and proclaimed King in 1881;[1] Frederick Eugene John (Prince "Fritz"), born June 25, 1843; Maria Louise Alexandrina, born November 17, 1845, and married in 1867 to Prince Philip of Belgium, Count of Flanders.

Prince Leopold was married September 12, 1861, to Antonia Maria Fernanda Micaela Gabriela Rafaela, daughter of Ferdinand and of Dona Maria da Gloria, late Queen of Portugal, born February 17, 1845. Thus the Princess Leopold was the daughter of the widowed King Consort of Portugal, and the sister of King Pedro V, who died in 1861, and of King Luiz, who reigned in 1870. King Luiz married Donna Maria Pia, daughter of Victor Emanuel.

Finally, Prince Leopold's aunt, Frederica Wilhelmina, married in 1844 Joachim Napoleon, Marquis of Pepoli, Italian Ambassador at Vienna in 1870. He was born in 1825, and was the grandson of Joachim Murat, King of Naples, through his daughter Letitia, who married the Marquis of Pepoli in 1822.

It will be seen that, outside of the candidate's German

[1] King Charles — Carol I — is still reigning over Roumania (1912).

APPENDIX 437

connections, he was most closely akin to the royal house of Portugal, and to the Murats. His relationship to the Bonapartes was rather shadowy: his maternal grandmother was an adopted daughter of the first Napoleon, his paternal grandmother a niece of the husband of Caroline Bonaparte, and his aunt the wife of a grandson of the said Caroline.

Prince Leopold himself, according to Bismarck, answered the question whether, in the event of trouble between France and Prussia, it would have been a disadvantage to the former to have him on the Spanish throne. "On the night after the battle of Sedan I was riding along the road to Donchéry, in thick darkness, with a number of our officers. . . . In reply to a question . . . I talked about the preliminaries to the war, and mentioned at the same time that I had thought Prince Leopold would be no unwelcome neighbor in Spain to the Emperor Napoleon, and would travel to Madrid *via* Paris, in order to get into touch with the imperial French policy, forming as it did a part of the conditions under which he would have had to govern Spain. I said: 'We should have been much more justified in dreading a close understanding between the Spanish and French crowns than in hoping for the restoration of a Spanish-German anti-French constellation after the analogy of Charles V; a king of Spain can only carry out Spanish policy, and the Prince, by assuming the crown of the country, would become a Spaniard.' To my surprise there came from the darkness behind me a vigorous rejoinder from the Prince of Hohenzollern, of whose presence I had not the least idea; he protested strongly against the possibility of presuming any French sympathies in him." Bismarck, *Reflections and Reminiscences*, English trans., vol. ii, pp. 87, 88.

Prince Leopold died in 1905.

APPENDIX E

THE DUC DE GRAMONT

ANTOINE AGÉNOR ALFRED, Duc de Gramont, some time Duc de Guiche (1819–1880), had held the seals of the Foreign Office only about a month when the Hohenzollern candidacy was made public, M. Ollivier having himself acted as Foreign Minister during the brief interim since the resignation of Comte Daru in April. Gramont had represented France in various foreign countries, notably at Rome in 1860, when Italian Unity became a fact, and had shown himself a consistent opponent of Italian independence. He was transferred to Vienna in 1861, where "he was at first rather coldly received by Austrian society, which was ultra-Catholic, because of some squabbles he had had with Cardinal Antonelli at Rome. But an event which took place in his family (his wife's conversion to Catholicism) changed this feeling." Delord, vol. vi, p. 123.

"The significance of this alteration" (in the ministry), says Walpole, "could hardly be ignored. Comte Daru's presence at the Foreign Office was everywhere regarded as an assurance of peace. The Duc de Gramont . . . was the partisan of the Pope against Italy, of Austria against Prussia." *History of Twenty-five Years*, vol. ii, p. 481.

"In a career already long, the new Minister of Foreign Affairs had learned diplomacy, and in despatches that were sometimes noteworthy, he had shown himself to be, at intervals, very shrewd in obtaining information; but he had never practised active politics . . . and he knew nothing of the perplexing responsibilities imposed by high office. Having lived long away from his country, he had faithfully retained in his heart the image of the France of an earlier

APPENDIX 439

day; and as he had been told in his childhood that no country surpassed, or even equalled, ours, he had reverentially become fixed in that conviction, and no critical education, no habit of revising his opinions, had enlightened him concerning the progress of our neighbors and our own weaknesses. Hence an ardent patriotism, readily led into recklessness, more justifiable in a soldier than in a statesman. A long residence in Austria had powerfully influenced the duke's mind. But that very influence had been to him more a source of error than of enlightenment. Heartily welcomed, because of his birth, in the aristocracy, he had lived on intimate terms with courtiers and military men who dreamed of revenge for Sadowa. It happened then, that having carried to Vienna the illusion of French omnipotence, he brought back to Paris another illusion, that of Austrian friendship for France. Taking the two illusions in combination, how far would the misconception not lead! Fast bound to the maxims of traditional diplomacy, M. de Gramont had, like most of his colleagues, bemoaned Italian Unity and German Unity. These regrets, which were those of a judicious mind, might, by taking the wrong turn, become a source of peril. They would be especially perilous if they should inspire a wish to seek in hot haste, at whatever cost, compensation for France and humiliation for Prussia. On joining the ministry M. de Gramont had disavowed any warlike opinions, and there was reason to rely upon his sincerity. Despite these protestations, those who knew him best did not feel altogether reassured. They were the less at ease in that they detected in him a certain overbearing, self-satisfied disposition, quick and irritable, inexperienced yet arrogant, not at all suited to a precarious fortune and a political situation surrounded by pitfalls." La Gorce, vol. vi, pp. 216, 217.

The most recent historian of the war, M. Henri Welschinger, who was employed in the Archives of the Corps Législatif from 1868 to 1870, and claims to have been present at all the sessions of the Chamber, is much more severe in his judgment of the Foreign Minister, as, indeed, he is a most bitter and unsparing critic of every act of the ministry of January 2. After quoting, with something very like a sneer, M. Ollivier's "extremely flattering" portrait of the duke, he says: "It is certain that the Duc de Gramont was more solemn than shrewd, more pretentious than subtle, more arrogant than insidious. He plumed himself on all occasions on the motto of his family: 'Gratia Dei sum id quod sum' (Thank God that I am what I am). He was about to have to deal with an extraordinarily skilful rival, who knew all the tricks of his trade and disdained neither stratagem nor perfidy, neither audacity nor imposture. Bismarck had, it seems, in a moment of vulgar mockery, described M. de Gramont, who deemed himself a great politician, as 'the stupidest man in Europe.' He had even called him a calf (Rindvieh). This brutal description had wounded the pride of the French diplomatist, who had sworn to show the Chancellor that he would have to reckon with him sooner or later. That is one of the secret reasons which almost instantly aggravated the approaching conflict between Prussia and France. As soon as he heard of the appointment to the ministry of foreign affairs of the Duc de Gramont, who, during his embassy at Vienna, had more than once thwarted his policy, Bismarck represented the new minister as a man who was dangerous to the security of Europe. . . . He caused it to be said by the reptiles of the Prussian press that Gramont's intimate relations with Beust . . . were of a nature to endanger peace. . . . The Baron von Varnbühler [Prime Minister of Würtemberg] said to M. de Saint-Vallier [French minister at Stuttgart] that the appointment of that minister had aroused uneasiness in Germany, and that the Emperor of the French had certainly selected him to carry out an adventurous policy in which he needed a minister *more yielding than serious-minded.* . . . Thus the accession of the Duc de Gramont was not, as M. Émile Ollivier thought,

APPENDIX 441

a guaranty of peace. Although the new minister accepted the events of 1866, with the maintenance of the stipulations of the Treaty of Prague, and seemed to agree to the policy of abstention for the present, Prussian diplomacy attributed to him ambitious and threatening projects." *La Guerre de 1870* (1911), vol. i, pp. 24, 25.

Bismarck's uncomplimentary references to Gramont may be found scattered through Dr. Busch's various works and in Bismarck's own *Reflections and Reminiscences*. According to Jules Favre, the Chancellor, in the famous interview at Ferrières, spoke of Gramont as "the most mediocre of diplomats," and said that Napoleon so regarded him. *Gouvernement de la Défense Nationale*, quoted by M. Ollivier, vol. xiv, page 598.

"It was well known," says Von Sybel, "that the Emperor had no very high regard for the ability of the new Minister of Foreign Affairs. . . . That Napoleon suggested his nomination is not at all likely. Had the Emperor really cherished plans of war at the time, he would nevertheless hardly have selected for so important a post the man whom in 1869 he had excluded from participation in the consultations regarding the triple alliance, a preparatory step to war, because of his inefficiency. If, on the other hand, Napoleon was anxious to preserve peaceful relations with Prussia, Gramont's advancement is still more inexplicable; for the duke's hatred of Prussia was quite as notorious as was his indiscretion.

"And who may it have been by whom the Emperor was persuaded to this nomination? . . .

"It is more than likely that in Daru's place, Ollivier desired a colleague who was disposed . . . to conduct negotiations with Prussia with fitting firmness and spirit. . . . It mattered little whether the new minister possessed more or less information or talent, since the Prime Minister felt that out of his own superabundance he could supply any deficiency in this respect which might be found in charge of the Foreign Office. From this point of view we can readily understand that Gramont must have been just the man for Ollivier; for in his tendencies he was thoroughly clerical, and it would have been difficult to find in all Europe any one more eager for an opportunity to strike at Prussia, and above all else, at Bismarck.

"To estimate the achievements of the great German statesman according to his principles and methods of action was wholly beyond Gramont's capacity. He saw in them no more than the triumphs of a successful course of disregard of the impositions and restrictions of the ordinary sense of duty and honor. . . .

"Once having assumed a position, he was proof against all argument, the irritation caused by its refutation simply urging him on. He was as little open to conviction as Ollivier, although for a wholly different reason. . . . With him it was merely the naïve arrogance of the aristocrat of circumscribed education, who is undisturbed in his opinions by any annoying consciousness of the rest of the world." *Die Begründung des deutsches Reichs*, vol. vii, English translation, pp. 273, 276.

M. Welschinger draws this pen-picture of M. de Gramont, as he appeared in the Salle des Pas Perdus immediately after reading the declaration of July 6, "seated on one of the benches, with his back to one of the great windows looking on the court of honor of the Palais Bourbon. Before him stood seven or eight deputies of the Right, in rapt contemplation, gazing upon him with touching deference. Still under the spell of the enthusiastic applause that had greeted his words of menace, he smacked his lips over what he deemed a triumph. His lordly head emerged from a high collar encircled by a long and wide cravat of black silk. His slender hand rested on a portfolio stuffed with papers wherein everyone of his admirers imagined that all the secrets of Europe reposed. His superb presence was most imposing. He bore himself nobly. He seemed the living arbiter of our destinies. . . . Seeing the minister thus, surrounded, con-

APPENDIX 443

gratulated, fawned upon; looking at that grave and solemn face, that glance à la Metternich, that smile à la Talleyrand, I can understand that more than one member of the majority, having little knowledge of diplomatic affairs and regarding him as an oracle, might well have believed that Count Bismarck had at last found his master." Vol. i, page 94.

It would be much easier to multiply indefinitely unflattering references to M. de Gramont than to find one of a different tenor except in the pages of his colleague and *soi-disant* chief, M. Ollivier; and it hardly needs to be said that his encomiums of his Minister for Foreign Affairs are not borne out by what he has to say of the course pursued by him on and after July 12.

In the autumn of 1871, Comte Benedetti, moved thereto by criticisms of the way in which he performed his duties as ambassador, published a volume, under the title *Ma Mission en Prusse*, his main purpose, as was evident from the preface, being to defend his conduct of the negotiations at Ems from July 9 to July 14, although a large part of the book is devoted to a review of the early years of his ambassadorship, which began late in 1864. He maintained that he had successfully accomplished the original object of his mission to Ems, in that the King's explicit approval of the withdrawal of the candidacy of Leopold was forthcoming as a result of his representations; that the negotiation was unnecessarily complicated by the futile demand of guaranties, and that the situation created by that demand was made impossible of amelioration by Werther's report of his interview with MM. Ollivier and Gramont in the afternoon of the 12th, as to which no information had been sent to him.

The publication of Benedetti's book put an end to the hesitation which had long deterred M. de Gramont from giving to the world his answer to the criticisms of his enemies upon his conduct of affairs in July, 1870, and in 1872 he published his self-justifying work, *La France et la Prusse avant la Guerre*. He vigorously attacked Benedetti for having, as he claimed, violated all the traditions of diplomacy by publishing official despatches without the consent of the government, as well as his (Gramont's) private and confidential correspondence without his knowledge or concurrence. He denies that the Ambassador had succeeded in his mission *in any respect*, and strongly hints that his attitude toward the King was too conciliatory. But his book is, in the main, a vindication of his course, the nature of which will sufficiently appear from such passages as are quoted in the notes to this book, and in Appendices G, I, and M. Like most of his colleagues in the ministry, M. de Gramont disappeared from public life with the fall of the ministry on August 9. His testimony at the Inquiry concerning the 4th of September is in some respects more informing than his book.

APPENDIX F

THE PRINCIPLES OF INTERNATIONAL LAW APPLICABLE TO
THE HOHENZOLLERN AFFAIR

(From Ollivier's *L'Empire Libéral*, vol. xiv, pp. 54–63)

IN 1815, after establishing a certain equilibrium, each of the great powers agreed to respect it and not to profit by any changes that might occur in the internal system of any state, to obtain an exclusive influence there or an advantage not shared by the other powers. To seek, for the behoof of a member of his family, a vacant crown, had been regarded as one of the most dangerous methods of securing such an influence and advantage. . . . Each of the great powers had bound itself not to acquire, to the behoof of a member of its reigning family, a vacant throne, without the formal assent of Europe. It was not long before this rule was extended to a hypothetical case which had not at first been anticipated, "where a prince, not belonging to one of the five great powers, or even a private citizen, should become, by his accession to a vacant throne, a source of danger to a neighboring power."[1]

Palmerston extended still further this balance-conserving rule. "The choice of the Queen's husband, in an independent country," he said, "is clearly a question in which the governments of other countries have no right to intervene, unless it is possible that the choice may fall upon some prince belonging to the reigning family of some powerful foreign state, who would probably combine the policies of his adopted country and his native country in a manner inju-

[1] Protocols of January 27 and February 7, 1831.

rious to the interests of other states." [July 19, 1846, apropos of the "Spanish Marriages."]

Numerous examples have confirmed these rules. In 1830 the sovereigns of Russia, France, and Great Britain, the liberators of Greece,[1] excluded from the ranks of aspirants for the new throne all the princes belonging to their families. And they named at first Prince Leopold of Saxe-Coburg, afterwards King of the Belgians, only after establishing the fact that he had ceased to belong to the royal family of Great Britain. In 1831, after the revolution which separated Belgium from Holland, Palmerston, plenipotentiary at the Conference of London, invoked the Greek precedent and caused it to be agreed that " in case the sovereignty of Belgium should be offered to a prince of either of the families reigning in Austria, France, Great Britain, Prussia, or Russia, such offer should invariably be declined." [2]

And, despite the enthusiasm which greeted the election of his son, the Duc de Nemours, to the throne by the National Congress, Louis-Philippe refused his assent, as head of the family, to the desire of the Belgian people. Considering that the sovereign of Belgium must necessarily fulfil the condition upon which the existence of that country depended, — neutrality, — the Prince of Leuchtenberg, son of Eugène de Beauharnais, was also excluded, being allied through his mother, Amelia of Bavaria, to the Bonaparte family, although he belonged to neither of the five great powers.

As a result of these exclusions, the Belgian government, before offering the crown to Leopold of Saxe-Coburg, made sure that the French government, which was at first opposed, had abandoned its opposition; and the Prince himself, after the vote of the National Congress, accepted the crown only on the assurance of the representations of the great powers that his election would be recognized.

[1] Protocol of the Conference of London, February 3, 1830.
[2] Protocol of February 1, 1831.

APPENDIX 447

In 1848, despite the desire of the Queen Regent of Spain, Maria Christina, to give her daughter to so charming a youth as the Duc d'Aumale, England pronounced a formal decree of exclusion against that marriage, and renewed it later against the Duc de Montpensier, so that Louis-Philippe was fain to renounce that project so dear to his heart.

In 1859, a Tuscan faction offered the grand-ducal crown to Prince Napoleon (cousin of the Emperor). The Emperor would not even discuss the proposal; and with respect to Naples he peremptorily put aside the aspirations which the Murats were thought to entertain.

In 1862, after King Otho was expelled from Greece, Napoleon again refused to sanction the candidacy of a member of his family. Nor did the Tsar Alexander approve the candidacy of Romanowski, husband of the Grand Duchess Marie, daughter of Nicholas, although it was open to question whether the Prince had been admitted to the ranks of the princes of the imperial family; and it might fairly be claimed that he was in a position analogous to that of Leopold of Saxe-Coburg with respect to the royal house of England, when he was chosen as sovereign of Greece in 1830.

England followed the same course with respect to Prince Alfred (Duke of Edinburgh), one of the Queen's sons, and the Hellenic Congress having elected him none the less, the Queen would not allow him to accept.

And in respect to Spain herself, one of the reasons that led the Italian ministry to reject the suggestion of the Duke of Genoa as a candidate, was that it was not certain that the powers would consent.

We evolved therefore this first rule: that when the choice of a sovereign is in question, a foreign government never has the right to claim, but always has the right to exclude, if the candidate proposed belongs to one of the reigning families of the great powers, or if, not so belonging, he constitutes, by his individual position, a source of danger without or within.

We asked ourselves another question. The rule being certain, ought we to invoke it? Would it not be more in conformity with the principles of modern society to disregard it? Had it not become obsolete since modern institutions had withdrawn from crowned heads the unlimited powers which formerly made their will supreme in the matter of peace and war and alliances, and had subordinated them to the will of their peoples and to the votes of legislatures? Guizot had already swept that paltry argument from the field of political discussion. "Superficial minds affect to despise the ties of family between sovereigns, and to consider them as of no account between states. A strange display of ignorance! Of course such ties are not inevitably decisive, or always salutary; but all history, ancient and modern, and our own history, are at hand to prove their importance and the advantage that political skill can derive from them."[1]

This rule is so great a safeguard of European good order, that even since the war brought about by its violation, it has been enforced several times. At the very outset of the war, when Don Ferdinand of Portugal seemed on the point of reconsidering his refusal, the first condition that he laid down was the antecedent consent of the powers, especially of the cabinets of Paris and London. Prince Amadeus of Savoy was not authorized by his father to accept the crown of Spain until he had formally consulted and obtained the consent of all the great powers. Prim resisted this demand at first, for it was a retrospective condemnation of his conduct toward us. But as the Italian government insisted, he was compelled (October 19) to request the sanction of the powers — a formality which he had thought it his duty to neglect in the case of the Hohenzollern. Finally, Article 3 of the Treaty of Berlin, of July 13, 1876 [1877] at the conclusion of the Russo-Turkish War, stipulates that "no member of the reigning dynasties of the great powers shall be elected Prince of Bulgaria."

[1] Guizot, *Mémoires*, vol. ii. p. 265.

And so it only remained for us to ascertain in what way this right of exclusion reserved to the great powers had been exercised without violating the higher law of the independence of the nations. The Conference of London had started with the principle that every right, of nations as well as of individuals, is limited by the rights of others, and that, while every nation is free to organize itself, and to choose as its king whomsoever it pleases, it is not to be allowed to threaten the tranquillity of a neighboring people by its choice. And it had authorized Louis-Philippe to prevent, by force if necessary, the election of the Duke of Leuchtenberg. This decision of the Conference came to be regarded as an abuse of its power, and Europe did not insist upon it. Europe regarded as overstrained the doctrine that the mere choice of a monarch, independently of any special facts, could be considered an aggressive act authorizing intervention: a nation was not required to account to anybody for the use, good or bad, that it might make of its sovereignty. On the other hand, Europe had confirmed the right of asking the head of the royal family to which the sovereign elect belonged to refuse his consent, lacking which the election could lead to no practical result; thus the European balance of power was maintained without any blow being dealt to the independence of a nation.

This procedure has always been followed in cases where there was occasion to resort to international exclusion. On the occasion of the candidacy of the Duc de Nemours, the protest of England was addressed to France, not to Belgium. She informed Louis-Philippe of her purpose to prevent, even by war, the accession of his son to the Belgian throne. In like manner, in 1862, the powers brought pressure to bear on England and Russia, not on Greece, to exclude from the throne the son of the Queen and the Tsar's kinsman. Again, it was to Louis-Philippe and not to Spain that England intimated her veto of the marriage of Queen Isabella to a prince of Orleans. . . . In 1866, the Russians and Turks, displeased by the election of Prince Charles of Hohenzollern to be Prince of Roumania, expressed their displeasure at Berlin, not at Bucharest.

Thus we had at our service a second unquestionable rule: to prevent the enthronement of a foreign prince whose family would gain in influence thereby, one must apply to the head of that family and not to the electing nation.

APPENDIX G

THE DECLARATION OF JULY 6

On pages 89–92 of this volume will be found what M. Ollivier has to say as to the wording of the declaration and the responsibility therefor. In the *Éclaircissements* to his volume xiv, pp. 573–577, he cites numerous examples of similar declarations.

In his testimony at the Inquiry concerning the 4th of September, Marshal Le Bœuf testified: "In the morning of the 6th the Council of Ministers deliberated concerning the reply to be made to M. Cochery's interpellation. The Council was divided concerning the form, several members, while agreeing that the draft submitted to them was justified by the conduct of Prussia, thought the form a little too sharp. Allow me to say that the Emperor was of that opinion. The words were softened but, on our arrival at the Chamber, we found great excitement among the deputies. We allowed ourselves to be swept away and the original draft, or something very like it, was read from the tribune. At least, that is what I seem to remember."

Gramont, in his testimony, flatly contradicted this version, which is so improbable that it seems hardly worthy of the arguments by which M. Ollivier demolishes it. Vol. xiv, *Éclaircissements*, pp. 571, 572.

"The declaration read from the tribune of the Corps Législatif," says Gramont, "had been discussed in the Council of Ministers that same morning at Saint-Cloud, the Emperor presiding. On this subject it is well to correct an error which has gained some credence among certain persons. It is alleged that a first draft, which was couched in very sharp terms, was corrected and softened after a prolonged discussion; so that there were two drafts: the first more vigorous in form, which the Council rejected; the second more conciliatory, which was the final result of the deliberation. On arriving at the Chamber, the Minister of Foreign Affairs — or, it may be, the whole Cabinet — seeing the prevailing excitement and the superintensity of the outbursts of patriotic feeling, allowed himself to be carried away by this manifestation of the general opinion and read from the tribune the first draft, the more vigorous of the two, which had been rejected in the morning as too sharp.

"According to another somewhat similar version, the minister did not substitute the first draft for the second, but simply omitted to read the modifications that had been made by the Council in the first draft in order to make it milder.

"These two stories are absolutely false. It is true that the draft first submitted to the Council was modified in the course of the discussion. The final form once agreed upon, I read it once more to the Council, and it was voted that I should read it to the Corps Législatif at the opening of the session.

"I left the palace of Saint-Cloud about half-past twelve, carrying in my portfolio the minute of the declaration as it had been agreed upon. I went directly to the Foreign Office, and, sending for two of my clerks, I myself dictated to them the official text of the declaration. I had not seen a single deputy, nor, in fact, any one, since I left Saint-Cloud; consequently I was in no way exposed to the risk of allowing myself to be carried away by an excitement of which I knew nothing. In any event, nothing on earth could have made me forget my duty to the point of changing a syllable in an official document agreed upon in Council.

"As soon as I had finished the dictation, I started for the Chamber, and, going up at once into the tribune, I read the declaration from one of the copies which I brought from the department. On coming down from the tribune, I gave that

APPENDIX 453

copy to one of the clerks whose duty it was to write the report of the sessions. The other has remained among my papers. . . .

"The text that I read to the Chamber was, word for word, that which had been agreed upon in Council at Saint-Cloud; I know it better than any one, for the minute did not leave my hand for a moment before it was dictated by me in my private office." *La France et la Prusse*, pp. 49–52.

In 1902 the manuscript of Gramont's minute, with the interlineations made during the session of the Council, turned up in an auction room, and was sold for 350 francs to an unknown buyer. It is described by Welschinger (vol. i, pp. 50–52) from a personal examination. It substantially confirms M. Ollivier's account, but shows in a little more detail the changes made, in Ollivier's handwriting at least, if not at his suggestion. For instance, he added the phrase, "by placing one of its princes on the throne of Charles V." M. de Gramont himself wrote on the minute: "The conclusion was discussed in the Council, and transcribed by M. Ollivier after it was accepted and unanimously voted by the Council."

A Brussels newspaper, the *Independance Belge*, printed on March 6, 1874, an article to the effect that after the Cochery interpellation on July 5, a council was held at Saint-Cloud, the Emperor presiding, and that, while he was thus engaged, the Empress, who had been in a very excited state since the 3d and had been talking in a most warlike strain, had an interview with Baron Jérôme David, as a result of which, she laid hold of the Emperor as soon as he was at liberty and talked with him till nearly one in the morning. When the ministers assembled at ten o'clock on the 6th, they were instantly stricken with amazement by the change in the Emperor's attitude, manifested by a determination to give a more emphatic tone to the declaration; and, after due remonstrance, they yielded to his wishes in great measure; so that the final draft represented the Emperor's views so far as it was couched in provocative language, but did not entirely satisfy him in that respect.

This version is adopted by Lehautcourt (vol. i, pp. 228–230 and notes), on the somewhat inconclusive ground that Darimon asserts that it came directly from Gramont's office, and that it is not contradicted by Gramont. La Gorce, however, with the better reason, rejects it, not only on the ground of its improbability, but because it is directly contradicted by Gramont, both in his book and in his testimony at the Inquiry concerning the 4th of September, and by his colleagues, especially M. Louvet, "whose testimony deserves the fullest confidence, for he was the very soul of uprightness and integrity," and who wrote on this subject: "The *Independance Belge* has dared to assert that the Emperor contributed to make the declaration more emphatic in a bellicose sense. This assertion is absolutely contrary to the fact."

This question of the responsibility for the *form* of the declaration is important in view of the fact that it has been often alleged to have been the first misstep that made the avoidance of war more difficult at least, if not impossible, having regard to Bismarck's now generally admitted purpose "to force France to the brink of the precipice."

M. Welschinger, one might almost say with glee, fastens upon M. Ollivier's admission that he wrote the concluding paragraph, as the foundation of an attack on the Keeper of the Seals as the approximate cause of the catastrophe that ensued. "These few lines, the importance of which was not realized until the session of the Corps Législatif . . . were, to mean, in the very near future, the inevitable clash of two great nations, deaths by tens of thousands, frightful destruction, and, for ourselves, billions to pay and two provinces to surrender. It is an extraordinary thing, which indicates the frivolity of its author, that it was M. Émile Ollivier, who claimed to be most inclined to pacific measures, — that it was he who, by that final sentence, set about leading us infallibly into war" (vol. i, p. 52). This unreasonably harsh judgment is explicable perhaps, in a measure, by the fact that it was written after the publication of M. Ollivier's fourteenth volume. It exaggerates the importance of the modifications of the original draft, and disregards the fact that the declaration was unanimously accepted by the Council of Ministers.

M. Jules Favre insists that Gramont, "instead of hurling an unusual sort of challenge from the tribune, should have requested, by a note, explanations which would have been forthcoming." (*Gouvernement de la Defense Nationale*, vol. i, p. 26.) But M. Favre's criticisms are not unbiassed, to say the least, and the ministry certainly was justified in believing that the Prussian government did not propose to enter into explanations. That it was indispensable, in view of the state of public feeling, to make some official announcement, cannot be questioned.

On the 7th Lord Lyons wrote to Lord Granville (*Blue Book*, p. 7): "I observed to the Duc de Gramont this afternoon that I could not but feel uneasy respecting the declaration which he had made the day before in the Corps Législatif. I could not, I said, help thinking that milder language would have rendered it more easy to treat both with Prussia and with Spain for the withdrawal of the pretensions of Prince Leopold of Hohenzollern.

"M. de Gramont answered that he was glad I had mentioned this, as he wished to have an opportunity of conveying to your Lordship an explanation of his reasons for making a public declaration in terms so positive. Your Lordship would, he was sure, as Minister in a constitutional country, understand perfectly the impossibility of contending with public opinion. The nation was, he said, so strongly roused upon this question that its will could not be resisted or trifled with. He had seen me in the Chamber when he had made his declaration. I had, therefore, myself witnessed the extraordinary enthusiasm and unanimity with which the announcement of the determination of the Government to repel the insult offered to the nation had been received. He had kept within bounds, or he might have provoked a still more remarkable explosion of feeling. Now, the indignation out of doors was equally violent and equally general. Nothing less than what he had said would have satisfied the public. His speech was, in fact, as regarded the interior of France, absolutely necessary; and diplomatic considerations must yield to public safety at home."

Lord Lyons goes on to quote M. de Gramont as to the *external* considerations which necessitated the declaration; but it will be fairer, perhaps, to allow the Minister to state them in his own words. In his book he wrote (pages 38–43) : —

"It was no longer possible to entertain a doubt as to the intentions of Prussia, and it was necessary at any cost to place a barrier between her enterprise and the date of July 20 [when the Cortes were to reassemble]. At Berlin they refused to discuss the matter; and, indeed, what could we have added to the arguments which our ambassador had already urged a year before against the same possibility?

"At Madrid, Marshal Prim contented himself with replying : 'It is possible that the first impression in France will be adverse, but they will soon think better of it on reflection.'

"Time pressed : we had left only the single resource of a declaration to the Chambers, thus making known, by official promulgation, what Spain seemed not to understand, and Prussia was not even willing to hear.

"It was under the influence of these considerations that the government determined upon the declaration which was read July 6 in the Corps Législatif. As we could not give the Chambers incomplete information, and as we desired to avoid overexciting public feeling by disclosing the disloyal manœuvring of the Cabinet of Berlin, the government had perforce to confine itself to setting forth in precise terms its attitude toward the two powers, whose combination had

APPENDIX 457

been managed in a fashion so prejudicial to the legitimate interest of France. It could only express its confidence in the friendship of the Spanish people and the wisdom of the German people. But if the vagueness of those hopes had to be made up for by language more decided than usual, and by a categorical exposition of its duties, those persons must be held responsible who, by declining its first overture, made it impossible for it, at the outset, to lead the parliament to cherish the probability of a favorable outcome; those persons who, in contempt of all international proprieties, had created by their disloyal actions an abnormal situation and had made a crisis imminent; who, in the words of the English newspapers that were most hostile to France, had preferred to honorable negotiation a perfidious transaction which had all the appearance of a vulgar and impudent coup d'état. (*The Times*, July 8, 1870.) . . .

"Every one knows how the Chambers, the public, and the press received the government's declaration. . . . Nothing was further from the government's purpose than to lead the country into war, and the sequel of the negotiations proves this most convincingly to every honorable and impartial mind.

"If we had wished to inflame the public mind more, and to seek in its excitement the corner-stone of an aggressive policy, we should have begun by exonerating our agents from the unmerited reproaches heaped upon them for what was termed their culpable lack of foresight. We should have told the Chamber of the pourparlers of 1869, of the reassuring but misleading language of Herr von Bismarck in May of that same year; we should have placed the Chamber in a position to understand thoroughly the premeditated, hostile character of that Prussian conspiracy, plotted in the dark and perfected long beforehand against us, with entire knowledge of the resistance it was sure to arouse and of the sentiments it was sure to wound.

"Now, I ask, what would have been the effect upon the

Chamber and throughout the country, if, after a full and exact account of these aggravating circumstances, the Minister for Foreign Affairs had made known the first negative result of our overtures at Berlin? However great the emotion which the reply of the government then caused, it would have been vastly exceeded by the general indignation when people should have learned that, on the subject of that candidacy, concocted with so much secrecy, at which all Europe was beginning to take alarm, the Prussian government, which had planned it, refused to explain itself, proffering the absurd reply that it did not propose to bother about the matter, *that it had no existence for it.*

"By maintaining silence on all these matters the French government imposed upon itself a genuine sacrifice. In the first place, it deprived itself of the strongest arguments to justify the firmness of its language; in the second place, it allowed undeserved blame to rest on its diplomatic staff, for some time at least. Now, this sacrifice it made solely to its desire to avoid agitating men's minds and public opinion overmuch at the moment when recent evidence of Prussia's evil purpose caused apprehension of the difficulties of the negotiation upon which it was about to enter.

"It was essential to formulate our policy explicitly and to place a formal declaration athwart the Prussian schemes, in order to forestall the coup d'état of July 20. That done, we were ready for all expedients to safeguard peace coincidently with the honor and material interests of France."

M. de Gramont published his book in 1872, so that most of the writers on the war had his attempted justification before them as a text upon which to build their commentaries. In addition to the works mentioned in this appendix, any of the others quoted from time to time in the notes may be consulted for criticism of this declaration, unbiassed by too great friendliness for the Empire or for the Ministry of January 2.

M. Albert Sorel, whose great reputation as a historian

APPENDIX 459

gives peculiar weight to his judgment, has this to say on the subject: —

"The imperial government believed that it was playing a great political game by thus throwing down the glove to Prussia. In reality it was simply playing its adversary's game. Failing to measure the strength of the position taken up by Bismarck, it made the opening for a sortie upon which the Chancellor had reckoned. Bismarck had but one thing to fear: that France would show some prudence, and, with the support of Europe, would enter on a diplomatic campaign. He knew that, in that case, the King would not make up his mind to a rupture, and that the war would slip through his fingers. M. de Gramont relieved him from that anxiety at the very outset of the negotiation. In fact, Europe was thrust aside; that peremptory language closed the mouths of diplomatists. Supercilious in form, inexorable in its conclusions, the declaration of July 6 called upon King William either to submit to a diplomatic affront or to declare war. It was an ultimatum, and despite the halting commentary with which M. Ollivier accompanied it, no one was deceived. . . .

"In this fatal enterprise, the declaration of the 6th must be regarded as the first disaster of France. It was a diplomatic Woerth. Prussia must submit, or it was war. This dilemma embarrassed Europe, which did not want war and did not propose to force King William's hand. However, diplomacy did not give up the search for a compromise, but it sought it without much hope. The powers did not hesitate to tell France that, by that burst of passion, she had lost all her diplomatic advantage."

The effect of the declaration in Germany, North and South, and in the other European countries, is described by La Gorce in vol. vi, pp. 232-238. Of especial interest are the views of the statesmen who were at the head of affairs in Austria and Italy, as both the Emperor and Gramont seem to have counted upon the material support of those countries.

In addition to Bismarck's retrospective reflections on the declaration of July 6 (*Reflections and Reminiscences*, English translation, vol. ii, pp. 92, 93), Dr. Busch, under date of July 9, gives us the Chancellor's contemporaneous remarks thereon: "The Secretary of State handed me a telegram from Berlin to the Chancellor, which was returned by the latter with comments. I was to get these circulated in the non-official journals. The telegram was to the effect that Gramont had stated in reply to an interpellation by Cochery, that Prim had offered the Spanish throne to the Hereditary Prince of Hohenzollern (*Remark:* 'He can do nothing of the kind. Only the Cortes'), and that the Prince had accepted it. (*Remark:* 'He will declare himself only after he has been elected.') The Spanish people has not yet, however, expressed its wishes. (*Remark:* 'That is the main point.') The French government do not recognize the negotiations in question. (*Remark:* 'There are no negotiations excepting those between Spain and the eventual candidates for the throne.') Gramont therefore begged that the discussion might be postponed, as it was purposeless for the present. (*Remark:* 'Very.') The French government would maintain the neutral attitude which they had observed up to the present, but would not permit a foreign power to place a prince upon the Spanish throne (*Remark:* 'Hardly any power entertains such an intention, except perhaps France'), and endanger the honor and dignity of France. They trusted to the wisdom of the Germans (*Remark:* 'That has nothing to do with it') and to the friendship of the Spanish people. (*Remark:* 'That is the main point.') Should they be deceived in their hope, they would do their duty without hesitation or weakness. (*Remark:* 'We also.')"
Bismarck: Some Secret Pages of his History, vol. i, p. 29.

APPENDIX H

BISMARCK'S CIRCULAR NOTE OF JULY 18 TO THE POWERS

(Printed in *Blue Book*, No. 3, pp. 5–8)

BERLIN, July 18, 1870.

THE proceedings of the French Ministers at the sittings of the Senate and the Legislative Body on the 15th instant, and the misrepresentations of the truth there brought forward with the solemn character of official declarations, have removed the last veil from the intentions which could no longer be doubtful to any disinterested person, since astonished Europe learned two days before from the mouth of the French Minister for Foreign Affairs that France was not satisfied with the voluntary renunciation of the hereditary Prince and had further negotiations to carry on with Prussia. Whilst the rest of the European Powers were busied in considering how they were to meet this new and unexpected phase, and perhaps exercise a conciliatory and mitigating influence on these alleged negotiations, whose nature and object no one could divine, the French Government has thought proper, by a public and solemn declaration which, while misrepresenting known facts, added fresh affronts to the threats of the 6th instant, to carry matters to such a pitch as to render any accommodation impossible, and, as every handle of intervention was taken away from the friendly Powers, to make the rupture unavoidable.

For a week past it could be no matter of doubt to us that the Emperor Napoleon was resolved, regardless of consequences, to bring us into a position in which we should have the choice between war and a humiliation which the honourable feelings of no nation can bear. Could we have entertained any doubt, we must have been undeceived by the Report of the Royal Ambassador on his first conference with the Duc de Gramont and M. Ollivier, after his return from Ems, in which the first described the renunciation of the hereditary Prince as a secondary matter, and both Ministers demanded that His Majesty the King should write an apologetic letter to the Emperor Napoleon, the publication of which might pacify the excited feelings of France. The scorn of the French Government press anticipated the desired triumph; but the Government seems to have feared that the war might still escape it, and hastened, by its official declarations of the 15th instant, to transfer the matter to a field which no longer admitted of intervention, and to prove to us and all the world that no compliance within the bounds of the national feelings of honour would suffice to maintain peace.

As, however, no one doubted, or could doubt, that *we* sincerely desired peace, and a few days before considered no war possible, as every pretext for war was wanting, and even the last artificially and forcibly created pretext, as it was devised without our aid, so it had disappeared again of itself : as, therefore, there was no *cause* at all for war, there was nothing left for the French Ministers, in order to their seeming justification before their own people, really peaceably disposed and requiring tranquillity, but by means of misrepresentation and invention of facts, the falsity of which was known to them from official documents, to persuade the two representative bodies, and through them the people, that they had been affronted by Prussia, thereby to stir up their passions to an outbreak by which they might represent themselves as carried away.

It is a sad business to expose the series of untruths; fortunately the French Ministers have shortened the task, as they, by their refusal to produce the note or despatch, as demanded by a part of the Assembly, have prepared the world for the intelligence that it has no existence whatever.

APPENDIX 463

This is in fact the case. There exists no note or despatch by which the Prussian Government notified to the Cabinets of Europe a refusal to receive the French Ambassador. There exists nothing but the newspaper telegram known to all the world, which was communicated to the German Governments, and to some of our Representatives with non-German Governments, according to the wording of the newspapers, in order to inform them of the nature of the French demands, and the impossibility of complying with them, and which, moreover, contains nothing injurious to France.

We have addressed no further communications on the incident to any Government. In regard to the fact of the refusal to receive the French Ambassador, in order to set that assertion in its proper light, I am authorized by His Majesty to transmit the two enclosed official documents to your Excellency, with the request that you will communicate them to the Government to which you have the honour to be accredited: the first is a literally correct account of what took place at Ems, drawn up at the command, and with the immediate approval of His Majesty the King; the second is the official report of the adjutant in attendance on His Majesty, on the performance of the duty assigned to him.

It may be unnecessary to point out that the firmness in repelling French pretension was attended with all the considerate friendliness both in *matter* and *form* which comports so well with the personal habits of His Majesty the King, as well as with the principles of international courtesy towards the Representatives of friendly sovereigns and nations.

Finally, with regard to the departure of our Ambassador, I only remark, as was officially known to the French Cabinet, that it was no recall, but a leave of absence requested by the Ambassador for personal reasons, and that he had transferred the business to the First Councillor of Legation, who had often represented him before, and had given me notification thereof as usual. The statement is also untrue that His Majesty the King communicated the candidature of Prince Leopold to me, the undersigned Chancellor of the Confederation. I was casually informed in confidence of the Spanish offer by a private person concerned in the negotiations.

If all the reasons brought forward by the French Ministers to show that war is inevitable, are thus reduced to nothing, and appear to be grasped out of the air, there unfortunately only remains to us the sad necessity of seeking for the real motives in the worst traditions of Louis XIV and the first Empire — traditions stigmatized by the nations and Governments of the civilized world for half a century, but which a party in France still writes on its banners, and which Napoleon III, as we believed, had successfully withstood.

As motive causes of this lamentable phenomenon we can but recognize, unfortunately, the worst instincts of hatred and of envy of the independence and welfare of Germany, with the endeavour to keep down liberty in their own country by involving it in foreign wars.

It is painful to think that, by such a gigantic conflict as the national exasperation, the magnitude and the strength of the two countries give us the prospect of, the peaceful development of civilization and of national prosperity, which was in advancing bloom, will be checked and driven back for many years. But we must, before God and man, make over the responsibility of it to those whose outrageous proceedings compel us to accept the combat, for the national honour and the freedom of Germany; and in such a just cause we may confidently hope for the help of God, as we are already sure of the help of the whole German nation, throughout which there are ever-increasing signs of a glad willingness for the sacrifice; and we may also express our confidence that France will find no allies for a war which she has so wantonly and so unjustly conjured up.

(*Signed*) VON BISMARCK.

APPENDIX

INCLOSURES

MEMORANDUM OF WHAT OCCURRED AT EMS, DRAWN UP AT THE COMMAND AND WITH THE APPROVAL OF THE KING OF PRUSSIA

On the 9th instant, Count Benedetti asked at Ems for an audience by the King, which was at once granted to him. Wherein he required that the King should order the hereditary Prince of Hohenzollern to withdraw his acceptance of the Spanish Crown. The King replied that, as throughout the whole affair he had only been applied to as head of the family, and never as King of Prussia, that as therefore he had given no order for the accepting the candidature for the Throne, neither could he give any order for the retraction. On the 11th, the French Ambassador asked for and obtained a *second* audience, wherein he tried to exert a pressure on the King to the end that he should urge the Prince to renounce the Crown. The King replied, that the Prince was entirely free in his resolutions; moreover, that he himself did not even know where the Prince, who wanted to take an Alpine journey, was at that moment. On the Fountain promenade, in the morning of the 13th, the King gave the Ambassador an extra number of the *Cologne Gazette*, which had been just delivered to himself, with a private telegram from Sigmaringen, on the renunciation of the Prince, the King remarking that he himself had not yet received any letter from Sigmaringen, but might expect one to-day. Count Benedetti mentioned that he had received news of the renunciation from Paris the evening before; and as the King thereupon looked upon the matter as settled, the Ambassador now quite unexpectedly required of the King that he should pronounce a distinct assurance that he *never again* would give his consent if the candidature for the Crown in question should be ever revived. The King decidedly refused such a demand, and kept to that decision, as Count Benedetti repeatedly and ever more urgently returned to his proposition. Nevertheless, after some hours, Count Benedetti sought a *third audience*. On inquiry, what was the subject to be spoken of, he returned answer that he wished to *recur* to that spoken of in the morning. The King refused a fresh audience *on this ground*, as he had no other answer than the one given; moreover, that from thenceforward all negotiations were to go on through the Ministries. Count Benedetti's wish to take leave of the King on his departure was acceded to, as he saluted him at the station on the 14th, in passing on a journey to Coblentz. According to this, therefore, the Ambassador had *three audiences* of the King, which always bore the character of private conversations, as Count Benedetti never conducted himself as a Commissioner or negotiator.

REPORT OF THE ADJUTANT IN ATTENDANCE ON THE KING OF PRUSSIA AT EMS

His Majesty the King, in consequence of a conversation with Count Benedetti on the Fountain promenade, early on the 13th of July, graciously sent me, about 2 in the afternoon, with the following message to the Count: —

His Majesty had received an hour before, by written communication of the Prince of Hohenzollern from Sigmaringen, the full corroboration of what the Count had communicated to him in the morning, as learned direct from Paris, in regard to the renunciation by Prince Leopold of the candidature to the Spanish Throne. His Majesty therewith looks upon this affair as settled.

Count Benedetti said, after I had delivered this message to him, that since his conversation with the King, he had received a fresh despatch from M. de Gramont, in which he was instructed to request an audience of His Majesty, and to submit once more to His Majesty the wish of the French Government: —

"1. To approve the renunciation of the Prince of Hohenzollern; and

"2. To give an assurance that this candidature would not again be taken up, even in the future."

APPENDIX 467

Hereupon His Majesty caused answer to be given to the Count through me, that His Majesty approved the renunciation of Prince Leopold in the same sense and to the same extent as His Majesty had previously done with the acceptance of this candidature. His Majesty had received the written communication of the renunciation from Prince Antony of Hohenzollern, who was authorized thereto by Prince Leopold. In regard to the second point, the assurance for the future, His Majesty could only refer to what he had himself replied to the Count in the morning.

Count Benedetti thankfully accepted this answer of the King's and said he would mention it again to his Government, as he was authorized to do.

But with regard to the second point, he must persist in his request for another conversation with His Majesty, as he was expressly instructed to do so in the last despatch from M. de Gramont, and even if it were only to hear the same words from His Majesty again; the more so as there were fresh arguments in this last despatch which he wished to submit to His Majesty.

Hereupon His Majesty caused answer to be given to the Count through me, for the third time, after dinner, about half-past 5 o'clock, that His Majesty must positively decline to enter into further discussions in regard to this last point (a binding assurance for the future). What he had said in the morning was His Majesty's last word on this matter, and he could do no more than refer to it.

On the assurance that Count Bismarck's arrival at Ems could not be positively depended upon, even for the next day, Count Benedetti declared that he, on his part, would rest content with the declaration of His Majesty the King.

(*Signed*) A. RADZIVILL, Lieutenant-Colonel, and
Adjutant-Major to His Majesty the King.

Ems, July 13, 1870.

APPENDIX I

THE NEGOTIATION AT EMS

M. OLLIVIER admits the unusualness, to say the least, of the step taken by the French government in sending the Ambassador to treat directly with the King of Prussia while he was taking a cure at Ems. See page 107, *supra*. The Duc de Gramont by implication makes a similar admission when, after recapitulating the vain attempt to obtain any sort of satisfaction at Berlin, he says: "It was not, therefore, of our own will, and in contemptuous disregard of diplomatic customs, that our Ambassador appealed to the King of Prussia. He received orders to that effect only on the day when the official channel was with premeditation closed to us." *La France et la Prusse*, p. 57.

We owe to M. de La Gorce a remarkably clear statement of the difficulties of the task imposed upon Benedetti. "Upon the words to be uttered depended the repose of France, perhaps the future of the world. The negotiation began on the very heels of a manifesto which seemed to be the first act of a war, so that it seemed discredited even before it began. The Ambassador would have to handle carefully, at one and the same time, the dignity of the monarch, who was intent upon not making haste, and the feverish ardor of his government, who were urgent to the point of counting the minutes. A twofold danger would arise from the clamorous outcries that were kept up in France, and the deep-seated wrath that was accumulating in Germany. The rank of the sovereign multiplied the perils. The Ambassador must needs be respectful and obstinate at once, must detect the false lights without seeming to have divined them, and fathom the King's purposes while pretending never to have suspected them. A word not well weighed, a demand not clearly defined, or misunderstood, would suffice to put the honor of the crown at stake and to induce an irreparable explosion. The very place where the King was would facilitate his means of evasion: he could at his pleasure pretend that it was his hour for taking the waters or that he needed rest, or he could plead the slowness of the post. . . . The distance from the capital, instead of being a source of embarrassment to William, would be a valuable resource. If pressed too close, he would take refuge behind his ministers, to give himself time for reflection and to give his ministers leisure to await their adversaries' mistakes. From afar M. de Bismarck would watch events, would sharpen his master's sensitiveness, would hold himself in readiness to light the fire for which he had prepared the materials. Everything would be a danger, even the reassuring graciousness, the cordial courtesy of the King. They who knew him best knew that that equanimity of temper, half natural, half assumed, was never at fault, even in the greatest crises. It was, as it were, the misleading sign, which would prolong the sense of security and enable the monarch's servants to work under cover until the moment when the whole affair should be disclosed." La Gorce, vol. vi, pp. 239, 240. See, to the same effect, Sorel, vol. i, pp. 100, 101.

"In my judgment," said Bismarck, "His Majesty while at Ems should have refused every business communication from the French negotiator, who was not on the same footing with him, and should have referred him to the department in Berlin. . . . But His Majesty, however careful in his usual respect for departmental relations, was too fond, not indeed of deciding important questions personally, but, at all events, of discussing them, to make a proper use of the shelter with which the sovereign is purposely surrounded against importunities and inconvenient questionings and demands. That the King, considering the consciousness of his supreme dignity which he possessed in so high a degree, did not withdraw at the very beginning from Benedetti's importunity, was to be attributed for the most part to the influence exercised upon him by the Queen, who was at Coblentz close by." *Reflections*, etc., English translation, vol. ii, pp. 95, 96.

The course of the negotiation at Ems is substantially covered by M. Ollivier in this volume. It probably was foredoomed to failure in any event; for it is hard to see how the war could have been avoided, in view of the attitude of the extreme partisans of the Bonapartist dynasty and of the enemies of the existing government, together with the warlike tone of the Parisian press and the more or less artificial inflammation of public sentiment, on the one side, and of Bismarck's well-established determination on the other. But it is certain that the negotiation had reached such a point on the 12th that the *responsibility* for the inevitable clash — if it was inevitable — might have been avoided by the French government, but for certain matters over which Benedetti had no control.

As we have seen (in Appendix E, *supra*), Benedetti having published, soon after the war, a justification of his conduct in *Ma Mission en Prusse*, in which he made public all the despatches — whether confidential or not — which were exchanged during his stay at Ems between himself and Gramont, the latter, alleging his indignation at this breach of propriety as a pretext, replied, in 1872, with his volume, *La France et la Prusse avant la Guerre*, which he expanded into a vindication of his conduct during his brief service as Minister of Foreign Affairs. In 1895, Benedetti published a second volume, — *Essais Diplomatiques*, — including therein a chapter entitled *Ma Mission à Ems*, which was written, he says, immediately after the appearance of Gramont's book. "I was hesitating, however, about entering upon a discussion that was undesirable for certain reasons, when M. de Gramont's death occurred. Obeying a sentiment which everybody will understand, I thereupon determined to keep the work in my portfolio, reserving the right to publish it if new developments should make it my duty to do so. The contradictory versions which have constantly appeared, both in France and abroad, of my conduct and my acts, on an occasion of such great interest for the history of my time, impel me not to wait until I in my turn shall disappear without having met the reproaches, I might say the accusations, brought against me by the Minister of Foreign Affairs who was my last chief."

In this more elaborate discussion of the negotiation Benedetti devotes himself principally to combating Gramont's repeated assertion that, at the time that the aspect of affairs was entirely changed by the demand of guaranties, he had accomplished absolutely nothing. On his arrival at Ems, Benedetti received an official despatch from his chief, as well as a private letter (*supra*, pp. 140–142). In the former he was instructed to request the King to intervene, "if not by his command, at least by his counsel," and thus put an end to the candidacy. In the private letter he was told that the only reply from the King which would prevent war was this: "The King's government does not approve the Prince of Hohenzollern's acceptance, and *orders* him to abandon his decision made without the King's permission." "I obeyed M. de Gramont's official instructions," says Benedetti, "paying no heed to the suggestions contained in his private letter. I did not ask the King to *order* the Prince to revoke his decision; I asked him to *advise* the Prince to do so."

His audiences of the King on the 9th and the 11th were marked by the utmost courtesy and apparent good feeling on William's part, despite Benedetti's persistence in urging his demands, which were met by the no less persistent refusal of the King to intervene. It became evident, however, that William was willing enough to see the end of the affair, provided that he could avoid compromising his own dignity in the eyes of his people; while stoutly denying that France was justified in taking offence at the candidacy, he nevertheless admitted that he was in communication with the princes and was expecting a definite answer from them, and he urged Benedetti to telegraph to Paris to that effect.

Meanwhile Gramont in Paris was multiplying despatches to the Ambassador, dwelling upon the necessity of haste. In obedience to the request of the Council referred to by M. Ollivier on page 152, Gramont telegraphed: "You cannot imagine the degree to which public opinion is inflamed. It is submerging us on all sides, and we are counting the hours. You must absolutely insist upon obtaining a reply from the King, affirmative or negative. We must have it to-morrow, the next day will be too late." This was sent soon after midnight of the 10th, and at about 6 P.M. of the 11th, he followed it up with the despatch given on page 165, *supra*, to which Benedetti replied, on the morning of the 12th: "I had realized myself that at the point affairs have reached I ought to use stronger language and show myself more pressing. That is what I did yesterday, in a second interview with the King before receiving your last telegrams, as you will see by the report which will reach you to-day. You will be of opinion, I doubt not, that I could not make my language more emphatic without endangering the object of my mission."

"It is important to note," says Benedetti (*Essais Diplomatiques*, p. 361), "that on the morning of the 12th, before he knew of the telegram from Prince Leopold's father to the Spanish Ambassador, before he received M. Werther, before Duvernois's interpellation, M. de Gramont was fully informed of the King's intentions. He knew that he refused absolutely *to promise us* to give orders or advice to Prince Leopold, that he proposed that his nephew's withdrawal should have all the characteristics of a free, individual determination, but that he consented to acquiesce in it by a declaration which he authorized me to transmit to the Imperial government. And M. de Gramont knew that that declaration would be made in a short time.

APPENDIX 473

"Did this arrangement, which satisfied the King in form, and justified us in substance, meet our legitimate demands? Ought we to be content with the withdrawal, supposed to be voluntary, of the Prince with the King's simple acquiescence, or were there imperative considerations which forced us to insist that the King should openly take the initiative by a command or advice to the Prince?

"These questions must have been submitted to the judgment of the Emperor and his ministers. What was their decision? What I can assert is that the first communication that I received on the 12th, *immediately after* the arrival of my report despatched the day before, fully authorized me to believe that the government deemed the solution which I forecasted sufficiently satisfactory."

Here follow two despatches, the first of which is not printed in this volume; in it Gramont reluctantly consents to the delay requested by the King. The second is the one given on pages 204, 205,[1] sent after Gramont had unofficial notice of the Prince's withdrawal.

"What is the inference from these two telegrams?" Benedetti continues. "That, at noon of the 12th, I am no longer instructed to demand of the King that he *forbid* the Prince to persist in his candidacy, or even that he *advise* him to withdraw it. Which goes to prove once more that such was not, as M. de Gramont alleged, the sole object of my mission. It is, on the other hand, a fair inference that they had decided at Paris to accept the withdrawal under the conditions on which it was offered us.

"Moreover, the exact meaning of these telegrams is given us by M. de Gramont himself; this is how he expresses himself on this subject: —

"'Let us suppose that the Prince of Hohenzollern, without a command from the King, without advice from the King, alone, of his own motion, abandons his candidacy, and so

[1] In his later work Benedetti restores the correct text of this despatch. See *supra*, p. 205 n.

informs His Majesty: the King, making himself the direct interpreter of his cousin's spontaneous resolution, might himself announce the withdrawal, with the accompaniment of a few gracious words. The withdrawal, transmitted by the King, would thus become an official act, a Prussian act, and the government would have found therein the shadow of a guaranty which, for love of peace, it would have magnified to the proportions of a satisfactory assurance. . . . It was under the influence of these ideas that the two telegrams following were sent to Comte Benedetti.'" See Gramont, pp. 101, 102.

One can but wonder if the true explanation of Gramont's indignation at the publication of this "very confidential" telegram (*supra*, p. 205 n.) was not that it naturally, almost inevitably, suggests the inference that Benedetti draws from it. (See *supra*, p. 228.) At all events, the King had already agreed to do, and actually did do later, the very thing that Benedetti was therein instructed to use all his skill, "I will even say cunning," to induce him to do. Whether the King's action was already in his mind, or was due to Benedetti's urging, it seems to me that M. Ollivier's general commendation of this part of the negotiation (page 168) does not need to be qualified by stigmatizing the Ambassador's claim to have brought it about as "vain braggadocio."

Then came the demand of guaranties and the fat was in the fire.

M. Ollivier maintains that it was the demand of guaranties which caused the King to determine not to receive Benedetti again,[1] and that the perusal of Werther's report of his interview of the 12th simply intensified his indignation. He elaborates the subject to the same effect, in the *Éclaircissements* to vol. xiv, pp. 598–600. Gramont, on the other hand, attributes the change to the intervention of Bismarck. "It is manifest that Bismarck's language to Lord A. Loftus on the 13th introduced a new phase in the relations between the

[1] A "commemorative stone" marks the spot where they exchanged their last words on the Promenade.

two governments. The ministers of Finance and of the Interior had joined the King, and his attitude was to coincide thenceforth with that assumed at Berlin by the Chancellor. Comte Benedetti is at fault in attributing this change to the unpleasant effect upon the King's mind produced by Baron Werther's report. . . . This individual opinion, admissible up to a certain point if one could put one's hand upon no other cause for the change in question, loses all semblance of probability when one knows the circumstances and details of that interview, and especially when one follows the logical interlocking of the things that happened simultaneously at Berlin and at Ems." Gramont, p. 196.

Benedetti contends with much vigor that Werther's report was the decisive factor, and he complains bitterly of the failure to inform him of the interview to which it related. He declares that, had he been informed of it, he would have been justified in arguing to the King that his own later despatches from Paris, being entirely inconsistent with the suggestion made to Baron Werther, proved that that suggestion had been abandoned and should be disregarded.

But the question seems to me to be entirely an academic one, for I cannot conceive that the effect of Werther's report could have been dissipated by such argument on Benedetti's part. Camphausen and Eulenbourg, representing Bismarck, arrived at the psychological moment, when the King's indignation, aroused by the demand of guaranties, was intensified by Werther's report; and thereafter no adjustment was possible except a complete back-down on the part of France. Declining to accord Benedetti another audience, as he had agreed to do, the King sent his aide-de-camp to him to say that he consented to give his full and unreserved approval[1] to the withdrawal of the Prince; but it was too late.

[1] But Radziwill, the aide-de-camp in question, in his report of the transaction (see Appendix H) declared the King's message to have been that he approved the withdrawal in the same way that he had previously approved the acceptance — that is to say, as head of the family, and not as king.

APPENDIX J

I. THE DUC DE GRAMONT'S CIRCULAR NOTE OF JULY 24 TO THE POWERS

(Printed in *Blue Book*, No. 3, pp. 39, 40)

The Minister for Foreign Affairs has addressed to the Diplomatic Agents of the Emperor the following despatch: —

PARIS, July 24, 1870.

MONSIEUR: —

The Cabinet of Berlin has published, relative to the negotiations at Ems, various documents, in the number of which is a despatch from Baron de Werther, giving an account of a conversation we had together during his last stay in this capital. These papers do not present the veritable aspect of the course pursued by the Emperor's Government under these circumstances, and the Report of M. de Werther especially attributes words to me which I believe my duty requires me to rectify on several points.

The Ambassador of Prussia, in our interview, dwelt particularly on this consideration, that the King, in authorizing the candidature of Prince de Hohenzollern, had never had any intention of wounding the Emperor, and had never supposed that this combination could give umbrage to France. I observed to my interlocutor that if such was the case a similar assurance given would be of a nature to facilitate the accord we were seeking. But I did not ask that the King should write a letter of excuse, as the Berlin journals have pretended in their semi-official commentaries.

APPENDIX 477

Nor can I agree to the observations which the Baron attributes to me on the subject of the declaration of the 6th of July. I did not admit that this manifestation had been determined by Parliamentary necessities. I explained our language by the sharpness of the wound we had received, and I in no way put forward the personal position of the Ministers as the motive determining their conduct. What I said was, that no Cabinet could preserve in France the confidence of the Chambers and public opinion in consenting to an arrangement which did not contain a serious guarantee for the future. I must add, contrary to the recital of M. de Werther, that I made no distinction between the Emperor and France. Nothing in my language could authorize the Representative of Prussia to suppose that a strict solidarity of impressions did not prevail between the Sovereign and the whole nation.

Those reserves made, I arrive at the principal reproach made against us by the Cabinet of Berlin. We are said to have voluntarily opened the discussion with the King of Prussia instead of with his Government. But when on the 4th of July, in accordance with my instructions, our Chargé d'Affaires called upon Count de Thile to speak to him of the news we had received from Spain, what was the language of the Secretary of State? According to his own expression, 'the Prussian Government was completely ignorant of this affair, which did not exist for it.' In presence of the attitude of the Cabinet, which affected to have nothing to do with the incident, and to consider it as solely regarding the Prussian Royal Family, what could we do except apply to the King himself?

It is thus that, against our will, we requested our Ambassador to place himself in communication with the Sovereign instead of treating with his Minister.

I have resided long enough in the Courts of Europe to know how disadvantageous that mode of negotiation is, and all the Cabinets will put faith in my words when I affirm that we only pursued that path because all others were closed to us. We regret that Count de Bismarck, as soon as he was aware of the gravity of the affair, had not gone to Ems to resume his natural position as intermediary between the King and our Ambassador; but are we in reality responsible for the isolation in which His Majesty doubtless desired to remain, and which the Chancellor probably found favourable to his designs? And if, as the Cabinet of Berlin states, the declaration of war remitted by our Chargé d'Affaires constitutes our first written and official communication, whose is the fault? Are notes addressed to Sovereigns? Could our Ambassador so far derogate from customary usages when he was treating with the King, and is not the absence of any document exchanged between the two Governments the necessary consequence of the obligation under which we were placed to pursue the discussion at Ems, instead of continuing it at Berlin, where we had first raised it?

Before closing these rectifications, I must refer to one observation of the Prussian Cabinet. According to a telegram from Berlin, published by the journals of the 23d, MM. de Bismarck and de Thile, contesting a passage in my circular despatch of the 21st of July, declared that "since the day they heard of the offer addressed to the Prince de Hohenzollern, the question of that candidature to the Throne of Spain had never been the subject of the least conversation, either official or private, between themselves and M. Benedetti." In the form in which it is produced, this affirmation is ambiguous; it seems to refer solely to the relations of our Ambassador with the Prussian Ministry, posterior to the acceptance of Prince Leopold. In that sense, it would not be contrary to what we have ourselves said; but if it is extended to anterior communications, it ceases to be true, and to establish that fact I cannot do better than cite here a despatch dated the 21st of March, 1869, addressed by Count Benedetti to the Marquis de Lavalette, then Minister of Foreign Affairs.

APPENDIX

It is thus conceived: —

"BERLIN, March 31, 1869.

"M. LE MARQUIS,

"Your Excellency requested me by telegraph yesterday to assure myself whether the candidature of the Prince de Hohenzollern to the Throne of Spain had a serious character. I had occasion this morning to see M. de Thile, and I asked him if I was to attach any importance to the rumours in circulation on this subject. I did not conceal from him that I was anxious to be exactly informed, remarking that such an eventuality was of too direct interest to the Emperor's Government for my duty not to compel me to point out the danger if any reason existed to believe that the project might be realized. I made him aware that I intended to communicate our conversation to you.

"M. de Thile gave me the most formal assurance that he had not at any moment been aware of any indication whatever which could authorize such a conjecture, and that the Spanish Minister at Vienna, during the stay he made in Berlin, had not ever made any allusion to the subject. The Under-Secretary of State, in thus expressing himself, and without anything I said being of a nature to induce such a manifestation, believed himself called upon to pledge his word of honour.

"According to him, M. Rances had confined himself to talking to Count de Bismarck — who perhaps was anxious to take advantage of the passage of this diplomatist to obtain some information on the state of things in Spain — of the manner in which affairs were advancing in what concerned the choice of the future Sovereign.

"That in substance, is what M. de Thile stated to me, several times repeating his first declaration, that there was not, and could not be, a question of the Prince de Hohenzollern for the Crown of Spain.

"Accept, etc.,
"BENEDETTI."

After this quotation I believe I have no occasion to enter into any further explanations on a point we must consider as definitely established.

GRAMONT.

II. BARON WERTHER'S REPORT OF HIS CONVERSATION WITH GRAMONT ON JULY 12

PARIS, July 12, 1870.

I arrived at Paris this morning, soon after ten, accompanied by a messenger from Count Benedetti, Baron de Bourqueney. The Duc de Gramont at once sent his secretary, Count de Faverney, to me to ask if I could call upon the minister. I replied that I was ready to do so, and I was received by the Duc de Gramont with his customary affability, as one would expect between two old acquaintances. Before reporting our interview, I will say that it was interrupted by the arrival of the Spanish Ambassador, who had an official communication to present. This consisted of a telegram from Prince Antony of Hohenzollern (the father), in which he announced that his son, the hereditary prince, in view of the complications caused by his candidacy, renounced the throne of Spain, and had advised Marshal Prim directly of his decision.

Our interview, begun by the Duc de Gramont, turned principally upon the subject brought up by M. Benedetti: namely, that His Royal Majesty, by his authorization of the Hohenzollern candidacy without having first entered into any understanding thereon with the imperial French government, had not realized that he had thereby offended France.

He asked me if that were really the fact. I explained to him that His Royal Majesty could not officially have refused such authorization, when the Prince of Hohenzollern felt disposed to accept the crown proffered him, and that, having regard to the relations of the Prince's family with the Emperor, His Majesty could not have thought that that candidacy would be ill-received in France.

APPENDIX 481

The Duc de Gramont cited the cases of the Duc de Nemours and the throne of Belgium, and of Prince Alfred and the throne of Greece, as cases in which a similar authorization had been refused. I denied all analogy with the present case.

The Duc de Gramont went on to say that France, as Spain's nearest neighbor, must be interested in the occupancy of the throne of that country. The secrecy in which the negotiations concerning the Hohenzollern candidacy had been shrouded could not fail to give great offence here, especially as the court of the Tuileries had constantly shown the greatest consideration for our government in all political questions. Such conduct had deeply wounded the public mind in France and one found the expression of that feeling in the attitude of the Chamber, which was, unfortunately, now in session — which fact aggravated the situation.

The Duc de Gramont added that he regarded the withdrawal of the Prince of Hohenzollern as a secondary matter, for the French government would never have permitted his installation; but he feared that, by reason of our conduct, there might be a permanent misunderstanding between our two countries. This germ must be destroyed, and to that end we must take as our starting point that in our actions toward France we had not used friendly methods, which fact had been recognized, to his knowledge, by all the great powers.

In all sincerity, he did not desire war, but cordial and friendly relations with Prussia, and he knew that I was aiming at the same result; we ought therefore to work together to find out whether there was any way of exerting a soothing influence in that direction, and he submitted to my judgment the question whether the true expedient would not lie in a letter from the King to the Emperor. He appealed to His Royal Majesty's heart, and he would give his just consent.

It would be simply a matter of saying in the letter that His Royal Majesty, in deigning to authorize Prince Leopold of Hohenzollern to accept the crown of Spain, had not intended to impair the interests or the dignity of the French nation; that the King associated himself with the Prince's withdrawal, and that he did so with the desire and the hope of seeing every subject of disagreement between our two governments vanish therewith. Such were the words, destined to bring about the tranquillizing of public feeling, which the letter in question should contain; but there must be no mention, observed M. de Gramont, of [Prince Leopold's] relationship to the Emperor. That argument would be particularly offensive here.

I directed the Duc de Gramont's attention to the fact that such a proceeding would be made extremely difficult by the remarks made by him in the Chamber on the 6th instant: they contained declarations which might well have wounded the King very deeply. The Duc de Gramont sought to combat this argument by reminding me that Prussia had not been named at all, and that his speech was absolutely necessary at that moment, to pacify the extraordinary excitement of the Chamber.

At this moment the Minister of Justice, M. Émile Ollivier, joined in our interview, the subject of which the Duc de Gramont made known to him. M. Émile Ollivier maintained most urgently the salutary necessity of acting in the interest of peace, and earnestly begged me to submit to His Majesty the King the idea of a letter to that effect. They both said that if I felt that I could not undertake it, they should find themselves compelled to instruct Count Benedetti to raise the question. The two ministers, while dwelling upon the point that they required some arrangement of this sort to calm the public agitation, having regard to their ministerial situation, added that such a letter would authorize them to come forward in defence of His Majesty the King against the attacks which would inevitably be made upon him.

Finally they both informed me that they could not conceal from me that our conduct in the Spanish-Hohenzollern affair had excited the French nation much more than it had affected the Emperor.

In our conversation the Duc de Gramont made this remark: that he believed that the Prince had withdrawn under pressure from His Majesty the King. I contradicted this idea, and asserted that the withdrawal unquestionably emanated from the Prince on his own initiative.

In their intense desire to hasten matters, the ministers wished me to report this interview by telegraph, but I did not consider it necessary.

WERTHER.

APPENDIX K

THE EMS DESPATCH

TELEGRAMS had been exchanged between the King and Bismarck on the subject of the Werther report. In reply to the King's request for his opinion as to the letter to be written by him, Bismarck had telegraphed: "It is impossible to sign it."[1] So that there is nothing strange in the silence thereon of Abeken's despatch to Bismarck, dated at Ems, July 13, 3.50 P.M. The Chancellor's purpose in handling the despatch as he did was disclosed by himself with his usual cynicism twenty years later, and is made clear enough in the text of this volume. According to the version read by von Caprivi in the Reichstag, on November 23, 1892, Abeken telegraphed: —

"Seine Mäjestät der König schreibt mir: 'Graf Benedetti fing mich auf der Promenade ab, um auf zuletzt sehr zudringliche Art von mir zu verlangen, ich sollte ihn autorisiren, sofort zu telegraphiren, das ich für alle Zukunft mich verpflichte, niemals wieder meine Zustimmung zu geben wenn die Hohenzollern auf ihre Kandidatur zurückkämen. Ich wies ihn zuletzt etwas ernst zurück, da man *à tout jamais* dergleichen Engagements nicht nehmen dürfe noch könne. Naturlich sagte ich ihm, das ich noch nichts erhalten hätte, und das er über Paris und Madrid früher benachrichtigt sei als ich, er wohl einsähe, das mein gouvernement wiederum ausser Spiel sei.'

"Seine Majestät hat seitdem ein Schreiben des Fürsten

---

[1] Interview with Bismarck, printed in the *Neue Freie Presse* of Vienna, November 20, 1892, three days before Count von Caprivi's address to the Reichstag concerning the Ems despatch.

APPENDIX 485

bekommen. Da Seine Majestät dem Grafen Benedetti besagt das er Nachricht von Fürsten erwarte, hat Allerhöchstderselbe, mit Rücksicht auf die obige Zumutung, auf des Grafen Eulenburg und meinen Vortrag, beschlossen, den Grafen Benedetti nicht mehr zu empfangen, sondern ihm nur durch einen Adjudanten sagen zu lassen: das Seine Majestät jetzt von Fürsten die Bestätigung der Nachricht erhalten, die Benedetti aus Paris schön gehabt, und dem Bostschafter nichts weiter zu sagen habe.

"Seine Majestät stellt Eurer Excellenz anheim ob nicht die neue Forderung Benedetti's, und ihre Zurückweisung sogleich sowohl unseren Gefandten als in der Presse mitgetheilt werden sollte."

In his interview in the *Neue Freie Presse*, Bismarck interpreted the last paragraph thus: "I was authorized to make such erasures as seemed to me necessary. It was left to my discretion to publish the despatch *in extenso* or by extracts. I have never regretted that I did the latter." In the course of a long and exhaustive discussion of the subject, M. Welschinger says: "Now, the paragraph as written by Abeken gave no such authorization. It simply left Bismarck at liberty to communicate to the German embassies and the newspapers Benedetti's latest demand and the King's refusal, without a word as to extracts. . . . It was not concerned with the refusal to receive the Ambassador, but simply with the refusal to accede to the demand of guaranties. He should therefore have published the despatch as it was, and then people would have learned that Benedetti had addressed the King on the promenade, to ask his authority to telegraph that he would undertake not to give his approval if the Hohenzollerns should ever renew the candidacy. And they would have learned, at the same time with the King's refusal, of his declaration that he considered that his government was out of the game, by reason of the Prince's withdrawal. In this part of the despatch, it will be seen, there was nothing brutal or particularly offensive."

He proceeds to argue that the second paragraph of the despatch is a commentary of Abeken and Eulenbourg on the King's own message contained in the first paragraph, but that their commentary was inaccurate. "The despatch was sent at 3.50 P.M., and two things had happened meanwhile since the interview between the King and Benedetti in the forenoon," namely, the King's announcements through his aide-de-camp to Benedetti that, the Prince having withdrawn, he considered the affair as concluded, and that he fully approved the withdrawal. "Abeken and Eulenbourg did not mention these two important facts . . . although they knew of them at 3.50, and still they left it to Bismarck to decide whether Benedetti's new demand and the King's refusal should be communicated to the Prussian ministers and the press. It is more than doubtful whether the King gave that authorization, for he would thereby infallibly provoke a rupture and place himself in disagreement with himself. In truth, how could he have written to the Queen on the 14th that he proposed to transfer the negotiations to Berlin? And how could he have said to Benedetti when he received him the same day at the railway station, that 'the negotiations which remained to be carried on would be conducted by his government?' . . . And there is his letter to the Queen of the 17th: 'The anecdote that is going about of a Prussian circular which provoked the declaration of war is outrageous, for such a circular never existed. It is wretched to lie so!' It is evident, therefore, that the sophistication resorted to by the Chancellor at the last moment was concealed from the King.

"But why did Bismarck act thus? Because the terms of the despatch dictated by the King, although silent as to the Prince's withdrawal and the assurance that the affair was settled, seemed to him weak and colorless. In the sentence: 'He could see that my government was out of the game,' the Chancellor saw a sort of apology. . . . In short, the despatch from Ems confined itself to saying that the King

APPENDIX 487

did not choose to receive the Ambassador again because he had nothing to add to the reply he had given him in the morning. To the Chancellor's mind that was neither short enough nor sharp enough. And so, seizing upon the permission given him by Abeken, to decide whether he should communicate to the German ambassadors and newspapers the demand of guaranties and the King's refusal, he does it in these few incisive words: 'His Majesty refused to receive the French Ambassador again, and sent the aide-de-camp on duty to say that His Majesty had nothing more to communicate to him.'"

Bismarck's "edition" of the despatch reads as follows: — "EMS, *Juli* 13, 1870: — Nach dem die Nachrichten von der Entsagung der Erbprinzen von Hohenzollern der Kaiserlich französischen Regierung von der Königlich spanischen amtlich mit getheilt worden sind, hat der französischen Botschafter in Ems an Seine Majestät nach die Forderung gestellt, ihn zu autorisiren, das er nach Paris telegraphiere, das Seine Majestät der König sich für alle Zükunft verpflichte, niemals wieder seine Zustimmung zu geben, wenn die Hohenzollern auf ihre Kandidatur wieder zurückkommen sollten. Seine Majestät der König hat es darauf abgelehnt, den französischen Botschafter nochmals zu empfangen und demselben durch den Adjudanten von Dienst sagen lassen, das Seine Majestät dem Botschafter nichts weiter mitzutheilen habe."

If space permitted it would be interesting to follow M. Welschinger's demonstration of Bismarck's recklessness of statement as shown in his previously quoted interview in the *Neue Freie Presse*, where he so described his handling of the despatch as to make it perfectly clear that he was talking about Radziwill's report of the occurrences of the 14th (printed as a part of Bismarck's Circular Note in Appendix H) instead of Abeken's despatch. In his *Reflections and Reminiscences* (English translation, vol. ii, p. 101), he says: "I made use of the royal authorization communicated to me

488 THE FRANCO-PRUSSIAN WAR

through Abeken, to publish the contents of the telegram; and in the presence of my two guests I reduced the telegram by striking out words, but without adding or altering. . . . The difference in the effect of the abbreviated text of the Ems telegram, as compared with that produced by the original, was not the result of stronger words, but of the form, which made this announcement appear decisive, while Abeken's version would only have been regarded as a fragment of a negotiation still pending, and to be continued at Berlin."

In a footnote to his *Political History of Europe* (Macvane's edition, p. 810), M. Seignobos says: "Bismarck having boasted later of having modified the terms of the note to make war inevitable, the German socialists reproached him with having *falsified* the Ems despatch; and the French press has repeated this accusation. It is enough to compare the two texts to show that there was no falsification. The despatch sent to Bismarck by Abeken in the King's name is in a confidential and obscure form, not suitable for publication, and ends thus: 'His Majesty leaves it to your Excellency,' etc. The note published by Bismarck adds nothing which is not in the despatch; it simply abbreviates it."

The suggestion that it was simply the German socialists who discovered a "falsification" of the original despatch in Bismarck's version, is sufficiently disproved by the extracts from German historians, given by M. Ollivier, all of whom, as he says, extol Bismarck for that falsification. The further suggestion, that in France only the press have repeated the charge, needs no refutation from any one who has glanced into any of the histories of the period. See, for example, La Gorce, vol. vi, p. 283.

In his *History of Twenty-Five Years*, vol. ii, p. 491, Sir Spencer Walpole says: Bismarck "saw that if he published it (the King's telegram) as it was received, it would create neither enthusiasm in Germany, nor resentment in France. But he saw also that by compressing the sentences he could create the impression that the King had met the demand of

APPENDIX 489

France by declining to see the French Ambassador, and had communicated the decision, *in a manner that was discourteous or even offensive*, through one of his aides-de-camp. In other words he saw that he could convert an innocuous piece of paper into what he himself called a red rag for the Gallic bull. He saw that he could produce a war which even at the eleventh hour might otherwise have been avoided."

To make it appear to his own countrymen that the French Ambassador had made an unreasonable demand, and to the French people that their representative had been insulted — that such was Bismarck's purpose there can be no possible question, nor that, in order to give that impression, it was essential to "denature" Abeken's despatch by some means. For, as Benedetti was never tired of saying, "at Ems there was neither insulter nor insulted." "I received no insult at Ems," he told the Commission of Inquiry concerning the 4th of September, "and my correspondence shows that I never complained of any ill-treatment." And he quotes the King as saying several years later: "M. Benedetti did his duty properly — that is all." (*Essais Diplomatiques*, pp. 20, 391.) "At Ems," says Sorel (vol. i, p. 160), "the King did not seem to suspect that M. Benedetti had failed in proper respect to him, nor did M. Benedetti suspect that the King had insulted France in his person." But "at Berlin no one doubted that the French Ambassador had insulted the King, just as, at Paris the next day, no one doubted that the King had insulted the French Ambassador. From this double-barrelled imposture sprang the twofold wrath which impelled two peoples, equally deceived, against each other." La Gorce, vol. vi, p. 284.

It is strange, to say no more, that it occurred to no member of the Council to interrogate Benedetti, in the light of this despatch. It seems to have been taken for granted that the bald statement contained therein was true. It is clear, however, from Gramont's own statements to Lyons, as reported by him to Lord Granville on the 15th, that he was not misled. "Nor indeed had the King really treated Benedetti with the rough discourtesy which had been boasted of by the Prussian Government. But that Government had now chosen to declare to Germany and to Europe that France had been affronted in the person of her Ambassador. *It was the boast which was the* gravamen of the offence. It constituted an insult which no nation of any spirit could brook." *Blue Book*, p. 40. So that, in Gramont's eyes, the insult consisted in the false pretence that there had been an insult. But this clearly was not the view of most of his colleagues, and, above all, not of the members of the Commission appointed by the Chamber to pass upon the government's proposed war legislation. As to the failure of the Commission to hear Benedetti, see Sorel, vol. i, p. 186; La Gorce, vol. vi, pp. 308, 309.

APPENDIX L

INTERVIEW BETWEEN COUNT BISMARCK AND LORD A. LOFTUS, BRITISH AMBASSADOR

(Reported by Loftus to Lord Granville. *Blue Book*, pp. 32, 33)

BERLIN, July 13, 1870.

I HAD an interview with Count Bismarck to-day, and congratulated his Excellency on the apparent solution of the impending crisis by the spontaneous renunciation of the Prince of Hohenzollern.

His Excellency appeared somewhat doubtful as to whether this solution would prove a settlement of the difference with France. He told me that the extreme moderation evinced by the King of Prussia under the menacing tone of the French Government, and the courteous reception by His Majesty of Count Benedetti at Ems, after the severe language held to Prussia, both officially and in the French press, was producing throughout Prussia general indignation.

He had that morning, he said, received telegrams from Bremen, Königsberg, and other places, expressing strong disapprobation of the conciliatory course pursued by the King of Prussia at Ems, and requiring that the honour of the country should not be sacrificed.

Count Bismarck then expressed a wish that Her Majesty's Government should take some opportunity, possibly by a declaration in Parliament, of expressing their satisfaction at the solution of the Spanish difficulty by the spontaneous act of Prince Leopold, and of bearing public testimony to the calm and wise moderation of the King of Prussia, his Government, and of the public press.

His Excellency adverted to the declaration made by the Duc de Gramont to the Corps Législatif, "that the Powers of Europe had recognized the just grounds of France in the demand addressed to the Prussian Government"; and he was, therefore, anxious that some public testimony should be given that the Powers who had used their *bons offices* to urge on the Prussian Government a renunciation by Prince Leopold, should likewise express their appreciation of the peaceful and conciliatory disposition manifested by the King of Prussia.

Count Bismarck then observed that intelligence had been received from Paris (though not officially from Baron Werther) that the solution of the Spanish difficulty would not suffice to content the French Government, and that other claims would be advanced. If such be the case, said his Excellency, it was evident that the question of the succession to the Spanish Throne was but a mere pretext, and that the real object of France was to seek a revenge for Königgrätz [Sadowa].

The feeling of the German nation, said his Excellency, was that they were fully equal to cope with France, and they were equally as confident as the French might be of military success. The feeling, therefore, in Prussia and in Germany was that they should accept no humiliation or insult from France, and that if unjustly provoked they should accept the combat.

"But," said his Excellency, "we do not wish for war, and we have proved, and shall continue to prove, our peaceful disposition; at the same time we cannot allow the French to have the start of us as regards armaments. I have," said his Excellency, "positive information that military preparations have been made, and are making, in France for war. Large stores of munitions are being concentrated, large purchases of hay, and other materials necessary for a campaign, are making; and horses are being collected. If these continue," said his Excellency, "we shall be obliged to ask

APPENDIX 493

the French Government for explanations as to their object and meaning.

"After what has now occurred we must require some assurance, some guarantee, that we may not be subjected to a sudden attack; we must know that this Spanish difficulty once removed, there are no other lurking designs which may burst upon us like a thunderstorm."

Count Bismarck further stated that unless some assurance, some declaration, were given by France to the European Powers, or in some official form, that the present solution of the Spanish question was a final and satisfactory settlement of the French demands, and that no further claims were to be raised; and if, further, a withdrawal, or a satisfactory explanation of the menacing language held by the Duc de Gramont were not made, the Prussian Government would be obliged to seek explanations from France. It was impossible, added his Excellency, that Prussia could tamely and quietly sit under the affront offered to the King and to the nation by the menacing language of the French Government. "I could not," said his Excellency, "hold communication with the French Ambassador after the language held to Prussia by the French Minister for Foreign Affairs in the face of Europe."

From the foregoing observations of Count Bismarck, your Lordship will perceive that unless some timely counsel, some friendly hand, can intervene to appease the irritation between the two Governments, the breach, in lieu of being closed by the solution of the Spanish difficulty, is likely to become wider.

It is evident to me that Count Bismarck and the Prussian Ministry regret the attitude and disposition of the King towards Count Benedetti, and that in the view of the public opinion of Germany they feel the necessity of some decided measures to safeguard the honour of the nation.

The only means which could pacify the wounded pride of the German nation and restore confidence in the maintenance of peace would be by a declaration of the French Government that the incident of the Spanish difficulty has been satisfactorily adjusted, and in rendering justice to the moderate and peaceful disposition of the King of Prussia and his Government, that the good relations existing between the two States were not likely to be again exposed to any disturbing influences. I greatly fear that if no mediating influences can be successfully brought to bear on the French Government to appease the irritation against Prussia, and to counsel moderation, war will be inevitable.

APPENDIX M

THE COMMISSION OF JULY 15 AND THE EMS CORRESPONDENCE

THE Commission chosen by the Corps Législatif on July 15 to examine and report upon the four war measures proposed by the government reported unanimously in favor of all four. *Supra*, pp. 356–358.

The Commission, in its report, said in part: —

"Certain diplomatic documents were laid before us, and very clear and full explanations concerning them were supplied to us.

"We knew that we should carry out the wish of the Chamber in making careful inquiry into all the diplomatic incidents. We have the satisfaction of informing you, messieurs, that the government, from the outset of the affair, and *from the first phase of the negotiations to the last*, has followed steadfastly the same end.

"Thus, *the first despatch sent to our Ambassador after his arrival at Ems* to talk with the King of Prussia, concludes with this sentence, which indicates that the government had clearly set forth its justifiable demand: —

"'That this withdrawal of Prince Antony may produce its effect, it is necessary that the King of Prussia shall associate himself with it, and give us the assurance that he will not again sanction that candidacy.'

"Thus, what continued to be the only point in dispute in that momentous discussion, was formulated at the very beginning, and you will realize the vital importance of this fact which has hitherto been unknown, it should be said, to the public.

"But, just as his Majesty the King of Prussia had already

refused to give the satisfaction justly demanded by the French government, which expected the best results from the unofficial courtesy of the Prussian Ambassador, who left Paris in order to smooth over the difficulty, so the French Ambassador, having intervened directly with King William, had done no more than obtain the confirmation of a fact which gave no guaranty for the future.

"Despite these facts, which are only too serious, your Commission thought it well to require, and has received, communication of the despatches from several of our diplomatic agents, the terms of which are identical and confirm, as has been stated to the Senate and Corps Législatif, what M. de Bismarck has officially made known to the Cabinets of Europe: that His Majesty the King of Prussia had refused to receive again the French Ambassador, and had sent word to him, by one of his aides-de-camp, that he had no further communication to make to him. . . .

"The profound conviction produced by examining these documents is that France could not brook the insult put upon the nation; that our diplomatists did their duty in confining their just demands to a field where Prussia could not escape, as she intended and hoped to do."

It is to be borne in mind in this connection that with the exception of the portion of one despatch quoted in this report, and of such of the other despatches, all later than the 12th, as were read by M. Ollivier to the Chamber on the 15th, the details of the negotiation at Ems were not publicly known until Benedetti printed all the despatches in *Ma Mission en Prusse*, in 1871. Not long after, came the sessions of the Commission of Inquiry concerning the 4th of September, and the testimony, among many others, of some if not all of the members of the Commission of July 15, — of Dréolle and Talhouët, at least.

As to the telegram sent broadcast by Bismarck's orders on the night of the 13th, it is unnecessary to say anything more than is said in the text and notes. Whoever cares to read

APPENDIX 497

a detailed report of the session of the Chamber of the 15th, as printed in almost any one of the historical works cited in the notes, will find that this telegram was the main subject of controversy both before and after the report of the Commission. We have seen that Jules Favre denied in 1871 that such a telegram existed, except by way of information to the different states of Germany (*supra*, p. 354 n., on p. 355). It may be of interest to add that M. Thiers chose to give the weight of his authority to a similar assertion. He had undertaken a mission to England and Russia at the request of the Government of National Defence, organized on the 4th of September. On September 13, he wrote from London to Jules Favre, Foreign Minister under that government, giving an account of his first interview with Lord Granville. "At first I took pains to prove, by a truthful recital of the events which brought on the war, that France did not desire the war, that the Chamber itself did not desire it and had yielded only to the pressure of those in power, always irresistible with the Chamber, and that notably on the last day, July 15, it had allowed itself to be swept off its feet only by the most culpable falsehood of an insult put upon France."

The despatch of which a portion is quoted in the report (see *supra*, pp. 218, 219) begins thus: "We have received by the hand of the Spanish Ambassador the withdrawal by Prince Antony, in the name of his son Leopold, of the latter's candidacy for the throne of Spain." And there are certain differences in the portions quoted, viz.: the original reads: "In order that this withdrawal may have its *full* effect, it *seems* necessary," etc. Furthermore, this despatch is of the 12th, and was, as we know, very far from being the first one sent to Ems.

It seems worth while to consider the allegations of wilful misrepresentation by Gramont to the Commission as evidenced by its statement of the grounds on which it based its conclusion that the only point in dispute (that is, the question of guaranties) was clearly formulated at the outset, and that the government "from the first phase of the negotiations to the last" had followed steadfastly the same end. The charge is supported by the authority of Albert Sorel in his *Histoire Diplomatique de la Guerre Franco-Allemande* (vol. i, p. 189), published in 1875, and has very recently (1910) been reasserted with the utmost solemnity by M. Welschinger, the latest historian of the war, who adduces the testimony at the Inquiry concerning the 4th of September of the Marquis de Talhouët, to the effect that the Commission of July 15 understood that guaranties had been demanded from the first day. *Guerre de 1870*, vol. i, pp. 184 ff.

In dealing with this charge, M. de Gramont first of all maintains the accuracy of the Commission's finding that his efforts had, from the outset, followed consistently the same end, that end being, in his own words, "to obtain, by means of the King's participation and concurrence in the withdrawal of the Hohenzollern candidacy, a sufficient guaranty against the return of similar complications." See *supra*, p. 226 n. Coming to the question of the misstatement of fact in the report, he says: —

"By a material error, which however, as I have just proved, in no wise invalidates the statement of the report, the despatch of July 12 was cited therein as being the first despatch sent to Ems at the opening of the negotiations. . . . This has aroused the heated, retrospective polemic, the refutation of which forces us to go into these details.

"This error, as I have already said, is to be explained in fact by the unwonted rapidity with which it was necessary to assemble, proceed to hear the ministers, deliberate, and draw the report in accordance with the deliberation and conclusions — all in a few moments. Nevertheless, instead of attributing it to that perfectly natural cause, some persons have preferred to accuse the government of having tried to deceive the Commission.

"The report, they say, would not have originated the confusion, and if it cited the despatch of the 12th as the first

APPENDIX 499

one sent to Ems, it was because the ministers did not produce those that preceded it; and, in order that the fraud might not be detected, they antedated the despatch of the 12th and presented it to the Commission as dated the 7th or 8th — that is to say, as the first one sent to Ems.

"It would, in very truth, have been difficult to do otherwise, for everybody knew that our Ambassador had arrived at Ems on the 8th in the evening, and it could not be conceived that he had been left there four days without instructions, which would have been the case if the government's first despatch had borne the date of the 12th. . . .

"But let us see. The despatch of July 12 has this peculiar characteristic, that it is not possible to antedate it since its date is fixed precisely in the text of the document itself. For we find therein these words: 'In order that this withdrawal may produce its effect, it is necessary that the King associate himself with it,' etc. Not only does it speak of the withdrawal of the Prince of Hohenzollern as an accomplished fact . . . but it points out what is necessary in order that it may produce its effect. Now, inasmuch as the Prince's withdrawal was not known until the 12th, at 2.40 A.M., it is impossible that the despatch was written earlier, and its date is automatically fixed as the evening of the 12th. . . .

"This once proved, it seems superfluous to add that the ministers could no more easily have concealed from the Commission the despatches preceding that of the 12th. Would the Commission have believed that Comte Benedetti was left without instructions from the 8th to the 12th? Furthermore, does not the government's communication to the Chamber a few hours earlier speak of the negotiations prior to the 12th, of representations to the King before that date? How could our Ambassador have done all this without despatches and instructions? . . .

"In the report of the Senate Commission, we read: 'The Minister of Foreign Affairs came before the Commission. He set forth at length, reading all the important despatches, the progress of the negotiations entered into at Ems, from July 6, with the King of Prussia.' Thus, on the one hand, the government laid before the Commission of the Senate all the important despatches from the beginning, and on the other hand it concealed from the Commission of the Corps Législatif the same documents down to that of the 12th. But we should have had also to prevent senators from talking with deputies, and above all, to prevent the publication of the report made to the Senate.

"When I reached the Corps Législatif during the night session of July 15, the report of the Commission had already been read, and I had no knowledge of it until 1 read it the next day in the *Journal Officiel*. Otherwise I should not have failed to call the honorable reporter's attention to an error, trivial in itself, which it would have been so easy to correct in an instant."[1] *La France et la Prusse*, pp. 264 ff.

M. Ollivier, in the fourteenth volume of *L'Empire Libéral* (pp. 452 ff.) goes into this subject at length. He gives some new facts concerning the testimony before the Commission, in support of his contention that the error in the report must have been a mere slip of the pen; facts which, uncontrolled, seem conclusive. He says, in the first place, that all the documents presented by Gramont were carefully arranged in the order of their dates, and that he read and explained the principal ones.

"No objection was raised except upon a single point. Albuféra had been impressed by the argument of the opposition that our demands had constantly increased with the concessions that had been made to us. He questioned Gramont closely. Gramont replied that on July 12, after the withdrawal of the candidacy was announced by Olozaga, when we had as yet obtained no concession from Prussia, not even a reply, he had *instantly* demanded, *at one and the same time*, both the King's approval and the guaranty for

[1] M. de Talhouët testified at the Inquiry concerning the 4th of September that Gramont was sitting in front of him when he read the report.

the future, and not, as the Left claimed, first the approval, then the guaranty. 'I understand then,' said Albuféra, 'that as soon as the withdrawal had been secured, you did immediately, at the very first moment, demand both concessions at once?' 'Yes,' Gramont replied. And he read and placed in Albuféra's hands the telegram to Benedetti of 7 o'clock of the 12th, which did in fact cover both demands. 'I am very glad to hear that statement,' said Albuféra; 'the report will surely take note of it, for it is of a nature to dissipate many misunderstandings.'"

M. Ollivier then repeats, without other comment than that it seemed to impress the Commission, Gramont's argument that the object of the negotiations had never varied. We know that he was not of that opinion.

In discussing the manifest error of fact in the report he follows the line of argument adopted by Gramont: that the despatch bore within itself the proof that it could not have been the first one addressed to Benedetti, and, moreover, that the error was corrected by the ministerial statements in their formal declaration read in both houses earlier in the day. He concludes his discussion with the following characteristic passage.

"When the war was at an end, there was a grand rush to deny all participation in the acts that had brought it to pass. The Bonapartist party, under their old leaders, adopted the plan of casting all the responsibility on the liberal ministry, which they denounced as the real artisan of our disasters. Dréolle[1] was one of the leaders of the campaign. He exhumed as a fresh argument the inaccuracy in the report of July 15, which everybody had forgotten: reversing the rôles, he charged to Gramont the error committed by himself, and characterized that harmless and involuntary error as being premeditated and of exceptional gravity. 'It was with full knowledge,' he said, 'that Gramont suppressed some portions of the despatch and put it back to the 7th, and, as it was upon that antedated and altered despatch that the war was

[1] A member of the Commission.

begun,[1] Gramont deceived the Commission and through it the Chamber and the country.'

"The authority of a Dréolle would not have given sufficient credit to the fable; he must needs obtain Talhouët's assent. If the real Talhouët had still been in existence, he would not have succeeded, but the poor fellow, stricken in the brain, inconsolable under the deadly burden which his report had imposed upon him, was only the shadow of his former self. When Dréolle went to him to tell him that there was a way to exonerate himself, he seized upon it without any scrutiny, and in his sudden sense of relief began to say to everybody: 'Did you know, the despatch was altered, the despatch was altered!'

"On a single point Dréolle could not move him. The important thing to that villain was, not to incriminate Gramont, who, after all, belonged to the absolutist régime, but to reach me, who was as ever the immovable personification of the régime that he detested. He declared, although he knew the contrary, that I was present (before the Commission) during Gramont's explanations. Thereupon the gallant man and true friend reawoke in Talhouët, and in his disposition he said that I had retired before my colleague arrived. . . .

"Dréolle's invention achieved a rapid success with the enemies of the Empire. . . .

"I had in my hands the text given to the Commission both before and after it was so given, and I declare that it bore its date at its head and that it agreed in every respect with the text published by Gramont and Benedetti in their books, and with the one preserved at the Foreign Office. Gramont would have been an idiot, not a rascal, if he had played a trick before the Commission which we had ourselves unmasked in the Senate and Corps Législatif, and which the text of the despatch, altered or not, put to confusion. . . .

"Every calumny *crescit eundo*. Ere long it was neither Gramont nor Émile Ollivier who had deceived the Com-

---

[1] This particular charge was made also by Gambetta.

APPENDIX 503

mission and the Chamber, and, through the Chamber, the country — it was the Cabinet. At this point we approach the monstrous. Here we have a dozen men, almost all eminent in some way, having held first rank, either in the army or navy, or at the bar, or in trade, or in finance, or in diplomacy; they were not ambitious of power; it was in some sense forced upon them by public opinion; they exercised it not without success and with devotion; and behold, scribblers who have never given any proof of capacity of any sort, having neither commanded a division nor even drafted a despatch, — alleged historians, forsooth, without competence or authority, — presume to pass judgment helter-skelter, without taking the pains, or without the intelligence to understand! Nor do they stop there: they accuse honorable men of having altered documents in order to win votes! That is too much! All the ministers were of pacific bent; they stood out as long as they could amid the public passion, in order to prevent war; they were compelled to decide upon it because they thought their country's honor wounded; they would have pressed the members of the Commission to their hearts if they had shown them that their sensibility was overdone, and that the Ems despatch was an amenity which we could afford to brook. And those men would have held back or altered documents in order to assure the triumph of an opinion which they would have been overjoyed to abandon, though their fall should follow instantly!

"Often, very often, I have felt indignation rumbling in my heart. How many times I have stricken out angry sentences as soon as I had written them, in order that this work should retain its character of mathematical clearness! But now I no longer contain myself, and I say to those who assert or insinuate that all or any of us deceived the Commission by a trick, in order to assure its vote and as a consequence that of the Chamber: 'You are cowardly impostors in whom I do not know which to detest more, your weakness of judgment or the perversity of your conscience.'"

There is no question, however, that some persons were deceived by the error. M. Fernand Giraudeau, for instance, in his *La Vérité sur la Campagne de 1870*, published early in 1871, bases his very vigorous defence of the ministry on the Commission's statement that the end sought at Ems had been absolutely the same from first to last.

On this point, as on so many others, M. de La Gorce takes what seems to be the more reasonable and saner view. "Did the error come from the reporter, who, having seized on the wing the despatches as they were read, set them down inaccurately? Or on the other hand — as is more probable — did M. de Gramont in his exposition neglect to follow the order of dates and confine himself to summarizing and putting together, according to his views, documents which it would have been more proper not to mix? On this point, which was discussed at great length by contemporaries, there prevails an uncertainty which in all probability will never be cleared away. One can only say that there was a twofold fault — on the minister's part in not presenting all the documents, and on the part of the Commission in not demanding them. The report concluded with a solemn approval of the action of the ministry. And in very truth it was no ordinary good fortune for the ministry to find, at the critical moment, the most worthy and venerable of men [the Marquis de Talhouët] to countersign its final resolution." *Histoire du Second Empire*, vol. vi, p. 310.

INDEX

ABEKEN, HEINRICH, his despatch of July 13 to Bismarck, 271; framed in consultation with Eulenbourg and Camphausen, 273; wherein the despatch was misleading, 273, 274; this despatch received by Bismarck, 282, and edited into the "Ems despatch," 283 ff.; 177, 184, 185, 266, 267, 269.

Albert, Archduke, of Austria, his visit to Paris, 89, 374, 375.

Albrecht, Prince, of Prussia, 184, 185, 244.

Albuféra, Duc d', president of Commission of July 15, 356, 357, 359.

Alexander II, Tsar, urges King William to order Leopold to withdraw, 118; refuses to intervene, 301; 32 and n., 66, 76, 91, 138, 300, 378, 380.

Alfonzo, Prince (afterwards Alfonzo XII), son of Isabella, 17, 66.

Alfred, Prince, of England, 150.

Ambassadors, duty of, as to strict obedience, 241, 242 and n.

Andrassy, Count, 375.

Antony, Prince, father of Leopold, 15; letter to Charles of Roumania, quoted, 18; and Strat's mission, 169 ff.; decides to withdraw candidacy, 171; on Leopold's refusal, acts in his name, 172–174; induces Leopold to submit, 175, 176; his despatch not official, 202; but accepted as official, 254; his authority denied by the Right, 222; possible effect of his despatch in Spain, 230, 231; 20, 21, 30, 37, 49, 76, 106, 114, 138, 140, 159, 189, 199, 206, 218, 219, 227, 228, 232, 246, 272, 385: And see Père Antoine.

Arago, Emmanuel, 95, 162, 164, 362.

Army, French. See French army.

Army, Prussian. See Prussian army,

Augusta, Queen, of Prussia, 136, 137, 139, 140, 147, 158, 165, 166, 178, 183, 247, 268.

Augustenburg, Duke of, 222.

Aumale, Duc d', 118, 123, 150.

Austria, after Sadowa, 13; Ollivier opposed to alliance with, 86; conditions in, 86, 87; Gramont favors alliance with, 87; Napoleon's secret negotiations with, 88 and n., 89; exclusion of, from Germany, 376.

BACHON, M., 215, 257, 258.

Balaguer, Victor, 44 and n.

Bartholdi, M., his mission to Serrano, 128 ff.; 48, 106, 107, 110.

Bazaine, François Achille, 395, 396.

Belgium, precedent of, 150.

Benedetti, Vincent, French Ambassador to Prussia, public opinion adverse to, 132; criticised by the *Constitutionnel*,

132; his recall demanded, 132; his record, 132; sent to treat with King William at Ems, 133; his failings, 134, 135; his good qualities, 135, 136; at Ems, 140; his double instructions, 140, 141; interview with Werther, 143; his first audience of the King, 144–147; his report criticised, 150, 151; deprecates open military preparations, 156; his second audience, 158, 159, 160, 165; result of his efforts to July 11, 166, 167; his book criticised, 166 and n.; his conduct praised, 167, 168; and Gramont's first despatch of July 12, 204, 205 n.; receives Gramont's modified despatch too late, 237; his opinion of the demand of guaranties, 241; his duty in view of that opinion, 241–243; his *Essais Diplomatiques*, 243; presents demand of guaranties to the King in the park, 244 ff.; reports to Gramont, 247; King's changed feeling regarding, 266, 267, not due to Werther's report, 267, 269; unable to obtain another audience, 270, 271; his "importunity" blamed, 271; on Abeken's despatch to Bismarck, 272; the King's final reply to, 272; misrepresented in Abeken's despatch, 274; Gramont's last instruction to, 299, 300; his last despatches, 302, 303, 305; and the Ems despatch, 332; rebuffed by Eulenbourg, 332; takes leave of the King at the station, 333; in Paris, July 15, 338; aggrieved by newspaper attacks, 338, 339; 33, 110, 111, 155, 175, 177, 184, 185, 186, 188, 212, 232, 233, 234, 254, 283, 284, 285, 309, 310, 311, 314, 322, 323, 356, 361, 378, 379, 385.

Berlin, excitement in, caused by Ems despatch, 289 ff.

Bernhardi, Major, his memoirs incomplete, 369; 24, 30, 374.

Bernstorff, Count von, 59, 125.

Berryer, Pierre Antoine, 392, 393.

Beust, Friedrich F., Count von, his "comic-opera" suggestion, 73; warns Gramont, 300; 35 and n., 65, 88, 108, 119, 375.

Bianchi, Nicomède, quoted, 388.

Bismarck, Countess Marie von, 33.

Bismarck, Otto E. L., Prince von, his policy after Sadowa, 13; discomfited by accession of liberal ministry, 13, 14; his understanding with Prim, 14 and n., 15; his connection with Leopold's candidacy, 15 ff.; and the Memoirs of Charles of Roumania, 19 n.; at Varzin, 26, 32, 33; and the *plebiscite*, 27, 28; writes to Prim, 29; his newspaper campaign, 60 and n.; and Benedetti's mission to Ems, 136, 177, 178; leaves Varzin for Ems *via* Berlin, 178, 179; learns of Leopold's withdrawal, 179; its effect on him, 180, 181, 187 n.; his *Reflections*, etc., quoted, 181, 182; offers resignation, 182, 183; regards war as inevitable, 183; effect of his resignation on the King, 185, 186; and the demand of guaranties, 266; again threatens to resign, 266; Abeken's despatch of July 13 to, 271; his state of mind July 13, 276; his interview with Loftus, 276–278; unmuzzles the press, 278,

INDEX 507

279; and Werther's report, 279; recalls Werther, 280; the historic dinner with Roon and Moltke, 281 ff.; determined to retire, 282; arrival of Abeken's despatch, 282; "edits" the despatch, 282, 283; his version (the "Ems despatch"), discussed, 283–285; how it was made public, 289, 290; seeks to cast responsibility for war on France, 366; the Ems despatch how described by him at the time, 366, and in later years, 368, 369; boasts of having forced France to fight, 367, 368; and the Emperor Frederick's journal, 368; his *Reflections*, etc., quoted, 368, 369, 376, 377; maintains his non-responsibility for the Hohenzollern plot, 369, 370; views of German historians on his responsibility for the war, 370 ff.; reasons for his action in 1870, 376 ff.; not ready for war in 1867, 377; his tactics changed by accession of liberal ministry, 378; quoted, on sudden changes of policy, 381; drove France into hostilities, 382, 383; alone responsible for the war, 402; Scherr's panegyric of, 402, 403; 37, 45, 51, 52, 55, 58, 67, 73, 76, 81, 102, 104, 105, 107, 113, 125, 130, 131, 135, 139, 140, 147, 168, 213, 261, 262, 267, 274, 311, 322, 323, 326, 331, 353, 355, 365, 384, 385, 393.
Bleibtreu, Karl, quoted, on Ems despatch, 288.
Blennerhassett, Sir Rowland, quoted, 14 n.
Blondeau, M., 152.
Bonaparte, Napoleon E. F. J., Prince Imperial, 249, 258.

Bonjean, M., 264.
Bouillé, Col., 204.
Bourbaki, Gen. Charles D. S., 52, 215, 216, 396.
Bray, Count Otto C. H., 120, 121, 323.
Brenier, M., 264.
Bucher, Adolf Lothar, sketch of, 23 n.; his mission to Spain, 23 and n., 24–26; his papers burned, 396; 29, 30, 32, 60, 178, 374.
Buffet, Louis Joseph (1818–1898), Minister of Finance, 11 n.; resigns, 11 n.; demands production of Ems despatch, 354, 355.
Busch, Dr. Moritz, his *Bismarck* quoted, 23 n., 60 and n.; his revelations concerning Bismarck, 367; 291.
Bylandt, Herr von, 291.

CADORE, DUC DE, 120, 323, 356, 361.
Camphausen, Baron von, 267, 269, 273.
Canrobert, Marshal, 396.
Cassagnac, Granier de, 306.
Cassagnac, Paul de, 221 n., 232, 233, 295–297, 306.
Cavour, Count Camillo de, 52, 89.
Cerutti, Signor, 119, 120.
Charles, Prince of Roumania, his Memoirs quoted, 18 n., 22, 25, 25 n.; great importance of his Memoirs, 19 n., 369, 370; 18, 48, 170, 230.
Chateaubriand, René, Vicomte de, 4, 391.
Chevandier de Valdrôme, Jean (1810–1878), Minister of the Interior, 11 n.; quoted, on temper of the Chamber, 200; 84, 189, 190, 249, 253, 335.
Clarendon, Lord, 34 and n.
Clermont-Tonnerre, Duc de, 85.

INDEX

Cochery, M., Thiers's "Egeria," 77 and n.; his interpellation of July 5, 77 ff.; 91, 92, 94.
Cologne *Gazette*, the, Leopold's withdrawal published in, 244 and n., 374.
Comminges-Guitaud, M. de, and the Ems despatch, 293, 294, 322, 323, 356.
Commission of July 15 (Senate), report of, 364.
Commission of July 15 (Corps Législatif), membership of, 356 and n.; ministers appear before, 356, 357; report of, 358, 495–504.
Conference of the powers, suggested on July 14, 315, 316; the plan abandoned, 321.
Constitution of 1870, right to declare war under, 336.
Constitutionnel, the, Ollivier's relations with, 53 and n., 68 and n.; attacks Benedetti, 132, 133; Mitchell's editorial in, July 13, 248; 237.
Corps Législatif, session of July 11, 161–163; attitude of parties in, 164; session of July 12, 197, 198; withdrawal of candidacy, how received in, 197, 198; Chevandier on temper of, 200; session of July 13, 259 ff.; debate of July 15, 339 ff.; reception of ministerial declaration, 343; rejects Favre's motion for production of Ems despatch, 355; names Commission on proposed credit, etc., 356; report of Commission presented to, 358; votes the credit requested, 362, and other war measures, 363.
Correspondant, the, 97.
Cortes, sudden adjournment of, 42 and n.; summoned for July 20, 56.
Council, of July 6, 89 ff.; of July 10, and Benedetti's first report, 152; of July 11, decides to postpone military preparation, 156, 157; of July 12, 188; of July 13, votes against recalling reserves, 253, and adopts temporizing declaration, 254; of July 14, noon, 311 ff. (votes to recall reserves, 313); of July 14, evening, 322 ff.; of July 15, 334 ff. (votes unanimously for war, 336).
Cowley, Lord, 210.
Crémieux, Isaac M., 94, 95, 362.

DAGBLAD, the, 382.
Daily Telegraph, 100.
Dalloz, Paul, 97.
Daru, Comte Napoleon (1807–1890), Foreign Minister, 11 n.; resigns, 11 n.; 92, 94, 239.
David, Baron Jérôme, colloquy with Gramont, 259; his interpellation, 260, 261; 164, 187, 233, 262, 304.
Declaration of July 6, discussed in Council, 89 ff.; changes in, 90, 91, 451–454; text of, as read to the Chambers, 92, 93; Ollivier's opinion of, 93, 94; attitude of press on, 96 ff.; greeted with passionate approval, 99; how judged in Europe, 100; responsible for withdrawal of candidacy, 180, 181; remarks on, 454–460.
Declaration of July 15, read to Council, 334, and unanimously adopted, 336; simply a reply to the Ems despatch, 335; read in Chamber, 339–342; in Senate, 363, 364; equivalent to a declaration of war, 365.
Declaration of war, formal, made by France, July 19, 365, 381, 382.

INDEX 509

Delbrück, Hans, quoted, 21; on responsibility for the war, 371, 372.
Delbrück, Jules, 19.
Delisle, Hubert, 263.
Delord, Taxile, *Histoire du Second Empire*, quoted, 64.
Demand of guaranties. See Guaranties, demand of.
Denmark and the Duchies, 4 n.
Détroyat, Léonce, 195 and n.
DeWitt, John, quoted, 87.
Doubs, M., President of Swiss Republic, 294, 323.
Dréolle, M., and the report of the Commission, 358.
Duchies, the. See Schleswig-Holstein.
Dumouriez, C. F., 63, 387, 388.
Dupont, Léonce, and Benedetti, 338.
Duruy, Albert, 331.
Duvernois, Clement, his interpellation, 198 and n., 216, 220; 187, 260, 261.

EMS, negotiation with King William at, 132 ff., 468–475; Bismarck angered by, 177, 178.
Ems despatch, the (Bismarck's version of Abeken's despatch), discussed, 283–285, approved by Roon and Moltke, 286; divers judgments of, 287–289; how published, 289 ff.; excitement in Berlin and elsewhere caused by, 290–293; in Paris, 309; reported from Berne and Munich, 323, 324; Lyons on effect of, 330; declaration of July 15, a reply to, 335; production of, demanded by Favre, 354, and denied by Chamber, 355; Bismarck's first construction of, 366; his later admissions concerning, 368, 369; views of German historians on, 371 ff.; 332, 347, 348, 484–489.
England, relations of France with, 85; Gramont's appeal to, 108, 109; her policy of abstention shortsighted, 121, 122; attempts to avert war, 318 n., 352. And see Granville and Lyons.
English Cabinet, its attitude criticised, 122.
Escobar, Ignacio, 44.
Esquiros, M., 362.
Eugénie, Empress, in favor of war, 215 ff.; frowns upon Ollivier, 258; opposed to conference of powers, 317, 318; at Council of July 14, 322, 326; and Napoleon's alleged illness, 328, 329; at Council of July 15, 334, 336; 49, 153, 304, 306, 374, 375.
Eulenbourg, Count von, and Benedetti, 332; 182, 267, 269, 273, 293.

FAILLY, GENERAL, 82.
Favre, Jules, demands production of Ems despatch, 354, 355; dodges vote on war measures, 362; 64, 394.
Ferry, Jules, 362.
Figaro, the, 97.
Fleury, Comte de, French Ambassador to Russia, 66, 91 and n., 107, 118, 301, 380, 381.
Fournier, M., 118.
France, various causes assigned for defeat of, in 1870, 2 ff.; intervention of, after Sadowa, 13; and the Hohenzollern candidacy, 33; public opinion in, 63 ff.; alliances of, in 1870, 85 ff.; her responsibility for the war discussed, 366–383; had pretexts at hand, if she wanted war, 380;

and Germany, differences between not fundamental, 400, 401; cause of the conflict an "artificial fatality," 400, 401.
Francis Joseph of Austria, his letter to Napoleon, 88, 89.
Franco-Prussian War. See War of 1870.
Frederick, Prince Royal of Prussia (afterwards Emperor), and the candidacy, 19, 29, 30; extracts from his journal published, 368.
French army, readiness of, for war, 81 ff.
Fritz, Prince, Leopold's brother, suggested candidacy of, 22, 25, and n., 26, 58.
Frossard, General, 82.

GAMBETTA, LÉON, his speech on July 15, 358, 359, 360; 65, 164, 191 and n., 192, 233, 258, 259, 361, 362, 394.
Garde Mobile, the, 337.
Garnier-Pagès, M., 94.
Gaulois, the, 97, 214.
Gazette de France, the, 199.
German Unity, Ollivier's policy concerning, 10, 11; at the root of Bismarck's policy in 1870, 376.
Germany and France, nature of differences between, discussed, 400, 401. And see Prussia.
Girardin, Emile de, 195.
Girault, M., 362.
Gladstone, W. E., quoted, 123; his Prussian sympathies, 124; his dread of war, 125; 34.
Glais-Bizoin, Alexander, 94, 362.
Gortchakoff, Prince, quoted, 117; 91, 179, 394.
Gramont, Antoine Alfred Agénor, Duc de (1819–1880), Foreign Minister, 11 n.; letter of, to Ollivier, 50, 52; his character,

53; his first despatches, 53, 54 and n.; and Olozaga, 54, 55; and Werther, 55, 56; his early attitude commended, 56; inclined to generalize the dispute, 71; conference of Ollivier and, with Napoleon, 72 ff.; ordered to prepare declaration, 77; at Council of July 6, 81, 89, 90; opposed to Russian and favors Austrian alliance, 87, 88; reads declaration in Chamber, 92, 93; his instructions to Mercier, 103, 105, Lesourd, 105, Fleury and others, 107, 108; letter of Napoleon to, 111; seeks intervention of England, 108, 109; appeals to States of the South, 109; general tone of his instructions, 110; supports Napoleon's personal negotiation with Serrano, 128, 129; his official despatch and private letter to Benedetti, 140–142; his speech in the Chambers, July 11, 161 and n.; his despatch of July 11 to Benedetti, 165; and of July 12, 1.40 P.M., 204, 205 and n., 206; Olozaga communicates Leopold's withdrawal to, 206, 207; his momentous interview with Werther, 207 ff.; suggests that William write a letter to Napoleon, 208, 209; his action justified, 209, 210; did not demand a letter of apology, 210, 212, 213; at Saint-Cloud, 217; the "conscientious discussion," who took part therein? 217, 218 and n.; demands guaranties in despatch to Benedetti of July 12, 7 P.M., 217, 218; was pledged not to enlarge field of discussion, 221; acted as an am-

bassador rather than as a responsible minister, 226; Lyons remonstrates with, 227, 228; his inconsistency, 228, 229; letter of Napoleon to, on demand of guaranties, 232, 233; Ollivier remonstrates with, 235, 236; his later despatch to Benedetti, 236, 237 and n.; colloquy with David, 259; his last despatches to Benedetti, 299, 300; is warned against insistence on guaranties, 300, 301; letters of, to Ollivier, 303, 304; at Saint-Cloud, 304, 305; and the Ems despatch, 309; at the Councils of July 14, 311 ff., 322, 326; suggests conference of the powers, 314; reads declaration of July 15 in the Council, 334; replies to Thiers, 354; before the Commission, 356, 357; charged with having misled Commission, 364, 495–504; 40, 48, 49, 57, 58, 70, 114, 122, 137, 151, 152, 155, 160, 162, 163, 164, 168, 184, 199, 200, 243, 245, 247, 249, 261, 263, 264, 271, 277, 278, 281, 296, 314, 332, 359, 380, 385, 386.
Granville, Lord, quoted, 65; his attitude criticised, 122 ff.; his instructions to Loftus and Layard, 124; inclined to France, 124, but dreads war, 125; his letter read at Council of July 13, 251, 252; 34 n., 59, 143, 254, 262, 318 n., 330.
Greece, precedent of, 150.
Gresley, Colonel, 152.
Gressier, M., 197.
Grévy, Jules, 362.
Gricourt, M. de, his pamphlet quoted, 397, 398.
Grivard, M., 328.
Guaranties, first mention of, 198.

Guaranties, demand of, in Gramont's despatch of July 12, 7 p.m., 218, 219; an ill-advised step, 219, 220; precedents for, 223; an act of personal authority, 226; not an ultimatum, 227; Napoleon's letter to Gramont on, 232, 233; Benedetti's opinion of, 241; presented by him to William, 243 ff.; disastrous effect of, on foreign opinion, 300, 301; Ollivier's judgment of, 353; war not a necessary result of, 353; 379, 385, 386.
Guizot, F. P. G., quoted, 181, 389, 391.

HAVAS NEWS AGENCY, 48.
Herreros de Tejada, 44.
Hohenzollern candidacy, the, Bismarck's plans concerning, 32–34; when to be divulged, 36; attitude of Prussia toward, 58; effect of, on public opinion in France, 63 ff.; importance of, to France, 70; conference of Gramont and Ollivier with Napoleon concerning, 72 ff.; Benedetti and, 132, 133; attitude of King William toward, 137 ff.; withdrawn by Prince Antony, 173, 174; Bismarck and the withdrawal of, 180, 181, 182, 87 n.; withdrawal of, due to declaration of July 6, 180; withdrawal of, communicated to Napoleon, 188, 189, and to Ollivier, 189, 190; effect of Ollivier's disclosure of withdrawal, 196 ff.; withdrawal due to Olozaga alone, according to Napoleon, 202; Bismarck always denied responsibility for, 369; how his agency was disclosed, 369,

370; the sole cause of the war, 383; summary of history of, 384 ff., 422–434; 378, 379.
Hohenzollern family, statutes of, 17, 18 and n., relationship of, to Napoleon, 208.
Hohenzollern family council of March 15, 1870, 18, 21, 22, 339.
Hohenzollern-Sigmaringen, 15.
Holstein, Duchy of. See Schleswig-Holstein.
Hugo, Victor, 155, 392.
Hungarians, the, 86, 375.

ISABELLA II, OF SPAIN, 14 and n., 123, 419, 420.
Italy, question of alliance with, 85, 86.

JOSEPHINE (MURAT), PRINCESS, OF HOHENZOLLERN, Leopold's mother, urges withdrawal, 171.
Journal des Débats, the, 98.

KAUNITZ, HERR VON, 20.
Kératry, M. de, 95, 261, 262.
Keudell, Herr von, 32, 178, 183, 280.
King and State, distinction between, in Prussia, 148, 149.
Königgrätz. See Sadowa.
Kulturkampf, the, 381.

LARABIT, M., 263.
La Valette, Marquis de, French Ambassador to England, 108, 123, 260.
Lavedan, M., 97.
Layard, Sir A. H., 124, 127, 130.
Le Bœuf, Edmond (1809–1888), Minister of War, 11 n.; his character, 82 and n.; and the Council, 83 and n., 84, 85; and the demand of guaranties, 249; insists on summoning reserves, 249, 250, 253; attacks Ollivier, 257; 152, 154, 156, 204, 311, 313, 318, 335.
Lebrun, General, his secret visit to Vienna in 1870, 89.
Lenz, Herr, his *Geschichte* quoted, 180.
Leo XIII, Pope, 133.
Leonardon, H., his *Prim et la Candidature Hohenzollern*, summarized, 422–434.
Leopold, Prince of Hohenzollern-Sigmaringen, candidate for Spanish throne, 15, 435–437; refuses first overture, 19; Prussian view of his candidacy, 21; wavers in his refusal, 30; finally accepts, 30, 31; seeks King William's sanction, 37; the grandson of a Murat, 53 and n., 436; his candidacy published at Paris, 48 ff.; and Strat's mission, 169 ff.; refuses to withdraw, 172, 175; his father acts for him, 173, 174; finally submits, 175, 176; what he might have done, 230, 231; withdrawal approved by the King, 270; 33, 42, 56, 58, 63, 64, 73, 92, 103, 104, 108, 110, 111, 112, 118, 119, 127, 128, 129, 130, 131, 136, 138, 139, 141, 143, 146, 159, 160, 165, 207, 208, 219, 222, 228, 232, 245, 246, 248, 251, 259, 295, 301, 303.
Lesourd, M., French chargé d'affaires at Berlin, Gramont's despatch of July 3 to, 54; his interview with Thile, 57, 58; 79, 309, 310, 322.
Liberté, the, 331.
Limburg, Roest van, quoted, 66.
Loftus, Lord Augustus, British Ambassador to Prussia, his interview of July 13 with Bismarck and report thereon,

INDEX   513

276-278, 491-494; 59, 65, 124, 322, 393.
Lopez y Dominguez, Serrano's messenger to Leopold, 131, 176.
Lorenz, Ottokar, his *Wilhelm I* quoted, 18 n., 25, 28, 61, 149, 370, 371.
Louis XIV, 382, 387.
Louis Napoleon. See Napoleon III.
Louis-Philippe, 150, 389, 390, 391, 392, 393.
Louvet, M., Minister of Commerce, 11 n., 253, 315, 322.
Luxembourg affair, the, 210, 250, 378.
Lyons, Lord, British Ambassador to France, quoted, 63; his character, 80; interview of July 5 with Ollivier, 80 and n.; on the declaration of July 6, 99; on the demand of guaranties, 227, 228, 229 and n.; on the Ems despatch, 330; 108, 109, 110, 142, 143, 163, 221, 251, 252, 262.

MACCHI, MGR., 133.
MacMahon, Marshal, Duc de Magenta, 85, 152, 204, 250, 328, 395.
Main, the, boundary between North and South Germany, 13.
Malaret, M., 108.
Marcks, Erich, quoted, on the Ems despatch, 289.
Maria, Countess of Flanders, Leopold's sister, quoted, 66.
Maria Christina, Regent of Spain, 14 n.
Maria Luisà, Duchesse de Montpensier, Infanta of Spain, 123.
Massa, Philippe de, and Thiers's overture to Napoleon, 153-155.
Mège, M., Minister of Public Works, 251, 253.

Mehemet Ali, 389.
Mercier de l'Ostende, French Ambassador to Spain, his interview with Prim, 46, 47; Gramont's despatch of July 3 to, 53; and Prim, 103; public opinion adverse to, 132, 133; 39 and n., 40, 48, 51, 66, 101, 106, 126, 127, 128, 129, 130, 138.
Metternich, Richard, Prince, quoted, 63, 75, 108, 110.
Mexico, French expedition to, 2 and n., 3.
Ministry of January 2, pacific disposition of, 11; members of, 11 n.; effect of accession of, on Bismarck's plans, 13, 378; its attitude toward Germany, 14; fights against the current, 299; had abundant cause for complaint, without Hohenzollern affair, 380; surprised in works and thoughts of peace, 383; attitude of French historians toward, 386; its conduct of affairs defended, 386. And see Council, Gramont, and Ollivier.
Mitchell, Robert, his article in the *Constitutionnel*, 248; 237, 238, 258, 259, 305, 306.
Moltke, General Count von, dines with Bismarck, July 13, 281; the Ems despatch, 282 ff.; 2 n., 19, 376, 378, 395.
Mommsen, Theodor, on the War of 1870, 399.
Moniteur Universel, the, 97.
Montpayroux, M., 164.
Montpensier, Duc de, his candidacy for the Spanish throne, 26, 47, 123.
Mouchy, Duc de, 153.
Mouchy, Duchesse de, 153, 154, 155.
Mullert, Pastor, 178.

514   INDEX

Mun, Albert de, 99.
Murat, Prince Napoleon, 106.

NAPOLEON I, 155.
Napoleon III, and the Mexican expedition, 2 and n., 3; and the War of 1859, 3, 4; and the Schleswig-Holstein question, 5; and the principle of nationalities, 5 ff.; his disloyalty to that principle, 8, 9; and Ollivier's foreign policy, 11; and Prim, 16 n.; favors Prince Alfonzo for Spanish throne, 17; first hears of Leopold's candidacy, 48, 49; his attitude justified, 69; approves conclusions of Gramont and Ollivier, 71; their conference with him on July 5, 72 ff.; orders Gramont to prepare declaration, 77; quoted, on military and naval affairs, 82; supreme in military affairs, 83, 84; his secret negotiations with Austria and Italy in 1869, 88 and n., 89; and the declaration of July 6, 90, 91; how he was the first to utter the word "war," 91; appeals to Serrano, 106; objects to direct negotiations with Leopold, 110, 111; and Strat's mission, 112 ff.; his personal negotiation with Serrano successful, 128 ff.; military measures taken by, 152, 153; Thiers's overture to, and his reply, 153–155; learns from Olozaga of Leopold's withdrawal, 188, 189; withholds news from Council, 189, 190; letter to Ollivier thereon, 199; Ollivier's interview with, 201–203; seems content with the withdrawal, 204; relations between him and the Hohenzollerns, 208; and the war party at Saint-Cloud, 215 ff.; and Duvernois's interpellation, 216; pledged not to enlarge field of discussion, 221; blamed for not demanding guaranties in 1869, 224; his hesitation, 225; demand of guaranties an act of his personal authority, 225; his letter to Gramont thereon, 232, 233; source of the letter, 233; favors summoning reserves, 251, then opposes, 253; his alleged syncope during council of July 14 denied by Ollivier, 328, 329; at the Council of July 15, 335, 336; on responsibility for the war, 362; his pacific disposition, 374, 375; had no motive for desiring war, 377; plan of the Right to exonerate, at expense of Ministry, 397; letter of Ollivier to, thereon, 398, 399, and his reply, 399; his attitude as between peace and war, 401, 402; 33, 45, 47, 85, 125, 126, 127, 140, 169, 170, 207, 210, 231, 245, 246, 254, 257, 258, 296, 304, 305, 306, 310, 311, 313, 314, 315, 317, 318, 321, 322, 366, 379, 382, 385, 386.

Nationalities, principle of, defined and discussed, 5–9; denial of, by Prussia, 8; Napoleon not loyal to, 8, 9; 71.

Nemours, Duc de, 150.

Niel, Marshal, his plans of military reform, 2 and n.; quoted, 82; 250, 294.

Nigra, Count Costantino, quoted, 180, 203.

North German Confederation, 13.

North German Gazette, Ems despatch published in, 289, 291, 309, 312, 330.

INDEX 515

OLLIVIER, ÉMILE, his ambition on taking office, 10; his attitude toward German unity, 10, 71; his foreign policy outlined to Napoleon, 10, 11; Keeper of Seals and Minister of Justice, 11 n.; learns of Leopold's candidacy, 50; how affected thereby, 51, 52; and Werther, 55; and the *Constitutionnel*, 68 and n.; his relations with other journals, 68 n.; his view of significance of candidacy, 70; conference of Gramont and, with Napoleon, 72 ff.; proposes ministerial declaration to Chambers, 75, 76; his official reception on July 5, 79, 80; interview with Lyons, 80 and n.; opposed to Austrian, and favors Russian alliance, 86, 87; and the declaration of July 6, 90, 91, 93, 94; his speech thereon, 95, 96; his letter to Napoleon on attitude of parties, 164; learns of Leopold's withdrawal, 189, 190; and Olozaga, 192, 193; discloses fact of withdrawal to deputies and others, 193–195 and notes; letter of Napoleon thereon, 199; his conversation with Thiers, 201, and with Napoleon, 201–203; and the Werther-Gramont interview, 210 ff.; effect of his intervention, 211; not consulted as to demand of guaranties, 218; attacked by the Right, 220, 221; learns of demand of guaranties, 232; is wounded and disturbed, 233–235; remonstrates with Gramont, 235, 236; urges mitigation of demand, 236; his impulse to resign, 238; result of his meditations, 239, 240; opposes recalling reserves, 253; attacked by Le Bœuf, 257, 258; the Empress frowns on him, 258; cause of irritation against, 264; his argument against war, 298, 299; believes peace assured at midnight of July 13, 307; proposes to ignore Ems despatch, 313, 314; on the proposed conference of the powers, 315–317, 319 ff.; and the declaration of July 15, 334; his promise to the Chamber, 336; reads declaration in Chamber, 339, 342; replies to Thiers, 346 ff.; "we accept with light hearts," 349–351, 351 n.; before the Commission, 356; colloquy with Gambetta, 360, 361; his letter to Napoleon on Gricourt's pamphlet, 398, 399, and the reply, 399,

Ollivier, Madame Émile, 190, 231, 317.

Olmütz, Conference of, 81 and n.

Olozaga, Don Sallustio, Spanish Ambassador to France, and Gramont, 54, 55; and Strat's mission to the princes, 111, 112 and n., 113–115; Prince Antony's despatch to, 174, 175; informs Napoleon of withdrawal of candidacy, 188, 189, and to Ollivier, 192, 193; alone responsible therefor, according to Napoleon, 202; communicates withdrawal to Gramont, 206, 207; 49 and n., 51, 104, 105, 180, 200, 202, 203, 231, 232, 301, 302, 305, 310, 385.

Oncken, Dr., his *Unser helden Kaiser*, quoted, 292.

Ordinaire, M., 362.

Orléans, Duc d', son of Louis-Philippe, 390.

516 INDEX

Orsini, Felice, his assault on Napoleon, 210.

Pall Mall Gazette, the, 100.
Palmerston, Lord, 123, 389, 392, 393.
Parieu, Marquis de, President of the Council, 11 n., 238, 256,
Paris, excitement in, 295. And see Press, Parisian.
Pays, the, 220, 221 n., 295–297.
Père Antoine, Prince Antony so-called in derision, 222, 232, 233, 251, 258, 259, 295, 296.
Persigny, Duc de, 210.
Pessard, M., 214.
Peuple Français, the, 317.
Philis, M., 317.
Picard, Ernest, 362.
Piennes, M. de, 328.
Pietri, F., 48, 257.
Pinard, M., 164.
Piré, Marquis de, 344, 345.
Plebiscite, the, of May 8, 1870, 27; effect of, in Prussia, 28, 374.
Plichon, Charles (1814–1888), Minister of Public Instruction, 11 n., 253, 315, 322, 326, 337.
Plombières, conference of Napoleon and Cavour at, 89.
Polish insurrection of 1862, 87.
Polo de Bernabé, Admiral, 56, 175, 176.
Prague, Treaty of, 192, 195, 263, 380.
Press, German, its subservience to Bismarck, 278, 279; and Werther's report, 279; on the Ems despatch, 292.
Press, Parisian, attitude of on the candidacy, 67, 68 and n.; on the declaration of July 6, 96 ff.; on the Ems despatch, 331.
Prim, Juan, Marquis de los Castillejos, Spanish Minister of War, 14 and n.; his understanding with Bismarck, 14 and n., 15; and Leopold's candidacy, 15, 16 and n., 40 n., 422–434; and Napoleon, 16 n.; and Bucher and Versen, 25, 26; Bismarck's letter to, 29; and the premature disclosure of the candidacy, 44, 45; his interview with Mercier, 46, 47; and Olozaga, 49 n.; induces approval of candidacy by Spanish ministry, 56; notifies foreign governments, 56; and Mercier, 103; continues his preparations, 103, 104; his circular note, 104; his difficult position, 126, 127; his disingenuous conduct, 127, 128, 130, 131; Prince Antony's letter to, withdrawing candidacy, 173, 174; 33, 34, 37, 38, 48, 51, 64, 67, 73, 74, 76, 92, 106, 108, 109, 111, 129, 130 n., 127, 138, 140, 159, 162, 199, 206, 230, 379.
Prussia, and the principle of nationalities, 9; position of, after Sadowa, 13; attitude of, toward Leopold's candidacy, 59, 60, affirmed by William to Benedetti, 147; rejects England's proffered mediation, 352.
Prussian army, mobilization of, ordered July 15, 365.
Prussian Monitor, the, 291, 292.
Public, the, 220.
Public opinion, its proper relation to a constitutional sovereign and to his ministers, 69.

RADZIWILL, ANTONY VON, 243, 270, 271, 272, 333.
Randon, Marshal, his Memoirs quoted, 2 n.
Rascon, Señor, Spanish Ambassador to Prussia, 67.

INDEX 517

Raspail, M., 94, 362.
Rathlef, Georg, quoted, 273, 275, 287, 288, 372.
Rémusat, M. de, 389.
Reserves, recall of, demanded by Le Bœuf, 249, 250; council declines to order, 253, then orders, 313; order for, partially countermanded, 316, 322, then confirmed, 326, 327.
Rezonville, battle of, 395, 396.
Richard, Maurice (1832–1888), Minister of Fine Arts, 11 n., 251, 253, 256, 257.
Rigault de Genouilly, Charles (1807–1873), Minister of Marine, 11 n., 85, 156, 157, 253, 257, 365.
Right, the, attitude of, on July 11, 163, 164; turns victory into defeat, 186, 187; and the withdrawal, 197, 198; predominance of, at Court, 215; determined on war, 220; attacks Ollivier, 220, 221; denies Prince Antony's authority, 222; insists on guaranties, expecting refusal, 223, 225; seeks to exonerate Napoleon at expense of ministers, 397.
Rivero, Señor, 42.
Roeder, Count von, 293, 294, 323.
Roger, Madame, 153.
Roman Question, the, and a French-Italian alliance, 35 and n.
Roon, General Count Albrecht, dines with Bismarck on July 13, 281; the Ems despatch, 282 ff.; 19, 158, 159, 179, 376.
Rouher, Eugène, President of the Senate, former prime minister, advises Duvernois, 260: 364.
Roumanian conspirators in Paris, 114.
Russia, Ollivier favors alliance with, 87; Gramont, *contra*, 87, 88; closely united to Prussia, 87. And see Alexander II, Fleury, and Gortchakoff.

SADOWA, battle of (1866), results of, 13; question of revenge for, 70, 71; Thiers on, 345; 352, 358, 376.
Sagasta, Praxedes M., 104, 126, 127, 301.
Saint-Hilaire, Barthélemy, 362.
Saint-Marc Girardin, quoted, 98.
Saint-Privat, battle of, 396.
Saint-Vallier, Comte de, 109, 120, 300.
Salazar y Mazaredo, and Leopold's candidacy, 16 and n., 422 ff.; divulges the secret, 42, 43, 45; 30, 32, 33, 37, 38, 39, 104.
Saxony, and the candidacy, 67.
Scherr, Johannes, his *1870–1871* quoted, 148, 149, 372, 373, 402, 403.
Schleinitz, Herr von, 19.
Schleswig, and the Treaty of Prague, 380, 381.
Schleswig-Holstein, Duchies of, and the War of 1864, 4 and n., 5.
Schultze, Walter, his *Die Thronkandidatur Hohenzollern* quoted, 373, 374.
Schwartzenburg, Prince von, 81.
Segris, Émile (1811–1880), Minister of Public Instruction, 11 n.; of Finance, 11 n.; 253, 256, 257, 322, 335.
Senate, warlike demonstration at session of July 13, 263, 264; declaration of July 15, how received in, 363, 364.
Serrano y Dominguez, Francisco, Regent of Spain, Napoleon appeals to, 106, 107, 128 ff.; quoted as to origin of can-

518 INDEX

didacy, 130 n.; 14, 56, 109, 110, 126, 301, 385.
Silvela, Señor, 301.
Simon, Jules, quoted, 64, 65; 362, 394.
Slavs, the, 86.
South German States, treaties of alliance with Prussia, 11 and n.; attitude of, toward the candidacy, 67, 120; a foreign war necessary to unite, to North Germany, 376, 377; 13.
Spain, should France have addressed remonstrance to, rather than to Prussia? 101 and n., 102; fruitless negotiations with, 126 ff.; possible effect of Prince Antony's despatch in, 230, 231; approval of withdrawal by, 301, 302, and n.
Spanish marriages, the, precedent of, 150, 391.
Spicheren, battle of, 395.
Standard (London), the, 100, 222.
Stoffel, Baron, 311.
Strantz, Colonel, sent by King William to Sigmaringen, 158, 175.
Strat, Roumanian agent at Paris, his mission to the princes, 112 ff. and notes; his mission successful, 169 ff., 171 n.; 180, 189, 385.
Sybel, Heinrich von, his *Begründung des Deutsches Reichs* quoted, 266, 291, 366, 371.

TALABOT, PAULIN, 194.
Talhouët, Marquis de (1819–1884), Minister of Public Works, 11 n.; resigns, 11 n.; reporter of Commission of July 15, 357, 358, 359, 360, 502.
Thiers, Adolphe, quoted, 65, 68, 75, 181, 387, 389, 396; and Cochery, 77 and n.; his overture to Napoleon, 153–155; and Ollivier, 201; his speech of July 15, 343; opposes ministerial declaration, 343, 344; his past conduct responsible for public agitation, 345, 346; Ollivier replies to, 346 ff.; his second speech, 351–354; Gramont's reply, 354; 3, 164, 358, 361, 362, 394.
Thile, Herr von, disclaims all knowledge of candidacy, 57, 58; quoted, 125, 126; 19, 33, 59, 72, 79, 105, 107, 137, 141, 147, 366, 384.
Times, the, 100, 222, 290.
Tocqueville, Alexis de, quoted, 352.
Topete y Caballo, Admiral, 14, 66.
Treaties, inchoate and complete, discussed, 89.

Univers, the, 97.

VAILLANT, MARSHALL, quoted, 64, 82, 215, 331.
Varnbühler, Friedrich G. K., 120.
Versen, Major von, his mission to Spain, 23–26; 14 n., 28, 29, 37, 38.
Veuillot, Louis, quoted, 97, 98, 392.
Victor Emanuel II, of Italy, his letter to Napoleon, 88, 89; 36, 375.
Victoria, Queen, 124, 138, 150, 210.
Visconti-Venosta, Marquis Emilio, 108, 119.
Vitzthum, Herr, 336.

WALEWSKI, COMTE ALEXANDRE, 10 and n.
War, right to declare, under the Constitution of 1870, 336, 337.
War of 1859, 3 and n., 4.

INDEX 519

War of 1870, the first cause of, 5; Napoleon on responsibility for, 362, 363; question of responsibility discussed, 366–383; a necessary step in achieving German Unity, 376, 377; considerations fixing responsibility for, 378, 379; Hohenzollern candidacy the sole cause of, 383; early stages of, 395; a justifiable war, 400; Mommsen on, 400.

War measures, proposed by Ministry, July 15, 337 ff.; passed by Corps Législatif, 362.

Werther, Baron von, Prussian Ambassador to France, 55, 56; his interview with Gramont on July 12, 207 ff.; an honorable but dull-witted person, 213; his report of the interview contradicted by Gramont, 213; his report reaches Ems, 267; its effect, 267 ff.; his report reaches Bismarck, 279; he is recalled, 280; text of his report, 480–483; 122, 137, 143, 168, 169, 179, 192, 193, 200, 310.

Werthern, Freiherr von, his life of Versen, quoted, 24 n.

Westmann, M., quoted, 380.

William I, King of Prussia, at first opposed to Leopold's candidacy, 16, 17, 18; Versen's report to, 26; and the Tsar, 32, 118; finally assents to candidacy, 37, 38; French ministers decide to appeal directly to, 107; Benedetti sent to, at Ems, 133; Bismarck's protest to, 136; disturbed by Hohenzollern affair, 137, 139; and the declaration of July 6, 138, 146; urges withdrawal of Leopold, 139, 140; Benedetti's first audience of, 144–147; declines to put pressure on Leopold, 145; his dual personality, 145, 148, 149, 160; his power to forbid the candidacy, 149, 150; his motive questioned, 150, 151; Benedetti's second audience, 158, 159, 160; sends Strantz to Sigmaringen, 158; desires to "save his face," 166, 167; Bismarck offers resignation, 182, 183, 184, 185; rejoices at withdrawal, 183, 184; his purpose unchanged by Bismarck's threats, 185, 186; his influence in the withdrawal denied by Werther, 207, 208; Gramont's suggestion of a letter from, to Napoleon, 208, 209; Benedetti instructed to demand guaranties from, 219; unlikely to sanction renewal of candidacy, 224, 241; demand of guaranties presented to, 243 ff.; his peremptory refusal, 246; effect of demand on, 266, 267, and of Werther's report, 267 ff.; sends Radziwill to Benedetti to communicate definitive withdrawal of candidacy and to refuse him an audience, 270, 271; approves the withdrawal, 270, 272; wearied by Benedetti's "persecution," he appeals to Bismarck, 271; his final reply to Benedetti, 272; his authorization of publicity a disloyal act, 274, 275; his attitude to Benedetti falsified in Ems despatch, 283, 284; and the Ems despatch, 293; leaves Ems, 332; sees Benedetti at station, 332; ordered mobilization, night of July 15, 365; 22, 28, 29, 45, 58, 76, 94, 105, 106, 109, 110,

127, 131, 143, 153, 165, 168, 171, 175, 177, 178, 179, 199, 202, 203, 237, 239, 251, 261, 301, 302, 303, 305, 309, 312, 314, 323, 324, 353, 358, 361, 366, 376, 378, 385, 386.

William II, German Emperor, 368.
Woerth, battle of, 395.
Würtemberg, attitude of, 120.

ZORRILLA, SEÑOR, 38, 43, 44.

DATE DUE